ARGUMENTATION AND DEBATE
Principles and Practices

CONTRIBUTING
AUTHORS

JOHN T. AUSTON   *University of Akron*

GIFFORD BLYTON   *University of Kentucky*

WALDO W. BRADEN   *Louisiana State University*

BERT E. BRADLEY, JR.   *University of Richmond*

PAUL D. BRANDES   *Ohio University*

MERRILL G. CHRISTOPHERSON   *University of South Carolina*

NICHOLAS M. CRIPE   *Butler University*

DOUGLAS EHNINGER   *State University of Iowa*

WAYNE C. EUBANK   *University of New Mexico*

DWIGHT L. FRESHLEY   *Vanderbilt University*

ANNABEL D. HAGOOD   *University of Alabama*

ALBERT C. HINGSTON   *Pacific University*

ROBERT B. HUBER   *University of Vermont*

JAMES H. McBATH   *University of Southern California*

RALPH Y. McGINNIS   *Montana State University*

CULLEN B. OWENS   *University of New Mexico*

GREGG PHIFER   *Florida State University*

DAVID POTTER   *Southern Illinois University*

W. CHARLES REDDING   *Purdue University*

RONALD F. REID   *Purdue University*

ARGUMENTATION
AND DEBATE · Principles
and Practices

JAMES H. McBATH, Editor

REVISED EDITION

HOLT, RINEHART AND WINSTON, INC.
NEW YORK · CHICAGO · SAN FRANCISCO · TORONTO · LONDON

EDITOR'S PREFACE

The first modern textbook in argumentation and debate was published in 1895; its author was George Pierce Baker. As Diderot was to encylopedia makers, so Baker was to writers of scores of texts in argumentation and debate. In 1954 the forensic honor society Tau Kappa Alpha published a volume unusual to the shelves of its companions. The Tau Kappa Alpha book was a collaborative venture with more than a dozen national authorities writing in their fields of special competency. Editor of this pioneering collection was David Potter.

In late 1960, conferences with Holt, Rinehart and Winston, successors to the original publishers, encouraged us to consider revision of the TKA textbook. Consultations with more than a hundred argumentation teachers and debate directors convinced us that no work would add more distinctively to the literature of forensic speaking than would full revision of the earlier TKA volume. On the basis of our survey, selected chapters of the original edition were retained and improved, while additional chapters were written to cover new material and topics. Every effort was made to promote continuity and consistency as we blended the collective experience of twenty teachers into this text.

Responsible for developing the present volume are members of the Editorial Board: Wayne C. Eubank, Owen Peterson, David Potter, W. Charles Redding, and James H. McBath, Chairman.

JAMES H. McBATH

February 24, 1963

v

FOREWORD

On March 4, 1963, the national offices of Delta Sigma Rho and Tau Kappa Alpha announced the formation of a single forensic honor society—Delta Sigma Rho–Tau Kappa Alpha. The united society preserves the names, the traditions, and the essential characteristics of both societies. It also represents a realization of the basic purpose of each group of founders—creation of a Phi Beta Kappa of forensics.

CONTENTS

ARGUMENTATION AND DEBATE

Principles and Practices

I.

chapter 1

INTRODUCTION TO ARGUMENT

by James H. McBath

Not long ago the Educational Policies Commission of the National Education Association attempted to define the chief goal of education in this country. The Commission concluded that "the purpose which runs through and strengthens all other educational purposes—the common thread of education—is the development of the ability to think." [1] Just as the cultivated power of the free mind is today a pervasive concern of American education, the emphasis upon man's rational ability has long motivated the study of argumentation and debate. For, whenever confronted with problems personal or social, the reliance in democratic societies has been upon an individual's capacity to think through problems and to submit conclusions to personal or group verdicts.

This preference for thought and talk before action is woven tightly into the fabric of the American tradition. In fact, our history is illuminated by a succession of great debates which have crystallized the thinking of citizens and certainly have shaped the course of our nation. We are all familiar with landmark debates such as those of the Constitutional Convention in 1787; the debates on ratification of the Constitution; the Webster-Hayne debate in 1830; the Webster-Calhoun clashes; the Lincoln-Douglas debates of 1858; the debates concerning advisability of joining the League of Nations; the neutrality debates, 1939–1941; and, of course, the Nixon-Kennedy debates on issues of the 1960 Presidential election. "From now on," predicts Walter Lippman, "it will be impossible for any

[1] *The Central Purpose of American Education*, 1961, p. 12.

candidate for any important elective office to avoid this kind of confrontation with his opponent." [2] Indeed, most men and women with public responsibility have already equipped themselves formally in the art of argument. When a national publication recently surveyed government leaders —including senators, congressmen, governors, Cabinet members, and Supreme Court justices—an impressive 62.5 percent reported participation in school debate.[3] Ninety percent of these respondents replied that experience in debating had helped either "greatly" or "invaluably" in their careers.

But great occasions are by no means the only ones when debates have taken place and arguers are not necessarily national figures. Whenever people deliberate critically to reach decisions, the tools of argumentation and debate may be employed: from campus groups or business conferences to court cases and Congressional lawmaking—whenever people determine to reach conclusions, test ideas, and influence the thought and action of others.[4] This book is concerned with the fundamentals of argumentation and debate by which a person derives his own conclusions and then tests them in the laboratory of controversy.

FUNDAMENTAL ASSUMPTIONS

Underpinning argumentation and debate are four cardinal assumptions or premises that give direction to our study.

INEVITABILITY OF CHOICES

In everyday life the individual and his group are necessarily confronted with innumerable courses of action. Should I major in economics? Should the campus abandon its fraternity system? Should our community build a new civic auditorium? Should the nation adopt a program of free trade? Should the Western nations establish a political federation? Such propositions emerge from the prospect of optional avenues of action. Some choices are on trivial matters where a wrong selection makes little difference, while others involve personal security or group welfare where a wrong choice can be painful. Similarly, when currents of popular opinion congeal into public decision, or policy, we bear the consequences of the

[2] "Television Debates Could Be Improved," *Los Angeles Times*, October 2, 1960, Section C, p. 4.

[3] *Freedom & Union*, November 1960, p. 5.

[4] James L. Robinson identifies the principal current occasions for public debate as *forum*, before popular groups, *legislative*, and *legal*. "Are We 'Overlegalizing' School Debate," *The Speech Teacher*, 10 (March 1960), 111–112.

option selected. "In life," commented Arthur Schlesinger, Jr., "one must make a choice and accept the consequences; in Doughface fantasy, one can denounce a decision without accepting the consequences of the alternative."[5]

WORTH OF INDIVIDUAL AND GROUP DECISIONS

If a decision is not disconsonant with prevailing social standards, it stands until modified by the group. We tend to presume, until shown otherwise, that people have decided correctly. Even if we doubt the wisdom of a decision, we say in effect: "Determine freely your course of action, and if it does not violate canons of public interest, it will be respected." This assumption reflects a deep-seated attitude of innate worth in responsible private and popular choices. Although in our age of science we sometimes wistfully hope that white-coated men huddled around computers will provide the difficult answers, social verdicts obviously require widespread personal involvement and sanction. Without a general confidence in the integrity of individual and group conclusions, the whole process of decision-making loses its vitality. Basic to our idea of freedom is respect for each person's ability to decide creatively the course of his life or action.

FREEDOM TO TEST IDEAS

Implicit within the democratic creed is opportunity to verify one's ideas through confrontation with opposing ideas. Thus, while liberal democracy presupposes a willingness to accept the consequences of popular verdicts, it offers wide latitude for investigation and verification. Decision-makers can if they wish explore their problem, recheck objectives, conduct pilot studies, argue the merits of alternatives—all before ultimate commitment. William O. Douglas gives a reasoned explanation for this pragmatic idealism when he writes that

> Public opinion—the basis upon which our society rests—must be responsible and responsive. To be such it must be disciplined and informed. It cannot be disciplined and informed unless those who shape it have the opportunities for critical inquiry, for the cultivation of open-mindedness, for the search for truth in every recess of the universe.[6]

From conference room to Congress the optimum condition for wise decision-making is in the reflection promoted by genuine debate as a

[5] *The Vital Center* (Boston: Houghton Mifflin Company, 1949), p. 43.
[6] *The Right of the People* (Garden City, N.Y.: Doubleday & Company, 1958), p. 27.

prelude to action. "Democracy," observed Pendleton Herring, "provides an ideology conducive to criticism, experimentation, and change." [7] The basic premise of a democratic society is that when given access to reliable information and free discussion, men and women can decide constructively.

INTELLECTUAL–EMOTIONAL BASES OF BELIEF

Man is neither an amalgam of predispositions, biases, and biological impulses nor is he an immaculate instrument of rationality. The truth is a blend of both views. Man can be both impulsive and reasonable. So while rational responses are preferred, we recognize that our judgments, attitudes, and social values are a function of some net resultant of past experiences, and that these events are perceived through the filter of our own personality. In writing of man's rational powers, his emotions or affects, and his instincts, Alexander Leighton reminds us that "these distinctions are, of course, purely analytic. In the successive patterned events which make up a personality system, affect, cognition, and basic urges are not separate faculties but aspects" of a self-integrating unit.[8] The successful arguer recognizes that choice involves the whole man, that reason and emotion do not operate segmentally, but are inseparably interrelated at any given moment. Man is a dynamic unity, and as such he participates in the life of his society.

CRITICAL DELIBERATION

Discussion and debate are two principal modes of critical deliberation. Their prime aim is to supply reasons for belief and action; both modes encourage delayed, critical response from listeners. Neither discussion nor debate has great appeal for special pleaders, rabble-rousers, or super salesmen who are understandably wary of the reflective process.

Discussion is organized group discourse under the guidance of a leader. It aims at problem-solving through orderly give-and-take conversation among a number of participants. *Argumentation* usually is defined as the broad process of developing ideas through a reasoned discourse employing logical, emotional, and ethical proof. *Debate* is the specific process of reaching decisions by subjecting propositions to the method of argument. It involves a conscious attempt by participants with conflicting points of view to educate or persuade through arguments pro and con on

---

[7] *The Politics of Democracy* (New York: W. W. Norton & Company, Inc., 1940), p. 434.

[8] *My Name is Legion* (New York: Basic Books, Inc., 1959), p. 20.

a controversial subject. Debaters present their hypotheses to the scrutiny of informed opponents, appealing beyond themselves for judgment.

The term *propaganda* is frequently used to denote an extreme form of group persuasion that seeks acceptance of ideas or beliefs through deliberate short-circuiting of the reflective process. It seeks favorable audience response, immediate or ultimate, and its success is measured in the degree of attainment of a desired reaction. Emphasis upon the rational plays a secondary role in the propagandist's rhetoric, although he generally is more effective when his message is developed systematically with a façade of supporting information. Listeners, even the strongly committed, like to think of themselves as open-minded and reasonable. Sometimes the systematic efforts of social, community, religious, and educational institutions to recruit money or members are mislabeled "propaganda." But these campaigns, although embodying premeditated persuasive appeal, usually endorse the free discussion that propagandists shun. Conceivably, in periods of emergency, propaganda techniques to secure prompt, united action can be justified. But extraordinary times or unusual circumstances are needed to give a semblance of ethics to the propagandist's motive and method.

Far from inviting the free play of argument, as discussants and debaters do, the propagandist thrives upon censored information and one-way communication. Without access to facts or the privilege of questioning, his disarmed consistuency can be made to believe anything: Communist China does not exist; capitalists are criminals; Norway started World War II; or even that the new dentrifice "Glare" is one's only antidote to crumbling teeth. When a society is sufficiently informed to confront with fact the propagandist's plausible nonsense, his influence dwindles.

PERSUASIVE ARGUMENTATION

The student of argumentation and debate is perfectly aware that people do not always think and act "logically." He can easily document instances of emotional, irrational behavior. Commented a distinguished British scientist, Wilfred Trotter: "The dispassionate intellect, the open mind, the unprejudiced observer, exist in an exact sense only in a sort of intellectual folklore; states even approaching them cannot be reached without a moral and emotional effort most of us cannot or will not make." [9] Yet who will seriously dispute that crucial decisions are better made by

[9] Quoted in W. I. B. Beveridge, *The Art of Scientific Investigation* (New York: Random House, Inc., 1957), p. 120.

persons oriented to the facts, open-minded, and willing to exchange ideas? Our view does not ignore man as he is; it merely confirms that wiser choices are made through critical deliberation than through calculated appeal to man's cupidity.

Argumentation is uniquely concerned with the soundness and dependability of decisions. For this reason, we do not measure the merit of an argument solely in terms of a speaker's ability to influence his audience. Thus a valid argument may not gain popular approval, while an invalid point may be highly persuasive. If the emphasis of persuasion generally is upon what creates belief, argumentation is concerned mainly with the conditions of justifiable belief. Because argumentative deliberation is objective, critical, and self-testing, it has greater social utility than does persuason lacking the built-in checks of debate. The method of argument places responsibility for decision-making squarely upon the listeners, who are assumed to be capable of intelligent choices when they are sufficiently informed. For example, democratic practice affirms that informed individuals can be trusted to decide upon rational bases in careers, in purchases, and in politics.[10]

The massive annual contests for votes offer a convenient contrast between public argument and partisan harangue as means for attaining political decisions. A recent study of campaign communications concluded that an informed electorate is better built through voter exposure to orderly argument than through long-distance persuasion by candidates speaking to separate audiences. "Debate occurs," wrote Stanley Kelley, Jr., defining his terms, "when two parties advocating alternative courses of action bring their dispute before a common audience and ask that audience to favor one of the two proposals."[11] Campaign communication best meets its social objective of encouraging rational voting when it "clarifies differences between candidates; presents reasons for adopting alternative courses of action; comes from clearly identified sources; exposes voters to the arguments of both sides; and gives a voter an accurate view of the subjects with which it deals."[12] In short, public argument provides the voter a more reliable

[10] Burton H. Byers, "Debate as a Social Methodology," *Southern Speech Journal,* 18 (May 1953), 234–235, describes the "function of debate in a democracy" as the encouragement of "all men to consider all reasoned points of view on the problem at hand. . . . His function is to persuade as many people as possible to hear all sides before making a choice . . . and persuasion is misplaced which is used to cause unthinking listeners to follow blindly the lead of the speaker. The democratic debater uses his most persuasive appeals to get his audience to think, and he trusts the decision to his audience after he has done his best to insure that they understand the merits of his case."

[11] *Political Campaigning: Problems in Creating an Informed Electorate* (Washington, D.C.: The Brookings Institution, 1960), p. 19.

[12] *Ibid.,* p. 23.

basis for his election-day choices than does exploitative persuasion more concerned with results than with the method by which results are achieved.

Our view emphasizes that the most impelling argument possesses both logical and psychological validity. Principles of listener motivation are highly adaptable to the debate process. Audience analysis is needed to reveal the audience's attitudes, incentives, social values, and levels of information. Listener attention and comprehension can be heightened appreciably through a speaker's persuasive skill. Obviously useful to the arguer is knowledge of factors that promote understanding and good relations between speaker and audience in their pursuit of a common goal. The debater can formulate premises for his arguments which engage the attitudes of his listeners and motivate them to accept what the logic of the matter seems to dictate. He can enlist their interests, desires, hopes, and aspirations in causes which are shown to have reasonable claims for support, and can thus facilitate the communication and acceptance of ideas which are anchored in probative argument.

ARGUMENTATION AS A MEANS OF ACHIEVING ASSENT

Collective assent or consensus, the indispensable condition of a functioning society, may be achieved through force or the threat of retaliation. It may be achieved through propaganda with its calculated manipulation of human motives. It may be achieved through persuasive appeal that pays mere lip service to logic. Consensus also can be reached through the processes of critical deliberation which seek agreement through orderly, reasonable talk. Citizens of free societies traditionally prefer the latter method, as it is both an earmark and a condition of their freedom. On this democratic commitment Paul Woodring is emphatic: "In a free society, all individuals with the sole exception of infants and those in custodial institutions, must make these decisions for themselves; if they are unable to do so—if their lives must be planned for them—they are no longer free, however benevolent the controls may be." [13]

A society is known by the way it reaches its decisions. The method of decision-making in Hitler's Third Reich, by orders and their enforcement, reflected the nature of his totalitarian state. Verdict by edict, whether in labor union, industrial empire, or national government, reveals the social philosophy of that organization. Soviet states may describe themselves as "people's democracies," but their practice of decision by an enlightened few refutes the claim. In like manner, the preference of Western

[13] "The Meaning of Excellence," *Saturday Review*, April 15, 1961, p. 51.

democracies for decision by representative verdict explains them as no other means could.

What we are saying is that methods are inseparable from goals, that one is a dynamic description of the other. If a society purports to esteem the individual and respect his integrity, the way in which it reaches decisions will reflect its genuineness. Jacques Maritain illuminates our thesis: "And what of the means? Do we not know, as a universal and inviolable axiom, an obvious first principle, that means must be proportioned and appropriate to the end, since they are *ways to the end* and, so to speak, the end itself in its very process of coming into existence?" [14]

Encouragement of the process of decision by informed public talk is, by its very nature, a demonstration of oneness between ends and means in a liberal democracy. Argumentation and debate, by their very nature, are not merely ways of achieving popular assent but also comprise an operational definition of government by public consent.

SOCIAL RESPONSIBILITY OF THE INQUIRER-ADVOCATE

Because he is provided powerful rhetorical tools for the molding and testing of belief, the debater has a concomitant responsibility to use them judiciously and generously. Usually he will espouse his own beliefs; sometimes he may argue vigorously against his apparent convictions. In either instance, the debater shoulders an obligation to develop and advance the best case he can for his side of the proposition. Students in school debate occasionally express concern about the merit or morality of defending both sides of controversial topics. They miss a crucial point—that open-minded clash should precede the formulation of ideas and beliefs worthy of sustained advocacy.

"Full and free discussion even of ideas we hate," remarked Justice Douglas, "encourages the testing of our own prejudices and preconceptions." [15] To the student we say: "Argue fairly both sides of questions, employing the best proof discoverable, and *then* determine your ultimate conviction—after inquiry and argument, not before it has been tested." Debate itself cultivates open-mindedness through repeated demonstration that most public issues are many-sided, and that conclusions about them are best drawn after searching examinations of differing points of view.

Moreover, there are circumstances in which unpopular positions deserve a fair hearing and in which honest men will do their best to see that

---

[14] *Man and the State* (London: Hollis and Carter, 1954), p. 50.
[15] Dissenting opinion in Dennis *vs.* U.S., 341 U.S. 494, June 1951.

such positions are represented competently. This view is no endorsement of sophistry or moral compromise. Men who sponsor a fair hearing for all viewpoints that have any claim to acceptability are on sounder grounds than are partisans who suppress the strength in another's case or who permit a responsible position to languish for lack of a competent spokesman. As John Stuart Mill wrote in his cogent essay, *On Liberty,*

> . . . the peculiar evil of silencing the expression of an opinion is, that it is robbing the human race; posterity as well as the existing generation; those who dissent from the opinion still more than those who hold it. If the opinion is right, they are deprived of the opportunity of exchanging error for truth; if wrong, they lose what is almost as great a benefit, the clearer perception and livelier impression of truth, produced by its collision with error.[16]

The primary aim of the debater is to achieve belief or action by proving the probable wisdom of his proposition. He attempts to construct and present a case that will enlist the rational conviction of his listeners or readers. Whether his purpose is to investigate, educate, or to advocate by means of reasoned discourse, his attitude is one of uncompromising criticalness. Therefore, in the study of argumentation and debate we ask not simply what creates belief, but rather upon what standards belief may be justified. Our discipline seeks to introduce order and critical thought into conclusion-drawing and thus to facilitate sounder individual and collective decisions. The inquirer–advocate is responsible for participating honestly to achieve this goal.

ARGUMENTATION IS AN INSTRUMENT OF INQUIRY

The principles of argumentation offer powerful tools in the quest for correct answers. They encourage critical thinking in the molding of opinion and the making of choices. They also make imperative a deep respect for reliable information, a concern for workable definitions, a sensitivity to laws of valid inference, and an ability to sort the essential from the trivial. They prize objectivity over bias or prejudice, suspended judgment over impulse. Argumentation insists that conclusions must be congruent with reality, and that belief should be subjected to the scrutiny of reason.

Argumentation is a useful medium for inquiry because (a) its processes are self-testing and critical, (b) it requires a consistent application of

[16] *On Liberty* (London: John W. Parker and Son, 1859), p. 33.

reason to our thought patterns, and (c) its objective principles can be applied to the content of other subjects.[17]

Argumentation, as a strategy of inquiry, has its inception in a problem, proceeds to investigation and discussion, and culminates in systematic probing of hypotheses in the format of debate. There is high credibility in any hypothesis that can survive the intelligent scrutiny of persons other than those who advance it. Shallow ideas simply cannot survive the joust of challenge and response. While debate tests ideas through its competitive framework, debate is cooperative in that it can only occur when men agree to abide by guarantees of comparable access to the audience, equitable division of time, codes of fair play, and when they contract to submit their arguments to the arbitration of listeners or readers.

Productive inquiry is encouraged by the intellectual competition of debate because:

(a) arguers may contribute facts, interpretations, or judgments unknown to others;
(b) new ideas may emerge from the pooling of information and the contest of ideas;
(c) errors may be exposed, since arguments are subjected to rigorous tests of their proof and consistency;
(d) arguers may be jarred loose from rutted, unproductive patterns of analysis.

Argumentation and debate cannot in themselves produce sound ideas, but they can provide an orderly, self-regulative method for the formulation and weighing of ideas. Argumentative deliberation, with its mood of cooperative controversy, offers an environment conducive to the achievement of valid, socially responsible group solutions.

SUMMARY

The ability to solve problems by using the accumulated intellectual resources of the race is perhaps mankind's most distinctive possession. To

[17] Sidney Hook, *Education for the Modern Man* (New York: The Dial Press, 1946), p. 119, emphasizes the primacy of *method* in inquiry: "The validity of any specific conclusion depends upon the methods by which it is reached. Upon what does the validity of the methods depend? Without fear of circularity, we can say that these methods are justified by their historical fruitfulness in the solution of problems. That is why in any specific inquiry we are more likely to judge whether a problem is truly solved by reference to the methods of inquiry that have been followed, than we are to evaluate these methods by a specific result. This explains why we do not abandon

transmit this power of disciplined thinking is a central concern of our educational system. Just as history documents a democratic preference for settlement of national issues through constructive controversy, our individual lives also are shaped by our ability to reach personal decisions creatively.

A durable rationale for the study of argumentation and debate depends upon our acceptance of several critical assumptions: that choices are inevitable in group and individual life, that responsible group and personal decisions will be respected, that citizens must enjoy freedom to test and verify their ideas, and that belief has intellectual–emotional bases.

Although argumentation as an instrument of inquiry differs in emphasis and method from other modes of persuasion, knowledge of attention factors and motivation is useful to the arguer in building an atmosphere of receptivity for his ideas. Moreover, the argument itself will be more likely to gain audience acceptance if it is identified with listener attitudes. Arguments thus may simultaneously hold probative force and persuasive impact. But we have concluded that decisions themselves improve as the debater intentionally relies upon the tools of critical deliberation.

An able debater is a conscious thinker, a purposive problem-solver. He collects evidence, weighs and sifts it, and exhibits a developed capacity for separating the proven from the unproven. He does not mind disclosing his premises and defining his terms. He shows a willingness to subject his views to the free play of orderly argument. He squares his advocacy of policy with the best moral values of his society. The competent debater declares his faith in man's rationality, and thus becomes a creative participant in the quest for reliable belief and justifiable action.

---

the methods of scientific medicine when confronted by a patient who has been cured by an incantation after he has been given up by the physicians."

~~~~~~

chapter 2

THE DEBATE TRADITION

by David Potter

The last half century has witnessed the introduction of many interesting and important developments in debate such as new forms of debate, the debate tournament, the critic-judge, state and regional conferences, international debates, and the founding of the forensic honoraries. But with the possible exception of the forensic honoraries, the majority of our innovations were anticipated by the college students and the college administrators of the eighteenth and nineteenth centuries. Thus, as President Wadsworth of Harvard recorded in his diary well over a century ago, students would not willingly participate in a scholastic exercise which had little meaning and less practical application:

> There was but one opponent, thô many at College. The Batchelours had sundry time neglected stated disputations in ye Hall. I several times sent for several of 'em, read ye Law to 'em and ye power I had to punish 'em for their neglect, exhorted 'em to duty, but these private kind admonitions had not ye desired effects; so I this day ordered ye Butler to punish ye delinquents, It is, to set three shillings a piece on ye Heads. . . .[1]

A brief picture of the ancient form of debating, then a required part of the curriculum at Harvard and at the majority of the American colleges

---

[1] Benjamin Wadsworth, "Benjamin Wadsworth's Book (A. Dom. 1725) relating to College affairs," *Publications of the Colonial Society of Massachusetts*, 31, 453.

throughout the colonial period, might explain President Wadsworth's difficulties.

THE SYLLOGISTIC DISPUTATION

Practically unchanged since its inception in the medieval universities, the Latin syllogistic disputation was, at one time or another, a prescribed part of most early university curriculums as well as a primary exercise at the university exhibitions and commencements. Its format was strictly governed by rules laid down in the prevailing texts in logic and differed but slightly when employed as a teaching and testing device or as a medium for academic display.

CLASSROOM PROCEDURE

As indicated by Bartholemew Keckermann's *Systema Logicae*, which was popular at Harvard in the seventeenth century, and by *The Improvement of the Mind*, authored by the prolific eighteenth-century writer Isaac Watts, the classroom procedure followed this order. A tutor, usually the reverend president, selected a question from one of the arts or sciences taught in the college. A student, called the "respondent," was appointed to defend the side of the question which, in the opinion of the tutor, represented truth. The remaining students in the class were detailed to act as opponents, having the express duty of raising logical objections, in their best Latin, to the side of the question maintained by the respondent.

The disputation was opened by the respondent who first read a carefully worded Latin discourse which stated his thesis, defined and delimited the question, and presented his strongest logically constructed arguments. Then each of the opponents offered his objection in the form of a syllogism, either denying the major or minor premises or distinguishing between the accepted usage of key words and the usage of the respondent. Following this, the respondent attempted to re-establish his argument by presenting other syllogisms which the opponents denied or reinterpreted until their objections were silenced and "truth" triumphed logically. The tutor, of course, was always on hand to help out should the respondent falter in his command of logic and Latin.

THE EXHIBITION DISPUTATION

The commencement and exhibition disputation differed from the classroom exercise primarily in the manner followed in the selection of questions. As in the classroom, the disputants were appointed by the tutor.

In the seventeenth century and in the early decades of the eighteenth, such appointments were highly prized. The theses, or questions for debate, however, were usually collected from the entire college curriculum by specially selected students. The collected theses, in turn, were studied by the faculty so that nothing blasphemous, sacrilegious, or humorous might be introduced. Finally, the censored lists were assembled into broadsides which, with the Latin questions marked for delivery and the names of the contestants indicated, were printed and distributed among the members of the audience. Following the short debates, rarely longer than fifteen minutes, the reverend president presented a learned opinion in which his conception of truth was clarified and embellished and his mastery of Latin was demonstrated. Then the lengthy program of oratory continued.[2]

DECLINE OF THE SYLLOGISTICS

There was once good reason for the syllogistics. During the Middle Ages and even during the Renaissance when Latin was the language of educated persons and when Aristotle's Organon was accepted as the proper measure for determining truth, debate was to a large extent the armor and armament of the scholar and the cleric. The academician needed to cultivate the intricate art so that he might verify accepted truths and win or maintain a following among the students at the university. The cleric relied upon the disputation to defend the church against proponents of heretical (or rival) postulates.

In addition to these practical applications of argumentation, debating was a most economical and useful means of testing a student's mastery of his subject matter. Moreover, without the severe competition of non-oral forms of communication, the syllogistics furnished academic diversion to the scholars who once made up the bulk of commencement audiences.

However, as the effects of the Enlightenment spread over the academic world, as dialectic began to yield to the pressure of experimentalism, as Latin bowed before the increased prestige of the vernacular, and as pressing political issues arose to challenge the student's mind, the rigid format of the ancient scholastic form of debating was found to be inadequate and, worse still, boring.

Even before the administration of President Wadsworth, Harvard students had questioned the worth of the syllogistics. As early as 1716 a commencement thesis boldly proclaimed: "The Socratic method of reason-

---

[2] Keckermann's treatment of the syllogistics may be found in translation in Colyer Meriwether's, *Our Colonial Curriculum 1607–1776* (New York: Capital Publishing Co., 1907), pp. 238–247. Many editions of *The Improvement of the Mind* are extant. Chapter XIII is of especial interest.

ing is preferable to the syllogistic." Fourteen years later a protesting Yale student upheld the thesis: "Syllogisms do not aid in exploring the truth." But despite students' protests and absenteeism, the exercise lingered on in the curriculum and in the commencement program. As late as June 14, 1786, John Quincy Adams, then at Harvard, complained to his father:

> Syllogistic disputes . . . are held in detestation by the scholars and everyone thinks it a reflection upon his character as a genius and a student to have a syllogistic; this opinion is the firmer, because the best scholars almost always have other parts. There are many disadvantages derived from these syllogisms, and I know of only one benefit, which is this. Many scholars would go through college without studying at all, but who would idle away all their time, who merely from the horrors of syllogisms begin to study, acquire a fondness for it, and make a very pretty figure in college. . . .[3]

Many "scholars" were not so completely resigned to their academic lot. Young Adams thus describes the reaction of another group of Harvard students who were appointed to participate in the commencement syllogistics in 1786:

> . . . the syllogists all got together . . . and drank till not one of them could stand straight, or was sensible of what he did. A little after 9 they sallied out, and for a quarter of an hour made such a noise as might be heard at a mile distant. . . . Mr. ———— [a tutor?] had two squares of his windows broke.[4]

Perhaps this and similar outbursts influenced the Board of Overseers, for the last syllogistic disputation was exhibited only six years later.

THE FORENSIC DISPUTATION

While some dismayed undergraduates were finding excuses to absent themselves from the required Latin exercises and some more determined young men were demonstrating their physical dislike of the syllogistics, other graduate and undergraduate students were engaged in an earnest search for a more satisfactory vehicle for reasoned discourse. In 1722 a select group of Harvard students, members of the newly constituted Spy

[3] John Quincy Adams, *Writings* (New York: The Macmillan Company, 1913), Vol. 1, p. 24.

[4] "Student Diary of John Quincy Adams," in Henry Adams, *Historical Essays* (New York: Charles Scribner's Sons, 1891), p. 113.

Club, found such a vehicle, prescribing as a featured exercise of the society "A Disputation on Two or more questions at every Meeting, one part of the Company holding the Affirmative, the other the Negative part of ye Question." [5] Significantly, the disputations were conducted in English, and the syllogistic method of proof was not decreed.

It must be admitted, however, that the topics debated were more nearly akin to the Roman *declamatio* collected by Seneca in his *Controversiae* [6] than to the propositions debated by twentieth-century collegians. Nevertheless, we can visualize the enthusiasm with which the "liberated" Cambridge collegians forensically considered "Whether the World will be annihilated or only refined" and "Whether humans Souls are Equal."

ENGLISH LANGUAGE DEBATES

Although the forensic disputation, as the new form of academic debating was called, was similar in form to the mode used in the assemblies of Athens, in the forums of Rome, and in the parliaments and assemblies of the contemporary powers (as well as in the local governing bodies), it was not recognized by the college administrations until the middle of the eighteenth century. By 1747, however, Yale was featuring English-language debates in the forensic manner,[7] and in 1765 forensics were required of the two upper classes every Tuesday during the academic year. In 1766 forensics appeared on the commencement program at the New Haven college, and by 1783 the upper class at Yale debated in English "all . . . Mondays except for the first in each month which was still reserved for the Syllogistics and every Tuesday." [8]

CHANGE IN SUBJECT MATTER

At first, the questions debated in English by American college students in society halls and in classrooms were largely theological. Thus, Yale students in 1747 somberly discussed "Whether, by the Sin of Adam his Posterity could be brought into a State worse than Non-Existence"

[5] William C. Lane, "The Telltale, 1721," *Publication of the Colonial Society of Massachusetts*, XII, 220–231.

[6] For an interesting defense of Seneca and of the value of *declamatio*, see Donald C. Clark, "Some Values of Roman Declamatio," *Quarterly Journal of Speech*, 35 (October, 1949), 280–283.

[7] See Naphtali Daggett, Argumenta recita in Aula Yalensi, 1947. Ms. in the Yale University Library.

[8] Ezra Stiles, *Literary Diary*, 3 (New York: Charles Scribner's Sons, 1901), p. 99.

and "Whether the Gift of Salvation after the Conditions be performed is an Act of Grace." [9] Gradually, however, the field of interest shifted to the "literary" questions and the secular problems of the day. An examination of the Princeton commencement broadsides from 1760 to 1774 reveals this change. In 1760, for example, the student debaters and their audiences were entertained by a debate on the topic, "The elegance of an Oration much consists in the Words being consonant to the Sense," a thesis strikingly similar to the rhetorical theses debated syllogistically in previous centuries. In 1765 the classically inspired topic was "A wicked man can not be an accomplished Orator." By 1768, however, the aroused Princetonians heard an impassioned discussion of a burning issue of the day: "It is lawful for every man, and in many cases his indispensable duty, to hazard his life in defense of his civil liberty." But by 1771 the advocates of culture, disputing the dominance of the politically minded, discussed the ageless question, "Does Ancient Poetry excell Modern?"

Throughout the remainder of the eighteenth century and far into the nineteenth, the "academic" and the "vital" battled for supremacy in the classroom and commencement forensics, with honors fairly well divided. In the halls of secret societies, already integral parts of every American college, the same distribution of interest was evidenced. However, members of the societies were relatively free from faculty interference and could occasionally divert their energies to the consideration of such important questions as:

"Is matrimony advantageous to 'men of learning.' "—Athenian Society of Queen's College [Rutgers], 1782.

"Whether the wearing of low bosoms in compliance with custom and fashion, be any impeachment of a lady's modesty."—Phi Beta Kappa of Harvard College, 1812.

"Supposing a man pull a rope tied to a pig's snout whether the man or the rope would pull the pig."—Phi Beta Kappa of Harvard College, 1813.

"Should Bachelors be taxed for the support of old maids."—Philo-Lexian Society, Columbia, 1817.

LITERARY AND DEBATING SOCIETIES

The importance of literary and debating societies in the history of American debating should not be glossed over too quickly. For many years

[9] Daggett, *op. cit.*, pp. 16, 28.

they were the chief source of forensic training in colleges and universities. And in their halls were nurtured such speakers as Alexander Hamilton, James Madison, Daniel Webster, Rufus Choate, Albert Beveridge, William Jennings Bryan, and Woodrow Wilson.

Almost from the beginning of higher education in America, secret literary and debating societies were sharpening the minds and polishing the manners of their members. As we have seen, the Spy Club of Harvard was featuring debates on questions of interest to its members as early as 1722. At William and Mary the Flat Hat Club was attracting the attention of such undergraduates as Thomas Jefferson in 1750. And in 1776 Phi Beta Kappa began its illustrious career in the nearby Raleigh Tavern.

GROWTH OF SOCIETIES

Throughout the country literary and debating societies experienced a rapid growth. In 1795 the Debating Society of North Carolina was featuring debating, composing, reading, speaking, and parliamentary procedure. And in the nineteenth century, at such representative institutions as Wabash, Ohio University, Alabama, Mississippi, Denison, Utah, Willamette, and the Michigan Agricultural College, active societies were catering to the literary and social needs of undergraduates within a few years after the opening of the college portals or in some instances, as soon as classes began.

College administrations were very well aware of the good work done in the "halls" in preparing students for the very vocal contemporary world. Brown College, for example, dropped the once required forensics from their catalog in 1829–1830, explaining that student societies were already doing the job. And the trustees of Columbia were informed on January 4, 1873, that "No exercises in extemporaneous speaking or debating were required from the Students, as there are two Societies formed amongst them which meet once every week in apartments appropriated to their use, of which these exercises constitute the principal objects." [10]

SOME TYPICAL LITERARY AND DEBATING SOCIETIES

A brief examination of the constitutions and minutes of the Columbia and the Brown literary and debate societies in the early nineteenth century indicates that the confidence of the college administrators was not misplaced. In 1820, for example, the "Constitution of the Columbia Philo-Lexian Society" prescribed:

[10] Minutes of the Trustees of Columbia College, 3, Part 2, 6 May, 1828–4 December, 1837, p. 1738.

The regular exercises of this society shall be delivering orations, reading compositions, and criticisms, reading select passages from approved authors and discussing questions.

At every meeting of the society members shall support a forensic discussion either by appointment or by a voluntary offer and the society shall decide on the merits of the question.

The members appointed to debate shall take sides on the question the evening previous to discussion, and the President shall be empowered to select one from the Affirm. and one from the Neg. to open the debate with a prepared speech, in writing or exmemoria.

No member of the Junior or Senior class (unless appointed to open the debate) shall be permitted to read off a written discussion.

When any member is about to speak in debate, or deliver any observation to the society he shall with due respect address himself to the President confining himself strictly to the point in discussion.

No member shall speak twice on the same motion without leave of the President.

On December 19, 1823, the minutes of the society further inform us: "The members of the society shall be divided into four classes who shall alternately perform the duties of speaking, reading, giving in compositions and debating." For those brothers forfeiting their turn in the rotation of exercises, severe and restrictive fines were ordered and collected.

The members of the United Brothers Society of Brown were even more debate-conscious than their New York confreres. As early as 1810 the constitution stated: "The only exercises of this society shall be the discussion of questions by extemporaneous speaking."

Just how the debates were to be judged, however, was not clearly defined by the Brothers. The 1810 constitution merely states that "After the debates, the decision of each question shall be made by taking votes in favor of the affirmative, and those in favor of the negative, which shall be recorded."

More specific than the United Brothers was the Philermenian Society, also of Brown. On June 12, 1858, the Philermenian constitution was amended to read: "After the discussion of the question [by the disputants and the house], the President shall sum up the arguments advanced on either side and decide the question from the merits of the arguments. The Ayes and Nays of the house shall then be taken on the merits of the questions."

By 1858, however, all was not well in many of the older college debating societies. The first signs of decay were evinced in the East where the minute books of such former stalwarts as Dartmouth's United Fraternity and Social Friends and Rutgers' Philoclean and Peithessophian recorded the frequent postponement of exercises or the absence of the disputants. With the outbreak of the Civil War, the decline spread throughout the South, where, as at William and Mary, the Phoenix and the Philomathean societies collapsed. Shortly afterward, the majority of the eastern societies succumbed to the pressure of the period. At Yale, for example, the once great Linonian Society had nearly ceased to exist in 1869. And at many other colleges the competition of the specialized clubs and the Greek-letter social fraternities made for a situation similar to that reported by Columbia's *Cap and Gown* on October 15, 1868:

> [Should you enter the rooms of either Columbia society] the meeting will not probably be called to order until an hour after the appointment time, with scarcely enough members present to form a quorum. . . . Very possibly an adjournment will take place before any literary exercises have been held . . . [and when a debate is heard] a levity of manner ill-suited to the subject, if it be a serious one, will be manifest. All this while the order in the room will be of a very questionable character; . . . and when fines are imposed much time will be wasted in frivolous or unconstitutional appeals. When we depart it will be with feelings of disappointment, dissatisfaction and regret.

THE RETURN OF DEBATING
TO THE CURRICULUM

Although there was a widespread lack of interest in debating during the decades following the Civil War, especially in the East and South, there were individuals who still believed that reasoned discourse deserved a place in the curriculum of the nation's schools and colleges. Such a believer was Francis Parkman, a member of the Harvard Corporation in 1878. Observing that the university had made no provisions for training men to speak on their feet, he urged the adoption of the necessary course work. The famous "English 6, Oral Discussion" was the result.

Without much fanfare, colleges throughout the rest of the country began to re-examine their curriculums. Gradually the emphasis on elocution and declamation was diminished, and, as at the Michigan Agricultural College (now Michigan State University) in 1884, seniors were given their choice of two essays or two debates during the first term. The old terminology lingered on, however, for when the University of Pennsylvania inaugurated its version of curricular debating in 1887, the course was entitled "Declamation (voluntary)." But the course description provided for "Exercises in Debating and Original Speaking."

THE REVIVAL OF EXTRACURRICULAR DEBATING

Not to be outdone by the administrations of their colleges, the undergraduates also intensified their efforts to rejuvenate the expiring societies. In the East, for example, the new Harvard Union was established in 1880. At Yale, where debating was practically extinct for nearly twenty years after the collapse of the Linonian Society, a partial renaissance occurred, and in 1890 both the Yale Union and the Kent Club were organized. Similarly, in 1892 unions modeled after those functioning at the British universities were organized at Brown and Dartmouth, and the Zelosophic Society was reconstituted at Pennsylvania. By 1887 Columbia witnessed the rebirth of active debate societies, and in 1899 Rutgers experimented with a congress closely resembling the House of Representatives, duplicating an experiment performed at Brown seventy years earlier.

In the South many of the older societies were reactivated shortly after the Civil War. Thus, the Phi Sigmas resumed their literary and forensic exercises at the University of Mississippi in 1865, and the Erosophic and Philomathic Societies of Alabama started anew in 1871. But the societies in the East and South, with the notable exception of several like Princeton's Whig and Clio, never regained their former popularity. As one Southern editor lamented in 1887: "With our hand upon its pulse, so to speak, we have felt the sinking, weakening throb, which has almost subsided." [11]

THE RISE OF INTERCOLLEGIATE DEBATING

While the eastern and southern schools were attempting, without much success, to regain their ancient debate prestige, the societies of the small western colleges were busily carrying on their relatively new business. In the spring of 1881, for instance, the campus of little Illinois College was the scene of great activity. On the evening of May 5, the Phi Alpha Society of Illinois and the Adelphi Society of Knox College clashed in one of America's earliest intercollegiate literary and debate contests. President Charles Henry Rammelkamp, of Illinois College, describes the occasion nicely:

> The oratorical contest took place that evening in the opera house, and brought out, in spite of the rain, such an audience . . . as even the

[11] *The Alabama University Monthly*, 14 (April, 1887), 254.

Athens of the West itself has seldom, if ever seen. . . . Although Phi
Alpha won the debate, Adelphi of Knox won the competition in essay,
declamation and oratory, and therefore, was declared the winner of the
contest as a whole. . . . The *Rambler* made its contribution to the occasion by publishing a special Interstate Edition of 1,220 copies. One
wonders whether it would be possible in these later days, when athletics
have become the main interest of our American undergraduates, to arouse
such interest in oratory in any college or university of the land.[12]

The spirit of intercollegiate competition encouraged so greatly by
the introduction of collegiate athletics was largely responsible, as we shall
see, for the renewed strength of the old societies and for the restoration of
debating to the curriculum in the last decades of the nineteenth century.

Rutgers, the site of the first intercollegiate football game, was also the
site of one of the first eastern intercollegiate debates. Just one day after
the contest at Illinois College, members of the feeble Peithessophian Society defeated the Philomathean debaters from New York University before
a partisan audience at old Kirkpatrick Chapel. The question, interestingly
enough, was, "Resolved, That the only limitations on suffrage in the United
States should be those of age and sex." Peitho had the negative.

PUBLIC INTEREST

For some reason intercollegiate debating did not catch the fancy of
the public at first. Perhaps it was the fault of insufficient publicity. For
again in 1887 without attendant fanfare, Rutgers and New York University "crossed" arguments, this time victory going to the visiting Philo-
matheans who upheld the negative of "Resolved, That Constitutional Prohibition is the only practical solution of the Liquor Problem."

Then Harvard stepped into the picture! As early as 1887 the Boston
Latin School, the Newton High School, and the Dorchester High School
were engaging in interscholastic debates. In 1889 several members of the
Harvard Union who had participated in these interscholastic contests proposed that the collegians adopt a similar practice. But in 1889 and again
in 1890 they were voted down. In 1891, however, correspondence was
exchanged with the Yale Union, and in 1892 Yale challenged her arch
athletic and cultural rival from Cambridge to a series of two debates.
The Harvard Union, of course, accepted the challenge, the "first of the
modern intercollegiates" taking place at Cambridge on January 14, 1892,
the second, chairmaned by Chauncey M. Depew, at New Haven on
March 25, 1892.

As might be expected, when institutions like Harvard and Yale joined forces, the rest of the academic world sat up and paid attention. Throughout the country, student journalists examined, editorialized and, in general, approved. Also, as might be expected, the editors of the *Princetonian* of March 28, 1892, had something critical to add:

> The question of Joint Debates so prominently brought up in the college world by the action of Yale and Harvard serves to show the growing interest in this most important feature of college work. . . . The real principle of Debate, however, was lacking in great measure inasmuch as no second speeches were given. There was but little attempt at rebuttal. Princeton has ever been proud of her position in regard to this form of literary work. While Yale and Harvard are just starting a new era in this respect the work of Clio and Whig Halls has been going steadily on. . . .
>
> The idea, however, of a joint debate between the large colleges undoubtedly puts a keener stimulus in such contests and arouses more enthusiasm from a mixed college audience. A joint debate and oratorical association is a possibility of the future, and none would be more glad to see such a league in existence than Princeton.

On March 24, 1895, Princeton met and lost to Harvard "before the largest audience which has assembled in Princeton this Year!"

Desirous of emulating their elders and besting their rivals, the freshman unions formed at Yale and Harvard also tried their hands at intercollegiate competition. On May 10, 1895, Yale's neophytes took the first encounter at New Haven. The following year, Harvard won at Cambridge. Princeton freshmen, however, were denied the privileges extended to the upperclassmen. The *Daily Princetonian* on March 24, 1899, explained why:

> The faculty considers that the members of the Freshman class are not mature enough intellectually, to be able to take part in a debate that will be a credit to the Universities concerned without an amount of preliminary work altogether disproportionate to the benefit received, or else without faculty coaching to an extent that would make the debate not representative and an artificial production.

Inspired by the success and perhaps by the publicity attending the debate activities of Harvard, Yale, and Princeton, colleges throughout the country soon established their own leagues, usually along the patterns already set up for the athletic contests. As early as 1894, for example, such worthy baseball and football rivals as Chicago and Michigan met in forensic combat. The following year intercollegiate debating moved to the West Coast and attracted large audiences at Stanford and California. And in 1897 two important Middle Western leagues, which were to set debate fashions for the next three decades, were established. They were the Ohio Intercollegiate Debate League and the quadrangular association of Michigan, Northwestern, Minnesota, and Chicago.

Also in 1897, on March 9, the Columbia Debating Union, inspired by the presence of President Seth Low, met and defeated the Harvard Union at the Carnegie Lyceum in New York City. Spurred on by the success of their venture, the Columbia debaters contracted for a debate with the University of Chicago. On the evening of March 25, 1898, the first forensic contest between universities of the East and West was held and won by Columbia.

The following year, however, the tables were turned, and Chicago evened the series. This second intersectional debate is of special interest to modern debaters. It brought into sharp focus the problem of obtaining competent judges for, if we can believe the partisan editors of the *Columbia Spectator* on April 18, 1899, Columbia won the debate but lost the decision:

> . . . the judges stated that the debate was very close. They said the mass of evidence brought forward by Columbia showed the Chicago side to be intrinsically so weak, that they would give the decision to Chicago because of the difficulty of her task.

Possibly because of this difficulty in selecting competent and unbiased judges and, more probably, because the society rules varied so greatly that no single set of regulations could be easily adopted, the representatives of the competing colleges spent long and arduous sessions determining the dicta under which their league should operate.

ADOPTION OF STANDARDS

An example of the seriousness with which students undertook the formation of their intercollegiate relationships is furnished by the first Cornell-Pennsylvania debate contract as recorded on the front page of the *Pennsylvanian*, January 9, 1894:

> Art. I. The first debate shall be held in Ithaca, April 20, 1894 and the second in Philadelphia, not later than March 10, 1895. The subject of debate shall be chosen by the University under whose auspices the debate shall be held and shall be submitted to the other university at least three months in advance. The choice of sides shall rest with the visiting university, and shall be made within two weeks of the receipt of the subject chosen. The names of the representatives chosen shall be exchanged by two universities at least one month from the date of the debate.

Art. II. The university conducting the debate shall assume all financial obligations except the expenses of the visiting delegation.

Art. III. Each university shall select three representatives from its student body without limitation. Each debater shall be allowed two speeches, the first of ten minutes duration, and the second of five minutes. The first series of speeches shall be opened by the affirmative and negative speakers. The second series shall alternate between the negative and affirmative speakers.

Art. IV. The contest shall be judged and decided by these judges who shall be disinterested persons, not connected with either institution in any relation; one chosen by the Provost of the University of Pennsylvania, the second chosen by the President of Cornell University, and the third, who shall also preside, chosen by the President of the University holding the debate and with the consent of the contesting institution. No person shall act as judge whose appointment is not sanctioned and verified by both institutions. Two points shall be considered by the judges in rendering their decision, (1) the merit of the subject-matter presented and (2) the method and manner of its presentation.

It is interesting to note that although the majority of colleges followed the pattern promulgated by Cornell and the University of Pennsylvania, there was no set procedure. As the *Princetonian* observed, the first Harvard-Yale debate provided for no rebuttals at all, each team delivering three 15-minute speeches. In 1893, perhaps at the insistence of the men from "Old Nassau," the Yale-Princeton debaters were granted 6-minute rebuttals, which, however, followed the same order as the constructive addresses. Indeed, it was not until October 21, 1899, that the *Daily Princetonian* was able to report that "a radical change was decided upon for the coming year; namely, that the order of speeches [for Harvard-Yale-Princeton debates] will be reversed and the affirmative will close the debate." But even as late as 1900, Rutgers and New York University were adhering to a 12–12–12–5 order, with the negative rebuttalist closing the debate.

SELECTION OF DEBATERS

As we have already noted, the spirit of competition nourished by intercollegiate athletics was in a large degree responsible for the rapid acceptance of intercollegiate debating. This desire to best an important academic or athletic rival was responsible for the setting up of rigorous methods for selecting potential winning debaters. And, as might be expected, members of the faculty were often called upon to add their brains to the common cause. Thus, in 1899, Professor George P. Baker, speaking for the Harvard Advisory Committee, informs us:

. . . until within a year our contestants were selected at one trial. Their power as debaters was judged from a five-minute speech. Fortunately, since the Princeton trials last year, we have had a good system of selection. Now we have three trials—the first with speeches of five minutes, simply to rule out students undoubtedly not to be considered seriously; the second, with ten-minute speeches, to show how each man can develop a case for a side; and the third, with three men on a side, in order to judge from the work in team play and rebuttal which four men should be chosen as main speakers and as alternate for the debate.[13]

Carefully observing the activities of its respected rival at New Haven, the *Harvard Crimson* of November 18, 1892, observed that the "Yale Union has been taking energetic steps to secure the best speakers by calling for competitive written speeches and hearing the best fifteen of these delivered." Soon, however, the Yale debaters were ready to try out a new plan that might deliver them from the ever-lengthening series of losses to Harvard. The *Yale Daily News* hopefully announced on November 19, 1894, that preliminary trials were to be held at both the academic and the law schools at which each contestant was to deliver an 8-minute speech before a board of judges specifically instructed to pay particular attention to extemporaneous work. Six undergraduates and three law school speakers were to be selected from this preliminary contest. At a second elimination round, similarly judged, the three varsity debaters were to be chosen. With some modification, this plan of selection was employed at New Haven for the remainder of the century.

In general, the elimination contest procedure for selecting varsity representatives was adopted by most of the American colleges throughout the nineteenth century and the early decades of the present century. The practice of opening the competition to graduate students as well as to undergraduates, however, met the early opposition of smaller colleges without graduate departments. In 1893, for instance, the University of Pennsylvania was forced to quit the newly formed Pennsylvania Debating and Oratorical League, which had been promulgated by her own debate societies, because her competitors insisted that law school students be declared ineligible for league competition.

PREPARATION FOR DEBATES

Once the contracts had been signed and the debaters chosen, the real work of preparing for the debate was begun. R. C. Ringwalt, a member of the Harvard team in 1895 and coach of the Columbia debaters in 1897

---

[13] George P. Baker, "Debating at Harvard," *The Harvard Graduates' Magazine*, 7 (March 1899), 365–366.

and 1898, describes the procedure followed by the Columbia teams during the early years of intercollegiate debating:

On the day after the final preliminary contest, the hard work begins. The debaters set about reading at once. They find little use in talking. From his preliminary work each man has derived a different idea as to how the question should be treated; and it is beyond his power to bring the others to his position. So the first thing is to get a common ground, and this can be had only by hard reading. Usually a bibliography of books, pamphlets, and articles is prepared, and divided among the debaters. Each man is instructed to look into everything on his list, to read what is pertinent, and take notes and report to the others all that has especial value. When this has been done, the general outlines of the questions begin to be discussed. Next comes the making of the brief—in which each debater, since he may have to defend an attack on any part of it, must have a share—and the partition of the subject. The first part of the debate is usually given to a man who has a clear head for exposition and is a graceful speaker; he must get the question before the audience clearly and in such a way as to win their sympathy. To the second speaker is given the brunt of the argumentation; he presents the argument so far as time permits him. The last speech always goes to the best man, the most facile in rebuttal; he takes up that part of the argument which the second speaker has failed to touch upon, and in general strengthens the case wherever he can. After the divisions have been made, each man turns to the preparation of his own particular part. He determines the points he will bring up, the evidence he will introduce under each, and the order. He may write his speech out, and learn portions of it, or the brief may be the final form; this will depend on his method as a speaker. When the parts have been put into some kind of shape, a week or ten days before the contest, by far the most exhilarating part of the preparation begins,—the practice debates. Old debaters, graduate students, all men, in fact, who have any knowledge of the topic, and who are willing, are called in to speak against the contestants. Meetings are held every day, different assignments being made, although the old debaters are usually on hand each afternoon. The contestants speak in the order they are to have at the debate; while the outsiders take the place of the visiting team, and try to present such arguments as they will offer. There is also constant criticism by all present of the most unsparing kind. The least mis-statement, the slightest tendency to be dry or verbose or to miss a point, is caught up, and the attention of the speaker called to it. This is exasperating at first, almost discouraging; but it is salutary discipline. For, as a result, when the men go on the platform for the debate, their knowledge of the questions and the best way to state it is well-nigh perfect. They are the masters of themselves and of their whole line of proof.[14]

[14] Ralph C. Ringwalt, "Intercollegiate Debating," *The Forum*, 22 (January 1897), 636–637.

As has been indicated, the amount of research done by the intercollegiate debaters of the 1890's was prodigious. The Reverend N. S. Reeves, who debated under Woodrow Wilson at Princeton, recalls: "From the time that the subject was announced and the team finally chosen, it was something like two months to the debate. I know my cuts from classes mounted at these periods to some weeks." [15]

Nor was this characteristic only of Princeton. The *Brown Daily Herald* of May 7, 1900, in describing Brown's preparation for the debate with Dartmouth records: "Both teams have made great efforts in preparation. At Dartmouth the faculty granted the team a week's leave in which to visit the Boston Libraries in preparation for the contest."

FACULTY ASSISTANCE

As we have already seen, members of the college faculties, as well as prominent graduates of the college, were often called in to assist the undergraduates in preparing for a debate with an important intercollegiate rival. As the nineteenth century drew to a close, faculty assistance became the general rule. In 1896, however, the Harvard Advisory Committee on Debating, worried by the intensified concern of the student body for victory rather than self-improvement and a consequent reliance upon faculty assistance, decided to abolish all faculty coaching other than in elocution and in giving information as to materials and the value of evidence.

Despite Harvard's adherence to this ruling during the remainder of the century, her rivals blithely continued to make use of all the faculty assistance that was available. As might be expected, therefore, the victory of the Yale debaters in 1896 was bitterly resented by the "amateurs" of Harvard. The attitude of the Cambridge student body was reflected by the editors of the *Harvard Crimson*, who complained on November 27, 1896:

> At Yale . . . the practice of giving Faculty assistance is carried to its extreme. Their faculty members may not only furnish references . . . and give material and information [as at Harvard], but may criticize the speeches of the debaters, change and amend their arguments and general plan of debate, and even select a team of Faculty members to actually debate with the student team and lecture to them on the subject chosen for the debate. Yale graduates, not connected with the university, who have become authorities on the question for discussion, may also come to New Haven and coach for as long a time as they see fit.

[15] Quoted in Dayton D. McKean, "Woodrow Wilson as a Debate Coach," *Quarterly Journal of Speech*, 16 (November 1930), 459.

It should be observed, however, that although faculty coaching was no longer permitted, there was no provision prohibiting the use of alumni and friends of the university. Furthermore, the Harvard debaters had, for the most part, already received or were receiving the critical supervision of such experts in debate as Professors Albert Hart and George P. Baker in English 6 or English 30, courses expressly designed to train students in the principles of argumentation and debate.

By 1900 modern courses in forensics had become part of the curriculums of schools other than Harvard and Pennsylvania. In 1894, for example, the Yale catalog announced a course in Economic Debates, and in 1896, perhaps in order to overcome the Harvard jinx, a new course called "Argumentation" was offered as an elective. And in 1893, Princeton required that all sophomores take a course in "Argumentative Composition."

COMPENSATION

Although it was honor enough to the competition-conscious undergraduate and graduate student of the 1890's to be selected through vigorous elimination contests to represent his *alma mater*, his compatriots often thought highly enough of his efforts to reward him financially. In 1895, for example, the Yale Alumni Association of New York presented gold medals to the triumphant Yale debaters. In 1896 a $75 prize was offered to the best speaker from the academic department in the preliminary contest to determine the Yale team. Harvard, not to be outdone, rewarded the two highest contestants in her try-outs with $100 prizes, which were provided by the Coolidge fund established in 1899. And the same year Spencer Trask donated a fund of $3,000 for the rewarding of outstanding contestants in Princeton's preliminary trials. The taint of "commercialism" spread quickly. By the end of the century, it had spread as far west as the University of Michigan, where varsity debaters divided $180.

Thus, in 1900, blessed with a program of incentives and rewards as well as faculty supervision, debating once again occupied a place of honor in the college curriculum. And intercollegiate debating, its youngest offspring, had come of age—ready to do battle with conflicting student and faculty interests and the competition of newer forms of argumentation.

SUMMARY

Before we discuss present-day concepts of debating and argumentation, it is advisable to reflect for a few moments upon the main currents of debate history as we have traced them in American colleges and universities. We recall that the first major type of academic debating, the syllogistic disputation, was a cultural holdover from the Middle Ages. Stringent in its interpretation of the rules of logic, merciless in its insistence upon the use of a language which increasingly taxed the patience of its users and their audiences, and largely restricted in its scope to academic questions, the syllogistic disputation was despised by the "duller" or more secularly minded students from the early years of the seventeenth century on. But it took a century for the faculties and administrations of the colonial colleges to realize that conditions called for a more flexible and adaptable form of argumentation.

Early in the eighteenth century students took the lead in devising a more malleable form of debate, adapted from the assemblies of the ancients and the contemporary controversial declamations of American orators. The format of this new academic exercise was flexible, well suited to the abilities and interests of students and their auditors. The language was English, and the argument was based not only upon logic but upon persuasion as well. Moreover, its questions were increasingly popular—taken from current topics of interest.

Prodded by students and faced with their resistance to older forms of debate, the faculties of American colleges adopted the forensic disputation as their own until, first, the popularity of the debate societies and, later, the decline of interest in oratory and debate on the part of the less academic students of the 1870's forced its exclusion from the curriculum.

The changing complexion of the American college student and the world in which he lived, plus the effects of the Civil War, the competition of secret Greek-letter social societies and specialized clubs, and the rise of athletics to intercollegiate proportions also undermined the older debate societies. But the intercollegiate spirit nurtured by athletics resulted in the popularization of debating as an intercollegiate activity. Anxious to best important rivals, undergraduates and their academic mentors reinstalled debating as a curricular exercise. Thus, by 1900 institutions of higher education throughout the country were fostering debating as a competitive collegiate enterprise.

chapter 3

FORENSIC
HONOR SOCIETIES

by Annabel Dunham Hagood

The formation of forensic fraternities was a logical development in the expanding pattern of forensics in the late nineteenth and early twentieth centuries. The moves, first to challenges between literary societies and then a few years later to the formation of debate leagues, made almost inevitable the development of large organizations to provide opportunities for forensic competition. The arrival of the debate director, the expanding program on the college and the high school levels, and the increasing emphasis on awards perhaps determined that these societies would have as their main purpose the recognition of excellence in forensics.

ORGANIZATION OF FORENSIC
HONOR SOCIETIES

DELTA SIGMA RHO

The first forensic fraternity, Delta Sigma Rho, was founded in Chicago, Illinois, April 13, 1906, by representatives of the following universities: Chicago, Illinois, Iowa, Michigan, Minnesota, Nebraska, Northwestern, and Wisconsin. Fifty years later, and again on April 13, Delta Sigma Rho representatives met in Chicago to commemorate the Golden

33

Anniversary of a society which numbered over eighty chapters and nineteen thousand alumni.[1]

What were some of the objectives and goals of those representatives who met in 1906? Such answers are difficult more than half a century later, but certain key expressions seem to permeate Delta Sigma Rho literature and perhaps they can provide the insight we need. Dedicated to encouraging "effective and sincere public speaking," the founders envisioned a society which would attain the prestige in forensics which Phi Beta Kappa has in liberal arts colleges. The requirement that each member must have been a fully participating representative of his alma mater in intercollegiate debate or oratory meant, interestingly, that some of the founders could never be members.[2]

The representatives at the 1906 meeting elected Thomas C. Trueblood, of Michigan, chairman and Ray Files, of Iowa, secretary. Committees were appointed to prepare a constitution and to submit designs of a badge and pin.

From 1906 through 1911 the Council met annually at the time and place of the Northern Oratorical League, a convenient arrangement since most of the original Delta Sigma Rho members also belonged to the Northern Oratorical League.

At the 1907 meeting, the secretary was able to report that "he had received inquiries from almost every college and university in the land"— perhaps the result of the printing of one thousand copies of a four-page leaflet "issued by the national secretary and the National Propaganda Committee of Delta Sigma Rho." Only one charter was granted at that 1907 meeting, however; "for a time the unwritten policy was to grant charters to Ivy League institutions, the older state universities, and to defer applications from state agricultural colleges, teachers colleges, and municipal colleges." [3] This unwritten policy is especially significant as one considers the developing pattern of forensic fraternities.

TAU KAPPA ALPHA

Tau Kappa Alpha was founded in the State House of Indiana on May 13, 1908. That meeting, held in the office of the lieutenant governor of the state, Hugh Th. Miller, was the result of a year of investigation and planning by Oswald Ryan, then an undergraduate debater at Butler Col-

[1] Thorrel B. Fest, "For Effective Speech in a Free Society," *Delta Sigma Rho Golden Anniversary* (Booklet prepared and distributed by the National Office of Delta Sigma Rho, 1956), p. 2.

[2] Henry L. Ewbank, Sr., "Bits and Pieces of Delta Sigma Rho History," *Delta Sigma Rho Anniversary*, p. 7.

[3] *Ibid.*, p. 8.

lege. Miller, Ryan, and nine undergraduate forensic speakers in Indiana colleges and universities became the charter members of Tau Kappa Alpha.

Oswald Ryan, former chairman of the Civil Aeronautics Board and now an attorney in Washington, maintains a keen interest in the forensic fraternity which he was instrumental in founding. Addressing the members of the Tau Kappa Alpha National Council he repeated the question which had prompted him to organize the fraternity: "Why, I asked myself, shouldn't there be a national honorary fraternity dedicated to excellence in public speech, a 'Phi Beta Kappa' for orators as well as scholars?" [4] Ryan, in his message written for the Tau Kappa Alpha Golden Anniversary brochure, described the role of the fraternity in challenging terms.

> Tau Kappa Alpha's role is clear: it must be in the open forum that man first states, then tests, then urges his conception of truth. Tau Kappa Alpha will continue to use its historic medium of debate and exhortation to search out the truth that makes men free.[5]

With Hugh Th. Miller as president and Roger W. Wallace, a Butler College debater, as secretary-treasurer, Oswald Ryan and others "began a campaign of promotion by correspondence" among outstanding students of debating and oratory in other sections of the country.[6]

Organized originally with the state as the chapter unit, each state was to be governed by a state council which would select for membership the outstanding debaters and orators from the colleges under its supervision. This procedure was abandoned in 1913 in favor of individually chartered college chapters. The fraternity expanded rapidly from a Hoosier organization and now numbers more than ninety-five chapters representing every section of the country.

PI KAPPA DELTA

Apparently no single meeting marked the origin of Pi Kappa Delta. The National Council has listed the years 1912–13 [7] as did an article written by one of the founders.[8]

[4] Charles R. Layton, "History of Tau Kappa Alpha," *Argumentation and Debate*, ed., David Potter (New York: Holt, Rinehart and Winston, Inc., 1954), p. 476.

[5] Oswald Ryan, "A Message from Tau Kappa Alpha's Founder," *Tau Kappa Alpha Golden Anniversary* (Booklet prepared and distributed by the National Office of Tau Kappa Alpha, 1958), p. 2.

[6] Layton, *op. cit.*, pp. 477–478.

[7] *What is Pi Kappa Delta?* (A pamphlet prepared and distributed by the National Council of Pi Kappa Delta).

[8] E. R. Nichols, "A Historical Sketch of Intercollegiate Debating," *Quarterly Journal of Speech*, 22 (December 1936), 599.

Pi Kappa Delta was created to provide a means of recognition for orators and debaters in the smaller colleges.[9] Although three men are listed as the founders of the society, John A. Shields, a student at Ottawa University, and E. R. Nichols, professor of English at Ottawa for two years, 1909–11, and later head of the Department of Composition at Ripon College in Wisconsin, were responsible for the idea which resulted in Pi Kappa Delta, now the largest forensic society with over two hundred chapters.

The idea moved toward reality when Professor Nichols and the Ripon College debaters adopted a constitution and sent it to the Ottawa College debaters where it was adopted with some changes. John A. Shields and Edgar A. Vaughn of Kansas State College at Manhattan met for a week end to make a final draft of the document. They then flipped a coin to see who would have the privilege of signing it first. Copies of the constitution were sent to seven other coaches and leaders of debate for their approval. All signed and local chapters were admitted by these founders as they applied. Ottawa qualified for the first charter, followed by Washburn College, Iowa Wesleyan College, and Kansas State College.

With the advent of this third fraternity, we note a distinct difference in philosophy and type of membership. Delta Sigma Rho and Tau Kappa Alpha were founded with the hope that each would become a Phi Beta Kappa of forensics. Membership was to be the ultimate goal and distinction. Pi Kappa Delta, perhaps as a result of the Masonic influence—two of the founders were Masons—established degrees of achievement and orders of membership. In this fraternity one becomes a member early in his forensic career and acquires additional orders and advanced degrees of membership as he becomes more proficient in debate and/or oratory.

The Constitution of Pi Kappa Delta provides for three orders of membership: oratory, debate, and instruction; and a member may be of one, two, and three orders, depending upon his qualifications. In addition, the organization has four degrees of membership: Fraternity, Proficiency, Honor, and Special Distinction. The degree of Fraternity is bestowed upon the candidate in oratory who shall have represented his college in a recognized contest in oratory or extemporaneous speaking, upon the candidate in debate who shall have participated in five decision or eight non-decision debates, and upon the candidate in instruction who is an instructor in public speaking or a director of oratory or debate in a recognized college. The other degrees, Proficiency, Honor, and Special Distinction, are granted to candidates as they meet specifically stated standards, which include the extent of participation and the degree of achievement.[10]

[9] "The History of Pi Kappa Delta," *The Forensic*, Series 45 (March 1960), 16.

[10] *Constitution of Pi Kappa Delta* (1957).

NATIONAL FORENSIC LEAGUE

Bruno Jacob of Ripon College frequently is referred to as "Mr. NFL" and the title accurately reflects his role in the organization and development of the National Forensic League. Jacob described the events leading to the formation of the organization in a booklet prepared and distributed by the NFL.

> In October, 1924, Ray Cecil Carver, head of the department of English in the high school at Albany, New York, wrote to the Pi Kappa Delta chapter at Ripon College, Wisconsin, asking, "Do you know of any association of debaters in which high school debaters are welcome to membership?" The letter came to my attention and brought this reply: "As far as we know there is at present no organization for high school debaters . . . we would be willing to go to considerable effort to sponsor such an enterprise."
>
> These letters mark the beginning of the National Forensic League. During the next several weeks I outlined the proposal to a selected list of debate coaches, inviting their co-operation. Fifty-five responded with enthusiasm." [11]

Ray Cecil Carver became the first president of the National Forensic League, an office which he held until 1933, when he was succeeded by Karl E. Mundt, now Senator from South Dakota and president of the NFL for more than twenty-five years. Bruno Jacob has served as secretary since the founding of the NFL. In July 1934, the national office of the League moved with him to the University of Denver. In September 1936, both returned to Ripon College.

The early years of the National Forensic League were marked by rapid growth. By March 28, 1925, twenty schools representing fifteen states from coast to coast had ratified the constitution. One hundred schools were chartered by 1926, and in 1933, despite the economic depression, four hundred chapters were chartered. In 1936, a limit of five hundred chapters was established and a waiting list set up. This limit was changed as schools clamored for membership, first to six hundred, then to seven hundred, and finally in 1960–61 to a quota of one thousand chapters. So great was the demand for a National Forensic League chapter that the Council authorized a comprehensive plan of affiliate membership for schools awaiting a charter vacancy.[12] This keen interest in the National Forensic League is graphic

---

[11] Bruno E. Jacob, "History of the National Forensic League," *Constitution and Regulations* (Booklet prepared and distributed by the National Office of the National Forensic League, 1962), p. 24.

[12] *Ibid.*, pp. 26–31.

indication that this society is fulfilling its primary purpose of interesting high school students in public speaking and holding their interest until they acquire a high degree of effectiveness as speakers.[13]

The National Forensic League uses a system of credit points as the basis for all honors in NFL.

> They are earned in interscholastic speech competition and in community service speaking . . . Every speech appearance earns some points, more of course for winning debates and highest contest honors, but still some recognition for every contestant.[14]

A student may apply to the local chapter for membership in the National Forensic League when he has earned twenty-five credit points, ten of which were gained in competitive speaking. The secretary of the local chapter ascertains from the high school office whether the student ranks scholastically in the upper two-thirds of his class. Membership is automatically deferred for the students in the lower one-third except in special cases where the chapter, with the approval of the principal, petitions the Executive Council to elect in spite of scholastic or credit point deficiencies.[15]

Advanced degrees of Honor, Excellence, and Distinction are available to members who have earned the required number of credit points. Instructors receive one-tenth as many points as the students they coach. They qualify for membership and advanced degrees according to the same schedule provided for the student members.[16]

PHI RHO PI

Phi Rho Pi was formed to promote the interests of debate, oratory, extemporaneous speaking, radio, and other speech activities in the junior colleges. Rarig and Greaves, in their brief discussion of Phi Rho Pi, listed Roland Shackson, coach of forensics at Grand Rapids Junior College, Michigan, as the single founder of this society, organized in 1928.[17]

[13] *The National Forensic League* (Booklet prepared and distributed by the National Office of the National Forensic League), p. 2.
[14] *Ibid.*
[15] *Chapter Manual* (Booklet prepared and distributed by the National Office of the National Forensic League, 1962), pp. 5–6.
[16] *Ibid.*
[17] Frank M. Rarig and Halbert S. Greaves, "National Speech Organizations and Speech Education," ed., Karl R. Wallace (New York: Appleton-Century-Crofts, Inc., 1954), p. 510.

Phi Rho Pi maintains orders of membership and degrees of achievement for student members and chapter sponsors similar in principle to Pi Kappa Delta. The orders of membership are: debate, oratory, extemporaneous speaking, public speaking, and impromptu speaking. The degree of Fellowship is open to any candidate recommended by the Phi Rho Pi sponsor and the local chapter. All Phi Rho Pi sponsors are automatically members of this degree. Candidates for the degree of Honor must have won first place in two intercollegiate contests or reached the finals in the national contest. Sponsors must have coached five students who have won the degree. The degree of Highest Achievement is reserved for winners of first or second place in the National Phi Rho Pi contest and those sponsors who have coached five students who have won the degree. The order of public speaking incorporates speech activities promoted by established tournaments but not otherwise specified in the orders, for instance, discussion, dramatic reading, and declamation. In submitting the name of a candidate for the degrees of Honor and Highest Achievement the sponsor must list the speeches, the dates the speeches were delivered, and the audiences. Notice of eligibility must be received before initiation is permitted.[18]

OTHER SOCIETIES

Compiling an historical account of forensic honor societies is at best a frustrating task. Little has been written about these societies, even about those in operation for forty years or more. Golden anniversaries seem to have generated an enthusiasm for historical accounting but even the anniversary booklets and brochures indicate that much of history is locked in memories and fraternity files.

The several societies in existence for only brief periods of time present an especially difficult problem. An occasional reference may be found to the existence of these societies but no information seems to be available on their founding or operation. References usually are to dissolution or merger.

E. R. Nichols listed two forensic societies which were organized for women, Zeta Kappa Xi in 1913 and Delta Phi in 1915. Nichols indicated that these societies were killed when Delta Sigma Rho and Tau Kappa Alpha began admitting women to membership about 1920.[19]

Equally sketchy was the statement in *The Speaker* of Tau Kappa Alpha announcing the merger of Alpha Phi Epsilon and Phi Delta Gamma

[18] *Constitution of Phi Rho Pi.*
[19] Nichols, "A Historical Sketch of Intercollegiate Debating," p. 599.

into TKA.[20] Considerable investigation failed to produce any information about the founding or the purposes of these two societies.[21]

The status of Phi Alpha Rho, a society listed by Gregg Phifer in his chapter on "Organizing Forensic Programs," was clarified by Phifer in a letter dated July 9, 1961.

> It [Phi Alpha Rho] was established at Loyola University in Chicago, intended to be a national Catholic forensic fraternity. This organization never got off the ground, never established chapters beyond the campus of Loyola, and was abolished by the student council at Loyola in 1952.[22]

THE DEVELOPMENT OF THE FORENSIC SOCIETIES

By 1935 the pattern of the forensic societies was established. Several societies had been disbanded or merged and there remained five societies which were to become increasingly important in the years ahead. These five: Delta Sigma Rho, Tau Kappa Alpha, Pi Kappa Delta, National Forensic League, and Phi Rho Pi, had solved many of their early financial problems by assessing initiation fees, charter fees, and, in some cases, chapter dues. Each published a magazine for its members—*The Gavel*, Delta Sigma Rho; *The Speaker*, Tau Kappa Alpha; *The Forensic*, Pi Kappa Delta; *The Rostrum*, National Forensic League; *The Persuader*, Phi Rho Pi.[23] The necessity of sponsoring a program of forensic activities which would make fraternity membership more meaningful was becoming increasingly apparent.

The original purposes of the founders remained fundamentally unchanged. Delta Sigma Rho and Tau Kappa Alpha continued to emphasize both academic and forensic excellence. The goal of a forensic society with the prestige of Phi Beta Kappa continued to influence fraternity policy. Pi Kappa Delta, while not restricting its membership to the smaller colleges, continued to provide a means of recognition for students in smaller colleges. Phi Rho Pi, Pi Kappa Delta, and the National Forensic League continued to use the incentive method in granting degrees of membership.

Undoubtedly the prime reason for the success which some societies

---

[20] *The Speaker*, 27 (May 1935), 5.

[21] Charles R. Layton, Historian of Tau Kappa Alpha, was unable to furnish any details concerning the founding or merger of these societies.

[22] Information in a letter to the author from Dr. Gregg Phifer of Florida State University, July 9, 1961.

[23] Phi Rho Pi did not publish *The Persuader* during the years 1937–47; Tau Kappa Alpha made available columns in *The Speaker* to Phi Rho Pi.

were enjoying by 1935 and others were destined to enjoy in the years immediately ahead was the inauguration of a program of forensic activities in which the members could participate. To understand the operation of these programs is to know much of the history of the fraternities in the years which followed.

PI KAPPA DELTA

E. R. Nichols, one of the founders of Pi Kappa Delta, attributed the rapid growth of his society to two factors, the membership plan and the practice of holding contests at national conventions.[24] This custom is almost as old as the fraternity itself for the second Pi Kappa Delta Convention, held at Ottawa University in Ottawa, Kansas, in 1918 featured an exhibition debate between Redlands University and Ottawa. The third convention, held two years later at Morningside College, Sioux City, Iowa, included an oratorical contest in addition to an exhibition debate between the host school and Redlands University. In 1922, the society decided to establish contests for men and women in oratory and extemporaneous speaking.

The introduction of a debate tournament resulted from a proposal by W. H. Veatch, the coach of debate at South Dakota Wesleyan College, who agreed to conduct the first tournament if Pi Kappa Delta would accept his proposal on a trial basis.[25] Thus, in 1926, in Estes Park, Colorado, the first national debate tournament was held, an innovation which was to have marked effect on future programming by the forensic societies.

Apparently this first tournament passed its trial with flying colors for Pi Kappa Delta has continued to sponsor a national tournament biennially since 1926, with the exception of the World War II interim. In 1923, the provincial convention was inaugurated for the alternate years when a national convention was not held. The format of the tournament has been changed from time to time, but a strong emphasis on debate has been retained.

NATIONAL FORENSIC LEAGUE

Many regard the academic year 1930–31 as the most significant year in the history of the National Forensic League. In August 1930, Secretary Bruno Jacob proposed to the Council that it sponsor a national speech tournament.[26] District tournaments were held in nine states to select con-

---

[24] Nichols, "A Historical Sketch of Intercollegiate Debating," p. 601.
[25] *Ibid.*
[26] Jacob, "History of the National Forensic League," *Constitution and Regula-*

testants for the national event. On May 7–9, 1931, forty-nine high schools representing seventeen states participated in the first National Forensic League tournament at Ripon College. In the 1932 tournament, ninety-two schools were registered. The national tournament continued to gain in popularity, and in 1962 the society held its largest national tournament to date.[27]

The first National Student Congress was held in conjunction with the national tournament in 1938 and was continued, even after the events of World War II necessitated the suspension of the national tournament, until 1945, when it was suspended in compliance with a ban on conventions. The Student Congress was restored to the national program in 1952.

The National Forensic League limits participation in the national tournament to those students who have won a state championship or placed first in a National Forensic League district tournament. It thus brings together some of the finest high school speakers in the nation to compete in the national tournament. This tournament now includes, in addition to debate, contests in extemporaneous speaking, original oratory, and dramatic interpretation. The Tau Kappa Alpha trophy is presented at the close of each national tournament to the participating chapter which then has the largest number of tournament points. These points are recorded for each round of participation in an individual contest event and each round of debate participation in the national tournament. The record begins in 1931 and all points gained by a school remain to its credit until it has received the trophy.

DELTA SIGMA RHO

The first National Student Congress of Delta Sigma Rho was held in the nation's capital in 1939, with 125 delegates from thirty-eight chapters in attendance. The Congress was the result of a proposal presented to the National Council by Milton Dickens of the University of Southern California and the investigation by a special committee which Dickens chaired.[28]

Senator Josh Lee of Oklahoma, Delta Sigma Rho member and former debate coach, addressed the opening assembly, and many other distinguished alumni of Delta Sigma Rho attended a banquet with the students that evening.

As a result of the success of the 1939 meeting, the National Student

tions (Booklet prepared and distributed by the National Office of the National Forensic League, 1962), p. 25.

[27] *Ibid.*, p. 26.

[28] Milton Dickens, "Origin and Development of the National Student Congresses of Delta Sigma Rho," *Delta Sigma Rho Golden Anniversary*, pp. 17–18.

Congress became a biennial program of Delta Sigma Rho. At the second Congress, held in Chicago, 250 delegates from forty-four chapters were in attendance.

Evaluation and self-criticism have been a consistent aspect of this program. When the third Congress met in 1947, an evaluation committee was provided to systematize criticisms and assist in planning future programs. Committee activity later was expanded to include the use of trained observers who made thorough studies of certain aspects of the Congress. This work by Delta Sigma Rho has provided a more effective student congress for the society and has added to the theory and practice of legislative discussion and debate.

TAU KAPPA ALPHA

The annual convention of the National Association of Teachers of Speech meeting in Chicago in December, 1939, marked the beginning of Tau Kappa Alpha's national speaking program. Under the direction of Hale Aarnes, chairman of the Department of Speech of the University of South Dakota, nearly one hundred students participated in "The Forensic Experience Progression in Contest Form." The progression combined extemporaneous speaking, discussion, and debate on the question, "To what extent should the United States follow a policy of isolation (economic and military) toward nations outside the Western Hemisphere engaged in armed international or civil conflict?" [29]

The three-day speech event continued to be an annual program of Tau Kappa Alpha until interrupted by World War II. The program was resumed in 1946, and became a yearly spring event on a college campus. In 1949, the "Forensic Progression" was dropped and debate, discussion, and various individual speaking events became the format. Today, the annual national conference is a vital aspect of Tau Kappa Alpha activity. Two divisions of debate, two-man and four-man, and a three-day program in discussion are the main events of the conference. The individual speaking events have been changed from time to time with public and extemporaneous speaking considered to be the most popular contests.

A distinct feature of each Tau Kappa Alpha national conference is the presentation of awards to men and women who have distinguished themselves in their chosen professional fields.

The first of these awards, the Speaker of the Year Award, was created in 1949. Through the selection of prominent men and women who have demonstrated effective, intelligent, and responsible communication, Tau Kappa Alpha vitalizes the goals of the fraternity for the American public.

[29] Keith S. Montgomery, "The National Student Conference and Student Council," *Tau Kappa Alpha Golden Anniversary*, p. 20.

From 1950 through 1958 awards were made to speakers in five broad areas of human endeavor: national affairs, business and commerce, religion, labor, and education, scientific, and cultural activities. In 1959 the National Council of Tau Kappa Alpha directed the Speaker of the Year Board of Award to select only one area of the five and to designate the outstanding speaker in that area as the Speaker of the Year.

The TKA Distinguished Alumni Awards were first presented at the Golden Anniversary banquet in 1958. The National Council approved the continuation of this award and each year Tau Kappa Alpha chapters are invited to nominate alumni for the awards. The nominations are reviewed by the Committee on Distinguished Alumni Awards and those selected for the award are presented with plaques at the national conference banquet.

PHI RHO PI

The national convention of Phi Rho Pi is an annual event affording competition in debate, oratory, extempore, impromptu, and after-dinner speaking. Preliminary rounds in the individual events are followed by semifinal and final rounds. Six preliminary rounds of debate are held and all teams which have lost no more than two of the six debates continue into the elimination rounds.[30]

THE FUTURE OF FORENSIC SOCIETIES

Examination of the founding of the forensic societies and the development of their programs indicates that distinct purposes and philosophies were evident in the organization and development of each society. In one sense, the societies have shared a common purpose—the recognition of excellence in public speaking. Beyond that common purpose certain marked differences continue to exist. Delta Sigma Rho and Tau Kappa Alpha demand high standards of academic excellence in addition to competence in forensics. The National Forensic League denies eligibility to those students who rank in the lower one-third of the academic class. In this sense, these three societies are appropriately termed honor societies. Pi Kappa Delta and Phi Rho Pi may more accurately be termed recognition societies since they do not adhere to academic standards of eligibility.

These five societies now serve almost fifteen hundred member schools. The chapter roll of each society includes schools from every section of the

---

[30] The author was unable to obtain the detailed information on Phi Rho Pi activities which was provided by the national offices of the other societies.

nation. Among the three senior college societies, the early restrictions on institutional size and prestige have vanished. Each society numbers among its member chapters both small colleges and universities. The applications for charters which each society has pending indicate a continuing interest in this type of fraternal affiliation and an expansion of forensic programs on the high school and college levels.

In looking ahead to the future of forensic societies, predictions should be based on the contributions which these societies have made to the field of speech and to the education of the students they have served.

Considerable evidence exists to indicate that the contributions have been significant. In many ways, the pattern of forensics in the twentieth century has been determined by the leadership provided by the forensic societies. Five contributions merit special attention.

1. *The crystallization of standards in forensic programs.*

A quick glance at the constitution of any society will indicate that the organization operates on specific principles designed to insure excellent training for the student in the area of public speaking. Charters are granted only to those schools whose forensic programs meet specified standards including faculty supervision and adequate financing. The program of each chapter is subject to constant review, and disciplinary action, such as probation or deactivation, may be taken when the chapter fails to maintain the standards of the society.

2. *The publication of forensic journals.*

The journals which are published quarterly by the societies contribute significantly to the field of speech. In addition to news about the chapters and messages from the officers, they contain articles of interest to students and teachers in the area of forensics. Not only do these publications provide additional outlets for articles of note, but they afford a medium of instruction for the students and alumni who are regular subscribers.

3. *The encouragement and recognition of excellence in public speaking.*

This, of course, was the basic purpose for which the societies were organized, and they have been highly successful in fulfilling the purpose. In our educational system it is vitally important to encourage excellence and stimulate the better-than-average student—the type who tends to find forensic programs attractive.

Indeed, in this period, when man seems to move more and more in the direction of negotiation with his fellow man, the cultivation of excellence in public speaking is a national necessity. The forensic societies are of inestimable value in seeking out, encouraging, and training future leaders in education, government, industry, law, medicine, and the sciences.

4. *The opportunity for national forensic competition.*

A quick glance at the listing of debate tournaments held during a given year reveals that the term *national* has become a popular description. It should be remembered that the first national tournament was sponsored by a forensic society. Indeed the national programs sponsored by the societies provide far more extensive opportunities than any currently popular national tournament limited to two or four students from a small select group of schools.

The constant study of the national programs, the evaluation, and the redesigning of format have enabled the forensic societies to provide valuable forensic experiences for their members. In addition, they have contributed in both design and standards to the dozens of tournaments which are held each year.

5. *The cultivation of a public appreciation of forensic activities.*

Beyond question this is one of the most valuable services forensic societies have rendered to the field of speech. Not only have prominent national figures held major offices in forensic societies, Karl Mundt, president of the National Forensic League, and Lowell Thomas, president of Tau Kappa Alpha, but many of the nation's most prominent men and women are members of one or several of the societies.

Furthermore, the societies endeavor to maintain contact with these members. The attendance at national meetings by distinguished alumni, programs of recognition such as those inaugurated by Delta Sigma Rho and Tau Kappa Alpha at the occasion of the Golden Anniversary, the use of newsletters and journals, all serve to maintain the interest of the alumni.

The Tau Kappa Speaker of the Year program has brought national recognition to forensic societies by vitalizing the standards of public speaking in a free society.

These and other contributions made by the societies indicate that the future of forensic societies is promising. The objectives of these societies are finding increasing expression in the objectives of American education. The cultivation of excellence in communication and the recognition of those who have met specific standards of achievement will enable the forensic societies to contribute significantly both to the field of speech and to education in general in the years ahead.

SUMMARY

The formation of forensic honor societies logically followed the development of debate leagues in the late nineteenth and early twentieth centuries. The first society, Delta Sigma Rho, was founded in 1906, followed two years later by Tau Kappa Alpha. The success of these societies undoubtedly led to the establishment of Pi Kappa Delta for students in small colleges, the National Forensic League for high schools, and Phi Rho Pi for junior colleges. Several other societies existed for brief periods of time, but the occasional references to their existence fail to provide information on their founding or operation.

These forensic societies have shared a common purpose—the recognition of excellence in public speaking. Their original purposes and present requirements for membership characterize Delta Sigma Rho, Tau Kappa Alpha, and the National Forensic League as honor societies. Pi Kappa Delta and Phi Rho Pi are recognition societies, having no stipulated academic achievement as a prerequisite to membership.

These organizations have contributed significantly to the field of speech and to the education of the students they have served. They have aided in the crystallization of standards in forensic programs, afforded the opportunity for national forensic competition, and encouraged and recognized excellence in public speaking. Through fraternity journals and programs they have maintained alumni interest and cultivated a public appreciation of forensic activities. In many ways, the pattern of forensics in the twentieth century has been determined by the leadership provided by the forensic societies.

II.

chapteR 4

ANALYSIS OF
THE PROPOSITION

by Ronald F. Reid

Intelligent, responsible debating requires thorough advance preparation which includes analyzing the proposition to be debated, research, outlining the argument, and developing a case. Although these four aspects of preparation frequently overlap and interact with one another, they are sufficiently distinct to justify separate consideration. This chapter will consider analysis of propositions, a process which is basic to other aspects of preparation.

THE NATURE OF A PROPOSITION

Before describing the process of analyzing a proposition, we should first understand what we are analyzing. In other words, what is a proposition? The famous nineteenth-century rhetorician and logician Richard Whately devised a concise and useful definition when he called a proposition a *judgment expressed in words*.[1]

Whately's definition does not limit itself to propositions for formal debate, for the average person expresses judgment in words in many situations other than debates. Anyone might, for example, casually observe that

[1] *Elements of Logic* (Boston: James Munroe & Co., 1843), p. 74.

"The sun is shining," or that "Professor Smith is a good teacher," or that "We ought to see the movie at the Ritz." Such statements are judgments expressed in words and therefore are propositions. However, they would probably not be suitable propositions for formal debates. This section of the chapter will discuss various types of propositions without specific reference to formal debating; the next section will consider propositions from the standpoint of their suitability for formal debate.

Propositions are classified into three general types: (1) fact, (2) value, and (3) policy. Any proposition is potentially controversial.

PROPOSITIONS OF FACT

Let us begin with propositions of fact. These are classified into four general types: (1) Statements which affirm or deny the occurrence of events or actions. For example, "Mr. X killed Mr. Y." (2) Statements which affirm or deny the existence of things. The frequent allegations and denials of the existence of "flying saucers" and of the so-called "abominable snowman" are examples of this type of proposition of fact. (3) Statements which affirm or deny the classification of objects or events. For example, both sides of a legal dispute might agree that Mr. X killed Mr. Y but disagree as to whether the act should be classified as "self-defense" or as "murder." (4) Statements which affirm or deny a relationship between events or objects. For example, one might affirm or deny that crime comics contribute to juvenile delinquency.[2] In summary, *propositions of fact are judgments expressed in words which affirm or deny the occurrence of events, the existence of things, the classification of things or events, or the relationship between events or objects.*

PROPOSITIONS OF VALUE

People not only perceive and infer facts, but they also relate what they perceive and infer to their attitudes and make value-judgments. One might observe various actions of Mr. Doe, relate these observed actions to one's attitudes, and then adjudge Mr. Doe to be "good" or "bad." Or one might observe various actions of the United Nations, relate these observed actions to one's attitudes, and then say that the U.N. is "useful" or "useless." In either case, one is attributing a quality to something.

Statements of value assume the existence of certain facts. The as-

---

[2] This classification of propositions of fact is a slight modification of the scheme presented by Horace G. Rahskopf in his "Questions of Fact vs. Questions of Policy," *Quarterly Journal of Speech*, 17 (February 1932), p. 62.

sertion that Mr. Doe is good assumes the existence of Mr. Doe. However, propositions of value go beyond the mere allegation or denial of facts; they also allege a quality such as "goodness-badness" or "usefulness-uselessness" about some object, idea, or event. In summary, *propositions of value are judgments expressed in words which attribute some quality to an event, idea, or object.*

PROPOSITIONS OF POLICY

The values which one has attached to something will affect his actions toward it. For example, if we decide that a certain politician is good, we probably shall decide to support him in the next election. The decision to support the politician is a decision to take a certain course of action. Similarly, if your roommate suggests that you quit studying and go with him to the movies, he is expressing in words a judgment as to a course of action which should be taken. In short, *propositions of policy are judgments expressed in words which allege or deny that a certain course of action should be taken.*

Just as value judgments presuppose certain factual propositions, so does our acceptance or rejection of propositions of policy depend upon our acceptance or rejection of certain related propositions of fact and value. For example, your reaction to your roommate's suggestion that you go to the movies will depend upon your beliefs about a number of facts (such as what is on at the movie and the likelihood of tests in your classes tomorrow) and upon your values (such as the importance you attach to grades).

Similarly, to use a more sophisticated example, during the moratorium on nuclear testing, some United States governmental officials advocated a policy of resuming tests. This proposal involved a course of action to be taken and was therefore a proposition of policy. One of the issues in the protracted debate on this proposal was the factual one of whether the Soviet Union was testing secretly, and another concerned propositions which alleged or denied the value of nuclear weapons and the morality of developing such weapons. Clearly, then, a proposition of policy has within it a number of subpropositions of fact and value, but it is differentiated from propositions of fact and value in that it advocates that a certain course of action should or should not be taken.

Thus far in this chapter we have considered propositions in general, and it is obvious that people allege or deny propositions in a variety of situations, including private thinking and informal conversation as well as in formal debating. We shall now turn our attention to propositions as they relate specifically to formal debating.

THE DEBATE PROPOSITION

CHARACTERISTICS OF A GOOD DEBATE PROPOSITION

A proposition, to be suitable for a formal debate, should be timely and significant. Furthermore, it should be sufficiently controversial to permit both the advocates and opponents of the proposition to find good arguments and evidence to support their positions.

Some people have difficulty in understanding that a debate proposition can have good arguments and evidence on both sides. In order to realize that there can be two good sides to a proposition we must disabuse ourselves of the common tendency to think in "either . . . or" terms. We should think of a man not as being either good *or* bad but as partially good *and* partially bad; we should think of propositions not as being true *or* false but as partially true *and* partially false. It is important for a debater to realize that the truth or falsity of a good debate proposition is seldom absolute and beyond dispute. To appreciate this point, it will be helpful to consider three closely related concepts: the possibly true, the probably true, and the certainly true.

A proposition is considered possibly true when the statement is (1) internally consistent and (2) consistent with other known facts. For example, the statement, "John Doe got out of bed this morning at 8:00 a.m. and remained in bed all day today" is not possibly true because the statement is internally inconsistent. Similarly, the statement that "John Doe walked to the moon this morning" is not possibly true because it is inconsistent with other known facts.

However, the statement, "John Doe painted his cow green" is possibly true; for the proposition is internally consistent and consistent with other known facts, such as the existence of cows, green paint, and abnormal behavior. The *probability* of such an occurrence, however, is obviously remote.

Probability involves not only internal and external consistency but also positive evidence which supports the judgment. The next question which arises concerns the amount of positive evidence necessary before one can say that a statement is certainly true. Philosophers have yet to agree on an answer to this question. Indeed, some deny that anything can be known for certain. Others maintain that something must be observed directly before a person can be certain of its truth.

Using the latter definition, it is important (and sometimes frightening) to reflect on how few of the things we "know" are really known as a certainty. We can look at the sun today and know, as a certainty, that it is there; but we cannot know as a certainty that it will be there tomorrow.

Indeed, any prediction about the future cannot logically be stated as a certainty.

It is true (it is probably true) that we confidently expect various things to happen in the future. Most of us expect the sun to rise tomorrow. The proposition, "The sun will rise tomorrow," however, is not true as a certainty but only as a high-grade probability.

Realizing that propositions vary on a continuum from the possibly true to the certainly true, we can see that the most debatable propositions, those for which sound arguments can be developed on both sides, are those which are somewhere near the center of the continuum. We can also see that on most propositions suitable for formal debate the speakers cannot "prove beyond the shadow of a doubt" or "prove conclusively" that the debate proposition is or is not true. Unfortunately, many debaters use such phrases, but to the rational man these debaters succeed only in revealing their own ignorance of the probable nature of most of our knowledge.

PHRASING A GOOD DEBATE PROPOSITION

At first glance, phrasing a suitable debate proposition might appear to be a simple task, requiring only the use of words which are defined clearly by a dictionary. Unfortunately, the task is more complex; for, in an ultimate sense, meanings of words exist in people, not in dictionaries. Words are not objects, actions, or ideas; they are *symbols* which represent objects, actions, or ideas. It is true that groups of people, through custom and usage, assign similar meanings to the same word; but two people, hearing the same word, might still attach slightly different meanings to the word. For example, suppose you say the word *automobile*. One listener might visualize a compact, rear-engine, blue-colored foreign-made car while another might imagine an American-made, black, front-engine limousine.

In some situations, such differing images do not interfere seriously with communication. In other situations they result in so much ambiguity that a complete breakdown in communication occurs. The problem of ambiguity is especially severe when people talk about abstractions and use words which symbolize ideas. Words such as *democracy, useful, socialism,* and *beauty* do not symbolize objects; they symbolize abstract concepts. As a general rule, the more abstract the word, the greater the chances that different people will attach different meanings to the word.

On the basis of the foregoing discussion, we can set forth the first requirement of a well-phrased debate proposition: the wording should be as specific and unambiguous as possible. An ambiguous debate proposition will result in a confusion, rather than a clarification, of the issues.

The second characteristic of a well-phrased proposition for formal debate is that the proposition be worded in an unprejudiced manner. To say that "The serious problem of unemployment should be solved by reducing taxes" is to give proponents of the proposition the crucial argument that unemployment is serious and leaves open only the question of whether a tax reduction is the best method of reducing unemployment. By giving one side an important argument, certain potentially important issues are left unexplored, thereby impairing the usefulness of a formal debate to identify and clarify the issues involved in a given subject.

Similarly, "loaded words," that is words with strong emotional connotations, should be avoided in the phrasing of a debate proposition. To say that "A program of socialized medicine should be established in the United States" is to slant the resolution in favor of the negative; for the phrase "socialized medicine" is a loaded phrase in view of the fact that a majority of Americans tend to oppose "socialism." It would be better to call for "compulsory national health insurance"—a relatively more specific and unprejudiced phrase—and leave the loaded term *socialized medicine* to the propagandists who devised it in the first place.

It is customary, when phrasing propositions for formal debates, to word the proposition affirmatively. Thus, it is usually better, when wording a proposition of fact for formal debate, to say that "X exists" rather than "X does not exist," or when phrasing a proposition of policy to say that "X policy should be adopted" rather than "X policy should not be adopted." When debating propositions of policy, it is customary to phrase the resolution so that the affirmative upholds the adoption of a new policy, thereby giving the negative the option of defending present policy or advocating a different new policy.

Finally, a good proposition for formal debate contains only one main idea. A proposition such as "Resolved: That the United States should increase its capability for fighting conventional limited wars and should reduce its stockpile of nuclear weapons" obviously contains two proposals. Theoretically, it would be possible either to favor both proposals, to oppose both, to favor the first and oppose the second, or to oppose the first and favor the second—and even these theoretical possibilities do not consider the possibility that a person might be neutral toward both proposals or be neutral toward one and have an opinion toward the other. Even supposing that two people, or teams of people, could be found to stage this debate, one favoring both proposals and the other opposing both, the arguments for and against one proposed policy would probably become blurred with arguments for and against the other. Clarity is enhanced if debaters consider one general proposition at a time.

THE GENERAL NATURE OF DEBATE PROPOSITIONS

Even if a debate proposition contains only one main idea, its truth will very likely rest upon the truth of one or more subpropositions. For example, if, in a court of law, the prosecution upheld the proposition that "Businessmen X and Y engaged in a conspiracy to fix prices" (a factual proposition), it might base the assertion on a series of meetings which were supposedly held by the alleged conspirators; but each assertion that such-and-such a meeting was held would constitute a subordinate factual proposition and conceivably could be disputed. Thus a series of subordinate factual propositions would have to be established before the general proposition of fact could be demonstrated. Similarly, a congressman might propose a bill (a proposition of policy) which, to be acceptable to others, would require the demonstration of a variety of subordinate propositions of fact and value.

Thus, even if a debate proposition has all the characteristics of a well-phrased proposition, including the specific statement of only one central idea, it will still need to be analyzed to find relevant subordinate propositions. And even if the proposition is phrased in clear-cut, unprejudiced language, the fact remains that language is inherently ambiguous. It is clear, therefore, that the analysis of a debate proposition involves two major steps: (1) analysis of the langauge of the proposition and (2) analysis of the subordinate propositions which must be demonstrated in order to demonstrate the truth of the general proposition.

ANALYSIS OF THE LANGUAGE OF A DEBATE PROPOSITION

Analyzing the language of a debate proposition involves finding definitions of the terms within the proposition. It is important that a debater understand that a "term" is not necessarily a word. It may consist of a group of words, and one of the first tasks for the debater is to group properly the words in the proposition and, where appropriate, to define phrases rather than individual words. This is necessary because words, when grouped together, sometimes mean something quite different from what the words mean when standing apart from one another.

Having grouped the words of a proposition into units, where such grouping is necessary, the debater should proceed to look for reasonable definitions of the words and phrases. The following discussion of definition will be divided into three parts: (1) the requirements of a good definition, (2) the basic methods of definition, and (3) sources of definition.

REQUIREMENTS OF A GOOD DEFINITION

Basically, most good definitions consist of verbally placing an object or concept within a general category and then differentiating it from other things within the same category. If a person defines orange as fruit, he has placed orange in a *category*. Such a classification helps clarify the meaning, but because orange has not been differentiated from other fruits, the most specific and meaningful definition has not been obtained. Only when a person has described some of the specific distinguishing characteristics of an orange—its color, size, shape, taste, smell, and so on—will he have differentiated it from other fruits, and only then will the definition be as meaningful as desired.

This example shows one of the basic requirements of a good definition: the definition should be more specific and clear-cut than the word or phrase being defined.

However, clear definitions are not automatically reasonable definitions. A reasonable definition is not only specific and clear-cut but also is commonly accepted in light of the present social context of a debate proposition. For example, when Congress debated the so-called Full Employment Act of 1946, proponents of the bill sometimes called it a "right-to-work" law. Opponents of the bill objected to this phrase, arguing that no person has a "right" to work. For the sake of compromise, the phrase was dropped and disappeared temporarily from common usage. Later, the term reappeared, this time to describe legislation prohibiting union shop contracts; and the term *right-to-work* currently is used in connection with laws outlawing union shop contracts. If, at the present time, a debater were defining right-to-work laws, he could go back to authoritative works written in 1946 and probably find a definition suggesting that right-to-work legislation means a full-employment law; but such a definition would hardly be reasonable in light of usage in the present social context.

Similarly, a number of years ago the national intercollegiate debate proposition called for the establishment of a *federal world government*, a term which most debate teams defined as a political organization of world-wide scope based on the political principles of federalism. One team discovered the existence of a theological doctrine called *federal* and then proceeded to define "federal world government" as a world-wide theocracy based on the principles of federal theology—ingenious, perhaps, but hardly reasonable in light of present usage and the present social context of the phrase "federal world government."

METHODS OF DEFINITION

Although the basic method of definition is one of classification and differentiation, there are numerous variations from the basic method which are often useful in analyzing the meaning of terms. Some of the common variations are as follows:

1. *Definition by negation,* as the name implies, consists of determining what a term does *not* mean. This method is useful when a given term is often, though mistakenly, confused with another. Definition by negation does not tell what a term does mean, but the method is often helpful when used in conjunction with another method.

2. *Definition by etymology* involves tracing the history of a word or its component parts back to the origin of the word. The term *democracy* can be traced to the Greek words *demos,* meaning "the people," and *kratein,* meaning "to rule." Although etymological definitions sometimes do not provide the current usage of a term, they often provide valuable insights as to the meaning of a word or phrase.

3. *Definition by synonym* simply involves the finding of another word or phrase which means the same, or approximately the same, as the word or phrase being defined.

4. *Definition by illustration* consists of determining the meaning of a generic term by studying the particulars within the category. If a debater were trying to define the term *profit-sharing plan* in the proposition, "Resolved: that American industries should adopt profit-sharing plans," he might study particular plans which were commonly called *profit sharing* in order to determine the characteristics of those plans.

None of the above-mentioned methods of definition can be used in a vacuum. The debater cannot—or at least should not—simply spin synonyms out of thin air or trace the history of a word or locate illustrative cases simply by armchair thinking. In order to find clear and reasonable definitions, the debater must use certain mechanical aids and research tools. A full consideration of research sources and procedures can be found in the next chapter, but a few questions about sources need to be considered in connection with analysis.

SOURCES OF DEFINITION

When thinking of sources for finding definitions, we are likely to think first of the standard dictionary. How useful is the standard dictionary? The answer is that dictionaries are extremely useful; but the debater should remember that they are not intended to deal adequately with highly technical terms. Hence, if debating an economic, literary, or sociological proposition, it is best to consult authorities in economics, literature, or sociology.

Debaters sometimes become alarmed if they find that various authoritative sources define a term in various ways. What should the debater do if authorities disagree in their definitions of crucial terms? Inasmuch as the affirmative is advocating the proposition, it is generally agreed that the affirmative has the prerogative of defining the terms as it chooses, provided that the definitions are reasonable and rest with authoritative sources.

Once a debater shows the meaning of the proposition he is debating, he is ready to undertake the final step in analysis, that of determining the subordinate propositions which must be established in order to demonstrate that the debate proposition should, or should not, be accepted. No textbook can tell a debater precisely how to proceed with this task, for the precise procedure depends upon the specific subject being debated. However, argumentation theorists have constructed sets of "stock issues," which are phrased in a general manner and which constitute general guidelines for locating the specific issues in a particular proposition of policy. By judicious use of the "stock issues" concept, the debater can be helped in finding the subordinate propositions which are relevant to a particular debate proposition.

STOCK ISSUES IN A PROPOSITION OF POLICY

Any institution, whether it be a family, a club, or a government, holds to certain values and follows certain policies which the institution thinks are consistent with those values. Sometimes these policies are written into laws and decrees; sometimes they are unwritten and exist as myths, customs, and mores. Regardless of whether they are written or unwritten, however, anyone proposing a new policy finds that an old policy is already being adhered to by those whom he hopes to persuade. To use Whately's metaphor, he finds that the ground which he hopes the new policy will occupy is already preoccupied by existing policies and that this preoccupation of the ground by existing policy "implies that it must stand good till sufficient reason is adduced against it. . . ." [3] In other words, people do not usually accept a new policy unless they are dissatisfied with the present system, unless there is some "felt need" to change the present way of doing

[3] Richard Whately, *Elements of Rhetoric* (Boston: James Munroe & Co., 1862), p. 139.

things. Thus, the first stock issue in a proposition of policy is the _need_ issue, which asks whether present conditions are unsatisfactory enough to warrant a change from present policy.

The existence of weaknesses in present policy, however, does not necessarily mean that the proposition calling for the acceptance of a specific new policy should be adopted. One must also consider whether the new proposal could appreciably improve the present system, whether it could ameliorate the problems within the status quo. Thus, the second stock issue is the _practicality_ issue, which asks whether the new policy can solve the needs.

However, even if a new policy is both needed and practical, it might not necessarily be a desirable policy to adopt, for it might have certain "side effects" which would create problems worse than those being remedied. Thus, there is a third stock issue which considers the relative importance of *the advantages versus the disadvantages* which might result from putting the new proposal into operation.

In summary, there are three possible stock issues concerning any new proposed policy: need, practicality and advantages versus disadvantages. In other words, debaters should analyze propositions of policy to determine whether a "yes" or "no" answer should be given to each of the following three questions:

1. Is the present situation unsatisfactory? Debaters frequently phrase this, "Is there a need?"
2. Is the proposed plan (the proposition) the best plan for solving the problems that make a change desirable?
3. Will the advantages of the new plan be more important than any disadvantages that might occur? [4]

If all three questions are answered affirmatively, it would be desirable to accept the debate proposition; but if the answer to any of the questions is negative, the proposal would be useless or undesirable and should therefore be rejected. Let us now consider each question separately.

THE NEED ISSUE

What constitutes a need for an institution to change from its present policy? We can answer this question in a general way by saying that *a need exists when the facts show that an institution is failing seriously to*

[4] The phrasing of the questions is taken from Jimmie Douglas Trent, A *Manual for the Beginner in Tournament Debate* (M.S. thesis, Kansas State Teachers College, Emporia, 1959), p. 27.

achieve a worthwhile goal(s) to an optimum degree under present policy.
It is important to note that this definition of *need* implies that an analysis
of the need issue requires the debater to examine both facts and goals.
For example, in the college debate in the appendix of this textbook, the
first "need" contention of the affirmative is that "the neglect of health
today is causing needless death and suffering." (See page 370.) This argument, although stated as a factual proposition, is a need argument only
because it implies an unstated subordinate proposition of value (that the
prevention of needless death and suffering is a desirable social goal).
Values to which individuals adhere are often unstated and so deeply felt
that they are frequently difficult to detect; yet, when we remember that
what we consider a need depends upon our values, we realize that sound
analysis demands that we examine values, as well as facts, when analyzing the need issue. In short, need arguments, as the example demonstrates, usually are a mixture of subordinate propositions of fact and
value.

Keeping in mind that the establishment of a need involves basing
factual propositions upon value premises concerning the institution's goals,
a debater can best begin his analysis of need issues by determining the
goals which the present policy is designed to achieve. If, for example, a
debater is preparing for a resolution concerning United States foreign
policy, he should begin his analysis of the need issue by determining the
goals of that policy. If he is preparing to debate a piece of proposed labor
legislation, he should determine the goals, the aims, of labor legislation.

Mere determination of the goals of present policy, however, is not
enough. Inasmuch as goals imply values, the debater should consider if
these goals are based upon sound value premises. For example, had students
in Germany in the late 1930's been permitted to debate Hitler's Jewish
policy, they might have discovered that the policy, though successful in
attaining its goals, was undesirable because the goals were based upon
unethical values.

If the debater finds that present policy is designed to achieve goals
which are based upon unsound values, he has, of course, located a reason
to change present policy. Let us assume, however, that, in a given instance,
he has decided that present goals are satisfactory. He should then determine
whether present policy is achieving these goals to an optimum degree.
Returning to the example given above concerning health insurance, let
us assume that a debater determines that the goal of preventing needless
death and suffering is a worthwhile social goal, one based upon a sound
set of values; he will then need to look at the facts to determine whether
the present system of providing medical care for people is achieving the
desired goal.

It frequently happens that a debater, upon examining the facts, finds that a given policy is neither a total success nor a total failure. For instance, few persons who favor the present system of providing medical care think that it is adequate for *every* person, and few persons who oppose the present system think that *no* person receives adequate medical care. Thus, since the answer to the question, "Is the present system achieving its goals?" is usually a matter of degree, not of absolutes, debaters will usually find that it is an over-simplification to answer simply "yes" or "no." Instead, the debater will usually have to decide whether any failures are serious enough to justify a change from the present system.

Unfortunately, no clear-cut, generally accepted formula exists for determining when a policy is seriously deficient. The line between the success or failure of a policy is broad and hazy rather than fine and clear-cut. However, it is helpful to remember three factors when trying to determine whether a problem is sufficiently serious to justify a change from present policy. First, definitions of key words are usually necessary. Thus, returning again to the question of adequate medical care, a debater should attempt to determine what constitutes *adequacy*. Or if a debater, in analyzing present United States foreign policy, decides that maximum security for United States citizens is a worthwhile goal of foreign policy, he should attempt to determine what constitutes *maximum security*.

Second, the debater should keep in mind the implications of the last phrase in our definition of a social need: "a need exists when the facts show that an institution is failing seriously to achieve a worthwhile goal(s) *to an optimum degree under present policy*." We have already pointed out that few policies *are* total successes or total failures. It is equally important to remember that few policies *can possibly be* total successes or total failures. Too many factors other than the policy itself influence its success or failure. The debater must, therefore, consider the "optimum success" of a given policy at a given time and under given circumstances. For example, if a nation were engaged in a war with a powerful enemy and lost a battle, we might not necessarily be right in assuming that the policies being pursued by the governmental and military leaders were unsound, for the strength of the enemy and other factors beyond the control of the leaders would have to be taken into account. Present policy might not be very successful, but it might be as good as could be expected under the circumstances.

Conversely, a policy which seems at first glance to be satisfactory and reveals few examples of dire hardship might reasonably be expected to be doing a much better job. For example, let us return to our hypothetical war and assume that the battle was won. It is possible that the policies of the military leaders were very unsound but that the battle was won because of the weakness and stupidity of the enemy. Sometimes the circumstances in which a policy is operating are so favorable that even a bad policy will appear to the superficial observer to be producing good results.

In short, the debater should examine the circumstances surrounding a policy and, in light of such circumstances, determine whether the present policy is achieving desirable goals *to an optimum degree.*

Third, the seriousness of a problem cannot be determined simply by arm-chair thinking. The debater should, of course, think about the seriousness of problems; but thinking must be based upon factual information.

Having determined the goals of present policy, the desirability of the goals in terms of the soundness of the value premises on which they are based and the relative success or failure of present policy in achieving the goals, the debater is now ready to take a fourth and final step in his analysis of the need issue. This step is to determine the inherency of any problem(s) he has found to exist.

Inherency involves the question of whether the failure of a policy is related to the particular phase of the status quo which the debate resolution proposes to change. For example, consider an approach taken by a negative debate team on the 1960–61 intercollegiate debate proposition, "Resolved: That the United States should adopt a program of compulsory health insurance for all citizens." The team acknowledged that present methods of financing medical care were inadequate in certain respects; but it argued that the particular phase of the status quo which the resolution proposed to change was the principle of voluntary participation in insurance programs and maintained that existing problems were in no way related to that principle. The team proposed a number of modifications in the present system to correct certain problems; the modifications concerned regulations of insurance companies and welfare programs and, according to the team, could be implemented without changing the principle of volunteerism. In other words, this team acknowledged the existence of certain problems but argued that they could be solved without changing the particular phase of the status quo which the resolution proposed to change.

The task of analyzing inherency is not too easy; the basic process is one of (1) determining precisely which phase(s) of the status quo the debate proposition proposes to change and (2) determining whether the existing problems are caused by, or at least are related to, those specific phases of the status quo. Only if the problems are in some way a result of the basic features of the status quo which the resolution will change can the problems be considered inherent. If the problems are not inherent, there are good grounds for rejecting the proposition.

In summary, we have seen that need arguments can be found by seeking answers to the following questions:

1. What are the goals of present policy?
2. Are the goals of the present system worthwhile? In other words, are

the goals consistent with a sound set of values? If not, a problem exists.

3. Is the present system achieving its goals to an optimum degree? If not, is the failure serious? If it is, a problem exists.

4. Are the failures of the present system related to features of the status quo which the proposition will change? In other words, is the problem inherent?

THE PRACTICALITY ISSUE

Having located the need issues, the debater should attempt to determine whether the proposed policy would be able to correct the needs which are alleged to exist. One of the first steps in this process is to consider the administrative feasibility of the proposal. This step is not required if the proposition simply calls for the adoption of a statement of principle, such as the abolition of capital punishment; but if the debate proposition calls for a policy requiring an elaborate administrative set-up, such as would be necessary for something like compulsory arbitration of labor-management disputes or a public fall-out shelter program for civil defense, the issue of administrative feasibility must be considered.

In most formal debates the debater will not have time to inquire into the minutiae of administrative organization. Nevertheless, debaters should remember that a proposed policy, to be effectuated, will often have to be administered by an agency which is properly organized, staffed, and financed. Thus, in his analysis of the proposition, he should ask such questions as the following: Can an administrative structure be organized so that it will be efficient? Can competent personnel be procured? Can adequate financing be provided?

In some cases, new proposals have to be analyzed in terms of their enforceability. For example, if laws were proposed calling for the prohibition of union-shop contracts or driving over fifty miles-per-hour on the highway, these laws would correct no problems unless they could be enforced. Thus, the debater should determine whether a proposition would, if adopted, present an enforcement problem and, if so, whether an adequate enforcement agency could be devised.

The question of enforcement often entails the question of the public's attitude toward the proposal. Of course, the word "should," which is either stated or implied in a proposition of policy, implies only the desirability of a proposal, not the public's attitude toward it; and it is generally agreed (except, perhaps, among the most rabid believers in the popular will) that the desirability of a proposal is not determined simply by a public-opinion poll. However, if public opposition to a proposed policy is deep-seated and widespread, there is likely to be a very serious problem in enforcing the policy.

If a debater decides that the proposal is administratively unworkable, he has found a good reason to reject the proposition. However, the converse is not true; in other words, the administrative feasibility of a plan is not enough to ensure its practicality. Debaters should also analyze the practicality of the proposition in terms of the probable effect of the proposal on the alleged needs. The author recalls judging one debate on the proposition calling for compulsory health insurance in which the affirmative team built its need arguments around the fact that private health insurance contracts contained co-insurance features and other features which made the insurance considerably less than comprehensive. Then, to his surprise, the team proposed a plan of compulsory health insurance which contained similar features. The negative team acknowledged the administrative feasibility of the plan, but it effectively pointed out that the proposed plan, regardless of its administrative feasibility, would have no effect on the alleged needs. Clearly, the proposal presented by the affirmative in this particular debate would have had no appreciable effect on the alleged problems if it had been adopted; thus it could be termed *impractical*.

The probable effect of some plans is to remove the *causes* of a problem while other plans remove only *symptoms*. A plan which can solve the causes of a problem is probably superior to one which removes only the symptoms; but despite occasional assertions by debaters to the contrary, a plan which cannot remove causes is not necessarily impractical, as an analogy from the field of medicine shows. There are instances in medicine when a certain program of therapy will not cure the causes of an ailment but will mitigate the symptoms. For example, the use of insulin will not cure the causes of diabetes; however, it will control the symptoms and keep the patient alive. Thus, only a very foolish physician or a very foolish diabetic patient would reject insulin treatment on the grounds that the insulin will not cure the causes of the ailment. In this instance, since the causes cannot be removed, controlling the symptoms is better than doing nothing.

Analogous situations arise in the field of social policy. We do not reject unemployment-compensation programs, for example, simply because they do not remove the causes of unemployment; rather, we recognize that other plans, designed to remove the causes of unemployment, cannot be completely successful, and maintain unemployment compensation in order to lessen the adverse effects of unemployment where it occurs. In short, we recognize that the most desirable plan is usually the one which will remove the causes of a problem, but we also realize that in some cases the causes cannot be removed and that, in such instances, a plan to mitigate the adverse symptoms of the problem is better than nothing.

In summary, we have seen that practicality arguments can be found by seeking answers to the following questions:

1. Is the proposal administratively feasible? If not, the plan is impractical.
2. Can the proposal be enforced? If not, the plan is impractical.
3. What effect will the proposal have on the alleged needs? If there will be only an insignificant effect, the plan is impractical.

ADVANTAGES VERSUS DISADVANTAGES

Debaters should consider not only the probable effects of the proposed plan on the alleged needs but also other results of putting the plan into operation, results which we might call *side-effects*. In some cases, the debater may conclude that no serious ill effects will occur; indeed, some desirable results, in addition to solving the needs, might accrue. In other instances, he may conclude that the proposed solution for a social ill would have such adverse side-effects that it would be an obviously unacceptable proposal despite its ability to solve existing problems.

In many cases, if not in most, adoption of a new plan will result in both good and bad effects; and an important step in analyzing a debate proposition is to weigh the good effects against the undesirable ones. Such a weighing of advantages against disadvantages is not easy, but it can be approached systematically if the debater will establish a priority of goals. Let us take as an example the controversy over legalizing wire-tapping. Proponents of legalized wire-tapping argue that the low rate of detection and conviction of criminals constitutes a serious need which could be solved by legalizing wire-tapping. Opponents of the proposal seldom deny the existence of the problem or the practicality of the solution; they are more concerned about the adverse effects of legalized wire-tapping on civil liberties and individual rights. In short, proponents of wire-tapping tend to talk in terms of the goal of group security, opponents in terms of the goal of individual liberty. Indeed, the group security–individual liberty dilemma is a pressing one, for almost any proposal which helps achieve one puts at least a minor obstacle in the road of achieving the other.

Resolution of this and similar conflicts can come about only when a society assigns various goals certain priorities. Thus, in weighing the advantages of a proposal against the disadvantages, the debater should establish a priority list of the social goals which would be affected by the proposal. Then, to return to our wire-tapping example, if he decides that the social goal of individual liberty deserves higher priority than group security, or vice versa, he has a good basis for determining whether the advantages outweigh the disadvantages.

In summary, an analysis of the advantages versus the disadvantages involves (1) determining the probable side effects which would occur if the proposal were put into operation, (2) determining which of these effects are good and which are bad, and (3) weighing the advantages against the disadantages by establishing priorities among the social goals which would be affected by adoption of the proposal.

POTENTIAL ISSUES, ADMITTED MATTER, AND ACTUAL ISSUES

The stock issues and their subordinate issues which we have considered are always potential issues in a debate on a proposition of policy, but they are not necessarily actual issues in a particular debate. In a given situation, for example, all of the debaters might agree that there is a need to change present policy but disagree about the practicality or the desirability of the affirmative's proposal.

Theoretically, the negative has considerable flexibility in what it chooses to admit and what it chooses to make an actual issue. From the affirmative point of view, *all* of the stock issues must be established affirmatively; in other words, the affirmative's proposition has not been demonstrated until the affirmative has established a need *and* the practicality of the plan *and* the advantages of the plan. The negative can theoretically center its attack on only one of the stock issues. Even the subordinate issues within a major stock issue are sometimes interdependent; in other words, two or more subordinate propositions must be true before the major proposition is true. For example, to establish the need issue the affirmative must establish that there is a problem *and* that the problem is serious *and* that the problem is inherent. In short, individual arguments are seldom isolated entities; they usually are links in a chain which support a more general proposition. If a vital link in the chain is destroyed, the general proposition falls. Thus, an important step in the analysis of a debate proposition is to select from among the potential issues which subordinate propositions to admit and which issues to argue.

The selection of arguments to be admitted and to be contested depends upon a number of factors. The amount and nature of the factual evidence is one such factor. There is little point in trying to establish an argument if there is no good evidence to support it. Audience predispositions constitute another important factor; it is often better to identify one's arguments with certain of the audience's attitudes than to clash with them. We shall not pursue the matter of selecting issues because the process is a complex one to which many of the subsequent chapters in this textbook are relevant. The point to be noted here is that an important step in the analytical process is to select from the potential issues the subordinate propositions which can be admitted safely and those which should be argued.

SOME SUGGESTIONS FOR MORE EFFECTIVE ANALYSIS

REMEMBER THAT ANALYSIS AND RESEARCH ARE INTERDEPENDENT

This chapter began by pointing out that analysis is only one aspect of thorough preparation and that the various aspects of preparation overlap and interact with one another. After discussing analysis for so many pages as if it were a single entity, it might be well to remind ourselves that analysis does not take place in a vacuum. It takes place in a world of facts, and no analysis can be any better than the research on which it rests. Our first suggestion for more effective analysis, therefore, is that analysis and research should be thought of as interdependent and should be performed together.

REMEMBER THE LIMITATIONS OF PROCEDURAL GUIDES

This chapter has outlined a procedure for analysis—a logical and useful procedure—and the debater should remember that all procedural formulae have their limitations as well as their uses. First, a procedure does not automatically provide answers; it merely provides the way of getting answers. A debater analyzing a proposition calling for free trade cannot content himself with reading this chapter and then asserting that "There is a need for free trade, free trade will solve the need, and the advantages of free trade will outweigh the disadvantages." He will have to examine economic theory and economic data to find what specific situations currently are causing problems, what evidence and theory support the notion that free trade is practical, what economic and political effects free trade might have. In short, the procedures outlined in this chapter will not do the debater's work for him; they can only guide the debater in his work.

A second limitation of any procedural formula is that it often appears too simple. The debater should remember that the work of analysis is not done in the nice, neat stages which we have explained. If a debater is perceptive and hard working, new insights may occur frequently.

Finally, the debater should recall the ancient precept that virtues have counterparts in vices and it is sometimes difficult to tell the difference between them. This precept has relevance to our scheme for analyzing debate propositions, for it is easy to cross the line which separates the virtue of logical rigor from the vice of pedantry. It is easy for small minds to become so absorbed in the *mechanics* of analysis that the *product* of analysis is disregarded. Harold Lasswell reminds us: "Perhaps the ultimate paradox of logical thinking is that it is self-destroying when too sedulously cultivated. It asserts its own prerogatives by clamping down certain restrictive frames of reference upon the activity of the mind, and presently ends by impoverishing the activity which it purports to guide into creative channels." [5]

Because analytical procedures are merely guides, because they may appear too neat and simple, and because they can lead to pedantry, the debater should remember that the procedures outlined in this chapter have limitations as well as uses, drawbacks as well as advantages. On the other hand, the debater should recognize the value of the logical rigor inherent in the procedures.

SUMMARY

We have seen that a proposition is a judgment expressed in words and that propositions can be classified into three general types: (1) propositions of fact, which allege or deny the occurrence of events, the existence of things, the classification of things or events, or the relationship between events or objects; (2) propositions of value, which attribute some quality, such as goodness or badness, to an event, idea, or object; and (3) propositions of policy, which allege or deny that a certain course of action should be taken.

Propositions are expressed in a variety of situations, not just in formal debates. To be suitable for formal debate, a proposition should be timely, significant, and admit of good arguments and evidence on both sides. A debate proposition should be phrased in as specific and unprejudiced a manner as possible. Customarily, debate propositions are worded affirmatively. Finally, a debate proposition should contain only one central idea.

Even if a debate proposition is well phrased and contains only one central idea, the inherently ambiguous nature of language and the general nature of debate propositions require that analysis of debate resolutions consist of (1) analysis of the language of the proposition and (2) analysis of the relevant subordinate propositions.

Analysis of the language of a proposition involves finding definitions for the words and phrases within the proposition. Good definitions are more precise and specific than the word or phrase being defined and are

[5] "Self-Analysis and Judicial Thinking," *International Journal of Ethics*, 40 (April 1930), 358.

reasonable in light of current usage and the present social context. Although the basic process of definition consists of classification and differentiation, there are numerous variations from the basic method, such as definition by negation, etymology, synonym, and illustration.

When analyzing a proposition of policy to locate the relevant subordinate propositions, the debater should first attempt to determine whether there is a need to change present policy by answering four basic questions: (1) What are the goals of present policy? (2) Are the goals of the present system worthwhile? (3) Is the present system achieving its goals to an optimum degree? (4) Are any serious problems inherent within the present system?

He should then examine the practicality of the proposed policy by considering the administrative feasibility of the proposal and the probable effect of the proposal on the alleged needs. Finally, the debater should consider the probable side-effects of the proposal and weigh the advantages which would probably result from the proposal against the disadvantages.

The analytical system discussed in this chapter simply provides a guideline for the debater to follow in analyzing a debate proposition. Such a system provides the debater with a logically rigorous and useful procedure, but no procedure can serve as an adequate substitute for hard work and good sense.

EXERCISES

1. Identify which type of proposition each of the following statements is:
    a. Labor unions are (are not) monopolies.
    b. Flying saucers do (do not) exist.
    c. The concept of states' rights is (is not) outmoded and harmful.
    d. Smokers should (should not) give up smoking.
    e. The United Nations ought (ought not) to be abolished.
    f. Union wage demands cause (do not cause) inflation.
2. Criticize the phrasing of the following debate propositions and reword them so that they meet the requirements of a well-phrased proposition:
    a. Resolved: That strikes which are injurious to the public welfare should be outlawed.
    b. Resolved: That a public works program should be instituted to solve unemployment.
    c. Resolved: That Congress should repeal the Fair Labor Standards and Wagner Acts.
3. Define the following terms, using at least two of the methods of definition suggested in the text for each term:
    a. Profit-sharing plans in industry.
    b. States' rights.

c. Optimum national economic growth.

d. Socialism.

4. Apply the concept of *stock issues* to the following propositions of policy:

a. Resolved: That the United States Congress should enact legislation providing for federal aid to education.

b. Resolved: That the National Labor Relations Act of 1947, as amended, should be repealed.

SUGGESTED READINGS

COURTNEY, LUTHER W., and GLENN R. CAPP. *Practical Debating.* Philadelphia: J. B. Lippincott, 1949. Chaps. 3, 4.

DEWEY, JOHN. *How We Think.* Boston: D. C. Heath, & Company, 1933, Chap. 1.

EHNINGER, DOUGLAS. "The Classical Doctrine of Invention," *The Gavel,* 39 (March 1957), 59–62, 70.

HOWELL, WILBUR SAMUEL. "The Positions of Argument: An Historical Examination," in *Papers in Rhetoric,* ed., Donald C. Bryant. St. Louis: privately printed, 1940, 8–17.

KRUGER, ARTHUR N. *Modern Debate: Its Logic and Strategy.* New York: McGraw-Hill Book Co., Inc., 1960. Chaps. 2, 3, 4.

LAMBERTSON, FLOYD W. "The Meaning of the Word 'Should' in a Question of Policy," *Quarterly Journal of Speech,* 28 (December 1942), 421–4.

NICHOLS, ALAN. "Debate Propositions and Contexts," *Quarterly Journal of Speech,* 21 (June 1935), 355–70.

RAHSKOPF, HORACE G. "Questions of Fact vs. Questions of Policy," *Quarterly Journal of Speech,* 18 (February 1932), 60–70.

chapteR 5

••••••••••••••••••••••••••••••••••••••

RESEARCH
FOR DEBATE

by Waldo W. Braden

Many debates are won before the speaking starts; they are won in the library, at a study table, and in conference with colleagues. They are won because the advocate has a keen insight into the problem, has made a thorough analysis of his case, and has assembled the facts to support his views. In other words, the debater knows "what he is talking about."

Considered from another point of view, debating carries with it responsibility. When a speaker asks his listeners to follow a course of action, he has a moral responsibility to understand thoroughly what he advocates. The person who dares to make persuasive assertions, not based on fact and careful thought, is foolish and sometimes even dangerous. Such rashness may result in a needless waste of human energy, in misdirected effort, and sometimes even in tragedy. Therefore, complete preparation is essential in debating.

From the point of view of the debate class or debate squad, research may be divided into the following six steps:

1. Adopt a plan of procedure.
2. Acquire a general background.
3. Assemble a bibliography.
4. Locate and procure supplementary materials.
5. Do your individual research.
6. Record and arrange your notes for effective use.

STEP 1: ADOPT A PLAN
OF PROCEDURE

At an early meeting, the debate group should consider seriously a plan of study and the advisability of cooperative research. The old adage that two heads are better than one is certainly true in locating pertinent materials. Cooperative study conserves time, insures a broader coverage, and promotes a wider understanding. In planning joint efforts the members of the class or squad may wish to discuss the following questions:

1. As a group what do we already know about the proposition? What are the sources of our information? Hearsay? Prejudice? Thoughtful reading?

2. What persons on the campus and in the community may be able to give personal testimony about the problem?

3. What are the resources of the local library? Is it possible to have a special reserve shelf for debate materials?

4. Are there other libraries near by which may contain materials on the subject? State lending library? City library? Library of neighboring college or private institution?

5. What local, state, or national agencies are likely to have information on the subject?

6. What private groups, such as the League of Women Voters, the American Medical Association, and the AFL–CIO, are likely to have published materials on the subject?

7. Is it desirable to write to prominent men and organizations for their opinions on the subject?

8. How can we ensure thorough coverage of the current periodicals, that is, newspapers, magazines, and pamphlets throughout the season?

9. Should the squad adopt a plan of study in which each member assumes a definite responsibility for the coverage of certain sources?

10. Should the group appoint a librarian to be responsible for materials gathered by the group?

Answers to these questions envision the research of the squad for the entire season. As succeeding steps are discussed, additional suggestions which will aid in your research will be made.

STEP 2: ACQUIRE A GENERAL
BACKGROUND

Before he can intelligently read a map, a traveler must first orient himself to the terrain; he must find out where he is on the map, and he must be able to associate near-by landmarks with the symbols of the map. So it is in doing research. As a beginning step the debater or discusser must orient himself to the subject, determining how much he knows about it. He must examine the general implications of the problem and thereby decide what aspects will require investigation. Suppose, for example, that you are considering the proposition, Resolved: That the United States should adopt a program of compulsory health insurance for all citizens. To start your research, you will find it advantageous to inquire into the following and similar questions:

Why are we debating this topic at the present time?

What is compulsory health insurance?

What is the history of health insurance?

What is alleged to be wrong with present medical care?

What groups support and oppose compulsory health insurance?

To what other subjects is the problem of health insurance related?

STANDARD REFERENCE WORKS

The searcher will probably find the general reference works in the library—encyclopedias, dictionaries, and yearbooks—a convenient starting point in getting a comprehensive view of the problem.

The encyclopedias, true to their name, often embrace the "circle of arts and sciences." Recent editions contain valuable current information because publishers follow a policy of continuous revision, which involves making changes in some articles with each reprinting. In addition, they publish annual yearbooks which give facts concerning new developments. Of course the copyright date of the references will tell whether the information that it contains is dated. This check is especially necessary in using standard sets because libraries retain reference volumes, such as the *Encyclopaedia Britannica*, on their shelves for many years.

The question arises as to which of these sets is the most authoritative. As an aid in evaluating the various encyclopedias, a brief description of each is given.

The Encyclopaedia Britannica (24 volumes) is recognized as "the most famous encyclopaedia in English and for some purposes the best." [1] Many of its articles, particularly in the cultural fields, are extensive and authoritative. It also includes many short articles, definitions, and identifications of names, places, and subjects. The editors follow a policy of con-

[1] Constance M. Winchell, *Guide to Reference Books* (Chicago: American Library Association, 1951), p. 77.

tinuous revision and publish an annual supplement, the *Britannica Book of the Year.*

The *Encyclopedia Americana* (30 volumes) is another excellent reference work. It is especially strong in information about American towns and cities, including up-to-date statistics on population, institutions, and industries. It is also recommended in the fields of applied science, technology, business, and government. It, too, follows a policy of continuous revision, and issues yearly the *Americana Annual.* It ranks second only to *Britannica.*

The *Collier's Encyclopedia* (1950–51, 20 volumes) is written for students at the senior high school and junior college level. Some articles are comprehensive.

The *Compton's Pictured Encyclopedia* and the *World Book Encyclopedia* are for younger students at the upper elementary school and high school levels, but it is not planned for the scholar or advanced research worker. These sets are recommended for those who are seeking simpler treatments.

Among the more specialized encyclopedias the debater will find particularly valuable the *Encyclopaedia of Religion and Ethics* (edited by James Hastings; New York: Scribner, 1908–27, 12 volumes); and the *Encyclopedia of the Social Sciences* (edited by E. R. A. Seligman; New York: Macmillan, 1930–35, 15 volumes).

The *Encyclopedia of the Social Sciences* includes articles on political science, economics, law, anthropology, sociology, penology, and social work. In addition, it has discussions of some social aspects of ethics, education, philosophy, psychology, biology, geography, medicine, and art.

AUTHORITIES

A second means of getting a general background on a proposition is to enlist the aid of professors on your campus or local government officials who may have studied or had experience with the problem. Often the professors of economics, government, history, or sociology may be able to direct you to some valuable sources or give you considerable information on the proposition. If possible, persuade these specialists to talk to the entire class or squad. If the equipment is available, make recordings of what your guests say. These recordings will enable you later to quote accurately what was said and may be extremely helpful to students who join the squad later. A question period should always be a part of these sessions. Members of the squad should approach the questioning with a spirit of inquiry, not advocacy.

DISCUSSION MEETINGS

A third aspect of general preparation may embrace a series of round-table discussions among members of your group. The first meeting may be devoted to considering plans for research (see Step 1). Later meetings may be used to analyze the meaning of the terms of the proposition, the history of the problem, and the cause for discussion and other similar topics. Individuals may be asked to investigate and report on selected phases. Discussion and reflective thought should help members of the squad to reach a common understanding of the scope and implications of the proposition.

STEP 3: ASSEMBLE A BIBLIOGRAPHY

A bibliography is a list of available books, articles, pamphlets, and miscellaneous materials on the subject. For your purposes it will probably prove wise to limit your bibliography for the debate proposition to the items available on the local campus or in near-by libraries. Some persons may question the advisability of delaying the assembling of the bibliography until after preliminary study of the question. However, collecting sources is much easier if you have some understanding of the implications and various facets of the proposition.

STANDARD BIBLIOGRAPHIES

To conserve time you should start by attempting to locate other bibliographies on your subject in the *Bibliographic Index* (New York: H. W. Wilson Company) which indexes published bibliographies. Likewise you will want to investigate lists of references found in volumes in the *Reference Shelf Series* (New York: H. W. Wilson Company) and in standard works which may include selected lists of recommended readings.

The gathering of such a selective bibliography is a project in which all members of the group can profitably participate. As a point of departure the group should agree on a list of cross references, that is, other subject titles under which pertinent material may be located. For example, if you are investigating the subject of compulsory health insurance, you will want to consider such additional topics as the following:

Aged	Medical service
American Medical Association	Medical care
Blue Cross Hospital Services	Medicine–practice

Group insurance	National Health Insurance
Health benefit plans	State health service
Health insurance	Social insurance
Hospitalization	Socialized medicine

Any cooperative plan of assembling references must involve (1) a division of labor and (2) uniformity in the methods of recording items. In order to distribute the work fairly, each participant may be asked to check references found in a given source. For example, assignments might be made according to a division similar to the following one:

1. Card catalog in college library.
2. Card catalog in city library.
3. *Readers' Guide* 1955–57.
4. *Readers' Guide* 1957–59.
5. *Readers' Guide* 1959–61.
6. *Education Index* 1950–57.
7. *Education Index* 1957–
8. *The International Index.*

Uniform recording suggestions may include the following:

1. Record references on 3 x 5 cards.
2. Write only one reference on a card.
3. Print or type cards.
4. For books include the following: author, title, edition, place of publication, name of publisher, and date of publication.

> Example: Robert J. Harris, *The Quest for Equality, the Constitution, Congress, and the Supreme Court* (Baton Rouge: Louisiana State University Press, 1960).

5. For magazine references follow the exact form found in the *Readers' Guide* and other H. W. Wilson publications.

> Examples: Burton, Philip, Public funds for public schools only. Christian Cent. 78:415–17 Ap 5'61.
>
> Race in space: where U.S. leads and lags. U. S. News 50:41–3 Mr 13'61.

This practice is at variance with that recommended by some authorities, but since the H. W. Wilson Company publishes most of the periodical indexes, it conserves time and ensures uniformity to follow their forms.

6. For books found in the card catalog, include complete library call number. This practice will save the time of those who wish to find the book later.

7. For magazines, check each article and add a note concerning availability and location; for example, "available in Social Science Library," "Circulating copies at City Library," "additional copy in Speech Office," "at present at bindery, but available after November 15."

8. Whenever possible include brief evaluative annotation.

Example:

Becker, H., "How Families Meet the Costs of Hospitalization and Medical Care," *Marriage and Family Living*, 19:166–71, May 1957. 1957.

This article presents an argument in favor of the voluntary prepayment plan for meeting the costs of illness. It shows why such a plan is needed and how it meets this established need.

LOCATING BOOKS

Finding book titles on a given subject is simplified by the Card Catalog in your library, an alphabetical index file which libraries maintain. These files usually contain at least three cards for each book: one under the author's name, a second under the title of the book, and a third under the subject. Many libraries classify their holdings under the Dewey decimal system, which divides all knowledge into the following ten major classes:

000   General works: encyclopedias, newspapers, bibliographies.
100   Philosophy and psychology.
200   Religion and mythology.
300   Social science: sociology, economics, law government, education, and folklore.
400   Languages: English and foreign.
500   Science: mathematics, astronomy, physics, chemistry, geology, biology.
600   Useful arts: medicine, hygiene, engineering, agriculture, home economics, business, and manufacturing.
700   Fine arts: art, architecture, sculpture, music, theatre, photography, sport, and recreation.
800   Literature of all countries.
900   History and geography.

LOCATING GOVERNMENT PUBLICATIONS

Government publications published between 1893 and 1940 are indexed in the *Document Catalogue* (*Catalogue of the Public Documents of Congress*), volumes 1 to 25. This set lists documents under author, subject, and title (when necessary) including full catalog information for each item.

The *United States Government Publications Monthly Catalogue* (usually known by the last two words) indexes government publications to date. It appears as a monthly and has an annual subject index. Listings are by department issuing and by subject. It also includes price and general information for ordering.

The current publications for the several states, territories, and insular possessions may be located by referring to the *Monthly Check List of State Publications* (Washington, D.C.: the United States Government Printing Office), which is assembled by the Library of Congress. Publications are listed by issuing agencies in alphabetical order.

LOCATING MAGAZINE AND NEWSPAPER REFERENCES

Numerous periodical guides facilitate the assembling of a list of articles published in magazines. The most useful is the *Readers' Guide to Periodical Literature*, often referred to by the shortened title *Readers' Guide*. It indexes all subjects in selected general magazines from 1900 to the present and covers at present about 118 publications. It appears semimonthly, and in final form in composite editions which encompass the listing of two years. Many students naively assume that by checking the *Readers' Guide* they have covered the field and surveyed the titles of the most important magazines. How wrong they are. In truth there are many other valuable indexes, some of which are listed below:

Agricultural Index, 1916–, specializes in magazines, books, bulletins, and government publications in the field of agriculture.

Applied Science and Technology Index (formerly *Industrial Arts Index*) provides a guide to periodicals in fields of aeronautics, automation, chemistry, construction, electricity, engineering, geology, industrial and mechanical arts, machinery, physics, and transportation.

Business Periodical Index, 1958–, covers periodicals in accounting, advertising, banking, finance, business, insurance, marketing, management, public administration, and taxation.

Catholic Periodical Index, 1930–, indexes by author and title fifty to seventy-five Catholic periodicals published in the United States, Canada, England, and Ireland.

Education Index, 1929–, indexes about 150 periodicals, books, pamphlets, and reports in the field of education.

Industrial Arts Index, 1913–57, indexes magazines and books in the fields of engineering, trade, business and finance. *This series is no longer issued.*

International Index to Periodicals, 1907–, indexes about 174 periodicals, mainly scholarly journals and foreign titles in the fields of the humanities and social science in the English language.

Index to Legal Periodicals, 1888–, indexes material on technical and historical law subjects, legal biography, and many articles on political, economic, and sociological subjects. It covers some general as well as legal periodicals.

Public Affairs Information Service, 1915–, is a selective index of more than 1,000 publications—magazines, books, documents, and pamphlets—in the fields of economics, sociology, government legislation, and political science.

The New York Times Index, 1913–, is a subject index to the newspaper *The New York Times*. Each entry includes an exact reference to the day, page, and column. (Sections are given for Sunday editions.) Items are listed under subject. This index is a useful guide to other newspapers in that news stories, particularly those carried by the press services, may be located under the date given in this guide. Other newspaper indexes include the *Wall Street Journal Index* and the *Index to the* [London] *Times*.

STEP 4: LOCATE AND PROCURE SUPPLEMENTARY MATERIALS

At times the resources of local libraries may prove inadequate for the study of a debate proposition. Often a sympathetic librarian will procure specialized materials for you, but no debate group should be completely dependent upon such generosity. You should strive to gather specialized materials. Here are several suggestions to aid you.

1. Is it possible to borrow books from other libraries? Many state lending libraries and libraries of private institutions will lend materials directly to you if they understand the nature of your project. *Interlibrary Loan* provides means through which your local librarian can borrow books and microfilm from the Library of Congress and other libraries scattered over the entire country. Ask your libraian to explain how *Interlibrary Loan* operates.

2. What new books on your subject have appeared recently? The *Cumulative Book Index* (H. W. Wilson Company) provides a means of surveying all books published in this country. Listings are in alphabetical order and are made under author, title, and subject. In surveying new pub-

lications the *Publishers' Weekly* and similar magazines are helpful. If you find an interesting title, you may quickly evaluate it by reading *The Book Review Digest*, which publishes excerpts from current reviews. More information may be obtained by reading the whole reviews in the original sources.

3. What pamphlet materials can you find on your subject? Pressure groups sometimes issue information and arguments on questions which affect their interests. Obviously information of this type is biased, but such material is helpful if the slant is kept clearly in mind. The addresses of these organizations may be found in the annual edition of *The World Almanac*. Pamphlets, booklets, leaflets, and inexpensive materials are indexed in the *Vertical File Services Catalog* which gives title, author, publisher, and price. Many free materials are included. It provides an excellent means for locating little-known materials.

4. What government publications are available? A letter addressed to your congressman or to the Superintendent of the United States Government Printing Office, Washington, D.C., will bring information about government publications.

5. What plans can be devised for the coverage of newspapers and current periodicals? Clippings pertaining to the debate proposition many times contain the most recent developments on your subject. Ask each debater to buy a different newspaper and check its columns. If clippings are pasted in a squad scrapbook, soon your group will have a valuable source that is both current and original. Each clipping should be labeled clearly as to source and date.

STEP 5: DO YOUR INDIVIDUAL RESEARCH

The conducting of research for any project is a slow and often dull process. The bibliography prepared by the squad and the special materials will be of great aid, but how much reading you do and where your research carries you will be determined by your own eagerness and your own intellectual curiosity. Each debater must chart his own course and do his own reading. The good debater has an insatiable hunger for information; he never finishes his research.

SPECIAL AIDS IN YOUR PREPARATION

On most debate propositions there are available several specialized publications which bring together articles on various aspects of the topic. The most helpful of these collections are probably those volumes found in

The Reference Shelf Series, published by the H. W. Wilson Company. Each volume reprints "with some abridgement, articles and addresses on current issues and social trends" and generally includes an extensive bibliography. This set, which was originally initiated for school debaters, is widely recognized, and many libraries maintain a standing order for new volumes as they are issued.

Recent numbers have been devoted to the following subjects: "India," "The New Nations of West Africa," "Outlook for the Railroads," and "The Security of the Free World." Since 1938 a volume of "Representative American Speeches" has been issued annually. On the subject of compulsory health insurance there are at least six volumes which contained valuable articles on the subject.

The N.U.E.A. *Debate Handbook,* edited by Bower Aly and published by the National University Extension Association as a service to high schools, is another excellent composite of materials. Usually included also are an introductory analysis and a bibliography. A set of these paperback booklets brings together articles by prominent authorities on the annual high school debate topic.

The Congressional Digest—not to be confused with the *Congressional Record*—devotes each issue to a single controversial subject. It is published under the heading of "An Independent Monthly Featuring Controversies in Congress, Pro and Con. Not an official organ, not controlled by any party, interest, class or sect." An issue usually includes an impartial analysis of the problem followed by a number of pro and con opinions. Problems like the following are discussed: "Statehood for Hawaii"; "Federal Aid for Depressed Areas"; "Federal Housing Aid"; "Financing of R.E.A. Programs"; "Foreign Aid"; "School Construction and Teachers Salaries"; "Labor Union Abuses"; "Recent Decisions of the Supreme Court"; "Ceiling on Long Term U.S. Bonds"; and "Unemployment Compensation." The editor follows the practice of devoting one issue each year to the high school debate topic and another to the college proposition.

The Annals of the American Academy of Political and Social Science is a bimonthly scholarly journal which also devotes single issues to controversial topics. It considers such problems as the following: "Perspectives on Government and Science"; "Lagging Justice"; "International Cooperation for Social Welfare—A New Reality"; "Whither American Foreign Policy"; "Agricultural Policy, Politics, and Public Interest"; and "Religion in America." Since only recognized authorities are invited to contribute, the *Annals* publishes articles of the highest type.

The University Debaters Annual (H. W. Wilson Company), which appeared annually from 1915 through 1952, is a compilation of college debates, discussions, and symposiums, usually five to seven in an issue. In recent years the publisher insisted on printing only debates which were recorded at the time of delivery. This practice ensured verbatim reporting. In addition to the printed texts of the constructive speeches and rebuttals, the remarks of the chairman and a selected bibliography are included. These books provide excellent examples of how various collegiate teams developed cases on controversial questions and refuted the arguments of the opposition.

The weekly radio and television forums bring together in face-to-face situations leading authorities and advocates who consider controversial topics often of interest to the school debater. The best known of these programs are "Meet the Press" and "Face the Nation." You may find it profitable to record some of these broadcasts and telecasts in order to have them available for later study by the entire class or squad.

Another valuable source is found in the reports of the hearings of the committees of the United States Senate and House. A public hearing on a vital problem usually results in a wide expression of opinion by experts representing diverse interests. In addition, these witnesses and the members of the committees may submit pages and pages of supporting evidence for the record. If at all possible, subscribe to the *Congressional Record* which reports the deliberations of the two houses of the United States Congress. Congressmen often insert into the record, generally in the appendix, many valuable reports, editorials, speeches, letters, and miscellaneous materials. Material of this type may be purchased from the U.S. Government Printing Office, Washington, D.C.

OTHER HANDBOOKS

In addition to the items previously discussed, the debater will find available numerous other handbooks, some of which are published in mimeographed form by companies catering to the demands of interschool debaters. Such books may contain briefs, discussion of debate technique, and miscellaneous collections of quotations, pro and con, and even in some cases prepared speeches. Their intention is to make research easy. Some of them may give the student initial insight into a problem, and they may help identify the sources of some of your opponents' arguments (especially those who are foolish enough to confine their research to these canned materials).

Before using "canned material," that is, material on your annual debate question assembled exclusively for debaters, you should subject it to careful scrutiny and thoughtful analysis. The fact that an opponent may be foolish enough to build his case on arguments taken from a given handbook in no way establishes the soundness of the source. In evaluating any printed evidence you should consider (1) the qualifications of the compiler, (2) the standing of the publisher, (3) the make-up of the book,

(4) the amount and kind of material included, and (5) the accuracy of the editing. Ask your librarian to check such publications in recognized technical library journals and books which guide librarians in their purchases.

A searcher should be wary of any publication which lifts quotations out of context. Beware of cheap, mimeographed books which purport to pack into a few pages hurried hints and helps for winning debates. There is no shortcut to a thorough understanding of highly complex political, social, or economic problems.

FINDING STATISTICAL EVIDENCE

The most convenient sources of statistical facts are *The World Almanac* (New York: New York World-Telegram and the Sun) and *The Information Please Almanac* (New York: The McGraw-Hill Book Company) both of which are annual publications and draw information from many sources. Also valuable are the annual supplements of the encyclopedias: *The Britannica Book of the Year, Collier's Yearbook, The New International Year Book,* and *The Americana Annual.*

Students may wish to consult some of the principal sources of these compilations. At least for statistics concerning the United States the searcher will find great storehouses of information in the United States *Census Reports* and the *Statistical Abstract of the United States.* The latter, published annually by the Department of Commerce, presents important summary statistics on industrial, social, economic, and political organization of the United States and includes a representative selection from most of the important statistical publications, such as the *Census Reports,* and the findings of other departments.

READING THE AUTHORITATIVE BOOKS ON THE SUBJECT

The debater must base much of his thinking upon what he can learn from others, especially from those persons who have thought deeply about the problem and have conducted exhaustive investigations of it. Usually the abundance of material that exists on most topics is somewhat bewildering to the novice. Such questions arise as: What shall I read first? How do I know what is authoritative? How can I determine who is an authority? How can I locate the best books? Simple answers to such questions are difficult, if not impossible, to give. The following suggestions may aid you in locating authoritative material:

1. Ask the local expert (the professor who teaches the related subject) for recommendations concerning what to read.

2. In your reading of special debate materials, take note of persons who are quoted or referred to most often.

3. Study annotated bibliographies with reference to their evaluations of sources.

4. Ask your librarian for help.

In attempting to evaluate the standing of a given authority, find answers to the following questions:

1. What is his training?

2. What is his experience in the field?

3. Have his scholarly attainments been recognized by others, that is, has he won fellowships, awards, honorary degrees, and other recognition?

4. Has he written widely on his topic in recognized journals? Has he written any books on the subject? Who were the publishers of these books? Has he written extensively in other fields?

5. Is there reason to suspect that he is biased or may profit materially if his views are accepted? Who is his present employer? What are his political, racial, religious, and social affiliations? What organization has sponsored his publications?

The standard biographical dictionaries will help in finding answers to the questions listed in the previous paragraph. For identification of persons no longer living consult the *Dictionary of National Biography,* a set of volumes devoted to the biographies of famous Englishmen, and the *Dictionary of American Biography,* a 20-volume set devoted to famous Americans. For information about living persons, the best sources are *Who's Who* (for Englishmen) and *Who's Who in America.* Likewise, *Current Biography* (H. W. Wilson Company) publishes biographical sketches of persons who are currently in the public eye but as yet not listed in *Who's Who.* Similar reference works exist for other countries. In addition, there are also biographical dictionaries for specialized fields and groups, such as, theater, education, aviation, law, medicine, and labor.

STEP 6: RECORD AND ARRANGE YOUR NOTES FOR EFFECTIVE USE

NOTE TAKING

If you are to get maximum benefit from your research, you must be accurate and systematic in your note taking. You will probably find it desirable to record your materials on 4 x 6 or 5 x 8 index cards. Smaller sizes are insufficient for substantial amounts of material. Be sure to label each card as to subject and source. For example:

The braceros

"Under P.L. 78, a total of 457,600 Mexican farm workers known as braceros were imported for seasonal work in 1959, mostly by growers of cotton, vegetables, fruits, and sugar beets."

Arnold Mayer, "The Grapes of Wrath, Vintages 1961," *The Reporter*, 24:34 Feb 2'61

In note taking remember these instructions:

1. Clearly label and give full bibliographical information.
2. Record only one subject on a card.
3. Record from only one source on a card.
4. Do not crowd material; you may have to read it at a moment's notice.
5. Be careful not to distort meaning by lifting material out of context. Always ask yourself whether what you have copied represents what the author intended as his meaning?
6. In deleting material use three dots (...) if a portion of the sentence is omitted. If more than a sentence is omitted or if the end of a sentence is omitted, use four dots.

FILING YOUR MATERIAL

Taking notes is the first step, but filing these notes systematically is a necessary and important second step. If you are to find your note cards later, you must early devise a filing system that involves appropriate headings under which to group material. You will probably find a topical division more useful than an alphabetical one.

The size and kind of filing box or folder which you use is a matter of personal taste. Debates have often been lost because pertinent evidence could not be found when it was needed. Naturally, the best place for facts is in your head. But seldom can a speaker retain in some sort of mental filing system all the information that he needs in a given debate.

At the opposite extreme is the intercollegiate debater who struggles to his place on the platform with two overstuffed briefcases of books, pamphlets, and magazines, plus one or even two expansive card files jammed with cards. In fact one high school debater carried his material about in a small trunk which he flung open just before the debate. Aside from the psychological value that a great pile of material may have in bewildering the opposition and impressing the judge and audience, it probably serves little purpose but to harry the debater who attempts to dig out some pertinent card in those last seconds before taking his place before the audience.

Many debaters find it desirable to have two files: a reserve file and an active file. The reserve file, as large and expansive as necessary, may be used for background materials. The active file, small and compact, can be devoted to evidence that supports your immediate case and answers the arguments most frequently heard. The first stays on your study table, the second goes to the debate. In preparing for an audience debate or a tournament, the student should always check his active file and augment it with material from his reserve. This system keeps before the debater the evidence that he is most likely to need and avoids that last-minute confusion on the platform.

PLANNING FOR REBUTTAL AND REFUTATION

The inexperienced debater often feels that it is necessary to work out rebuttal arguments before the debate. He may wish to go so far as to brief or outline refutatory arguments and insert evidence. This type of material may be placed on index cards too and filed with the other notes. One year the author had a group of students who devised a useful notebook file. They briefed their answers on index cards (5 x 8). Each argument was labeled with an index tab, and holes were punched in the card at the proper places so that it could be placed in a small looseleaf notebook. Upon hearing a counterargument, the student would open his notebook to the proper place, remove the card, and insert it in the notes that he planned to take to the platform. By this means he had before him a complete outline of what he wanted to say.

Regardless of the system, give thought to the preparing and filing of your rebuttal materials.

SUMMARY

Debating which is not based upon sound arguments and facts is meaningless. Make it a rule to prepare thoroughly each time you appear before an audience. If you do, you will have greater self-assurance, a better chance to carry your point, and the inner satisfaction of knowing that you have not been guilty of misleading your listeners.

Thorough preparation is an essential of effective debating. The group which hopes to gain the maximum from the activity may wish to organize its research around six successive steps: (1) formulating a plan for research; (2) acquiring a general background; (3) preparing a bibliography;

(4) finding specialized materials which are pertinent to the proposition; (5) doing individual research; and (6) finally taking careful notes.

EXERCISES

1. Assemble a list of 25 cross references on a given subject (the one which the class has decided to study).
2. Prepare a bibliography through the cooperative efforts of the members of the class or the debate squad.
   a. Assign to each member selected years in one of the indexes:
      1. *Agricultural Index*
      2. *Education Index*
      3. *Catholic Periodical Index*
      4. *International Index*
      5. *Readers' Guide to Periodical Literature*
      6. *Business Periodical Index*
      7. *Index to Legal Periodical Literature*
      8. *Public Affairs Information Service*
   b. Put each reference on a 3 x 5 index card, following the form used by *Periodical Guide*.
   c. Check the availability of the reference in your local libraries. Write an annotation of 50 to 100 words. Sign your statement.
   d. Appoint a committee to collect the cards, to alphabetize them, and to eliminate duplicates.
   e. Appoint a committee to type, mimeograph, and distribute the complete bibliography.
3. Present a five-minute report to the group on the usefulness to the debater of one of the following sources:
   a. *Biography Index*
   b. *Who's Who in America*
   c. *Current Biography*
   d. *Congressional Record*
   e. *The Britannica Book of the Year*
   f. *Statistical Abstract of the United States*
   g. *The Information Please Almanac*
   h. *Encyclopedia of the Social Sciences*
   i. *The New York Times*
   j. Another source of your own choice.

   In preparing your report, examine the source carefully, noting the kinds of materials included and the unique characteristics of the publication. Also consult Constance M. Winchell's *Guide to Reference Books*.
4. Study the list of private organizations published in the *World Almanac* Prepare a list of fifteen organizations (with their addresses) which probabl'

publish materials on the proposition under consideration by the class or squad. Put every entry on an index card.

In class or squad meeting prepare a combined list. Ask each member to write to several of the organizations inquiring whether they have materials on the subject. Letters should be typed or written neatly on business stationery (preferably the letterhead of the department), and a business letter form should be used. Ask the instructor to check the letter form and content before it is mailed.

5. Conduct a two-man debate (15 minutes long) on one of the following propositions:
   a. Resolved: That directors of debate should forbid the use of handbooks as a source of information.
   b. Resolved: That the use of prepared materials on a given subject is contrary to sound educational practice.
6. Have each member study available prepared materials (handbooks, and the like) and report to the class on their suitability for use. Be sure to check quotations against the original sources to ascertain whether materials have been lifted out of context.
7. As a group, assemble a scrapbook of clippings on the proposition under consideration. Ask one member to be in charge of keeping the scrapbook and of putting clippings into it. Each entry should be identified as to source and date.

SUGGESTED READINGS

ADLER, MORTIMER, J. *How to Read a Book; the Art of Getting a Liberal Education*. New York: Simon and Schuster, Inc., 1940.

ALDRICH, ELLA VIRGINIA. *Using Books and Libraries*. 3rd ed. Englewood Cliffs, N.J.: Prentice-Hall, Inc., 1951.

A Manual of Style. Chicago: The University of Chicago Press, 1949. Excellent sources on bibliographies, punctuation, and mechanics.

AUER, J. JEFFERY. *An Introduction To Research in Speech*. New York: Harper & Row, Publishers, 1949.

BRADEN, WALDO W., and EARNEST BRANDENBURG. *Oral Decision-Making, Principles of Discussion and Debate*. New York: Harper & Row, Publishers, 1955. Chap. 4.

WINCHELL, CONSTANCE M. *Guide to Reference Books*. 7th ed. Chicago: American Library Association, 1951. Librarians use this as a guide in evaluating reference works.

~~~~~~

chapter 6

OUTLINING
THE ARGUMENT

by Dwight L. Freshley

Now that you have gathered the raw material for your persuasive product, the debate argument, you will need a method of organizing and processing these myriad facts and opinions for successful delivery in the marketplace of ideas. This is a crucial step. For if you do not understand a chain of argument thoroughly, if you are hesitant or hazy about where this contention or that bit of evidence fits in on the assembly line of cogent ideas, you will fail to produce a competitive or defensible argument.

In this chapter we shall consider the purpose, application, and rules of effective outlining in a general sense. This will be followed by a discussion of the brief. Legal and nonlegal kinds of briefs will be explained, rules for the debate brief will be spelled out, and finally, some examples from a specimen brief will be presented for your guidance.

PURPOSE OF OUTLINING

One of the most important components in man's extraordinary thinking mechanism is that which enables him to place things in their proper order. In the process of social learning we develop a proclivity for organization. We grow up to the admonition, "A place for everything and everything in its place." As a matter of fact, we become such creatures of habit that too much change in our established method of doing things, such as jumping from the high school schedule of monitored daily recitations to the collegiate lecture and final examination, sometimes unnerves us.

Some of us, however, develop the habit of organizing less than others —especially in writing and speaking. The person who cannot put his thought in logical manner is difficult to talk to. Some are as trying as the lawyer for the plaintiff who was stating the case before an English judge. He began somewhere in the middle and jumped around from one end to the other until the exasperated judge implored, "Mr. So & So, I wish you would adopt some order in the statement of your case. The chronological order is ordinarily best, but for Heaven's sake have some order, even if it is only an alphabetical order." [1] When our writing or speaking lacks order, the inevitable result is a breakdown in communication.

The general purpose of outlining, therefore, is *to guide the speaker and, in turn, aid the listener in effective, meaningful communication.* When the speaker has decided in his own mind the logical sequence his presentation should follow, he will gain needed confidence and discover that the proper method is also the easiest method. Explanations which were derailed with such deviations as "I forgot to mention while explaining step one that . . ." will disappear. Those famous arguments "I would have won if I had thought of . . ." will begin to appear on the black side of the ledger. These gains in communication effectiveness will begin to accrue when you apply the following three specific purposes of outlining to help carry out the general purpose stated above. These are:

1. To insure logical relationships between points.
2. To determine proper emphasis of arguments.
3. To insure against omission of significant arguments or evidence.

Application and rewards for this discipline are legion. A friend of the author's, a successful college professor, was a debater in high school and college. His professors could always recognize his examination papers by their clarity of organization. The predisposition in his favor earned him high respect and, incidentally, consistently high marks. Lawyers are always rewarded in some way for the discipline which drawing up a good brief demands. Sometimes the reward will be more intangible than monetary— perhaps a favorable verdict in a public defender role; other times the handsome fee from the wealthy client will compensate the attorney for his hours of arduous preparation. Finally, public life abounds with examples of unusual successes of effective communicators whose ability to organize was recognized. General Nathan Twining, Air Force Chief of Staff under

---

[1] Henry T. Simmons, "How Lawyers Should Argue Cases on Appeal," *Advocacy and the King's English,* ed. George Rossman (New York: The Bobbs-Merrill Company, 1960), p. 349.

President Eisenhower, once proved the superiority of his Air Force budget over those of the Army and Navy through his clarity of presentation before a Congressional committee. These are examples of men who did their homework thoroughly before selling their ideas in the marketplace.

RULES FOR OUTLINING

Having considered the purpose and application of the outline, let us now set down six specific rules to be followed in its construction. They are:

1. Standard symbol system
2. Consistent indentation
3. Complete sentences
4. Logical subordination
5. Coordinate ideas
6. Discreteness

STANDARD SYMBOL SYSTEM. The first requisite for proper and satisfactory outlining is that symbols must be used consistently. The most widely accepted format is as follows:

```
I. — — — — — — —
   A. — — — — — — —
      1. — — — — — — —
            a. — — — — — —
            b. — — — — — —
      2. — — — — — — —
   B. — — — — — — —
II. — — — — — — —
```

In using this system for general outlining, one symbol should be used before each item and only one sentence behind each symbol. The latter rule is flexible in writing the brief. Though points following Roman numerals and capital letters should be one sentence only, further subordinated points can be expanded as in the samples under "Principles of Briefmaking." In the example from general outlining that follows, note how the two rules above are violated.

Incorrect
I. A. The services performed by the American Red Cross cover a broad spectrum.
   B. The unusual and dramatic services receive the most publicity.
      1. The A.R.C. provided forty pints of blood for a hemorrhaging

mother in New York and the A.R.C. furnished food, clothing, and shelter to the survivors of the Vicksburg tornado in 1953.

C. Follow-up services in disaster relief, though less dramatic than other services, are the most costly.

Correct

I. The services performed by the American Red Cross cover a broad spectrum.

A. The unusual and dramatic services receive the most publicity.

1. The A.R.C. provided forty pints of blood for a hemorrhaging mother in New York.

2. The A.R.C. furnished food, clothing, and shelter to the survivors of the Vicksburg tornado in 1953.

B. Follow-up services in disaster relief, though less dramatic than other services, are the most costly.

CONSISTENT INDENTATION.   Integrated with the use of these symbols should be uniform indentation with all the Roman numerals being equidistant from the left edge of the paper, all the capital letters being uniformly indented but farther from the left edge than the Roman numerals, and so on. Also, if a sentence is more than one line, it should not be returned to the extreme left-hand margin but should begin on the second and subsequent lines immediately below the first letter of that sentence. Let us illustrate:

I. The vote of the electoral college and not the individual ultimately decided the election of the President.

A. At the state level the popular vote is translated into electoral college votes.

1. The majority of popular votes decides the entire electoral vote in each state.

a. For example, the vote in Illinois in 1960 was 2,367,837 for the Republicans and 2,377,638 for the Democrats, with the Democrats winning all the twenty-seven electoral votes in the state.

COMPLETE SENTENCES.   Logical outlining demands complete sentences. While it is recognized that two other kinds of outlines are used, namely, the key-phrase and the key-word outlines, these are not satisfactory for our present purposes. These abbreviated types of outlines are most often used by experienced speakers who need only a word or phrase to jog their memories. Complete sentences aid the writer in thinking systematically. In addition, if the outline is to be of use to anyone besides the speaker, complete sentences will provide the thoroughness needed. Note how sketchy the first outline is compared with the full-sentence outline which follows:

Key Word

I. Parthenon's religions
  A. Greek
  B. Christian
  C. Moslem

Complete Sentence

I. The Parthenon has been the center of three different religions in its history.
  A. In the beginning it was the Temple of the Greek goddess Athena Parthenos, Goddess of Wisdom.
  B. It was a Christian Church from 426 to 1458.
  C. It was a Mohammedan mosque from 1458 to 1687.

LOGICAL SUBORDINATION. Of all the important rules of outlining, perhaps none should be heeded more seriously than proper subordination. This reveals how logically rigorous you have been in establishing the proper relationship between points. If your thinking has been fuzzy, your outlining will reflect this. For example, in the incorrect example immediately following, note that B does not relate significantly to I. In the corrected example, however, observe how A and B are clearly coordinate and help to prove the truth of the statement to which they are subordinate. Likewise, 1 serves the same purpose for A, and a provides evidence for 1. Furthermore, checks for logical order can be made by applying the conjunction *for* after the statements organized in deductive order as below, or if you want to read the line of reasoning from the bottom, use the connective *therefore*.

Incorrect

I. Conditions in the area of labor unions are harmful to the continued success of labor unions themselves, *for*
  A. Some unions have become dominated by racketeers and gangsters.
  B. The Taft-Hartley Act has helped remove some of the evils in unions.

Correct.

I. Conditions in labor unions are harmful to the continued success of labor unions themselves, *for*
  A. Some unions have become dominated by racketeers and gangsters, *for*
    1. The International Teamsters Union has continually been under fire by the McClellan Committee, *for*
      a. Evidence has proven that Johnny Dio, known racketeer and

friend of Jimmy Hoffa, was a specialist in organizing "paper locals," that is, local unions without working members.
B. Financial abuses of union funds have been widespread, *for*
1. Etc.

COORDINATE IDEAS.   Consonant with logical subordination is the use of coordinate ideas. This implies that you choose a series of generically related ideas. These points, under each series of Roman numerals or capital letters, will be alike in one or more significant aspects. One incorrect example below should suffice in demonstrating this rule. Note how E is out of keeping with the rest of the supporting fields.

I. Fields of Psychology
   A. Industrial Psychology
   B. Clinical Psychology
   C. Educational Psychology
   D. Social Psychology
   E. Salesmanship

DISCRETENESS.   Accurate division of points or discreteness is a final logical necessity for good outlining. To avoid unnecessary overlapping of ideas, you must see that one classification is maintained throughout each series. Note in the incorrect example below the switch from the chronological to the topical pattern.

Incorrect	*Correct*
I. Beethoven's works covered a wide range	I. Beethoven's work covered a wide range
A. Early works	A. Concertos
B. Sonatas	B. Sonatas
C. Symphonies	C. Symphonies
D. Church music	D. Church music

PRINCIPLES OF BRIEFMAKING

DEFINITION

The outlining rules we have just been discussing are for general use. They are of immediate relevance, however, as we consider now how to construct the brief. To Webster, under the classification of *Law*, a brief is an "abridgement or concise statement of a client's case made out for the instruction of counsel." The legal profession does not have standardized requirements for the brief. However, there are certain items that most lawyers agree should appear in the preparation of a case. A

recent survey of prominent trial lawyers across the United States disclosed
that the majority of them recommended the following matters be included
in a trial brief: [2]

1. A statement of issues or an analysis of the pleadings and pretrial
   orders.
2. A diagram and outline of proof.
3. Notes for the opening statement.
4. A resume of expected testimony of each witness or the statements
   of each witness.
5. Notes about each witness to assist the lawyer in handling the witness.
6. Notes for cross-examination.
7. Briefs of law.
8. An exhibit file.
9. An index and cross index.

The nonlegal brief used by debaters may also vary in format and style.
Some see it as "a complete, logical outline which organizes and records all
the available material on one side of the proposition." [3] Others maintain
"it is a complete written survey of all available material that is pertinent to
a given problem." [4] To gain the depth of understanding necessary for
analysis of a debate proposition, the debater should write a brief which
encompasses both sides of a given topic. Therefore, *the full brief is a comprehensive collection of written materials on both sides of a given proposition, outlined logically, from which the debater can develop his case.*

KINDS OF BRIEFS

While the *full brief* is recommended here, it is well to recognize the
use of other kinds of briefs which may be used in certain circumstances. The
traditional brief treats one side of the question as suggested above. This has
been used in the academic debate arena for some decades and, when one
is pressed for time or is utilizing some division of labor, has much to recommend it. However, probably most useful in the courtroom is the traditional brief. It fills the requirements for cases which demand that each
attorney apprise the other of his position in advance of a case being heard.

An outgrowth of the full brief is a third kind called the *flexible*

<hr/>

[2] Charles W. Joiner, "The Trial Brief," *Advocacy and the King's English*, pp.
46–47.

[3] James H. McBurney, James M. O'Neill, and Glen Mills, *Argumentation and
Debate* (New York: The Macmillan Co., 1951), p. 173.

[4] William A. Behl, *Discussion and Debate* (New York: The Ronald Press, 1953),
p. 116.

brief.[5] The chief feature of this approach is the provision for considering counterarguments to each side of the question. For example, the negative may well want to include an approach for the status quo and counterplan as well as straight refutation.

RULES FOR CONSTRUCTING THE BRIEF

Just as there is no one correct method for drawing the legal brief, there is no single, iron-clad set of rules for constructing the academic debate brief. What follows is an acceptable set of ground rules which reflect the standards of recognized debate authorities in this century.

A. GENERAL RULES

1. The brief should be divided into three parts, the introduction, the discussion, and the conclusion. Each of these should be treated as a separate unit and your symbol system should show this by beginning each section with Roman numeral I.
2. Complete sentences should be used throughout the brief.
3. The style of writing should be impersonal. At this point you are writing with no particular audience in mind. Avoid subjective sentence introductions such as: "I think" and "We should." Also, don't begin a supporting point by saying "Ralph McGill says," but quote your authority and then document as follows: "The one way we may avoid atomic war is to face up to the possibility that we may have one." (Ralph McGill, *Nashville Tennessean*, September 20, 1961, p. 9.)

B. RULES FOR THE INTRODUCTION. The purpose of the introduction is to offer a meaningful background of the topic. This first section provides a preliminary summary of the main divisions of argument so that an intelligent reading of the brief can be made. Do not try to prove any points in the introduction. At this stage you are merely headlining your case. Your contentions will be supported in the discussion section.

The following points usually are included in the introduction of a full brief:

1. Statement of the proposition
2. Immediate cause for discussion
3. Origin and history of the question
4. Definition of terms
5. A statement of irrelevant and admitted matter
6. Clash of opinion

[5] Austin J. Freeley, *Argumentation and Debate* (Belmont, Calif.: Wadsworth Publishing Co., 1961), 156.

7. Statement of issues
8. Points in partition

A specimen introduction, prepared for use in debate, follows for your guidance.[6]

INTRODUCTION

RESOLVED: That labor organizations should be under the jurisdiction of anti-trust legislation.

I. The cause for discussion is as follows:
   A. The activities of labor organizations either directly or indirectly affect everyone in the United States.
   B. These activities are not always limited to the basic functions of labor organizations.
   C. The limitation and restriction of the activities of labor organizations have recently been discussed in Congress and by other governmental and academic agencies and committees.
   D. The plan of anti-trust legislation being used as a means to limit and restrict the activities of labor organizations has been suggested.
II. The history of the question is as follows:
   A. When anti-trust legislation was first passed in 1890, labor organizations were under its jurisdiction.
   B. In 1914 labor organizations received immunity from anti-trust laws under Section 6 of the Clayton Act.
   C. The 1932 Norris-LaGuardia Act and Supreme Court decisions, such as in the 1940 United States *vs.* Hutcheson case, upheld and added to the immunity of labor organizations under anti-trust legislation.
   D. Recent labor-management legislation, such as the 1947 Taft-Hartley Act and the 1959 Landrum-Griffin Act, was passed to limit and restrict labor organization activities.
III. Admitted and/or irrelevant matter:
   A. It is admitted that labor organizations should be allowed to pursue their legitimate objectives.
IV. The terms are explained in this way:
   A. Labor organization may be defined as any organization in which employees participate and which exists for the purpose of dealing with employers concerning grievances, labor disputes, wages, rate of pay, hours of employment, conditions of work and other legitimate objectives.

[6] The examples of briefmaking are taken from a brief prepared by Don Clements, undergraduate at Vanderbilt University.

B. Jurisdiction may be defined as sphere of authority, the limits within which any particular power may be exercised.
C. Anti-trust legislation may be defined as federal legislation governing and controlling monopolies and restraint of trade.

V. The conflicting arguments are as follows:
  A. The Affirmative argue:
    1. There is a need for labor organizations to be under the jurisdiction of anti-trust legislation.
      a. Present labor power is necessary for labor organizations to carry out effectively their legitimate objectives; however, today they can and do use this power to restrain trade.
      b. There are no effective curbs on these activities of labor organizations today.
    2. Anti-trust legislation would effectively meet these needs.
  B. The Negative argue:
    1. There is no need for labor organizations to be under the jurisdiction of anti-trust legislation.
      a. Labor organizations cannot themselves directly restrain trade unless this restraint is a by-product of pursuance of a legitimate objective.
      b. If restraint of trade does occur not as a by-product of pursuance of a legitimate objective, then present legislation is effective to curb the means used to restrain trade.
    2. Anti-trust legislation would not meet the needs.

VI. The main issues suggested are:
  A. Can and do labor organizations directly restrain trade except as a by-product of the pursuance of legitimate objectives?
  B. Can present legislation effectively curb the activities of labor organizations which are not in the pursuance of legitimate objectives?
  C. Would anti-trust legislation curb these activities of labor organizations which are not in the pursuance of legitimate objectives?

VII. The Affirmative will establish the following arguments:
  A. There is a need for labor organizations to be under the jurisdiction of anti-trust legislation.
    1. Labor organizations can and do directly restrain trade.
    2. Present legislation cannot effectively cover these activities.
  B. Anti-trust legislation would effectively curb these activities which restrain trade.

C. RULES FOR THE DISCUSSION

1. The main points of the discussion should correspond to the points in partition in the introduction.
2. The outlining should be logical and follow the rules set forth

earlier in the chapter. Keep in mind that each substatement should serve as proof of the statement to which it is subordinate.

3. Points should be adequately supported by reasoning and evidence. Evidence needs to be carefully documented. Choose one of the following methods: (1) in the margin at the left of the evidence being documented, (2) in a footnote, or (3) in parenthesis at the end of the evidence. The third method is used in the excerpted discussion specimen below.

This section of the brief does not exhaust the available supporting materials under the main points or subpoints. It merely illustrates how development should proceed. Additional evidence would be necessary to establish these points successfully.

AFFIRMATIVE DISCUSSION

I. There is a need for labor organizations to be under the jurisdiction of anti-trust legislation, *for*
   A. Labor organizations can and do directly restrain trade, *for*
      1. "Reported cases indicate, however, that some unions have engaged in some practices aimed directly at commercial market restraints by fixing the kind or amount of products which may be sold in any area at their market price. Such activities run counter to our national anti-trust policy." (Robert A. Bicks, Assistant Attorney General in charge of anti-trust prosecutions, *Hearings Before the Joint Economic Committee of the United States* (Eighty-sixth Congress, first session), Part 7, "The Effects of Monopolistic and Quasi-monopolistic Practices," September 22, 23, 24, 25, 1959, p. 2079.)
      2. That unions restrain trade may be documented in three areas *for*
         a. Restraint of trade is practiced by directly fixing the prices at which goods may be bought or sold.
            (1) Examples have been found in agreements covering wholesale bread delivery, milk distribution, and in the construction industry. (William M. Leiserson, "Restraints on Trade," *Union, Management and the Public*, E. Wight Bakke and others, 1960, p. 213.)
            (2) In a growing number of cities the price of your milk is set, not by the farmer or the dairy or the storekeeper, but by a local union leader. Teamsters Local 202 in New York City, for instance, established union approved price lists for dairy products. (W. L. White, "Should Unions Have Monopoly Powers?", *Readers Digest*, August 1955, p. 33.)

b. Restraint of trade is practiced by limiting the production and use of certain products, *for*

  (1) "In mid-1942 the Musicians Unions established a record ban, halting the production of phonograph records altogether. The attorney general brought anti-trust action against the ban . . . the court held the union's activity to be protected under the Clayton and Norris-LaGuardia Acts." (John Van de Water, "Work Restrictions in Anti-Trust Legislation," *Labor Law Journal*, September 1954, p. 602.)

  (2) The Sheet Metal Workers Union refused to install ventilators produced by nine corporations. This boycott has caused a great loss to all companies involved. The Burt Manufacturing Company of Akron, Ohio, lost an estimated $1,000,000 during the first two years of this boycott. (*Business Week*, February 27, 1957, p. 30.)

c. Restraint of trade is practiced by limiting the areas in which goods may be used, produced, or sold, *for*

  (1) The Chicago Roofers' Union limits the geographical territory in which contractors may take jobs. (Archibald Cox, "Labor and the Anti-Trust Laws," *University of Pennsylvania Law Review*, November 1955, p. 267.)

  (2) In San Francisco there was a union agreement to shut out all millwork and patterned lumber produced outside the area. (William M. Leiserson, *op. cit.*)

D. RULES FOR THE CONCLUSION

1. The conclusion should summarize the main points of the discussion, and, therefore, usually recapitulates the points in partition.

2. This summary should be followed by an affirmation or denial of the proposition.

The following conclusion is typical:

AFFIRMATIVE CONCLUSIONS

I. Since there is a need to govern the restraints of trade carried out by labor organizations; and

II. Since there are no effective laws today to govern these restraints; and

III. Since anti-trust legislation was meant to curb such restraints; and

IV. Since anti-trust legislation would be both practical and desirable,

V. Therefore, labor organizations should be under the jurisdiction of anti-trust legislation.

SUMMARY

A study of outlining in general and briefmaking in particular serves as a basic tool for many disciplines. Basic rules to follow in this method of organizing one's material are: a standard symbol system, consistent indentation, complete sentences, logical subordination, coordinate ideas, and discreteness.

There are several kinds of briefs, both legal and nonlegal. The nonlegal brief may be *traditional* (one side of the question), *full* (both sides of the question), or *flexible* (specific consideration of refutation). Many writers recommend the *full* brief for its completeness.

The rules for constructing the brief are: (1) The proposition should appear at the head of the brief; (2) the brief should be divided into three parts, introduction, discussion, and conclusion; (3) complete sentences should be used throughout; (4) the style of writing should be impersonal; (5) the introduction should include the background material needed for understanding the discussion to follow; (6) the main points of the discussion should correspond to the points of partition in the introduction; (7) the outline should be logical, with points adequately supported by reasoning and evidence; (8) points of refutation should be clearly marked; and (9) the conclusion should summarize the main points and affirm or deny the proposition.

EXERCISES

1. Outline the next public speech you hear. Observe whether the organization was topical, logical, or both.
2. Outline the first affirmative speech of the sample debate in the Appendix. Can a logical outline be developed without violating any of the general rules set forth in this chapter? Do the same thing for the first negative speech.
3. Take a topic recently discussed in class and exercise your deductive wit by playing what will be called the inside golf game, "For." The idea is for one to start with a conclusion and the next person to offer the probative subpoint preceded, of course, by the appropriate "for," until the stock of supporting points is exhausted. Do this same exercise after you finish your brief for the course.
4. Consider the following partial outline:

    Resolved: That H-bomb testing should be stopped.

I. Attention must be given to the strontium 90 which keeps its radioactive strength for many years and is now entering our food and water supplies.
 A. America's children gain most bone-building calcium from milk.
  1. Of greatest concern to American parents is the strontium 90 in milk.
   a. Strontium is taken into children's bones along with calcium.
  2. This odorless, tasteless element can cause cancer and leukemia.
 B. By peeling and washing the plant thoroughly the housewife can remove whatever strontium 90 that may have fallen on it.
  1. The strontium 90 that has entered a plant from the soil, however, cannot be washed off.
  2. Scientists have learned that much of the strontium can be removed in the normal preparation of some foods.

Are the following statements concerning the above outline true or false?

1. I is the main idea.
2. Neither A nor B is a proper subpoint under I.
3. Subpoint a should be main subpoint A.
4. I contains too many ideas.
5. Subpoint 2 under A is logically situated in the outline.
6. Subpoint 2 under B should be the second main supporting idea of I, and therefore, should be placed at B.

5. Rewrite the following partial outline following the logical pattern explained in the chapter:

I. There would be three benefits to free trade: lower prices, the elimination of union monopolies, and a higher standard of living.

II. Labor would be placed on the open price market with every other resource.

III. The unions would be forced either to conform to market prices or to retire from the industry.

IV. It would also eliminate many labor monopolies.

V. Many inefficient industries would be forced out of business because of lowered prices, but the labor resource would flow into other more efficient industries which would be expanding because of the increased market in international trade.

VI. Third, free trade helps improve the standard of living through the principle of comparative advantage.

VII. Free trade will help you by lowering prices.

VIII. Lower prices would be achieved through the free open-price market.

IX. To illustrate the principle of comparative advantage, we may be able to produce two products at a lower cost than another country (say, Brazil), and yet if we concentrate on the comparatively better one (by lower cost) such as steel and let the other country produce the second product such as cotton (which is presumably better for it), we will be able to set up trade exchange that will enhance the living standards of both countries.

X. Trade is based upon this principle of comparative advantage.

SUGGESTED READINGS

BAIRD, A. CRAIG. *Argumentation, Discussion, and Debate.* New York: McGraw-Hill Book Company, Inc., 1950. Chap. 7.

CROCKER, LIONEL. *Argumentation and Debate.* New York: American Book Co., 1944. Chap. 15.

DICKENS, MILTON, AND JAMES H. McBATH; *Guidebook for Speech Practice.* New York: Harcourt, Brace & World, Inc., 1961, Chap. 10.

FOSTER, W. T. *Argumentation and Debate.* Boston: Houghton Mifflin Company, 1932. Chap. 3.

FREELEY, AUSTIN, JR. *Argumentation and Debate.* Belmont, Calif.: Wadsworth Publishing Company, 1961. Chap. 12.

HUBER, ROBERT B. *Influencing Through Argument.* New York: David McKay Company, Inc., 1963. Chap. 12.

THOMPSON, ERNEST. "Does Organization Really Make a Difference?" *The AFA Register,* 8 (Spring 1960), 12–16.

chapteR 7

DEVELOPING
THE CASE

by Wayne C. Eubank

As employed by debaters, *case* simply means the issues, evidence, arguments, and strategy upon which a team bases its stand on a given debate proposition. Following a program of thorough investigation, analysis, and as many directors insist, briefing [1] (all prior steps to building a case), a team selects from the total possibilities of the proposition the major and minor issues capable of proper support on which it will debate. This is their *case* and on it they must win or lose. An illustration from the affirmative side of a recent college debate proposition may be helpful.

In a debate on the question, "Resolved: That the federal government should adopt a program of permanent wage and price control," the affirmative chose as the fundamentals in its case: (1) There is a need for the federal government to adopt such a program because of (a) great evils of inflation, (b) evils of deflation, and (c) continuing threat of military force, and (2) the affirmative plan (a specific plan was presented) will be (a) practicable and (b) desirable (each contention was supported with evidence and argument). In this debate, the affirmative chose certain evidence and arguments to prove the need for a change; they presented a plan of action; and they pointed out how their plan would work and correct the evils of the present system, thus affording benefits not possible under the status quo.

[1] For a discussion of briefing and an example of student briefs, see Chapter 6.

103

PURPOSE OF THE CASE

The purpose of the *case* is to give unity and clarity to the presentation. Through its use a debate team can work as a unit, centering all its evidence and argument around the given proposition which forms the basis for its case. It makes possible an orderly presentation of material. It leads to a selection of the strongest possible arguments and makes possible the elimination of the trivial.

The following suggestions will assist the debater in preparing his case:

CHOOSE POINTS THAT ARE CAPABLE OF PROOF

It is well to remember that each contention should be proved in a debate. Argument and evidence must be the basis for deciding on whether a contention should be included in a case. Do not use contentions that would require more time than you have available. It is foolish to include points in your case that are not subject to proof, for they will easily be destroyed by refutation.

THE MAJOR CONTENTIONS IN THE CASE SHOULD BE FEW IN NUMBER

It is a common fault of beginning debaters to try to prove too much. Within the time limits of a standard debate it is impossible to do justice to more than three or four major points. Resist the impulse to overcome the judge or audience with the completeness of your knowledge.

SELECT PROPOSITIONS FOR YOUR CASE THAT WILL HAVE AUDIENCE ACCEPTABILITY

In debating before various groups, you will find that certain arguments have more appeal. If you are to be persuasive, utilize the most powerful arguments you can for a given audience. Be versatile. Have a breadth of knowledge and variety of arguments sufficient to adapt to a variety of audiences.

DEVELOP YOUR CASE TOWARD A CLIMAX

Select contentions, arguments, and evidence that are cumulative in force. Avoid individual, isolated points. Such irrelevent material destroys the unity in your case. Unity throughout your presentation is imperative. Construct your case in such a manner that it will progress step by step toward a climax.

THE AFFIRMATIVE CASE

Because of its position in the debate, the affirmative traditionally has been held responsible for certain introductory and explanatory material. Usually it is responsible for citing the reason for the discussion of the question, defining the terms, outlining the main issues, and establishing criteria for the evaluation of the proposed solution. The length of the introductory material will depend to a large extent on the nature of the audience. If the debate is before a large audience, and if the question is new to them, it may be necessary for the affirmative to spend some time in explaining the origin of the question and the immediate cause for discussion and in other prefatory remarks. It has become customary in tournament debates to forego a lengthy introduction and merely outline the essentials in the introductory material. A more detailed listing of this introductory material as related to interpretation is presented on pages 116–117.

BURDEN OF PROOF

One of the fundamental parts of the affirmative responsibilities is the burden of proof. Each debater should understand its meaning and its importance. The burden of proof is the *risk of the proposition*. It is that burden which rests on a proponent of something new, the side which is proposing a change in the status quo, the side which would lose unless something is done. The burden of proof rests always with the affirmative. It never shifts from side to side. As will be pointed out later, a negative team may propose a counterplan and will then have the responsibilities for support for this given proposition, but the basic burden of proof for the original proposition still lies with the affirmative.

PRESUMPTION

The concept of burden of proof is directly related to that of presumption. In debating, the presumption rests with the negative at the beginning of the debate. The affirmative can begin to overcome this presumption by carrying the burden of proof. Presumption favors existing institutions. In 1834, Bishop Richard Whately stated clearly the concept of presumption and its relationships:

According to the correct use of the term, a "presumption" in favor of any supposition means not (as has been sometimes erroneously imagined) a preponderance of antecedent probability in its favor, but, such a "pre"-occupation of the ground as implies that it must stand good till some sufficient reason is adduced against it; in short, that the "burden of proof" lies on the side of him who disputes it.[2]

Thus, we can say that the burden of proof rests with the party who has the presumption against him.

Whately goes on to point out that it is a well-known principle of law that every man is to be presumed innocent until his guilt is established. This does not mean that we are to take his innocence for granted; nor does it mean that it is antecedently more likely than not that he is innocent. It means only that the burden of proof lies with the accusers; that the prisoner is not to be called on to prove his innocence or to be dealt with as a criminal until his accusers have established his guilt.

Whately sums up this important factor:

> There is a presumption in favor of every existing institution. Many of these (we will suppose the majority) may be susceptible of alteration for the better; but still the "burden of proof" lies with him who proposes an alteration; simply, on the ground that since a change is not a good in itself, he who demands a change should show cause for it. No one is called on . . . to defend an existing institution, till some argument is adduced against it; and that argument ought in fairness to prove, not merely an actual inconvenience, but the possibility of a change for the better.[3]

Thus, in debating the proposition "Resolved: That the United States should adopt a program of compulsory health insurance for all citizens," the affirmative would have to assume the responsibility of showing that the present system (voluntary, private, individual-payment medical service) demands reforms; that there are evils in this system; that the proposed plan of compulsory health insurance for all citizens is a practicable, workable system; and that the proposed plan will correct the existing evils without bringing about new and greater evils. Unless the affirmative can do this, the debate goes to the negative because presumption favors the present system. Actually, the negative need do nothing until the affirmative has begun to establish its case by showing a need for a change. The first thing that the affirmative must do, therefore, is overcome the presumption

[2] Richard Whately, *Elements of Rhetoric* (New York: William Jackson, 1834), p. 74.

[3] *Ibid.*, p. 76.

in favor of the negative. This can be done only by assuming the burden of proof.

PRIMA FACIE CASE

The affirmative can satisfactorily discharge its burden of proof by establishing a prima facie case. In law, prima facie means evidence sufficient to establish a fact, or to raise a presumption of fact, unless rebutted. It is a case which would stand logically complete if it were not attacked by the negative. Someone has defined it as the minimum which the affirmative must prove to establish its case. When the affirmative has presented a prima facie case, then it has swung the presumption which was in favor of the negative back to the affirmative. This immediately leads to another debate term, the *burden of rejoinder*, or the *burden of rebuttal*. After the affirmative has established a prima facie case, it is the responsibility of the negative to respond. By making this response, the negative attempts to regain the presumption which was in its favor originally. Thus, the initial responsibility for the burden of rebuttal rests with the negative. As pointed out previously, the burden of proof does not shift from the affirmative, but the burden of rebuttal shifts back and forth from the negative, who must initiate it, to the affirmative as the argument proceeds.

MAIN DUTIES OF THE AFFIRMATIVE

1. DEFINE THE TERMS IN THE PROPOSITION

Much time and temper can be saved if the affirmative and negative teams can agree upon definitions early in the debate. Consequently, the first affirmative should lay down clear-cut definitions early in his opening speech. The affirmative team should not only define the terms; they should be fair and just in their delineations. They should avoid hazy or restrictive definitions that might give them a seeming advantage, for if they resort to such definitions and the negative points up this fact, the affirmative is sure to lose some of the confidence of the audience.

2. ESTABLISH A NEED FOR A CHANGE

The first main duty of the affirmative team is to establish *a need for a change*. In advancing the need issue, the affirmative must show that the present system is beset with various inherent evils. In order to discharge this obligation successfully the affirmative must have thoroughgoing knowledge of the workings of the present system. An attack upon superficial evils is not sufficient. It must be shown that the alleged evils are inherent within the present system, not temporary, not incidental.

If the alleged evils can be eliminated by slight alterations in the present system, the affirmative has not established a sound need for a change. It is precisely at this point that many affirmative need cases fail. If the alleged evils in the present system are not of sufficient magnitude to warrant a complete change of policy, the negative will merely advance a few simple repairs for the present system and thus contend that the affirmative has not proved the status quo fundamentally and irreparably unsound.

Therefore, in establishing the need issue the affirmative must show that the present system is unsound because of certain evils and that the alleged evils are inherent and only the abolition of the present system will insure their elimination. An example of a skeleton affirmative need case under the proposition "Resolved: That the United Nations should be evolved immediately into a world federation" follows:

1. The United Nations is a weak confederation with no power to act.
2. Through unilateral action, nations sidestep the United Nations.
3. The veto power in the Security Council gives any nation represented there the power to block all proceedings.

It is evident that the above evils are a part of the present United Nations organization. Furthermore, it is clear that in order to eliminate those evils, the entire system would have to be changed.

Debating the proposition "Resolved: That the federal government should provide a complete system of medical care available to all citizens at public expense," the affirmative chose the following need contentions:

1. The American people need better medical care.
   a. Our health record reveals weaknesses.
   b. Preventative health services are woefully inadequate.
2. All Americans cannot obtain adequate medical care under the present system.
   a. The present medical program is poorly organized and uncoordinated.
   b. The cost of medical care is prohibitive to many citizens.

It is always necessary for the affirmative to prove the need for a change. Some debate directors contend that the affirmative can approach the need contention in either of two ways: touch the need lightly or stress the need. Few propositions are framed so as to eliminate the necessity of proving the *need* issue. Sometimes the negative will ignore the need and center its attack upon the plan. In such instances, the affirmative may conclude that it has wasted the first speech.

This conclusion is not always justified. If the need had been touched lightly by the first affirmative, the first negative might have taken advantage of the situation and amassed evidence showing no need for a change. Thus, the affirmative would be charged with dereliction of duty. The second affirmative would have to assume the responsibility of the first affirmative, thus placing them in a defensive rather than an offensive position. Furthermore, the affirmative plan usually is so constructed as to remedy the evils in the present system. Therefore, it is logical to set forth these evils in the need step. It is true that if the negative employs a counterplan much of the value of the need issue is lost to the affirmative. Since, however, the intent of the negative cannot be known in advance, it is strongly recommended that the affirmative stress the need issue.

3. PRESENT A PLAN TO SOLVE THE NEED

Following the establishment of a need for a change, the second duty of the affirmative is the presentation of a plan to supplant the status quo. Some authorities state that it is not necessary for an affirmative team to present a plan. This is true of questions of fact, but not of policy. However, some maintain that even with questions of policy, the affirmative can merely argue general principles. An occasional question of policy might lend itself to this type of development (arguing general principles rather than a definite plan). However, most astute negative teams will argue that before the new policy can be accepted, the affirmative must prove its workability, which necessitates the offering of a plan. The affirmative can do much to safeguard itself from strong negative attack if it presents a well-worked-out plan. Sometimes, the general principles upon which the plan is based may be sufficient. However, in many instances, a rather concrete or detailed layout of the machinery for putting the new policy into operation is necessary.

Experience leads us to suggest that at least a broad outline or framework of the plan should be presented. It is true that this gives the negative something concrete to attack. However, in view of the essentials that the affirmative must prove regarding the plan, this procedure seems plausible, because the affirmative must show that the plan remedies the alleged evils in the present system and that the affirmative plan does not introduce new evils.

Usually it is easier to show that the plan meets the requirements set set forth in the need issue if the plan has a definite framework. It should not be inferred that the affirmative is required to present a new system, minute in every detail. The following plan, as presented by Edward Stollenwerck, University of Kansas, debating the proposition "Resolved: That the Marshall Plan should be adopted," represents a rather carefully developed affirmative plan.

Well now, I know you are curious as to just how the Marshall Plan will be set up and administered and so, at this time, I should like to demonstrate to you a brief skeleton plan for administration. First of all, a European Planning Board should be established for Europe. That planning board will be composed of representatives from all the participating nations and likewise the United States to report upon conditions in Europe so that our country here can know exactly what conditions are over in Europe, so that we can understand just how well our funds are being used in the recovery program in Europe.

Still further, any European nation can be a part of the Marshall Plan. Any European nation can become a beneficiary of American aid. And thus, we realize that this does not stop any nation regardless of whether they are communistic or socialistic from enjoying the benefits of the Marshall Plan so long as they meet the requirements of mutual self-help and cooperation. And still further, a large part of the relief, that is, a large part of the money and commodities that the United States will ship to Europe, will be paid back. Plans for payment in cash and scarce commodities are already made. Now many of the European nations have colonies whose products are scarce in the United States and trade with these colonies would definitely be beneficial in restoring some of our natural resources. Plans have already been made for improved trade relations between those colonies and the United States. We would be definitely improving the whole economy of the United States in the long-run view by realizing that the whole European Recovery Program is not merely a gift or a donation.

Still further, all the European nations will be required to help themselves, and—this is an important item in the Marshall Plan—with the European Planning Board reviewing the situation and with the report three times a year, the United States will be able to determine whether or not these nations are cooperating and are helping themselves.

And now, just what form will European relief take? Well, for the first few years, essentially, most of the commodities will fall under these classifications: food and fuel, fertilizer, industrialized machinery, raw materials, and farm machinery. And thus, we have here a skeleton outline of the Marshall Plan. Seventeen billion dollars over a period of four-and-one-half years.[4]

4. *SHOW HOW THE PLAN REMEDIES THE EVILS IN THE PRESENT SYSTEM WITHOUT INTRODUCING NEW AND EQUALLY UNDESIRABLE EVILS*

This duty of the affirmative is frequently described as the development of the benefits that accrue from the adoption of the affirmative plan.

[4] Dorothy Ulman, *University Debaters Annual*, 1947–48 (New York: H. W. Wilson Company, 1948), pp. 96–97.

It is not sufficient for the affirmative to show that evils exist in the present system. The affirmative must prove, not assert, not declare, that the proposed plan corrects the alleged evils. This most important task of the affirmative is accomplished only when each evil in the present system is considered individually and shown to be absent from the proposed plan. The process of proving how your plan eradicates the evils inherent in the present system is the most difficult task of the second affirmative. It is appalling how many affirmative teams either overlook this fundamental entirely or else muddle through it. Avoid this fatal mistake by carefully analyzing your list of alleged evils. You will propably find it desirable to select certain evils that sufficiently indict the present system and evils that you can eliminate with your plan.

Debating the *National Medical Program for All Citizens* proposition, Gene Berrodin of Kent State University did a good job of showing how the plan of the affirmative answered the first affirmative need issue (American people need better medical care):

> I would now like to continue with the affirmative case to show how our plan would operate to give the American people better medical care. By instituting, first, a nationwide system of prepaid health benefits through which all the population would be guaranteed comprehensive preventative and curative health services. Second, federal grants to non-profit institutions and agencies for medical education to help furnish the additional doctors, dentists, and others needed to provide the necessary services would be provided along with grants to medical research to increase the scope and effectiveness of the benefits, and to reduce their cost. Third, federal grants to states for more adequate public health programs, services for the aged, chronically ill, and others would be provided. Fourth, increased federal grants for hospital and health-center construction, and liberalization of the Hill-Burton Bill to make it helpful to rural and low-income communities.[5]

It should be evident that close unity between the *need* and *plan* issues is essential. This necessitates understanding and acquaintance, on the part of each speaker, with the other's case, even to the point of minute evidence. An astute negative team will always try to drive a wedge between the need and plan contentions of the affirmative. Only through meticulous care in planning the merger of the need and plan issues can the affirmative avoid the hazard of inadequacy or inconsistency.

On the surface, the task of setting up a plan to cure the evils in the present system is not too difficult. However, arriving at a plan that does not introduce new evils is another matter. Frequently an inexperienced

[5] *Ibid.* (1950), p. 150.

affirmative team will arive at a seemingly perfect plan that remedies existing evils only to find in the first encounter that a sharp negative has discovered that the new policy introduces more striking evils than are present in the status quo.

Any plan, if practical, is likely to possess some failings or evils. The affirmative must be able to show that the evils in the present system are far greater in number and severity than those possibly introduced by its plan. The affirmative must be ready to prove that the evils are minor, that in time the new policy will outgrow them, or that the benefits of the proposed plan far outweigh the few relatively unimportant ills. In short, the affirmative, in the light of the plan's overwhelming benefits, must be ready to justify whatever evils attend its adoption.

TYPES OF AFFIRMATIVE CASES

The affirmative side has little latitude in its choice of procedures or methods. Because of the forensic custom, the affirmative must do certain things in order to carry its burden of proof. Fundamentally, the best affirmative case is that one which meets the problems head on, frankly, and endeavors to debate the question on its merits. This means that the affirmative will select strong arguments for its case, will document them thoroughly, and will be prepared to defend them against the negative attacks. This approach can be labeled as the traditional or conventional case. Its merit is that the affirmative without strategy or trickery comes to grips with the question and is prepared to debate the resolution on its merits.

It is possible for the affirmative to develop an unusual interpretation of the debate question. The advisability of this procedure will depend upon the nature of the question and the type of interpretation used. It has happened too often that a team has used a surprise interpretation as a substitute for good sound work on a debate proposition. If this has been done, the purposes of debate have been subverted. An example of an unusual type of interpretation occurred in a debate on the question "Resolved: That the federal government should adopt a permanent program of wage and price controls." One team decided that it would offer a plan of democratic socialism, that it would go beyond the boundaries of the proposition. This interpretation of the proposition won a few debates, but many judges were not willing to accept this interpretation of the question. Many of these debates settled down to an argument over the merits of capitalism versus socialism. Granted that it is possible to work out surprise interpretations for an affirmative case, such interpretations should never be substituted for thorough investigation, analysis, and complete documentation of the proposition.

THE NEGATIVE CASE

The negative has certain responsibilities with respect to case and at the same time it has many possibilities or approaches. At the outset, the negative has a responsibility for making a response to the affirmative interpretation and analysis. If the negative disagrees with the opening remarks of the affirmative in respect to definition of terms, issues, importance of the question, or any other phase, they should present these exceptions in the first speech. The negative should not merely quibble over small matters. If there is a fundamental difference, it should be pointed out. After having made this exception to the affirmative analysis, the negative should proceed to debate the question on its merits.

As stated earlier, the affirmative has the burden of proof, but the negative has the original responsibility of *rebuttal* or *rejoinder*. Thus, after the affirmative has endeavored to establish its prima facie case, the negative must make an adaptation to it. One of the cardinal rules of debate is that the participants must clash on the issues, the arguments, and the evidence of the given debate. Debate is not conducted in a vacuum. Each side cannot present its case, ignoring its opponent. Refutation should not be withheld until the rebuttal periods. One of the first rules for the negative is to adapt to the affirmative case and make a definite clash with each of the major arguments of the affirmative.

After the first affirmative has presented his speech (usually centered around the need issue), the negative must make clear its approach to the proposition. If the negative has two or three important questions to ask the affirmative, these should be written out and handed to the affirmative after they have been asked orally. If the questions are asked, they must be followed up by the second negative debater. They should become an integral part of the debate, and not merely something to waste the time of the affirmative.

The negative has at least four case possibilities or a combination of the four. Theoretically, the negative needs to demolish completely one major issue, and it will win the debate. Most negative teams prefer to spread their case and attack two or three of the issues presented by the affirmative.

THE DENIAL OR PURE REFUTATION CASE

The first case possibility of the negative is that of straight refutation or what is sometimes called the *denial case*. In this attack, the negative does not stand for anything directly. It merely attacks each of the affirmative contentions. Hence, on the question of permanent price and wage controls, the negative would be content to show that there was no need for such a program by attacking each specific evil pointed out by the affirmative; it would show that such a plan would be unworkable; and finally it would show that the affirmative's plan would be undesirable because it would not correct the alleged evils, or would produce greater evils.

Obviously, this is not a very constructive stand. Many authorities in debate dislike this position because it puts the negative in the position of being purely obstructionist. If the negative is really interested in *searching for the truth* and is interested in the problem, many say that it should do something constructive. However, technically, the negative does not have to present a constructive program or plan. It may make a valuable contribution by preventing any action being taken. The negative stands not for something but against something. In the above example the negative stands against permanent price and wage control by the federal government. Also, when the negative merely attacks the affirmative position, it is saying by implication that it supports the status quo. In other words, it likes the way we are doing things now. This position of straight refutation becomes much more powerful when combined with one of the other case possibilities.

THE STATUS QUO OR STAND-PAT CASE

The second case possibility is a *defense of the status quo* or a stand-pat case. Here the negative argues that the present system is satisfactory. Hence, on the question of a federal world government, the negative would say that a federal world government is not needed, is impracticable, and is undesirable and that our present method of working through the United Nations, NATO, and other organizations is satisfactory in meeting the problem of world peace. The negative would spend some time in this approach in documenting the accomplishments made under the status quo. The major negative attack would be on the affirmative issue of need.

UPHOLDING THE STATUS QUO WITH REPAIRS

The third case possibility is *upholding the status quo* (present system) *with repairs*. In this situation, the negative admits that the present system is not perfect. It attempts to minimize the need argument of the affirmative. Many negative debaters try to point out that there is no need to adopt the radical affirmative proposal when the existing machinery is adequate and merely needs minor repairs. For example, in a debate on the federal world government question, one negative team tried to show how the United Nations and other pacts offered a satisfactory plan for peace.

This team took each of the affirmative attacks and showed how they could be met under the status quo with certain adjustments in the machinery. Thus, to counteract the evil effect of the veto in the Security Council, the negative suggested the shifting of power to the General Assembly. In addition to taking each evil presented, the negative went on to show that a federal world government was impracticable and undesirable. They pointed out that if the people of the world really wanted peace, they could have it under any plan. They pointed out that nations would not be willing to give up their sovereignty; that nations, especially Russia, would not join; that there is not enough time; and so on. This whole approach, then, says that we can improve our present system with changes, that the status quo is basically sound, and that the affirmative proposal is impracticable and undesirable. Many debaters prefer this method to the others because it gives them a very strong basic stand.

THE COUNTERPLAN

The fourth and last stand of the negative is that of the *counterplan* or *alternative proposal*. This is perhaps the most radical and unusual negative approach. In this position, the negative admits the need contention of the affirmative, but contends that there is a better solution to the problem than the affirmative proposal. This approach, especially in the early part of the season, may catch the affirmative unprepared, but the advantage decreases as the forensic year goes along.

It is sometimes alleged that when the negative employs a counterplan, the affirmative first speech, which is usually restricted to the need issue, has been wasted. Such is not the case. Although the negative, when employing a counterplan, may admit the affirmative need issue, the affirmative has not wasted its time since any plan advanced by the affirmative must solve a need previously advanced. When the negative employs the counterplan approach, it changes the nature of the debate. Instead of the question, "Should we have a federal world government?" the question becomes "Should we have a federal world government or some other type of program?" For instance, on the federal world government question many negatives were admitting the need and utilizing such counterplans as Anglo-American alliance, declaration of immediate war on Russia, alliance of the democracies, an armed truce, a United States of Europe, or a United States of Asia.

The negative must assume the responsibilities for proof of its counterproposal. The negative should present its counterplan in the first speech so that the affirmative will have one constructive speech in which to consider it. The negative must state its counterproposal very clearly. It cannot be too similar to that which the affirmative is proposing but must be truly counter. If the counterplan is not truly counter, but merely slightly different, it will be possible for the affirmative to incorporate that argument in its own proposal.

The negative should attack the affirmative proposal as being impracticable and undesirable, while at the same time presenting the merits of the counterproposal. The negative must show that the counterproposal is superior to the affirmative proposal.

No one can say that a given negative approach is the best. It will depend upon the specific debate and the specific debate proposition. A variety of case possibilities should be tried by the negative. However, the usual negative case is a two-way combination of straight refutation and a defense of the status quo with repairs.

DUTIES OF AFFIRMATIVE AND NEGATIVE SPEAKERS

Having discussed the obligations of the affirmative and negative in regard to cases, we now direct our attention to the specific duties of each speaker of each team. It should be clear at the outset that the following suggestions are only suggestions, that what occurs during a debate cannot be too well determined in advance. Nevertheless, the following general remarks should be of value to the beginning debater.

MAIN SPEECHES

FIRST AFFIRMATIVE SPEAKER

The first affirmative speaker is the only debater who should have a set speech. The phrase *set speech* does not mean that the speech is memorized. It implies that the speech is well organized in advance and that the speaker is very familiar with the material. However, the exact wording of the speech should be determined by the audience reaction during delivery.

Since refutation is not required of the first affirmative in a constructive speech, he has the opportunity of presenting a smooth, excellently organized and persuasive case. After having been introduced by the chairman of the debate, the first speaker acknowledges the chairman and proceeds to the lectern. There was a time when speakers made quite an exercise out of their salutation, that is, "Mr. Chairman, Mr. Timekeeper, Honorable Judges, Most Worthy Opponents, Ladies and Gentlemen." In addressing the audience, modern debaters usually say "Ladies and Gentlemen" or "Friends," and go directly into the debate in a pleasant and businesslike fashion. If the first speaker of the affirmative represents the host school in a dual debate, he should next extend a warm, friendly but brief welcome to the visiting team; for example:

> We are pleased to welcome Mr. James and Mr. Thompson of the University of Florida to our campus. This meeting tonight represents the fifteenth time in eight years that our universities have met in friendly rivalry. We of Butler University always look forward to the annual visit of the squad from the University of Florida. Gentlemen, the facilities of our campus are at your command.

If the first affirmative represents the guest school, he should respond pleasantly but briefly to the welcome extended by the chairman of the debate; for example:

> Your Chairman, Mr. Hamilton, has been very kind in extending to Mr. Thompson and me the facilities of your campus. As some of you may recall, this is our second visit to Butler University. With the pleasures of last year's visit still fresh in our memory, we know that we will be royally entertained. We trust that members of the Butler Debate Squad will soon be visitors on our campus.

In tournament debating this sort of salutation is either omitted or held to a minimum.

Having completed the greetings, the speaker states the proposition and defines those terms that need clarification. Some debate directors insist that a history or background of the proposition be given. There may be times when such procedure is desirable; however, it is usually unnecessary, except when the historical background becomes a part of the argument or is needed to acquaint the audience with the proposition. If background material is used, it can either precede or follow the statement of the proposition. If the affirmative team has an over-all stand or position that it intends to assume and defend, this position is stated next. Then the first speaker outlines his case, usually the need issue, and proceeds to prove it. Occasionally, the first affirmative may also present the plan. However, if the need issue is stressed, there is seldom enough time to present the plan adequately.

The necessity for simple, clear-cut organization cannot be overemphasized. Following each main issue in the speaker's case, the argument should be clinched by a summary. This practice is called *internal summarizing*. At the close of the first affirmative case, the main arguments should again be summarized. The speaker closes with an appeal for a change from the present system to the plan called for by the proposition.

SECOND AFFIRMATIVE SPEAKER

The constructive duty of the second affirmative speaker is two-fold: to present the plan and to show how the plan eliminates the evils in the present system previously pointed out by the first speaker of the affirmative. However, before undertaking these fundamental tasks, the second affirmative should rebuild the case of the first affirmative. This presupposes on the part of the second affirmative speaker a thorough knowledge of his colleague's case. He should review the main issues of the first affirmative one by one, indicating the arguments that escaped attack by the negative and rebuilding those parts of the case impaired by negative refutation.

Having repaired his colleague's case, the second affirmative speaker presents the affirmative plan and shows how the plan will remedy the need presented by the first affirmative. Following a summary of the affirmative stand, the second speaker concludes with a plea for the adoption of the affirmative proposal. If the first affirmative presents both the need issue and the plan, the second speaker should employ his time in rebuttal and refutation, rebuilding the affirmative case (proving the practicability of the case) and refuting the negative attack. Regardless of the plan of attack employed by the affirmative, the second speaker should be quick in analysis and a master of refutation and rebuttal.

FIRST NEGATIVE SPEAKER

Unless the negative team presents a counterplan, it is their duty to meet the affirmative in direct clash. This means that the negative should refute the affirmative case as presented or show that affirmative analysis has been faulty—that the affirmative has ignored main issues inherent in the proposition. The negative may present and defend certain issues, but it should also meet and destroy the affirmative case. Today many negative teams prepare their cases in advance, even to the point of having prepared speeches. They make no attempt to clash, that is, to come to grips with the affirmative. This is poor debating and thwarts the very purpose for which debate procedures are practiced.

After acknowledging the chairman's introduction, addressing the audience, and responding to the greetings of the affirmative, the first negative speaker accepts or rejects the definition of terms advanced by the affirmative. Before engaging in direct refutation of the first affirmative speech, the first negative may clarify the negative stand in the debate. Normally this will embody its line of attack and any specific interpretation of the proposition.

In attacking the affirmative case, the negative speaker may refute each main contention advanced by the affirmative or single out two or three salient arguments (fundamental to the affirmative position) upon which to center his attack. If the negative has a constructive case, arguments upholding the status quo, it is usually more effective when presented after the direct refutation of the affirmative case. Like the affirmative, the negative should employ internal summaries.

Some negative teams follow the practice of presenting the affirmative with a long list of so-called pertinent questions at the close of the first negative speech, demanding that they be answered at once. Two or three pointed questions clearly on the proposition and basic in nature are legitimate, and the negative should rightly expect an answer. However, when a long list of questions, factual, psychological, sociological, and even philosophical in nature is adroitly prepared and obviously presented for the sole purpose of confusing the opposition, the negative has overstepped the bounds of good sportsmanship.

If the negative intends to introduce a counterplan, it can be introduced by either the first or second speaker. However, good sportsmanship would dictate that the counterplan be introduced by the first speaker.

SECOND NEGATIVE SPEAKER

The second negative speaker occupies a most enviable position in the debate *if* he is keen in analysis and astute in refutation and rebuttal. The entire affirmative case has been presented. It is his privilege to hold the affirmative case before the audience and "riddle it with light." It may be that the second affirmative will have so rebuilt the need issue that it will necessitate refutation by the second negative. After disposing of the need issue, the *big guns* of the second negative are leveled at the affirmative plan. Is it practicable? Workable? Does it elminate the evils as set forth by the first affirmative and does it perchance introduce new evils even greater than those existent in the status quo? These are some of the questions asked and answered by the argument of the second negative speaker.

Some speakers prefer attacking the plan of the affirmative at the outset, since it is usually the last concern of the second affirmative. Other speakers refute the second affirmative speech as presented, issue by issue. It matters little which procedure is followed so long as the second affirmative speech is refuted successfully. Since the first negative rebuttal follows the second negative constructive speech, a negative team may follow the plan of assigning the second negative constructive speech the duty of refuting the plan of the second affirmative, thus allowing the first negative rebuttal speaker to confine his efforts to the need issue. This kind of division of labor can work fairly successfully. Regardless of the plan of attack, the second negative should close the negative constructive case with an excellent summary. Unless the speaker is conscious of time, he may find that his time has run out before he has a chance to summarize adequately.

REBUTTALS

FIRST NEGATIVE SPEAKER

The first negative speaker is in a position to analyze the entire constructive arguments of both teams. Thus, he is able to point out where the affirmative has failed to establish its case. He may attack the affirmative arguments that have escaped major damage, taking each in turn, demolishing it, clinching his point, and then attacking the next one. He may center his attack on one or two paramount issues around which the remainder of the debate will revolve. These are sometimes called *ultimate issues* or the *final issues* of the debate. In any event, he should leave the audience with a clear picture of the final obligations resting upon the affirmative in the establishment of its case. The speaker will close with a summary of the negative case.

SECOND NEGATIVE SPEAKER

The second negative speaker has the responsibility of bringing the entire weight of negative evidence and reasoning to bear on the affirmative case. This is the time for keen analysis, for a sifting out of the vital affirmative arguments. They must be destroyed. The speaker usually opens his speech with a clear-cut presentation of the affirmative stand in the debate, centering his attack upon salient weaknesses in the affirmative case. He must show where the affirmative has failed to meet successfully its obligations in upholding the proposition. He may contrast the principal arguments of the affirmative and negative, indicating where the negative has overpowered the affirmative evidence and reasoning. The second speaker will close the debate for the negative with a summary of the negative stand and an appeal for the rejection of the affirmative proposal.

FIRST AFFIRMATIVE SPEAKER

The first affirmative speaker has the difficult task of overcoming the attack of two consecutive negative speakers. This is the most critical point in the debate for the affirmative. Usually the negative will have attempted to spread the affirmative defenses by pointing out a number of obligations and weaknesses in the affirmative position. There is danger that the speaker will be tempted to consume valuable time on minor issues. The affirmative must stick by its case—the main issues as presented in the constructive speeches. The affirmative should not accede to a negative attempt to saddle them with excessive obligations. A summary and clinching of each main point should terminate the presentation of successive arguments. The speaker must re-establish the *need* for a change and the *practicability* of the affirmative plan.

SECOND AFFIRMATIVE SPEAKER

The last affirmative rebuttalist has one final chance to establish a balance of probability on his side of the proposition. He should be quick in locating the holes in the affirmative dike and be thorough in mending them. The speaker may resort to a summary form of rebuttal, amassing the affirmative arguments which have not been successfully challenged or destroyed, then rebuilding the affirmative issues that have been seriously attacked. He should refute the main negative contentions, summarize the affirmative case, and conclude with an appeal for the adoption of the proposition.

We should like to issue a note of warning to the speaker. Realizing that the negative has no chance to answer, often the second affirmative rebuttalist will make sweeping generalizations, falsely accuse the opposition of failing to meet the affirmative case, misquote the negative and in general take unfair advantage of his position as closing speaker. Such behavior is unpardonable and displays the poorest type of sportsmanship. The audience is quick to recognize such unfair tactics and will rightly penalize the speaker for this breach of debate ethics.

SUMMARY

Case as ordinarily used by debaters means the arguments and evidence that a team, after careful research and analysis, employs in establishing its stand upon a proposition. In general, a team should choose a limited number of major points around which substantial proof can be massed. Furthermore, the main points selected should have audience appeal, and the proof should build toward a climax. The burden of proof in a debate lies with the affirmative. At the outset they must assume this burden by establishing a prima facie case. The main duties of the affirmative are to define the terms of the proposition, establish a need for a change, present a plan to solve the need, show how the plan remedies the evils in the present system without introducing new evils, thus affording benefits not possible under the present system.

At the outset of the debate, presumption lies with the negative. It must keep the presumption in its favor throughout the discussion. In maintaining its stand, the negative has four case possibilities: pure refutation or denial approach; defense of the status quo; support of the status quo with repairs; and presentation of a counterplan or alternative proposal. It is impossible to determine, in advance of the study of a given proposition, the best negative approach. However, the usual negative case consists of a combination of pure refutation and a defense of status quo with repairs.

Finally, debaters must realize that, depending upon the case employed, each member of a debate team has certain duties to discharge. These obligations should be met with dispatch.

EXERCISES

1. Why does the affirmative have the burden of proof in debate? What does this burden involve? Is it necessary for the affirmative to establish a prima facie case?
2. Does the affirmative have the right to interpret the proposition? Is the negative bound to adhere to the affirmative interpretation? Should the affirmative strive to develop a tricky interpretation of the debate proposition? Explain.
3. What are the usual stock issues present in a question of policy? How do stock issues vary between questions of policy and questions of fact? Using *University Debaters' Annual* or *Intercollegiate Debates* as references, find examples of stock issues for questions of policy and questions of fact.
4. If the negative team admits the *need for a change* after the first affirmative speaker has presented a *need*, has the first affirmative speaker wasted his time? Explain.
5. Select a question current on your campus and outline the major issues that might be used by affirmative and negative teams.
6. Prepare an introduction to a first affirmative speech setting forth definitions and issues to be employed by the affirmative team. Should the affirmative plan presented by the second speaker solve the need as presented by the first affirmative speaker? Explain.
7. What are the possible plans the negative team may choose in developing its case? Find examples of each of these stands in *University Debaters' Annual, Intercollegiate Debates,* or similar sources.
8. Using the current intercollegiate debate proposition, outline a possible case for the affirmative. Which negative alternative should be chosen to best counter the affirmative case? Why?
9. What ordinarily determines the stand that the negative may employ upon a proposition? Why is the presentation of a counterplan by the negative often a dangerous stand? What is the type of stand most frequently employed by negative teams?
10. Is it necessary that debaters have a division of duties? Explain.

SUGGESTED READINGS

CAPP, GLENN R., ROBERT HUBER, WAYNE C. EUBANK. "Duties of Affirmative Speakers—A Symposium," *The Speech Teacher*, 8 (March 1959), 139–149.

COURTNEY, LUTHER W., and GLENN R. CAPP. *Practical Debating.* Philadelphia: J. B. Lippincott Company, 1949, Chap. 2.

CROCKER, LIONEL. *Argumentation and Debate.* New York: American Book Company, 1944. Chaps. 4, 15.

EWBANK, HENRY L., and J. JEFFERY AUER. *Discussion and Debate.* 2nd ed. New York: Appleton-Century-Crofts, Inc., 1951. Chap. 25.

FOSTER, WILLIAM T. *Argumentation and Debating.* Boston: Houghton Mifflin Company, 1945. Chaps. 3, 12.

GIFFIN, KIM, and KENNETH MEGILL. "Stock Issues in Tournament Debates," *Central States Speech Journal*, 12 (Autumn 1960), 27–32.

GULLEY, HALBERT E. *Essentials of Discussion and Debate.* New York: Holt, Rinehart & Winston, Inc. 1955, pp. 106–114.

KRUGER, ARTHUR N. *Modern Debate: Its Logic and Strategy.* New York: McGraw-Hill Book Company, 1960. Chaps. 5, 7.

KRUGER, ARTHUR N. "Logic and Strategy in Developing the Debate Case" *The Speech Teacher*, 3 (March 1954), 89–106.

NEBERGALL, ROGER E. "The Negative Counterplan," *The Speech Teacher*, 6 (September 1957), 217–220.

III.

chapteR 8

~~~~~~

AUDIENCE ANALYSIS
AND MOTIVATION

by Cullen B. Owens

Traditionally, textbooks on argumentation and debate have touched lightly, if at all, on the topics of audience analysis and motivation. With formal intercollegiate debate as their model, students of argumentation have been prone to labor exclusively on such matters as analysis of the proposition, building an unbeatable case well-larded with evidence, amassing vast files for refutation and rebuttal, and devising strategy to bring down the opposition. No teacher could possibly wish to discourage this kind of labor on the part of his debaters; on the contrary, probably every teacher has at times felt a deep longing for debaters who would do more of it. It is nevertheless appropriate to remind students of argumentation and debate that, insofar as they are training themselves to become effective speakers on live issues before real audiences, the subject of this chapter is of crucial importance.

AUDIENCE ANALYSIS

As a subject, audience analysis has its roots deep in antiquity. Aristotle's *Rhetoric*, the most thorough and profound textbook on public speaking which has come down to us from ancient times, is centered on considerations of the audience. With his eye on Grecian culture, of course, Aristotle sets forth the goods, or goals, for which men strive, the virtues they admire; analyzes in fascinating detail the passions which move them, dissects for us the characteristics of young men, old men, men in their prime, of the well-born, the wealthy, the powerful. In short, Aristotle incorporated in his *Rhetoric* a practical psychology to assist the speaker in making a proper estimate of his audience. Turn where he may among the pages devoted to framing and constructing the speech, the reader will find that the audience is kept constantly in view.

Although no rhetoric since Aristotle's provides as searching a study of the audience, the works of rhetoricians over the centuries have stressed the importance of such study and have offered the speaker guidance in considering the audience. All would subscribe to this statement by a great eighteenth-century rhetorician: "The necessity which a speaker is under of suiting himself to his audience, both that he may be understood by them, and that his words may have influence upon them, is a maxim so evident as to need neither proof nor illustration." [1]

All too commonly, however, we passively assent to "evident" principles, yet fail to gather any fruit from them. The serious student of persuasive argument cannot afford such mistakes. It will not do to nod one's head to the authority of Campbell, or of Aristotle, and then go right on dully constructing argument, as it were, in a vacuum. The obvious principle must be analyzed, illustrated, and practiced. The effective speaker must unfailingly consider his audience, as Campbell urged, both as men in general, "thinking beings endowed with understanding, imagination, memory, and passions," and as "men in particular," as individuals whose differences from other individuals account for the special character of any one audience. In sum, the serious student will bring himself to a sharp realization of the indispensability of audience analysis. He will see that every facet of effective argument must be conditioned by the speaker's conception of his audience. He will understand that without proper audience analysis motivation is a shot in the dark. Let us turn now and deal more specifically with this topic of audience analysis.

PRIMARY PURPOSE OF AUDIENCE ANALYSIS

The main, though of course not the only, function of audience analysis is to reveal those audience attitudes which have particular bearing on the speaker's problem of motivation, which, simply put, is to lead his auditors to make the choice which he is asking them to make. Since the concept *attitude* is to be the key concept of this chapter, certain things need to be said about it at this point; we shall have more to say further

---

[1] George Campbell, *The Philosophy of Rhetoric*, 2nd ed., Book I, Ch. X, Sect. II, (London: Printed for A. Strahan, T. Cadell, Jun. and W. Davies; and William Creech at Edinburgh: By J. Moir, Edinburgh, 1801), p. 212.

on under the head of motivation. Few words are more common or more useful in everyday speech than attitude. But particular attention is called here to the fact that the concept of attitudes occupies a central position in social psychology. As early as 1935, Gordon Allport wrote of attitude as "probably the most distinctive and indispensable concept in contemporary American social psychology" [2] and called attention to the fact that several writers were then defining social psychology as the scientific study of attitudes. An examination of the field of social psychology since 1935 reveals that the main preoccupation of social psychologists has been with the study of how the individual becomes socialized through interaction with other human beings. And attitudes are, to use the words of an eminent social psychologist, "the psychological products par excellence of his socialization." [3] Although presented in various language, the chief features of attitudes emerge clearly enough. They are learned dispositions, more or less permanent and ingrained, and they vary widely in their inclusiveness and their importance in the life of the individual. They are often called direction sets, or states of readiness, because they both orient the individual toward objects and symbols and prepare, predispose, him to behave in more or less predictable ways with respect to them. The student will understand that the term *objects* in the preceding sentence is inclusive of everything about which one could acquire an attitude: other people, races, customs, institutions, policies, political parties, labor unions, religion, one's self, occupations, required courses, bridge, golf, jazz, classical music—and so on ad infinitum. Now when it is said that an attitude predisposes the holder of it to behave in more or less predictable ways toward the object with which it is related, behavior must be taken in a very inclusive sense, for attitudinal behavior involves the *whole person*. This is a most important fact for the student of motivation to keep in mind and one to which we shall revert further on. One's attitudinal behavior toward something includes the way he perceives it, or conceives of it, how he feels about it, thinks about it, acts toward it. We infer the existence of attitudes in persons by their rather characteristic and persistent reactions when confronted with particular objects (objects, remember, in the inclusive sense indicated above). For example, suppose you tell me that you have a friend who hates big labor unions. This means that you have inferred the existence in him of an intensely held attitude. How did you make such an inference? Very likely, simply by observing his responses on different occasions when the subject of big labor unions has been introduced. He conceives of them as menaces to the country, and he explains in so many words that he de-

[2] G. W. Allport, "Attitudes," *Handbook of Social Psychology*, ed. Carl Murchison (Worcester, Mass.: Clark University Press, 1935), p. 798.

[3] Muzafer Sherif, *An Outline of Social Psychology* (New York: Harper & Row, Publishers, 1948), p. 203.

tests them and intends to cast his vote for congressmen dedicated to curbing their power. An attitude thus represents a probability that a person or whole groups of persons holding a similar attitude will react in characteristic and consistent fashion toward the object with which the attitude is related. It follows that a knowledge of attitudes is crucial in the prediction of behavior, and that is why their discovery is, as we have already said, the primary function of audience analysis. None of us should be troubled by the fact that existence of attitudes is a matter of inference, that an attitude is a theoretical construct, something to be seen only in the mind's eye. The thing to be borne in mind is that it is a necessary assumption, for without it the understanding and anticipation of the behavior of others— whether of individuals, groups or nations—would be impossible. Although unseen, attitudes prove to be as "real" as sticks and stones. There is profound insight in the remark of a great sociologist that "the solid facts of our human life exist in the imagination." [4]

PRACTICAL SYNONYMS FOR ATTITUDE

As we have indicated, *attitudes* is the term most generally used by social psychologists to refer to the learned predispositions which are inferred as lying behind and accounting for observed uniformities in behavior. But we find in common speech, as well as in the pages of social psychology, many other terms that are really synonyms, more or less exact, for attitude. The relatively large number of such terms and their overlapping in meaning is doubtless attributable to their popular origin. It may serve to avoid confusion, as well as to sharpen the perception of the speaker when he comes to analyze audiences, if we call attention here to these terms in order to show that they all refer to the same kind of learned psychological formation that we designate by the term *attitude*. Take interests, for example. You say, "My friend has a strong interest in classical music." Though you may never have stopped to consider how you arrived at that inference, you did it by observing his behavior at various times. Perhaps you often heard him talk ardently about classical music, noted that he spent much of his spare cash on classical records, and listened for hours to them on his stereo-phonograph. The term *interest* represents here, in the same way that the term *attitude* always represents, a conceptual construction, a generalization, that expresses for you the meaning of the directly observable data. Interests, like attitudes, are acquired through experience and they serve to describe and explain and predict behavior in precisely the same way that attitudes do. The authors of one current textbook

[4] Ellsworth Faris, *The Nature of Human Nature* (New York: McGraw-Hill Book Company, 1937), p. 142.

in beginning psychology employ the term interest and define an interest in the same way that other psychologists employ and define attitude. They hold that if you wish to understand and predict a man's behavior you had better find out his interests instead of cataloging his physiological drives. In fact, they believe that to know a man's interests is pretty much to know the man himself and to hold a key to his behavior and the knowledge of how to appeal to him.[5]

Observe now the following list of additional concepts, all of which may be subsumed, just as we have subsumed the concept *interest*, under the general classification of attitudes: sentiments, prejudices, aversions, loves, fears, hatreds, desires, tastes, ambitions, ideals, values, stereotypes, purposes, aspirations, wants, loyalties, drives, sets, tensions, appetites, prepossessions, propensities, beliefs (many, not *all*, beliefs). By virtue of their common nature, origin, and psychological significance all of these concepts belong under the general label of attitudes. Note that they all have some objective reference. They orient the individual toward some object or goal and dispose him to act with reference to it. Typically, when we employ these terms we indicate the object or goal involved, often with a suggestion of the dynamic quality of the disposition. Thus we speak of one's "passionate love of freedom." (Obviously, it would make no sense to say "he loves" unless you were merely conjugating the verb.) Again, we may speak of "an aspiration to become a novelist," a "prejudice toward Tibetans," "ambition to become a doctor," "aversion to research in the library," "hatred of television commercials," "fear of nuclear war," and so on. All of the dispositions indicated by these terms have their origin in the individual's experiences in a society. They are indispensable in describing the nature of individuals and in accounting for the selectivity of their responses. In short, all of the terms in our list, as well as numerous popular terms of the same kind not included, refer to dispositions that have the same psychological significance we have already noted as belonging to the concept *attitude*. The term *attitude* thus turns out to be inclusive of many dispositions, which, although they go under a variety of names, really belong in a common class. If the speaker keeps in mind this unity in variety, his analysis of audiences should become more perceptive. When, for the sake of economy and convenience of reference, we hereafter use the single term *attitude*, the student will bear in mind its inclusiveness of all classes of disposition.

What has been said thus far about attitudes is designed to aid the speaker in considering the audience as "men in particular," if we may reiterate Dr. Campbell's expression. To discover the attitudes of an audience is to go a long way toward fixing in mind its special character and

[5] E. R. Guthrie and A. L. Edwards, *Psychology* (New York: Harper & Row, Publishers, 1949), pp. 115–6.

making it possible to suit the speech to it. Differences between audiences may be so great that a speech which would persuade one might merely provoke contempt in another. As Whately put it a long time ago, "There can be no excellence of writing or speaking, in the abstract; nor can we any more pronounce on the Eloquence of any Composition, than upon the wholesomeness of a medicine, without knowing for whom it is intended." [6]

INTELLECTUAL AND CULTURAL LEVEL OF THE AUDIENCE

In considering his audience as "men in particular" the speaker should strive not only to divine their attitudes, but also, and invariably, he should seek to gauge their intellectual and cultural level. Style, considered as an instrument for reaching men's minds, must in large measure be shaped by this knowledge. Persuasive argument must, above all, be understood; and it should, further, create a rapport between speaker and audience. The student of argument should read the speeches of outstandingly persuasive speakers and note how they have achieved this goal. Franklin D. Roosevelt, for example, became a master of speaking the language of his audiences and of putting complex issues to them in words that they could grasp. Facing Kansas farmers, he pledged himself to find a cure "for the condition that compels the farmer to trade in 1932 two wagon-loads for the things which in 1914 he traded one wagon-load"; and he promised to clear away "the governmental underbrush which has sprouted for years." [7] The student who follows one of Roosevelt's campaigns will be struck by this kind of adaptation to the varied audiences before which he spoke. If an earlier example is wanted, the student might well study the speeches of Richard Cobden, especially those made all over England during his years of agitation against the Corn Laws, tariffs against the importation of foreign grain, under which the masses of England suffered for so long. In his biography of this master agitator of the nineteenth century John Morley, in analyzing the secrets of his persuasiveness, notes "a singular facility of exposition . . . a curious ingenuity in framing the argument that happened to be wanted . . . the oratorial art of presenting it in the way that made its admission to the understanding of a listener easy and undenied." And Morley makes

---

[6] Richard Whately, *Elements of Rhetoric* (New York: Sheldon & Company, 1867), p. 241.

[7] Samuel I. Rosenman (Compiler), *The Public Papers and Addresses of Franklin D. Roosevelt.* 5 vols. (New York: Random House, Inc., 1938), pp. 698, 701. For the citations here the author is indebted to Robert C. Dick, "A Rhetorical Analysis of Franklin D. Roosevelt's 1932 Campaign Speaking," unpublished master's thesis, University of New Mexico, 1960.

special note of Cobden's "inexhaustible patience in dealing with the mental infirmities of those whom it was his business to persuade." [8]

As of Roosevelt and Cobden, so it may be said of all effective speakers that they seek genuinely and patiently to become acquainted with their audiences. If the primary goal in analyzing particular audiences is to discover their attitudes, with particular emphasis on those that may influence directly reactions to the speaker's message, the goal next in importance is to assess the intellectual and cultural level of the audience. But it should be obvious that *any* information about a particular audience may serve a speaker's purpose, for example, a knowledge of the region in which they live, the chief experiences arising from the way in which they make their living, the things of which they are proud, and so on. Getting acquainted with the people in an audience should be regarded not as a coldly analytical procedure but as a sympathetic effort to penetrate the quality of their lives. Only in this spirit may a speaker be able to "feel in" with them and reach them.

THE AUDIENCE CONSIDERED AS MEN IN GENERAL

Although the central concern in audience analysis must be to see each audience as a particular one differing, perhaps markedly, from others, there is also a need for the speaker to think of his audience as just a sample of human beings, as men in general. A right concept of the audience, which is of course the goal of analysis, will remind the speaker of certain obligations he owes the audience merely as "thinking beings endowed with understanding, imagination, memory, and passions." Isn't it true that any audience wants to be interested to the point of close and effortless attention to the arguments, wants to understand them, remember them, and see the relation of them to their lives? If so, a speaker should do his best to fulfill their expectations. He ought to feel a strong obligation to be interesting and to be clearly understood. And to the end that the audience may remember what is said, it needs and appreciates such qualities as vividness, order, proper divisions, transitions, and repetition of key ideas. Further, experience may teach the speaker what Richard Cobden discovered during his long campaign against the corn laws. On one occasion Cobden said:

> I defy anybody to keep the ear of the public for seven years upon one question, without studying to amuse as well as instruct . . . If they are simply lectured, they may sit out the lesson for once, but they will

[8] John Morley, *The Life of Richard Cobden* (Boston: Roberts Brothers, 1881), pp. 130, 132.

not come again; and as I have required them again and again, I have been obliged to amuse them, not by standing on my head or eating fire, but by kindred feats of jugglery, such as appeals to their self-esteem, their combativeness, or their humor.[9]

Finally, consideration of the audience as men in general should lead to some thought about the kind of qualities that any audience is likely to appreciate in a speaker. Once more, Morley's analysis of the persuasive power of Richard Cobden comes to mind. His audience, Morley wrote, "were delighted by mingled vivacity and ease, by directness, by spontaneousness and reality, by the charm, so effective and so uncommon between a speaker and his audience, of personal friendliness and undisguised cordiality." Cobden was inspired "with a peculiar respect for his great popular audiences, and they instinctively felt the presence of it, making a claim on their goodwill and their attention." [10] Cobden, it appears, possessed additionally many other qualities which move audiences to favorable response: modesty, fairness, good humor, self-control, tact, sincerity. Though the dissimilarities among audiences may be very great, it is probably safe to assume that they are similar to each other in their liking for such qualities; and the favorable attitude that an audience bears toward a speaker who exhibits them is always important, and may at times be crucial, in motivation.

THE PROBLEM OF MAKING AN AUDIENCE ANALYSIS

The difficulty of finding out what the speaker needs to know about a particular audience will of course vary greatly with the circumstances. There is no stock list of questions the answers to which will lead to proper analysis in all cases, even if we assumed, as we must not, that the answers can always be found. Yet the speaker who uses his best judgment and industry should, nevertheless, be able to unearth much useful knowledge about his audience, even when the task may appear discouraging. The unthinkable alternative for him is to prepare his speech in the dark. The suggestions which follow should prove useful.

The primary purpose of audience analysis is to discover audience attitudes. This being so, the speaker must search for clues, for various indices, to those attitudes. Unquestionably, the most valuable single clue will prove to be the groups with which the audience identifies itself. This is so be-

[9] *Ibid.*, p. 139.
[10] *Ibid.*, pp. 132–133.

cause man is primarily a group animal. Each of us becomes socialized—civilized—as a member of groups, beginning with such primary ones as family, neighborhood, school, church, from which we derive a host of attitudes, many of them—religious, political, moral, destined, as a rule, to be long lasting. Beyond the primary groups there exist, literally, hundreds of others with which the average American may become associated. In recent years the social psychologists have turned increasing attention to the far-reaching effects on individuals of their group affiliation. These groups include not only those in which one may be a member—membership groups—but also others to which one merely relates himself, or refers himself, psychologically, so-called reference groups. The reference group may be an actual organization, or it may represent a conception in the mind of the individual, as, for instance, when one conceives of himself as being a left-winger in politics, or an existentialist in philosophy. Obviously one's membership groups are also, as a rule, his reference groups, in the sense that he refers himself to them psychologically. In any case, both the maintenance and change of attitudes are found to depend in great measure on the groups to which one relates himself. Group members tend to share common norms —customs, traditions, standards, rules, values—which serve as frames-of-reference and determine, in the main, how they perceive many things. And the way we perceive a thing largely determines or constitutes our attitude toward it. If you are a devout Hindu, for example, you see a cow as a sacred animal, in no sense a candidate for the butcher shop. A communist sees American capitalism as an instrument for exploitation of the masses. A member of the S.P.C.A. sees the practice of vivisection in medicine as indefensible cruelty toward animals. Some groups see our federal income tax as the ultimate fiscal horror.

Find out then, if possible, the groups—economic, political, religious, social, occupational, professional, and so on—with which your audience is identified. Find out what those groups stand for, through their spokesmen, their publications, if any, or by other means. Any audience within our borders can, of course, be regarded as belonging to the great group known as Americans, a group which, despite divisions, shares many fundamental attitudes which serve to unify us as a people. Doubtless, such sameness as Fourth of July oratory exhibits is explained by the fact that it is addressed to us as Americans. And the comedian on a national television show feels confident that a widespread attitude will insure a laugh when he refers to his mother-in-law as "Khrushchev in a housecoat."

SOCIAL CLASSES REGARDED AS GROUPS

When considering groups with which the audience identifies itself as clues to their attitudes, the speaker should not overlook those large, inclusive ones called social classes. Although America may not have a very rigid class structure, sociologists do descry among us an upper, a middle, and a lower class; and, additionally, in the typical larger community, they subdivide each of these into an upper and a lower group, thus making six classes in all. The serious student who studies this aspect of the work of the sociologists will find significant correlations between social classes and attitudes. It is easier, of course, to classify people socially on the basis of objective data such as annual income or kind of occupation than it is to discover what kind of class label they place on themselves. Many waiters and bartenders, for example, subjectively identify themselves as middle-class. Either kind of information, it has been found, enables one to predict attitudes; but both kinds together are better than either alone.[11]

The investigation necessary to discover the social classes and the various other groups into which the audience falls will likely provide the answers to many specific questions that may be useful in analysis. These may include, for example, questions about occupations, income, level of education, reading habits, use of leisure time, racial background, place of residence, age, sex, and many others. Here, as in all aspects of speechmaking, the speaker's own good judgment must tell him what, considering his subject and purpose, he needs to know.

One who sets out to do significant speechmaking must become a student of the society in which he lives, as well as a student of human nature. He will therefore welcome as allies the social psychologist, the sociologist, the political scientist, the historian. Works in the special field of public opinion will provide him a view of all the forces that seek to mold the mind of the public and of the ever-growing business of research into opinions and attitudes. The card catalog of any good library will reveal historical works on particular states or regions—even cities—that may provide much information useful in audience analysis. Finally, the general literature of this country—novel, story, poetry, drama, special works of nonfiction—will tell a perceptive speaker much about Americans.

MOTIVATION

The necessarily brief discussion of motivation which follows here is based on the premise that the only fruitful approach to this subject is through a study of the process of social learning. In this process the individual is molded by his social milieu—the ideas, customs, values, prejudices, organizations, and institutions—which stand between him and the natural world about him. His eventual reactions, the stimuli which arouse them, the goals that he seeks, are seen to be chiefly a function of his cultural heritage

[11] Theodore Newcomb, *Social Psychology* (New York: Holt, Rinehart & Winston, Inc., 1950), pp. 555–559.

and of his specific experiences in a society. The discipline on which we rely for an account of how human behavior arises and of the ways in which human beings interact with each other is, of course, social psychology. Social psychology, it has been said, "studies individuals in their interaction when the fact of their interaction is of central interest." [12] Perhaps the act of public speaking may be taken as the example par excellence of the interaction of individuals. Public speaking theory tries to show the prospective speaker how to conduct his part in the interaction so as to achieve a predetermined end.

Because the concept of attitude occupies a central position in social psychology, it is the typical instrument of social-psychological analysis. This concept is indispensable in explaining most of the phenomena with which social psychology is concerned, such as variations in sentiment, practice, and belief from one cultural group or class to another, racial and religious prejudices, stereotypes, in-group and out-group sentiments, public opinion, propaganda, and crowd psychology. It follows that the concept of attitude is equally indispensable to the speaker who wants to predict the reactions of an audience and to influence its behavior. Hence attitude has already been designated as the key concept of this chapter, concerned as it is with audience analysis and motivation. If necessary, the student may turn back here and refresh his memory of what we earlier subsumed under attitude. Bear in mind that a host of popular terms such as *values, tastes, ideals, purposes, interests,* all indicate learned dispositions that are, in their essential nature, attitudes. These products of social learning are both descriptive of the nature of individuals and predictive of their behavior; and that is why their discovery is the necessary prelude to any successful attempt at motivation.

SHORTCOMINGS OF DRIVE THEORY

The view of motivation espoused here can make no use of the assumption, found in many current textbooks of public speaking, that human behavior must be explained in terms of a brief list of "basic" motives, drives, urges, needs or wishes common to all mankind. Lists of these "universal" impulses, which vary in length, exhibit a mixture of the innate and the acquired, with the former (those physiological in origin) generally predominating. Each drive is treated as a separate and distinct source of power, a kind of dynamo, which supplies the energy for all other lesser motives. Indeed all other motives are held to be "outgrowths," "modifications," "permutations," or "expressions" of a handful of primitive urges (often referred to as "mainsprings" of human action). By making a motive appeal

[12] G. Murphy, L. B. Murphy, and T. M. Newcomb, *Experimental Social Psychology* (New York: Harper & Row, Publishers, 1937), p. 24.

to some one or more of the numerous derived drives, the speaker, it is presumed, sets in motion a basic urge with which it is connected. The derived drive, it would appear, corresponds to a remote control switch which turns on the real source of power that pushes, pulls, or prods the individual into action.

Remove the whiskers from this mechanical model of motivation and you discover the old discredited instinct theory. William McDougall, who started the vogue for making lists of instincts back in 1908, characterized instincts as the "prime movers" of all human behavior. All thought, all bodily activity, he held, was sustained by these prime movers or by habits derived from them.[13]

There is no essential difference in motivational emphasis between this instinct theory and the drive theory which we have just outlined. The drive has simply been elevated to the role previously assigned to instinct. The assumption of separate drives, functioning as so many distinct motive spots, or sources of *directed energy* that push individuals about and serve as the dynamic underpinning for all their specific motives, is at variance with the facts of biology and neurology. For more than two decades outstanding social psychologists have criticized this assumption and called attention to the fact that names for drives are no more than abstractions from the total mass of life activity. To hypostatize these abstractions as real forces is to give a false picture of a living organism. Naturally, when a man is hungry or thirsty (here we are thinking of catalogs of physiological drives) he sets about to supply himself. To put the labels "hunger drive" and "thirst drive" on his reactions to these deficits is to add nothing at all to our understanding of his behavior. The *whole man* is hungry or thirsty, and unless he has something more urgent to do, he will seek food and water. Note that it is always the *man himself* who determines in any particular situation what is the most important thing to do for his self-actualization. The dog-tired student, for example, may resist the so-called "drive" for rest and review all night to pass that exam on which graduation depends. Our prime mover turns out to be the whole living, thinking man, and the energy that he uses in attaining his goals comes, not from some instinctual or visceral dynamo, but doubtless from that well-known process called metabolism. The postulation of a fixed number of drives common to all men as the central concern in motivation is a useless notion which can serve only to fog up the subject. Social behavior, in all its endless variety, cannot be understood by seeking its origin in the primitive motivation of the individual: his physiological needs, basic wants, dependable motives, primary motives, impelling motives, fundamental desires, wishes and the like. It is both unnecessary and impossible to trace all human motives back to a few hypothetical

[13] William McDougall, *An Introduction to Social Psychology* (London: Methuen, 1931), pp. 45–46. First published in 1908, this book went through twenty-two editions.

primary urges; and to regard each specific motive as getting its force by some assumed connection, analogous to an electric circuit, with one or more of these primary urges, is sheer fantasy. And yet this image, though generally not in as bald a form as indicated here, shows up in many textbooks of public speaking. These same books may give more or less recognition to attitudes, especially when audience analysis is discussed, but when the subject of motivation is taken up, attitudes are assigned a minor role.

ATTITUDES FUNCTION AS MOTIVES

But any useful scheme of motivation must assign to attitudes. the major role. Let us reiterate that under the general label of attitudes go the variously named acquired determinants of behavior. These dispositions, built up in all of us through experience, largely determine not only the kinds of stimuli to which we will respond, but also the ways in which the response will be made. Our attitudes, in short, function as motives, and the two terms have come to be used pretty much interchangeably. When a social psychologist writes on one page of acquiring motives, and on another of acquiring attitudes, he is not referring to two different things. The term *motive* is typically employed with references to the goal of behavior, as when we ask, "What is his motive?" A single dynamic attitude which one has developed toward something may account for various specific motivated acts with respect to it. The majority of doctors today can be depended upon to act in a variety of ways to combat "socialized medicine," toward which they hold a distinctly unfavorable attitude. Their attitude predisposes them to perceive, think, feel, and act in more or less predictable fashion toward "socialized medicine." The attitude is a dynamic set which functions as a motive whenever an opportunity is given for its release. Regardless of the origin of an attitude, the speaker has to deal with it in its own right as the efficient and contemporaneous cause of the observed behavior. Now it is' desirable, of course, to obtain the fullest understanding possible of the attitude by tracing, if we can, its genesis and trying to determine the kind of adjustment it represents. When, perchance, we discover the significance of an attitude in the life economy of an individual by examining its origin; and when we assume that the arousal of an attitude by some related object or situation produces tension that has a directive effect on behavior, we have included everything that falls within the phenomena of motivation. Needless to say, it is a far easier task to infer the existence of a particular attitude than it is to discover its origin and discern its "true" meaning. The speaker must, in any case, take account of the attitude as a present reality. To know the attitudes that people hold is to be in a position to estimate the likelihood that they can be motivated in certain ways. This is the crucial fact for the speaker to bear in mind.

ATTITUDE IS A MOLAR CONCEPT

Earlier, under audience analysis, we called attention to the fact that attitudinal behavior involves the whole person. Some social psychologists like to use the term *molar* to describe unified acts that involve all of a person's behavior. Such molar units, they insist, are the most useful ones in studying behavior. It is proper, therefore, to designate attitude as a molar concept, because it subsumes all aspects of experience: perception, thought, feeling, action. An attitude is a composite formation of perceptual, cognitive, motivational, and emotional elements, no one of which occurs in isolation, but are inseparably interrelated. An individual's attitude (a residuum of experience) disposes him to think, talk, write or otherwise act in a purposeful way with respect to an object which has for him some affective quality. Depending on the kind of attitude involved and the situation in which it is expressed, now one and now another of its aspects may occupy the foreground of attention; but no part of the unitary set occurs in isolation. Attitudes in which the cognitive aspect is usually most conspicuous are likely to go under appelations such as ideals, beliefs, stereotypes. If the motivational aspect seems generally uppermost, we may speak of aspirations, ambitions, desires, wishes. Dispositions in which the affective quality is typically displayed may be called interests, sentiments, prejudices, loves, fears, hatreds, aversions, and the like. We repeat, however, that each acquired disposition is a composite formation which includes all of these discriminable aspects; and depending on the situation any of the possible types of response may be predominant. In one situation, for example, an individual may merely talk ardently about one of his ideals. In another, he may grow angry when this ideal is challenged in a certain manner by someone. There is a story that John Keats, in his school days, deprived one of his associates of a tooth during an argument over poetry.

EMOTIONS

Here it is mete to bring up the topic of the so-called emotions: anger, fear, love, pity, shame, and the like. They should be regarded as components of attitudes, as states accompanying attitudinal behavior, not isolated, patterned entities having a free-floating existence in their own right. Emotions are felt in situations upon which the individual places some kind of interpretation. Aristotle, in his discussion of emotions, went to considerable length in delineating the situations in which various kinds of emotional behavior could be expected to occur. For example, a man can be expected to become angry if he interprets what another says as disparagement of that to which he attaches great importance (or, in other words, towards which his attitude is highly favorable). One who places a high value on philosophy may well take umbrage if I characterize that pursuit as "a search by a blind man for a black cat in a pitch-dark room where there is no cat." But here, as in all other cases, the felt emotion is a quality of the complex *whole* of the behavior. To reiterate, the term *attitude*, since it subsumes all aspects of our experience, discourages the tendency to think of any part of it as arising and functioning separately from any other part; as, for example, thinking of fear as being a pure entity which is to be aroused by some special appeal directed at the "seats of emotion." There are, of course, as many different kinds of fear as there are situations which we interpret as potentially painful and destructive to us.

Attitudinal description of behavior, then, makes no provision for dichotomies, as for example between reason and emotion, argument and persuasion. Expressions such as "appeals to emotion," "appeals to reason," "logical appeals," "psychological appeals," "good speaking combines both logic and persuasion," "sound argument but also strong motive appeal" are often seen in speech literature. The student should bear in mind, however, that these expressions are used for purposes of analysis, to indicate the various aspects of a unitary process. Taken literally, they would suggest a dichotomy where none is intended. It may easily be seen that a theory of motivation based on fundamental drives helps to perpetuate the argument-persuasion dichotomy. It leads us to think of the individual as having a number of these primal "springs of action" situated somewhere in him; and to think of persuasion as a skillful appeal which "touches off" the springs. But this persuasive appeal should also, it is held, be accompanied by a logical appeal aimed at man's reason, which, though regarded as weak (presumably because acquired late in his evolution), must apparently be posited as the "higher" agency which "makes the decision in the struggle between the single drives." The only alternative is to undertake the impossible task of arranging the fundamental drives in a hierarchy of potency. The theory of drives, leading as it does to artificial isolation of the potentialities of human beings, almost inevitably entangles us in the errors of faculty psychology.

In the past, a disproportionate amount of the psychological literature concerned with motivation has been devoted to experiments on the lower animals and to observation of infant behavior. The resulting mechanical model, which we have described, has had its day in social psychology. When, during World War II, many psychologists came out of their laboratories to work directly with adult human beings, they found their "threadbare models" (the expression is that of the noted psychologist Gordon Allport, in an address to his colleagues) quite useless. Allport's objection to the animal paradigm is that "the motivational structure of man and of lower animals seems to be in only a slight degree similar." [14] All the years of experiment on the white rat failed, it appears, to advance our understanding of the behavior of man as a political animal.

A proper theory of motivation must be centered on those distinctive capacities and possessions that set man apart from all other animals. Taking for granted the biological structures that make it possible, we come at once to the essential characteristic of man: his capacity for conceptual thought, for true speech that employs a symbolic language. All else that concerns us here flows from this unique capacity. Man's language made it possible to accumulate a tradition of knowledge, to perfect his tools and machinery, and thus to dominate the earth. By contrast, each generation of apes remains on the same level as previous generations. Their language of signs, or signals, lacking names for objects, lacking words for concepts, condemns them forever to the same old bag of ape knowledge. Apes can never add to their meagre store; whereas human beings, each generation standing as it were on the shoulders of the preceding generation, keep extending their horizon so that there appears to be no limit to their accumulation of knowledge.

But of particular concern here is that by-product of man's language which has special bearing on his motivation. This by-product is human culture, a civilized society into which each human being is inducted, is socialized. Language is the mediating agent. Through language man comes to be ruled by cultural values, by social attitudes, so that he is always a changing part of his environment in a sense that is true of no other animal. The most distinctive thing to note about human beings, when motivation is under consideration, is their virtually unlimited capacity for acquiring attitudes through interaction with each other. And this requires conceptual thought. A man could not, for example, acquire the attitudes of a particular group, or class, or occupation, without the ability to grasp their meaning and significance on a *conceptual* level.

It is safe to say, then, that social attitudes, mediated by conceptual thought, constitute no part of the psychological world of lower animals. By virtue of his language man dwells in a sphere of reality known only to man, a sphere in which words are the "ideational surrogates" of things themselves. The abstract level of functioning must be considered as the normal level of functioning for human beings. It is on this level—the level of the higher mental processes and of those distinctively human attributes called attitudes—that a speaker must deal with an audience.

[14] G. W. Allport, "Scientific Models and Human Morals," *Psychological Review*, 54 (July 1947), 185.

THE BASIC PROBLEM IN
MOTIVATION

In the final analysis, motivation turns out to be a process of identification. The speaker's role is as a guide to a choice which he is asking the audience to make among alternatives. The speech as a whole must be so designed that it leads the audience to identify this choice with their own best interests. For it must be assumed that rational people will always act in what they conceive to be their interests, that everyone seeks self-fulfillment, self-actualization. This is not a cynical view, nor is there in it the slightest implication that human nature is basically selfish. The question whether human nature is basically selfish, or basically one thing or another could come only from one unacquainted with the process of socialization through which human nature is achieved. Although selves within a particular culture may have much in common, there are as many different selves or egos, as there are people. When motivation is in view, the ego may be considered to be a constellation of attitudes that may vary from culture to culture and within cultures. The attitudes that may be said to constitute an ego are, like others, learned. They include how one conceives of himself, his status, his relationship to others, his most cherished values, his principles of right and wrong, his ideals, his aspirations, ambitions, long-term intentions. The directions of one's strivings, of his interests, are a matter of learning. If we agree, then, that people are going to make choices that appear to accord with their interests, the significant question is, What are their interests, what kind of selves have they acquired? The interests of some are such as to include the whole community, the interests of still others, short-sighted, piggish. When a human being of the stature of Albert Schweitzer acts in his own best interests, for self-fulfillment, the world profits; when a hoodlum acts in *his* interests, somebody is going to get skinned.

For making the identifications on which persuasive argument depends, the speaker's insight into human nature, a right estimate of his audience, and a proper conception of his own role are infinitely more important than prescriptions and devices. Persuasion is a complex and difficult art, not a matter of finding a specific motivational button leading to the past adjustments of an individual. A most serious defect of the kind of drive theory that we have criticized is that it points us in the wrong direction—backwards to some primal spring of action as the key to behavior. Admittedly, when we talk of attitudes, we have regard to past adjustments that people have made. And we have said that a knowledge of audience attitudes is the best clue to the directions in which they may be motivated. But this is only part of the picture. We must also focus attention on the present external situation which individuals are facing and keep in mind that they are trying to live their lives forward. They are trying to interpret the situation and arrive at a judgment or a choice which will harmonize with their values, as well as their immediate plans and long-range intentions. And this effort to arrive at a choice, more especially if it is a hard choice, brings into play, not one, but a whole complex of motives or attitudes that enter into the final decision. The response is thus a result of the interplay of inner determinants of behavior with external stimuli. We carry around our entire life history, so that our behavior at a particular time depends in part on the external situation, in part on the kind of history we have had and what we are trying to do at the time we act.

Now the speaker and his speech are the source of the external stimuli in a speaking situation. The speaker relies on those significant symbols of language that can create an environment of reality in the minds of an audience. When used with precision and vividness, words may lead an audience to respond as though they were in the presence of the things for which the words are surrogates. The speaker is therefore able to manipulate the perceptions of his audience. It appears certain that behavior springs largely from the way individuals perceive their world, and that differences in perceiving account for differences in behavior. People who have different attitudes toward a thing just don't see it in the same way. The perceptual part of an attitude includes a frame of reference (roughly speaking, a standard of judgment), and thus the holder of the attitude is predisposed to regard the object (the issue, for example) from that frame of reference and to feel and act accordingly. Now language may be used to cause the perception of a thing in one frame of reference rather than another. The persuasive speaker, after analysis of his audience, achieves the identification he seeks by using language for this purpose. Let us suppose, for example, that he is arguing that medical care for the aged should be placed under the social security system. He has reason to believe that the opposition from the audience stems from the fact that they see this proposal as "socialistic." Wisely, the speaker refrains from arguing about socialism. Instead he calls forth another attitude. He begins to talk about the principle of insurance, a principle which they have long accepted. He talks specifically about automobile insurance. He demonstrates that expensive, possibly bankrupting illness, is much more likely to occur than a serious automobile accident. He eventually presents the medical proposal as essentially an insurance arrangement, with the government, rather than an insurance company, paying the claims—and moreover without making a profit on the insured. If the speaker succeeds in getting the audience to see the proposal in this frame of reference, he may make the desired identification and win their approval.

The same method used in the foregoing hypothetical example was employed in a speech made by the great British orator, John Bright, on December 4, 1861. This speech is said to have had a powerful effect in allaying hostile sentiment aroused in England by the seizure of two Confederate envoys from the British steamer "Trent." The "Trent" affair furnished a rallying cry for those who wished to intervene in the American Civil War on behalf of the Confederacy. Bright's proposition was, "We should be neutral as far as regards mingling in the strife." How did he go about identifying this proposition with the best interests of the English? We note that he scarcely mentioned the "Trent" affair, or the motive of revenge, did not discuss the Northern blockade, which was depriving England of cotton. He let these "sleeping dogs" lie. What he did was to depict our Civil War as the kind of struggle for freedom that the British had always honored. He went into British history for examples to show England's traditional regard for freedom. In short, he called forth and stimulated the British attitude toward freedom, thus providing a frame of reference from which interference on the side of the Confederacy was perceived to be betrayal of a cherished ideal. The following portion of the concluding sentence of Bright's speech eloquently strikes the note of identification . . . "If all other tongues are silent, mine shall speak for that policy which gives hope to the bondsmen of the South, and which tends to generous thoughts and generous words, and generous deeds, between the two great nations who speak the English language, and from their origin are alike entitled to the English name." [15]

The complexity of human motivation affords the speaker many avenues to the mind of the audience. Their learned attitudes, or motives, may range from the most material to the most ideal. Within this gamut the speaker must feel his way to the possibilities for identification; and to the making of those identifications everything that goes into his speech should, directly or indirectly, contribute.

SUMMARY

Since the time of Aristotle rhetoricians have stressed the importance of audience analysis in persuasive argument. The cardinal aim of audience analysis is to reveal attitudes that have special relevance to the speaker's problem of motivation. An attitude is a learned formation, a residuum of experience, which predisposes an individual to behave in more or less predictable ways towards objects with which it is related. The term *attitude*

---

[15] John Bright, *Speeches*, I, ed. J. E. T. Rogers (London: Macmillan and Company, 1869), p. 195.

embraces the whole range of dispositions indicated by such popular terms as interests, sentiments, prejudices, loves, fears, hatreds, desires, purposes, ambitions, ideals, motives, values, stereotypes, and so on. In addition to discovering attitudes, analysis should seek to gauge the intellectual and cultural level of the audience and, by assessing a variety of information, acquaint the speaker with his auditors. Of particular importance in analysis is a knowledge of the groups with which the audience identifies itself. A serious speaker must become a student of society.

Motivation is best approached through a study of the process of social learning in which attitudes are rooted. The postulation of a fixed number of drives common to all men as the central concern in motivation must be abandoned. In concrete situations, we must know men's attitudes in order to estimate the likelihood that they can be motivated in certain ways. It is important to see that attitudinal reactions involve perception, thought, feeling, and action as discriminable dimensions of a unitary whole, not as separate segments. Attitudinal description of behavior makes no provision for dichotomies, as for example between reason and emotion.

Motivation may be said to occur when persons in an audience are led to identify the choice a speaker is asking them to make with their own best interests. Through a knowledge of audience attitudes the speaker uses language in such a way that the choice is seen in the proper frame of reference for making the desired identifications.

EXERCISES

1. Make an informative speech on interest groups in the United States.
2. Considering America as a single group, make a list of attitudes which you consider to be the most widespread in this country. Then analyze a Fourth of July oration and see whether the speaker adapted his speech to some of these attitudes.
3. Read Aristotle's analysis of the emotions in Book II of *The Rhetoric*. Then make a speech in which you either support or refute the following statement: "Emotions are not free-floating entities in experience."
4. Make a speech to support the following statement: "A syllogism is only a formal way of putting an identification."
5. Make an expository speech on the following statement: "The propagandist channels an already existing stream. Where there is no water, he digs in vain."
6. Assume you are to speak on the current intercollegiate debate proposition. Make an appropriate analysis of three different audiences.
7. Make an analysis of your class in argumentation and debate for a forthcoming speech.

SUGGESTED READINGS

ALLPORT, G. W. *Pattern and Growth in Personality*, New York: Holt, Rinehart & Winston, Inc., 1961. Chaps. 10, 13.

ARISTOTLE, *The Rhetoric*, trans., Lane Cooper. New York: D. Appleton-Century, 1932, Book 2, pp. 90–142.

GOLDSTEIN, KURT. *Human Nature in the Light of Psychopathology*, Cambridge, Mass.: Harvard University Press, 1940. Chaps. 1, 9.

MANNHEIM, K. *Ideology and Utopia*, New York, Harcourt, Brace & World, Inc., 1936. Chaps. 1–5.

MEAD, G. H. *Mind, Self and Society*, Chicago: The University of Chicago Press, 1934. Chaps. 1, 2, 10, 11, 23–25.

MURPHY, GARDNER. *Personality*, New York: Harper & Row, Publishers, 1947. Chaps. 8, 9, 15.

NEWCOMB, T. M. *Social Psychology*, New York: Holt, Rinehart & Winston, Inc., 1950. Chaps. 3, 4, 14.

SHERIF, M. *An Outline of Social Psychology*, New York: Harper & Row, Publishers, 1948. Chaps. 9, 10.

SHERIF, M. *The Psychology of Social Norms*, New York: Harper & Row, Publishers, 1936. Chaps. 4, 9.

SHERIF, M. and CANTRIL, H. *The Psychology of Ego-Involvements*, New York: John Wiley & Sons, 1947. Chap. 5.

chapter 9

EVIDENCE

by Paul D. Brandes

A proposition is seldom able to win acceptance of and by itself. A fact or a sign may be immediately acceptable to some or even many, but propositions concerned with generally accepted facts and signs are seldom the basis for argument. Most propositions require some degree of proof before they are accepted, and the more controversial the proposition, the more proof is required.

WHAT IS EVIDENCE?

The student of argument who is asked what types of proof are available may answer, "Well, of course, there is *evidence*." Evidence is indeed a form of proof used to win acceptance for a proposition. What is evidence and what unique functions of support does it fulfill?

To begin with, evidence is NOT any of the following:

1. Evidence is NOT any fact or opinion used to support a proposition.
2. Evidence is NOT necessarily reputable.
3. Evidence is NOT necessarily irrefutable.
4. Evidence is NOT exclusively logical or inherently scientific in nature, but has inherent ethical and emotional connotations as well as logical properties.

Evidence is not *any* fact or opinion, but those facts and opinions which the audience divorces from speaker bias. It may be defined as follows: *Evidence is that form of proof wherein the speaker confronts his audience with propositions which the audience establishes are relatively free of speaker bias.*

proof: Aristotle provides two types of proof. The first type is invented by the speaker and is automatically biased in favor of the speaker; the second is not invented by the speaker, but is someone else's invention which the speaker uses as part of his support for his proposition.[1]

audience confrontation: The speaker presents sufficient detail concerning his evidence to permit the audience to recognize it as relatively free of speaker bias.

audience acceptance: The audience must accept the proof offered by the speaker as relatively free of bias. It is not enough for the speaker to decide that he has not invented certain of his propositions. In order for evidence to serve as evidence, the audience must accept the speaker's judgment.

speaker bias: Any speaker who uses evidence influences it to some extent, if nothing else by the order in which the evidence is admitted. Yet an audience has the opportunity of deciding that a particular proposition is sufficiently free of speaker bias to be considered evidential.

When proof used is not invented by the speaker, when the audience is confronted with sufficient detail concerning the proof to establish the independence of the invention, and when the audience accepts this independence of invention, then and only then is the speaker using *evidence*.

WHAT ARE THE TESTS FOR EVIDENCE?

This definition of evidence distinguishes evidence from speaker-centered argument, but it gives to evidence no other properties. There may be good evidence and bad evidence; strong evidence and weak evidence; true evidence and false evidence. Evidence's only inherent property is its initial set of freedom from the bias of the speaker. Although evidence may support the speaker's bias, it does so, until proven otherwise, of its own volition and not because of the speaker's manipulations.

Yet, just because evidence is unbiased does not mean that it neces-

[1] See Paul D. Brandes, "Evidence in Aristotle's Rhetoric," *Speech Monographs*, 28 (March 1961), 21–28.

sarily belongs in a controversial speech. From all the evidence that is available to him, the speaker should choose for a particular occasion evidential proofs which meet these criteria:

1. The evidence should be material to the issue. The proof offered should be of real importance in seeking a solution to the problem. Evidence which is so out of date that it no longer is of importance in seeking a solution or is so trivial that its inclusion is of questionable merit should be excluded.

For example, in support of the proposition, *Fluoride should be added to drinking water to prevent tooth decay,* a debater should seldom offer the opinions of his own local dentist as evidence, unless his dentist has made more than a casual, subjective observation of the effects of fluorine. There are available such reports as the "Statement on Fluoridation of Public Water Supplies" by the House of Delegates of the American Medical Association (December 3–6, 1957), Philadelphia," or "Medical Aspects of Excessive Fluoride in a Water Supply," by Nicholas C. Leone *et al., Public Health Reports,* vol. 69, no. 10 (October 1954), pages 925–936. Although the information contained in these reports is several years old, it is still material to the proposition and is the result of a much more comprehensive and controlled type of induction than are the personal opinions of a local dentist. Similarly, the *Look* magazine article of June 24, 1958, by a *Look* staff writer can hardly be classed as material proof.

2. The evidence should be relevant to the issue. Material which is not germane should be excluded.

For example, persons advocating that fluoride should be added to drinking water may wish to introduce evidence to show how painful it is to have dental surgery resulting from infections caused by tooth decay. This evidence, no matter how reputable its source, is not relevant to the issue. The question is not *A solution should be found to prevent pain resulting from tooth decay* but rather, should fluoride be added to drinking water to prevent tooth decay. Opponents of fluorine should avoid putting themselves in a position where it could be said that they are in favor of pain and suffering by pointing out that evidence introduced to show the need for relieving pain is relevant to another issue not in question at this time.[2]

3. The evidence should be of probative value without introducing

[2] Dr. F. B. Exner explains: "Before going farther, I want to make one point clear. No one except the child's own parents is more concerned than I for the welfare of every child—and I mean *every* child, not just 'children' as a class. I do not go along with the idea that it is all right to damage a few children, or even a single child, if by so doing we can help the rest." See "Why Not to Fluoridate," *Journal of Applied Nutrition,* 10 (Spring 1957), 485.

too many extraneous side issues, particularly emotional issues, to distract the thinking of the audience.

For example, opponents of fluoridation sometimes advocate that fluorine in drinking water is injurious to elderly persons, particularly those who are already having trouble with their joints. Such evidence, if properly introduced, is of probative value. But, if the negative should present descriptions of the supposed effects of fluorine on elderly persons which, in their attempt to arouse pity in the audience, would so distort the issue at hand that the audience would no longer be concerned with whether fluorine may be safe for drinking water but rather that something should be done to help the old and infirm, then the proponents of fluoridation should seek to exclude such evidence as unnecessarily emotional.

WHAT ARE THE PURPOSES OF USING EVIDENCE?

A speaker who uses evidence is a speaker who announces to his audience that persons other than he have points of view which deserve consideration. He says: "I do not wish to offer only my own ideas on this issue" or "I am modest enough to offer you material which is not of my invention, which would have been available whether or not I had ever given my thoughts to the issue and which you may believe, even though you for some reason wish to reject me." A speaker who confronts an audience with such an attitude may gain increased acceptance for a number of reasons, all of which may be summarized as improved ethical, emotional, or logical argument.

EVIDENCE AND ETHICAL PERSUASION

The effective use of evidence may result in increased stature of the communicator and greater acceptance of the proposition, for the following reasons:

1. The *hostile audience* may respond favorably to the evidence presented, and such a favorable reaction may result, through association, with an improvement in the status of the speaker. There is not only "guilt by association," but also "gilt by association." A hostile audience which is resisting the communicator and his proposition may find itself accepting his evidence, since the evidence is disassociated from the communicator.

For example, persons favorably inclined toward fluoridation may have a set against any local communicator who is discouraging fluoridation. If Mr. "X" proposes dangers to health from fluoridation, a hostile audience may reject him. However, if Mr. "X" introduces as evidence a book review by S. J. Baudo, M.D., appearing in the *Archives of Pediatrics*, vol. 74, no. 5 (May 1957), which recommends consideration of the discouraging reports of Dr. F. B. Exner and Dr. G. L. Waldbott in their book, *The American Fluoridation Experiment,* then the audience's hostility to "X" may not be sufficient to develop a similar hostility to the *Archives of Pediatrics* and its book-review editor, Michael A. Brescia, and the author of the book review, Dr. S. J. Baudo. Mr. "X's" association with a source which the audience respects may not only win acceptance for his proposition, but it may also dispel part of the hostility toward him.

2. The *skeptical audience* may respond to evidence, where it would not respond to additional speaker-centered proofs. The skeptical audience may be seeking a preponderance of opinions or facts rather than a limited perspective on the subject which one speaker might offer. The skeptic often finds safety in numbers. He may be overwhelmed by a variety of evidence, which, when added to the persuasiveness of the speaker-centered proofs (the ethos, pathos, and logic of the speaker), may be too much for him to resist. If the communicator knows the reasons for audience skepticism, he may wish to choose his evidence selectively; if the reasons for the skepticism are unknown or are widely varied, he may wish to choose from a wide range of evidence in the hope of closing any escape hatches which the audience has kept open.

For example, the wide variety of proofs offered in the booklet, "Our Children's Teeth," prepared by the Committee to Protect Our Children's Teeth, Inc., 105 East 22nd Street, New York, with Dr. Benjamin Spock as chairman, would enable an advocate of fluoridation to quote such sources as the Commissioner of Public Health of the City of Philadelphia, the Mayor of St. Louis, Missouri, the President of the National Academy of Sciences, and a professor of oral pathology at Harvard University. Although the skeptic might well dismiss advocate "X," he would find it much more difficult to dismiss the wide variety of reputable sources found in the booklet cited above.

3. *The critical audience* may hold opinions that range from receptive to hostile. A protagonist, however, must be as concerned with his followers as with his opponents. Research in communication shows tendencies for audiences to respond negatively to communicators with whom they register initial agreement.[3] In other words, the audience was prepared to be enthusiastic, but its enthusiasms were not justified.

Have you ever been told that you *must* read a certain novel, or that you *must* see a certain play? Then, when you read the book or went to

[3] See T. N. Ewing, "A Study of Certain Factors Involved in Changes of Opinion," *Journal of Social Psychology,* 16 (August 1942), 63–88.

the theatre, the enthusiasm you expected to show failed to materialize and you registered a negative reaction. A similar negative shift appears to follow a communication favoring audience bias. If evidence is added to the proofs, however, the communicator may well avoid this dilemma by furnishing sufficient food for thought to the supporters in his audience to maintain their respect. A politician who is not careful to stimulate the interests of his supporters may unknowingly diminish their enthusiasms in an effort to gain the votes of his opponents.

On the other hand, critical audiences that are less in agreement with the proposition may need evidence to assist them in reaching an impartial agreement. If the speaker is relatively inexperienced and uninformed on his subject matter or if he realizes that his audience contains members who are as informed as he is, he should consider using evidence to increase the possibilities of gaining acceptance.

One of the best ways to maintain the respect of proponents of your proposition is to offer them new evidence to support their point of view. For example, audiences well familiar with older research on fluoridation might not be aware of the report by Dr. J. R. Blayney of Evanston, Illinois, entitled "A Report on Thirteen Years of Water Fluoridation in Evanston, Illinois," appearing in the *Journal of the American Dental Association,* vol. 61 (July 1960), pages 76–79. While the Newburgh-Kingston report in the March 1956 *Journal of the American Dental Association* may be "old hat" to a critical audience, the newer report may be sufficiently stimulating to satisfy the intellectual curiosity of the critical audience.

College and high school debaters who discuss the same issue for a given school year should be well aware of how fresh stimuli are required for judges already saturated with a year's earful of evidence.

EVIDENCE AND EMOTIONAL PERSUASION

A myth exists that evidence, being "logical," must therefore be unemotional. However, evidence is inherently emotional, and some evidence to some audiences has more impact emotionally than it does logically. The speaker must ask himself: "Which emotions shall my evidence assist?" and not "How can I be unemotional?" Persons who object to emotion are objecting to the type of emotion employed. They are perfectly willing to admit emotions whose implications they prefer.

Is there a strong emotion about "being unemotional?" Scientists become enthusiastic about their lack of emotion. But this enthusiasm is in itself emotional. How else can a scientist spend hour upon hour in his laboratory searching for a solution to cancer which he knows may never come—unless he is operating under some sort of an emotional drive? What the scientist may well mean when he says he is being unemotional is that he is being emotional in the particular way of which scientists approve.

Courts of law have long recognized the emotional properties of evidence. The judge may exclude evidence, not because it is irrelevant or immaterial, but on the basis that its emotional components may support propositions which the court is not interested in exploring at that time. For example, in an accident case, the court may object to the victim displaying his injuries to the jury, or, in a paternity case, the court may object to the mother displaying her child to show resemblance to the alleged father. The judge reasons that he is not interested in the propositions: *All persons who are so gravely injured are persons who need help* and *All little babies without fathers are babies who deserve support*, but rather in, *Defendant X is a person guilty of negligence under specific laws* or *Defendant X is the father of Y.*

A typical example of how courts react to evidence which is highly emotional exists in insurance liability cases. Most courts decline to have admitted that the defendant in an auto accident case is insured. The reasoning is that the jury may well shift from the proposition, *Defendant Z is a person who negligently injured Prosecuting A*, to *Defendant Z is a person who has sufficient insurance so that he may assist "A,"* regardless of whether or not he has injured "A."

Evidence may be able to engender in an audience any of the basic emotions: fear, pity, hate, love, scorn, pride. The speaker should remind himself that evidence, because it is divorced in some measure from the speaker, may be able to arouse a particular emotion in an audience when he, the speaker, may not be able to do so. Since an audience is always emotional (the only unemotional audience being one of corpses) and since the degree of motivation depends entirely upon the degree of emotional stimulation, the communicator should select his evidence carefully to stimulate in his audience the emotional reactions suitable to his case.

However, although the use of emotion with evidence is inevitable, the proponents of propositions should not use this as an excuse to enter maudlin sentiment into their arguments. Nor should they unnecessarily stimulate an audience to emotional reactions.[4] Nor should they use

[4] Research by I. L. Janis and H. C. Milholland, Jr., comparing many degrees of fear appeals reveals that subjects exposed to minimal threat appeals remembered the causes of the threats better than those exposed to maximal threat appeals. See "The Influence of Threat Appeals on Selective Learning of the Content of a Persuasive Communication," *Journal of Psychology*, 37 (January 1954), 75–80. I. L. Janis and S. Feshbach report that a minimal fear appeal was most effective in resisting counterpropaganda and in securing adherence to the recommendations of the communicator. See "Effects of Fear-arousing Communications," *Journal of Abnormal and Social Psychology*, 48 (January 1953), 78–92.

argumentum ad populum to smother the proposition with false issues which are not only highly emotional but also irrelevant to the debate. A proponent is obligated to introduce only those emotions which are inherently a part of his case. Otherwise he risks the disapprobation of the audience by employing questionable ethics.

EVIDENCE AND LOGICAL PERSUASION

The syllogisms and enthymemes of sources independent of the speaker are often more persuasive than those constructed by the speaker himself. Furthermore, the borrowing of such lines of argument may lift the communicator from the prosaic to the poetic. The speaker who lacks imaginative organization and who despairs of his knack of "putting things" must serve himself, with proper recognition, of course, to the superior talents of others. Otherwise he is doomed to boredom and mediocrity.

An advocate may borrow from another speech its entire logical structure, substituting his own propositions and his own supporting proof. For example, the structure used by John C. Calhoun in his March 4, 1850, speech on slavery using the rhetorical question followed by the elimination of false solutions and the proposing of a true solution could be used in many situations.

Or a speaker may need clarification for a subpoint, or a particular sentence may be giving him trouble. That subpoint may have been carefully worked out by a researcher specializing in the area and that particular sentence may have been said exactly right by a fellow advocate of his proposition. Just as Shakespeare did honor to the plots he borrowed, so can the communicator enhance the evidence he uses by giving it new purposes and new imports.

For example, a proponent of fluoridation may be experiencing difficulty in explaining just how the human body reacts to fluoride in drinking water. Then he reads a statement by Frank J. McClure, Senior Nutritionist for the National Institute of Health, which states the case in three parts: (1) that artificial fluoridation of drinking water affects the human body in the same way as does natural fluoridation; (2) that the human body eliminates fluorine added to water artificially in the same manner in which it eliminates fluorine added to water naturally; and (3) no adverse effects result from the presence of small quantities of fluorine in the calcified structures of the body.

Or if an opponent of fluoridation wishes to explain his reluctance to begin mass medication without further study, he may wish to quote the summarizing sentence of Sir Arthur Amies in the *Australian Dental Journal*, vol. 4 (April 1959): "Fluoridation of domestic water supplies involves the administration with therapeutic intent of a chemical preparation to young and old, dentate or edentulous, well and ill, without individual examination and regardless of individual desire." Such a key sentence may help the debater organize his ideas and start him on a new path of investigation.

The ways in which evidence may increase the logical persuasiveness of a communication may be summarized as follows:

Induction
    a. Evidence may furnish examples or a series of examples from which the speaker may draw a generality.
    b. Evidence may furnish a generality from which the speaker can supply examples, from his own experiences or from other evidence.

Deduction
    a. Evidence may furnish a series of enthymemes which the speaker may use as the structure of his speech.
    b. Evidence may furnish isolated enthymemes, which may form a major premise, a minor premise, or a conclusion of a syllogism. The speaker may wish to allow the audience to supply the missing portions of the syllogism, or he may wish to supply the missing parts himself.

WHAT FORMS OF EVIDENCE ARE THERE?

Anyone who attempts to categorize the forms of evidence risks making the same error that T. S. Eliot avoided when he would not define poetry because he knew of no definition which either did not assume that the reader already knew what poetry meant or which left out more poetry than it included.[5] Nevertheless, some categories are sufficiently helpful to risk minor error in an effort to find appropriate labels.

Therefore, this chapter will propose that evidence may be classified into five functional forms: evidence furnished by a witness, evidence furnished by a document, evidence furnished by recordings, evidence furnished by pictorial forms, and evidence furnished by relics. A successful debater should learn to use all five forms to advantage.

THE WITNESS

Evidence furnished by witnesses is limited here to include only that testimony given under observation by the audience (or judge), allowing

    [5] T. S. Eliot, *The Use of Poetry and the Use of Criticism* (Cambridge, Mass.: Harvard University Press, 1933), p. 155.

for the possibility of cross-examination. Therefore, a speaker who furnishes a deputation (or written statement) of an observation of a witness is furnishing a document rather than employing a witness.

The evidence of witnesses is not used often enough. Many communicators try to do themselves what others may do more easily for them. If a communicator finds his credibility limited, if he realizes that his own impact on an audience is minimal, if he finds that his own abilities to create demonstrative proof are handicapped, then he may do well to seek a witness who can supply the missing ethical, emotional, logical proofs. Yet, because of the lack of experience in handling the witness or because of the trouble involved in securing witnesses or a number of other factors, the communicator often goes down to defeat because he tried to do the job himself.

Woodrow Wilson, in his campaign to sell the people of the United States on joining the League of Nations, was certainly in a bitter argument. He knew what the reaction of the United States Senate had been; he knew the inherent isolationism of the Mid-West. Nevertheless, when he made his fatal tour of speaking engagements, aimed at changing the opinions of the undecided or opposed voters, he used only speaker-centered proofs.[6] There is little or no evidence in the speeches of the summer of 1919. Wilson was saying: "You Americans, you join the League of Nations because I, Woodrow Wilson, say you should join!" Such an appeal may have been greeted with cheers by the enthusiastic Wilson supporters, but it appears to have failed in its mission to change the votes of the undecided and opposed. What the difference might have been if Wilson had been willing to reduce his own arguments by half and had interspersed them with the appearances of local figures who favored his cause can only be a matter of speculation. But it can be asserted that Wilson, for all of his statesmanlike qualities, lost perspective on himself. Cheering supporters only accelerated the error. Did Wilson ask himself what were the reactions of the uncommitted voters to his Minneapolis address?

One of the more interesting documents pertaining to the controversy over fluoridation is *Hearings before the Committee on Interstate and Foreign Commerce of the House of Representatives,* Eighty-Third Congress, on the House Resolution No. 2341, concerning a bill to protect the public health from the dangers of fluorination of water. The flavor of the testimony is readily apparent from the record of the committee hearings.

A witness may furnish the ethical motivation needed for success, the emotional motivation needed for success, the examples for the speaker's generalization from the wide experiences the witness has had, or the

---

[6] Henderlider observes: "Wilson used authority sparingly. Quotations, direct or indirect were used less than twenty times in the thirty-three speeches." See Clair R. Henderlider, "Woodrow Wilson's Speeches on the League of Nations, September 4–25, 1919," *Speech Monographs,* 13 (January 1946), 29.

generalizations (or enthymemes) to which the speaker may add examples. In other words, the witness is an auxiliary speaker.

THE DOCUMENT

Many communicators prefer the document to the witness because they feel they are in better control of the document. College and high school debaters rely largely on the document as evidence because of its maneuverability. It is mobile; it is available; it is relatively inexpensive.

A document may be defined as any material written by someone other than the speaker and accepted by the audience on that basis.

The chapter on Research for Debate stresses the search for appropriate documents, since they are so predominant in argumentation. The search for documents may furnish the tools for induction: case histories, judicial decisions, narratives, analogies, and statistics; or the generalities for which examples may be furnished, completing the inductive chain, or the generalities for which minor premises and conclusions may be drawn, completing the deductive chain.

For example, a chart for a portion of the text from the hearings of the House of Representatives on H.R. 2341 [7] is reproduced here.

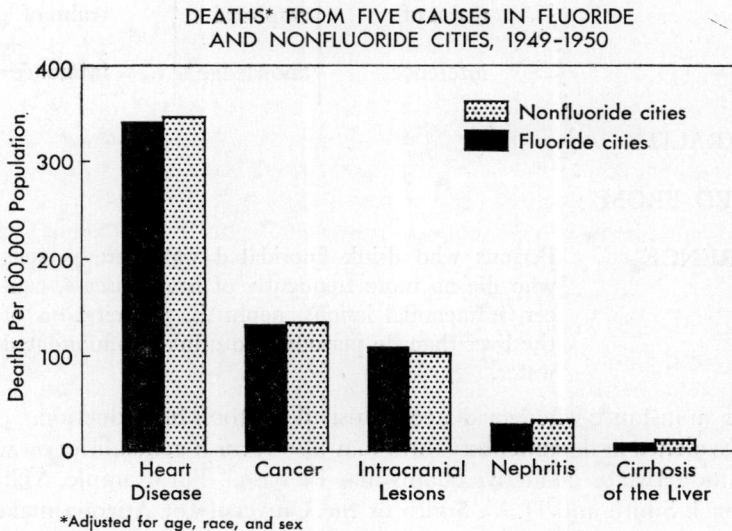

DEATHS* FROM FIVE CAUSES IN FLUORIDE
AND NONFLUORIDE CITIES, 1949-1950

*Adjusted for age, race, and sex

[7] See *Hearings before the Committee on Interstate and Foreign Commerce*, House of Representatives, 83rd Congress, 2nd session, on H.R. 2341, p. 374, Chart 6, of the testimony of Dr. John W. Knutson, Chief Dental Officer, Public Health Service. Minor changes in design have been made in the chart as it appears in this text.

This chart shows the distribution of mortality rates from heart disease, cancer, intracranial lesions, nephritis, and cirrhosis of the liver in 32 cities in the United States with fluoride and 32 with fluoride-free water supplies. As can be seen, no discernible difference exists between the mortality rates for these two groups of cities.

These data provide the multiple examples called statistics from which a generality may be drawn. The inductive chain of reasoning may be diagrammed as follows:

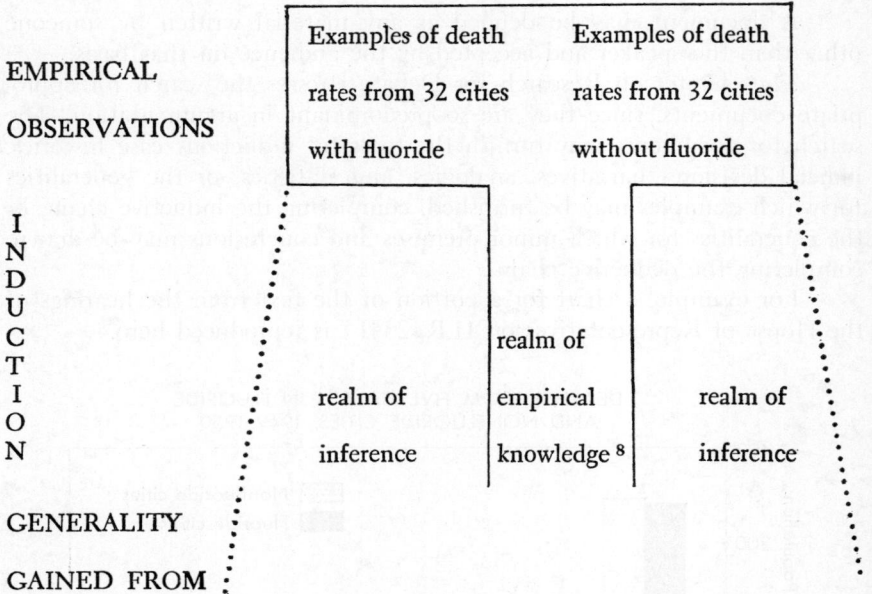

EMPIRICAL

OBSERVATIONS

Examples of death rates from 32 cities with fluoride	Examples of death rates from 32 cities without fluoride

I
N
D
U
C
T
I
O
N

	realm of empirical knowledge [8]	
realm of inference		realm of inference

GENERALITY

GAINED FROM

INFERENCE

Persons who drink fluoridated water are persons who die no more frequently of heart disease, cancer, intracranial lesions, nephritis, and cirrhosis of the liver than do persons who drink nonfluoridated water.

Here is an instance where evidence furnished the tools for induction.

Evidence in documentary form may also furnish generalities on which either inductive or deductive chains may be based. For example, Margaret Cammack Smith and H. V. Smith of the University of Arizona make the

---

[8] We know for certain only the limited conclusions that our sample from sixty-four cities will afford. But we generalize from this to many cases that we have not examined. This is the process of inference by which we go from the known (our sixty-four cities) to the unknown (the many other cities that we did not examine). Unless we make this inference, we have not induced; we have only summarized.

following statement in the September 1940 issue of the *American Journal of Public Health*: "It would appear therefore, that even though fluorine ingestion during the period of tooth formation may produce teeth which offer more resistance to bacterial invasion, the disadvantage of the resulting poorly constructed, internally weak, mottled teeth may far more than offset the advantage of a greater resistance to external invasion by bacteria." An inductive chain could be set up by furnishing the statistics on which the Smiths base their statement; a deductive chain could be set up by adding a minor premise and a conclusion to the Smiths' generalization:

Smith generalization: All persons who drink fluoridated water are persons who may have teeth more resistant to bacterial invasion, but may also have structurally defective teeth.

Supplied minor premise: New York is composed of persons who may drink fluoridated water if the City decides to fluoridate.

Supplied conclusion: New York, in such an event, will be composed of persons who may have teeth more resistant to bacterial invasion, but may also have structurally defective teeth.

RECORDINGS

Recent mechanical improvements in recording devices have accelerated the use of the recording in furnishing evidence. Tape recorders are now inexpensive and easily portable. Although the recording lacks the complete picture that the witness or an on-the-scene observation may give, it does furnish sound, which, despite the effectiveness of written symbols, often tells us much more than the document.

However, the recording, as well as the pictorial to be discussed next, somewhat smacks of the lamp. Unless it is used properly and with reserve, its ostentatiousness and premeditation may offset its persuasive abilities. All evidence may involve the same limitations of ostentation and premeditation as does the recording. The recorder accentuates the invasion of the arts by the sciences. The "art" of speaking is confronted with the "science" of mechanical recording. Persons who have a set in favor of an art, who feel that man's intelligence is sufficient to solve his problems without mechanical devices, may respond negatively to the intrusion of science. No little part of the court's reluctance to accept the recording may be attributed to such a prejudice. Yet, when an audience is set for science, as it is in radio or television, it welcomes the recording as a stimulating adjunct.

The persuasive power of the recording in many oral situations has yet to be explored. Even its introduction into courts of law is largely undefined. Further experimentation is required to establish its potentialities as a persuasive device.

PICTORIALIZATIONS

The chart, the graph, the sketch, the diagram, the photograph all present interesting problems when used as evidence. For example, do audiences consider photographs taken by the speaker as evidence? If so, do they consider them as less "evidential" than they do photographs taken by someone else other than the speaker? If a speaker is showing colored slides to a group, under what conditions does his argument improve if he disassociates himself from authorship of the slides? Are charts, graphs, sketches, and diagrams more effective to the degree that they are established as evidence?

The answers to these questions and to many others on pictorialization remain largely unanswered. It is rather well established that a speaker on a controversial issue will find his efforts at clarification and persuasion improved by pictorialization.[9] The picture magazine, television, and the motion picture have achieved such a following because of the operation of this theory. Our sight is so much faster than our ear and it can add so much detail so quickly that the vividness of the stimulus increases materially with the picture.

How pictorial evidence compares with straight pictorial argument remains to be tested. Pictorial evidence would have the usual assumption of freedom from bias operating in its favor. There is every reason to believe that the powers of pictorial evidence are considerable. Yet many scholastic debaters scorn charts and graphs, finding them unworthy of the level of conceptual thinking. The concepts of mathematics need continual visualization, and philosophy has created such assists as Euler's circles. But there seems to be no data to support the contention that pictorial material retards conceptual thinking.[10] It may be that a sophistic, involving artificially constructed values by interscholastic debaters and their coaches, has resulted in a decrease in persuasiveness of pictorial materials to persons so prejudiced in the limited area of debate. But this isolated position is not to be encouraged.

In debating the problem of fluoridation, there are many pictorializa-

[9] See Carl I. Hovland, Arthur A. Lumadaine, and Fred D. Sheffield, *Experiments on Mass Communication,* vol. 3 of *Studies in Social Psychology in World War II* (Princeton, N.J.: Princeton University Press, 1949), pp. 114–116.

[10] This may not be true of the extreme use of graphics. See Hovland, Lumsdaine, and Sheffield, pp. 108–112.

tions which could be used as evidence, one of which has already been reproduced in this chapter. A glance through the hearings on House Resolution No. 2341 demonstrates how important persons who testified before
the House Committee felt pictorialization was to explain their positions.
A debater who tries to use words to describe the detail that a pictorialization could simplify may be debating, but he is not an effective communicator.

RELICS

A relic is any presentation meeting the definition of evidence which
is not a witness, a document, a recording, or a pictorialization. Weapons,
fingerprints, hair, and similar items are often introduced as evidence in
criminal proceedings; scientific demonstrations, mathematical calculations,
and a wide variety of illustrative devices appear in informative discourse.

The concreteness of the relic and its familiarity to the audience are
factors which make it a valuable adjunct to persuasion. If each member
of the group handles the relics for himself, the increase in effectiveness
of the communicator is appreciable.[11] Therefore, the teacher-centered demonstration in biology has given way to laboratory work by each student.
Although the form is more efficient in many respects and certainly less
expensive, its effectiveness in comparison to participation is limited.

Yet school debaters seldom reproduce their evidence and furnish
copies of it to their opponents and their judges, for much the same reasons, it is supposed, that biology teachers clung to the demonstration for
so many years. However, the uninventiveness of the debater in this respect
is to be deplored. His reluctance to challenge existing debate procedures for
fear of losing a debate (and perhaps winning an argument) is unfortunate.

HOW MAY THE FORMS OF
EVIDENCE BE USED TO ACHIEVE
THE PURPOSES?

Now that the purposes of evidence have been discussed and the types
of evidence clarified, it is necessary to discuss some of the particular problems that arise in developing evidence to achieve its purposes.

A question of prime concern is, *To what degree should evidence be
documented?* It has already been asserted that evidence is not evidence

[11] See Carl I. Hovland, Irving L. Janis, and Harold H. Kelley, *Communication
and Persuasion* (New Haven, Conn.: Yale University Press, 1953), for studies reported
in Chapter 7, "Acquiring Conviction through Active Participation."

unless the audience so defines it. It is assumed that documentation is necessary to assist the audience in differentiating speaker-centered proofs from nonspeaker-centered proofs, else the audience would have no reason for assuming a shift of emphasis from one type of proof to another. The degree to which documentation occurs is important for two reasons:

1. The more documentation offered, the more time consumed.
2. The more documentation offered, the more complicated becomes the message, increasing the possibility of audience fatigue.

For example, a source on fluoridation has the following complete citation:

> Expert Committee on Water Fluoridation. *First Report.* World Health Organization Technical Report Series No. 146 (Geneva: World Health Organization, 1958).

Furthermore, there were in 1957, seven members of the committee, with Professor Yngve Ericsson of Sweden as Chairman and including Dr. Harold C. Hodge of the Rochester School of Medicine and Dentistry and Dr. John W. Knutson, Assistant Surgeon General, Chief Dental Officer, Public Health Service, Washington, D.C.

How much of this material should be offered an audience?

It appears that the more hostile the audience is to the communication, the more detailed the documentation should be. Research studies in this area are yet to be produced, but all indications lead in this direction. College audiences have failed to show increased shifts in opinion with increased documentation of sources [12] but have responded favorably to increased amounts of evidence.[13] However, the college audiences tested were not predominantly hostile. Further research is necessary before the effect of the degree of documentation and the amount of documentation is determined.

Until such research is concluded, the student of argument may wish to follow these rules of thumb in documenting his evidence:

1. Visualize the documentation whenever possible. In using pictorializations, have the evidence plainly marked as to source. Copies of

---

[12] R. S. Cathcart, "An Experimental Study of the Relative Effectiveness of Selected Means of Handling Evidence in Speeches of Advocacy," *Speech Monographs,* 22 (August 1955), 227–233.

[13] Eual M. Samples, "An Experimental Study of the Effectiveness of Scripture in Persuasive Speeches upon Attitudes of the Audience" (unpublished master's thesis, *University of South Mississippi,* 1956); and Gerard A. Wagner, "An Experimental Study of the Relative Effectiveness of Varying Amounts of Evidence in a Persuasive Communication" (unpublished master's thesis, *University of South Mississippi,* 1958).

written documents, available to all concerned, should show as much detail as possible concerning authorship. The blackboard may be used to list source details, particularly those which the audience might miss with only an audible stimulus. A list of the sources of the first affirmative speaker should be most impressive, and would certainly eliminate quibbling about source detail. A bibliography of sources, distributed to all concerned, would be very helpful.

2. If only an audible stimulus is to be used, the proponent of a proposition should not be surprised if a single exposure does not result in a clarification of his source. Repetition of the essential factors of the documentation should be considered. Since repetition takes time, the debater may wish to minimize the documentation of sources not critical to his case, and maximize through repetition of detail those that are important.

3. The debater should consider having all written documents in hand when citing from them. He should consider appearing as close to his audience as possible during these citations, avoiding the speaker's stand, so that the audience can sense the directness of the debater's approach.

A second question that arises is, *Should primary or secondary evidence be used?* Primary evidence is developed from first-hand observations, whereas secondary evidence is developed from hearsay or second-hand observations. Primary sources are generally preferable to secondary ones, unless the prestige of the secondary source is considerable. If a participating witness or document is not available, then the substitution of a secondary source may be necessary. But the communicator must be prepared for his audience to depreciate the value of the source in proportion to its secondary qualities.

In *Look* magazine of June 24, 1958, Dr. Louis I. Dublin, referred to as a former vice-president of the Metropolitan Life Insurance Company, is quoted as saying: "This opposition to fluoridation will disappear like a bad dream, once citizens make it their business to learn the facts." A debater who wishes to use this quotation should seek to locate the particular conditions under which the purported statement was made. He should locate the document containing the quotation in its original form, if such a document is available. Otherwise, he runs the risk of all the errors in interpretation that may have occurred during the process of publication. Such a secondary source—a quotation of one sentence already lifted from its context—lifted again from its context—should not be considered good evidence.

The debater must also ask, *Which type of evidence shall I use?* This question has been partially answered in the previous discussions, wherein the advantages and disadvantages of each of the five types of evidence were discussed. But there still remain the implications of variety in the use of evidence and the order of such variety to achieve the most effective results. Should a speaker feature more than one type of evidence in his communication? If he does feature more than one type, is there an ascending order of effectiveness for presenting the types?

At present, answers to these questions must be based largely upon speculation. It is assumed that audiences respond to a variety of evidence as they respond to variety in other phases of communication, and that because of the more exhibitory aspects of the recording, the audience should be carefully prepared for its introduction.

An interesting question arising from the use of evidence is, *How far removed from audience experience may the implications of evidence be?* Audiences are often conservative and incredulous. They must be wooed from their established beliefs and not shocked into accepting new concepts. An audience whose prejudices or biases or preconceived opinions have crystallized will often reject the implications of highly probative evidence, merely because it conflicts too abruptly with existing beliefs. In investigating the affects of advertising, Poffenberger found that what is true is not necessarily that which is believed.[14] Evidence which raises contentions highly contrary to existing audience beliefs should be examined carefully for possible exclusion, despite its probative value. If it is included, the audience should be well prepared for its introduction and it should fall relatively late in the sequence of ideas.

That there may be both good and bad evidence has already been stated. A quality of good evidence is that it is reputable; bad evidence is disreputable. The question arises, *What standards does an audience use to evaluate evidence?* An attorney who is confronted with testimony by a witness whose reputation for honesty is questionable will endeavor to point out to the court that the witness's integrity is vulnerable. A debater will endeavor to do the same. There is considerable reason to believe that audiences will discount the effect of sources they consider of low credibility,[15] but there is only rudimentary evidence as to how they make their decisions as to what sources are low in credibility and what sources are high in credibility.

Several hypotheses can be offered: (1) Educated audiences are more critical of source credibility than are uneducated audiences; (2) There is a direct relationship between knowledge of the source and an evaluation

    [14] A. J. Poffenberger, "The Condition of Belief in Advertising," *Journal of Applied Psychology*, 7 (March 1923), 1–9.
    [15] C. I. Hovland and W. Weiss, "The Influence of Source Credibility on Communication Effectiveness," *Public Opinion Quarterly*, 15 (Winter 1951), 635–650; H. C. Kelman and C. I. Hovland, " 'Reinstatement' of the Communicator in Delayed Measurement of Opinion Change," *Journal of Abnormal and Social Psychology*, 48 (July 1953), 327–335.

of its credibility; and (3) The degree of documentation affects the credibility of evidence.

The ironical problem involved here is that in some instances it is only sources of questionable origin which are available. If two cars are in an accident and the only witness happens to be a man who has a criminal record, he is still the best source of information on certain phases of the accident. Complaints by prisoners in penitentiaries may be highly justifiable, but they are often discounted. Certainly there is much evidence on fluoridation which is of questionable origin. Persons who appear to have selfish interests in promoting or discouraging fluoridation lack credibility to the degree that their selfish intent interferes with their ability to analyze the problem objectively.

The intent of the evidence appears to be one of the main factors by which audiences evaluate the sources presented to them.[16] In choosing his evidential proofs, the speaker should try to eliminate those sources which appear to gain advantage by the adoption of his proposition. The operation of this principle makes the endorsement of fluoridation by the American Dental Association highly probative, since the dentists not only have nothing to gain from reduced dental caries (except for their own personal welfare) but conceivably have much to lose.

WHAT ARE THE DELIVERY PROBLEMS INVOLVED IN PRESENTING EVIDENCE?

A technique for presenting evidence must be developed. Many communicators avoid using evidence because they have not trained themselves to handle its types with ease. They stumble in introducing a witness or appear awkward in finding a page in a document or experience power failure in using a recorder, and the uncomfortable experience is enough to discourage them from further efforts at using evidence. They then rationalize that evidence is really unnecessary and that they can fight their own battles without assistance.

Such rationalization is foolhardy. A speaker who cannot use evidence is like an army with rifles but no artillery. No matter how effective the rifles may be, there are certain instances when their effectiveness is negligible without larger weapon support. Speakers should be willing to make

[16] I. Hovland and W. Mandell, "An Experimental Comparison of Conclusion-Drawing by the Communicator and by the Audience," *Journal of Abnormal and Social Psychology*, 47 (July 1952), 581–588; R. K. Merton, *Mass Persuasion; the Social Psychology of a War Bond Drive* (New York: Harper and Brothers, 1946), p. 90.

mistakes in their early efforts at employing evidence in order to gain the proficiency that comes with practice.

A limited number of postulates will be offered here to be followed during practice periods. Written documents should be visible to the audience at the time of citation. If read from, the reading should conform to the standards of oral interpretation of literature, with book held high enough so that the voice can move out into the audience and the eyes can maintain contact with the audience. During reading periods, more energy, and not less energy, is needed to maintain desired levels of audience attention. A direct quotation from a document is not necessary. Unless the phraseology is crucial or the issue is highly controversial, an accurate paraphrase is often sufficient. While this paraphrase is underway, the communicator may wish to hold the document in his hands open to the page from which he is paraphrasing. Speakers should avoid saying "quote" and "unquote." An appropriate pause before and after citations will properly punctuate quoted material. The communicator should remember that as he introduces evidence, he is introducing variety and that perhaps a slight movement in position before and after the citation may punctuate the variety effectively for the audience and help it to maintain the separation between the speaker's argument and his evidence.

The extent to which a speaker should interrupt a quotation for clarification or repetition varies considerably for each occasion. Such interruptions are acceptable and should be encouraged to the extent that they assist the audience in gaining a more accurate understanding of the evidence. The French bishop Bossuet seldom presented quotations without interrupting his reading, working with the material, making it an integral part of his communication rather than an appendage or adjunct. Although the debater should hesitate to influence his citations to the point that their objectivity can be questioned, he should consider paraphrasing a complicated direct quotation after he has read it to give the audience two opportunities to grasp the concept. He may wish to interrupt his quotation to repeat an important statistic; he may find it desirable to repeat the whole quotation, word for word, to insure communication.

> [Suppose a debater wished to present the following:] When any substance is added to the public water supply, it is the duty of those who add it to establish beyond shadow of doubt that it is safe for everyone who will use the water, or at least that the water is safer with the addition than without. We add chlorine, another poisonous substance, because we are convinced that any slight harm the chlorine may do is less to be feared than the typhoid germs which might otherwise be in the water, and which the chlorine kills. Since fluoride does nothing to add to the safety of the water, the burden must rest on those who want it

added to prove beyond doubt that it is safe for everyone, not on opponents to prove it harmful.[17]

Here is a quotation composed of three long complex sentences. Each is philosophical in nature and requires time to be understood. A debater might read all three slowly, without interruption or repetition. Or he might repeat the first sentence verbatim, read the second sentence only once, since it is less complicated than the other two, and paraphrase the third sentence after its first reading.

A sentence with statistics requires particular attention. Suppose the debater wished to cite the conclusions to the Russell and Elvove study of fluoride-dental caries in adults:

1. Objective lists of natives 20–44 years old with verified histories of residence and water usage were prepared in Boulder, Colorado, where the communal water is virtually fluoride free, and in Colorado Springs, Colorado, where the communal water contains about 2.5 ppm of fluorides. The cities are otherwise similar and the two groups are comparable in race and occupation. Persons on the lists were given dental examinations with mouth mirror and explorer.

2. The prevalence of fluorosis was uniform through the age range at Colorado Springs. No fluorosis was seen in natives of Boulder.

3. Total rates for decayed, missing, or filled permanent teeth were about 60 percent lower in Colorado Springs than in Boulder for each age group. The phenomenon of caries inhibition continued undiminished through the age of 44 years.

4. Boulder natives had lost three or four times as many teeth from dental caries as had natives of Colorado Springs.[18]

Finding number three involves the statistic, "60 percent"; four, "three or four times as many." Both of these passages are strategically important to the conclusions of the study. Both should be given particular attention by the communicator. He may wish to repeat them, or pause after them, or paraphrase their implications. But he should not pass over them with one reading. Statistical reports more complicated than those given above from Russell and Elvove should be assisted with visual support.

Witnesses should be made as comfortable as possible and efforts should be made to prevent their embarrassment before the group. Leading

[17] F. B. Exner, *op. cit.*, p. 485.

[18] A. L. Russell and Elias Elvove, "Domestic Water and Dental Caries; VII. A Study of the Fluoride-Dental Caries Relationship in an Adult Population," *Public Health Reports*, October 26, 1951, pp. 1399–1400.

questions should be avoided. Witnesses should be briefed carefully on time limits and on the necessity to project their voices sufficiently to be heard easily. The speaker should not hesitate to remind the witness of time limits and volume requirements. If necessary, some concrete reminder, such as a time card or a bell, may be employed to remind witnesses of specified time limits.

Pictorializations should be easily visible. Fringes of rooms whose sight lines are questionable should be roped off ahead of time to prevent seating, since it is always cumbersome to move persons once they have located themselves. The documentation of pictorializations should not be overlooked. The communicator should rehearse his presentation, equipping himself with a pointer, if need be, to guide his audience through the graphics. Naturally, the speaker should avoid passing single copies of evidence. Unless he has a copy for everyone, he should maintain attention at a central point. If the communicator does have copies for all, he should perfect a technique for passing the material out quickly, making certain that his audience has dismissed it when it has passed the point wherein it was of service.

All recording and film equipment should be checked in advance, to make certain it is in working order. Supplementary tapes should be available, in case one is damaged. Sight lines for relics should be mapped out in advance. Demonstrations must be easily visible. Seating arrangements in rooms may have to be modified to present maximum sight lines.

SUMMARY

This chapter has attempted to do six things. First, it defined evidence as that form of proof wherein the speaker confronts his audience with propositions which the audience establishes are relatively free of speaker bias. Second, it pointed out that evidence should be material to the issue, relevant to the argument at hand, and of probative value without introducing unwanted side issues. Third, it stated that evidence is useful in building ethical persuasion with hostile audiences, skeptical audiences, and critical audiences, that it is useful in enforcing legitimate emotions, and that it can furnish both inductive and deductive elements in reasoning. Fourth, the chapter listed five types of evidence: the witness, the document, the recording, the pictorialization, and the relic. Fifth, it discussed some specific philosophical problems of how the various forms of evidence may be employed to achieve the goals desired, and sixth, it dealt concretely with certain delivery problems involved in using evidence effectively.

Lionel Ruby points up the frustrations that many students experience in their attempts to clarify the meaning of evidence:

> Adequate evidence is evidence which is relevant to the conclusion to which it is directed. We need not define "evidence" or "relevant" since we may assume that these words will be generally understood by most persons. Unless the meaning of these words were understood by the reader of a book on logic prior to his reading the book, he would not be able to follow the author's reasoning.[19]

This chapter does not assume an understanding of *evidence*, but its efforts to define the term must only be a beginning for the student of argumentation. Unless the student does pursue a comprehension of evidence, as Professor Ruby points out, his understanding of logic will be minimal indeed.

EXERCISES

1. Attend a public speech given by a person of considerable repute. Make a list of all items which qualify as evidence under the definition given in this chapter.
2. Attend a public speech where the audience is predominately hostile to the speaker. Make a list of those instances in which the speaker might have dispelled the hostility by substituting evidence for his own opinions.
3. Examine a recent speech by an important public figure as it is reproduced in *The New York Times*. Write an essay evaluating how well the speaker used evidence.
4. Prepare an outline for a controversial speech in which you use as much evidence as possible. Refrain from putting in any of your own wording whenever possible. Use evidence for the theme of the speech, the main headings, and the subheadings.
5. Choose a set of rather complicated statistics and prepare to deliver this information to the class. Be certain that the source of the statistics is made very clear. Consider using a pictorialization.
6. Choose a rather complicated quotation of at least five sentences for oral presentation to the class. Be prepared to paraphrase your quotation.
7. Choose a controversial speech subject which will permit you to bring a witness to class to offer evidence. Discuss with your witness his time limits and his duties as a speaker. Present your speech, calling on your witness to assist you in at least three different places. You and your witness may

---

[19] Lionel Ruby, *Logic: An Introduction*, 2nd ed. (Philadelphia: J. B. Lippincott Co., 1960), p. 131.

both remain seated, or you may stand and your witness may remain seated.

8. Choose a controversial speech subject which will permit you to record on tape the viewpoints of a well-known person in your area. Present your speech, using the tape recording to support your proposition in at least three different places.

9. Bring to class a primary source document and a secondary source document on the same subject.

10. Choose a proposition for debate. Bring to class evidence which seems to support the proposition but which is (1) immaterial or (2) irrelevant or (3) too involved with emotional side issues.

SUGGESTED READINGS

BENJAMIN, ROBERT L. "Authority: Its Nature and Influence on Oral Argument." Unpublished master's thesis, University of Wisconsin, 1947.

BRITTIN, MARIE ELEANOR. "Concepts of Evidence in Rhetoric." Unpublished doctoral dissertation, Northwestern University, 1949.

JOHNSON, ALLEN. *The Historian and Historical Evidence.* New York: Charles Scribner's Sons, 1926.

LARRABEE, H. A. *Reliable Knowledge.* Boston: Houghton Mifflin Company, 1945.

LUND, F. H. "The Psychology of Belief," *Journal of Abnormal Psychology,* 20 (April 1925, July 1925), 63–81, 174–196.

MAGUIRE, JOHN N. *Evidence, Common Sense and Common Law.* Brooklyn: The Foundation Press, Inc., 1947.

MILLS, GLEN E. *Composing the Speech.* Englewood Cliffs, N.J.: Prentice-Hall, Inc., 1952, pp. 155–162.

MOOS, MALCOLM and BERTRAM KOSLIN. "Prestige, Suggestion, and Political Leadership," *Public Opinion Quarterly,* 16 (Spring 1952), 77–93.

RUSSELL, BERTRAND. *An Inquiry into Meaning and Truth.* New York: W. W. Norton & Company, Inc., 1940.

SCHEFFLER, ISRAEL and C. N. WINSLOW. "Group Position and Attitudes toward Authority," *Journal of Social Psychology,* 32 (November 1950), 177–190.

VINCENT, JOHN M. *Aids to Historical Research.* New York: Appleton-Century-Crofts, 1934.

chapter 10

THE LOGIC
OF ARGUMENT

by Douglas Ehninger

The task of the debater is to confirm or negate a proposition. But not all disputed propositions admit of the same type of proof.

Some propositions may be confirmed or negated by subjecting their truth claims to the test of sense experience or to verification by laboratory methods. "The stove is hot," "The soil contains alkali" are propositions of this sort. A second class may be tested by straight-line reference to a single known fact. If, for example, one wishes to establish the proposition "Ten thousand students are enrolled at X University," the official total as recorded by the registrar provides a sufficient warrant.

A third class of propositions cannot be verified by any of the foregoing methods. "Knowledge is virtue," "The grading system used in most colleges is undesirable," "The minimum wage of factory workers should be increased fifteen cents an hour." In evaluating these propositions sense experience and laboratory tests are of no service, and no reliable conclusion can be based upon a single known fact. Here, unless one is to defer to authority, he must examine many diverse data—as the Scottish rhetorician George Campbell said, assemble "a bundle of independent proofs." [1] Moreover, through a series of steps or stages in reasoning he must show how these seemingly discrete data are related so as to imply a common conclusion.

Reasonable men do not argue about the truth claim of any proposi-

[1] *The Philosophy of Rhetoric* (London, 1776), 1.5.2.

tion which may be tested by sense experience, by laboratory procedures, or by reference to an established fact. To do so not only would be a waste of time, but would show a misunderstanding of the function of argument as a means of testing truth claims. Arguments are properly reserved for disputes concerning propositions of the third class—those propositions which can be verified only by comparing the relative worth of conflicting bodies of independent data.

ARGUMENTATION AS APPLIED LOGIC

Because proofs appropriate to arguable propositions characteristically entail several steps or stages in reasoning rather than proceeding directly from data to claim, they are said to employ *mediate,* as distinguished from *immediate,* inference. The process of arriving at a conclusion is suspended as thought rests at least momentarily upon certain premises which intervene between data and claim.

The discipline which describes and classifies the forms of mediate inference and determines the conditions each form must meet in order to be valid is *logic.* Hence a study of the modes of mediate inference, together with the body of doctrine which surrounds them, may be said to constitute the *logic of argument*—the logic which it is the purpose of this chapter to describe.

FORMS OF INFERENCE COMMONLY EMPLOYED BY THE DEBATER

In which of the forms of mediate inference studied by logic must the debater be skilled? To answer this question, let us review the problems in proof which commonly confront him during the course of a controversy. Without pretending that our list is exhaustive or that each of these problems invariably arises, we may say that more often than not he is called upon to prove the following:

1. Something that may be directly observed is a symptom of a state or condition that is not directly observable. ("The 200 divisions which X nation maintains under arms show that she has aggressive intentions.")

2. (a) Some present condition or circumstance will necessarily produce a given future condition or circumstance ("The present rate of government spending will result in the collapse of our economic system.") or (b) some present condition or circumstance is the necessary product of a prior condition or circumstance. ("Our precarious position in world

affairs today may be traced to mistakes made at Yalta, Potsdam, and Panmunjon.")

3. Certain propositions known or assumed to be true (or false) necessarily imply the truth (or falsity) of a different, but related proposition. ("Since the purpose of education is to train students to meet the problems of life, and since extracurricular activities provide such training in a realistic and stimulating environment, these activities are an essential part of a sound educational system.")

4. What is true of a representative sample taken from among the members of a given class will also be true of additional members of that class. ("Experience in colleges A, H, P, and W has shown that the honor system reduces cheating. Therefore, it would have this same effect in other colleges also.")

5. When two phenomena are closely similar in nature, the second will have the same characteristics or causes or effects as the first. ("Because stricter tests for driver license applicants have reduced the number of fatal automobile accidents in state A, they should likewise reduce the number of fatal automobile accidents in state B.")

6. When item B bears the same relation to item A that item D bears to item C, even though the pairs of items themselves be dissimilar, whatever is asserted concerning D–C may likewise be asserted concerning B–A. ("Just as an overly protective parent who coddles his child [D] undermines the child's initiative and sense of responsibility [C], so a nation which through welfare legislation coddles its citizens [B] undermines their initiative and sense of responsibility [A].")

The forms of mediate inference employed in meeting the six problems in proof just outlined we shall here refer to as argument from sign, argument from causal relation, argument from rhetorical syllogism, argument from generalization, argument from parallel case, and argument from analogy.

Let us examine each of these arguments in turn, inquiring into the nature of the thought relationship upon which it is based and the conditions under which that thought relationship may be said to yield a valid conclusion.

ARGUMENT FROM SIGN

When he undertakes to establish or negate a proposition, the debater who proceeds systematically first seeks to make clear those facts, conditions, or circumstances out of which the proposition grows or concerning which it is a summary judgment. For example, when arguing a proposition of fact ("Jones cheated on the examination."), he begins by describing the various actions and coincidences upon which the suspicion is founded. In a proposition of value ("National party conventions are an undesirable method of selecting candidates for President.") he opens by recounting the evils and deficiences allegedly present in the convention procedure. In a proposition of policy ("Our foreign aid program should be discontinued.") he first examines what the program consists of, what is wrong with it as it stands, and so on.

THE FUNCTION OF SIGN IN PROOF

Sometimes the facts, conditions, and circumstances with which the debater is concerned are overt, and may, therefore, be observed at first hand. Thus, if he were attempting to show that the school buildings in a particular city needed repair, he could point to broken windows, leaky roofs, and falling plaster.

Let us suppose, however, the debater wishes to show that the populations of countries behind the Iron Curtain are restive under Russian domination. The restlessness of an entire population cannot be directly observed, nor can mental or emotional dissatisfaction be seen as one may see a dilapidated school building.

Under such circumstances, how is the debater to proceed? He must single out certain observable indications or symptoms of unrest, and upon the basis of these symptoms attempt to prove that the alleged condition exists. In so doing, he reasons much as does the physician who is unable to see measles directly, but who, from the presence of a rash, fever, and other usual indications, infers the presence of the disease.

ARGUMENT FROM SIGN DEFINED

When the debater uses a symptom or outward mark to prove the existence of a state or condition that itself cannot be observed, he is said to be arguing from *sign*. Since in such instances his purpose is to supply knowledge or information, an argument from sign is a *ratio cognoscendi* —a way of knowing.

SIGN DISTINGUISHED FROM CAUSE

As a *ratio cognoscendi*, an argument from sign answers the question "What?" not the question "Why?" In the foregoing examples we did not ask why Jones cheated, or why there are evils in the convention system of nominating presidents, or why our foreign aid program is defective, any more than the doctor when making his diagnosis asks why the child has measles. Our concern was limited to establishing the existence of a given fact or condition.

Similarly, when we say someone has died because the flag is at half-mast or dinner is ready because the bell is ringing, we are only pointing to indications or signs by means of which these facts may be known. The reason for the man's death may have been heart failure or cancer, or he may have been struck by an automobile; the reason dinner is ready is that the cook has labored in the kitchen; the child may have caught measles because playing in the rain made him unusually susceptible. These, however, are quite different matters. They fall, not under the head of *sign*, but under the head of *cause*. Consequently, they will be discussed in the following section.

Unfortunately, the difference between sign and cause is not always easy to grasp at first trial. There are two reasons why this is so. First, at one point sign and cause coincide, since among the reasons for our knowing a thing is an awareness of its cause. Thus, triangular ripples in the water are both a sign that a boat has passed and are also the effect resulting from the boat's having agitated the water. Second, in English we commonly employ *because, hence,* and similar words to express both relationships.[2]

The point to bear in mind is that while in some instances—such as that of the boat passing through the water—cause and sign coincide, this coincidence is relatively rare. Usually cause and sign provide different types of information. Through sign we learn something about the condition of a person or thing; through cause we are informed concerning the reason for that condition. If a man looks thinner, we know he has lost weight (sign). The *cause* of the loss, however, may have been illness or deliberate dieting. From his appearance alone we cannot determine which factor produced the change.

RELIABILITY OF SIGNS

Signs vary greatly in reliability. Some invariably accompany the condition of which they are a symptom and may, therefore, be taken as a certain indication of the existence of that condition. Such signs we call *infallible*. ("He has a fever; therefore, he is ill.") Others usually, but not always, accompany the condition and, consequently, are only more or less probable indications of its existence. Signs of this sort are said to be *falli-*

[2] Richard Whately, *Elements of Rhetoric* (London, 1828), 1.2.3.; James H. McBurney, James M. O'Neill, and Glen E. Mills, *Argumentation and Debate* (New York: The Macmillan Company, 1951), p. 99.

ble. ("Falling wage rates in the basic industries show that the inflationary spiral has run its course.")

In short, the regularity with which a symptom accompanies a condition determines its reliability as a sign of the existence of that condition. The more nearly invariable the relationship, the more certain the sign.

THE USE OF SIGNS IN PROOF

When employing argument from sign the following considerations should be borne in mind:

1. *That which is alleged to be a sign of a particular state or condition must bear a necessary relation to that state or condition.*

To interpret mounting juvenile delinquency as a sign that the American people are reading fewer books, or to interpret decreased attendance at baseball games as a sign that they are going to the movies more frequently may in each case lead to a faulty conclusion since the relationships asserted to exist between these phenomena are not necessary and inevitable. Alternative interpretations of the data would yield equally probable claims.

Similarly, it would be unwarranted to consider a snub nose a reliable sign of intelligence because Socrates reputedly had such a nose. Such an assumption would accept as essential and therefore universal a relationship that was merely coincidental.

2. *That which at one time or under one set of circumstances may be a valid sign of a state or condition is not necessarily a valid sign of that state or condition at another time or under altered circumstances.*

In 1910, when automobiles were few and costly, car ownership may have provided a reliable sign of wealth. Today automobiles are numerous and, considered in relation to the income of the average individual, much less of a luxury. Therefore, the ownership of an automobile is no longer a reliable sign that a man is wealthy.

3. *While occasionally a single sign may be sufficient to establish the existence of a state or condition, usually the corroboration of several signs is necessary in order to establish its existence.*

A competent physician would not base his diagnosis of a serious disease upon a single symptom. Nor will the responsible debater contend the world is on the brink of war simply because one nation has massed three additional divisions on a neighbor's frontier. In matters as complex as human disease or war the corroboration of a number of signs is required if we are to derive a reliable conclusion.

ARGUMENT FROM CAUSAL RELATION

Having proved a certain thing to be so, the debater's next responsibility is to make clear *why* it is so. What external forces or inner motives led Jones to cheat? How are we to account for the presence of evils in the party convention system? Why is our foreign aid program failing? These questions must now command attention.

IMPORTANCE OF CAUSAL RELATION IN PROOF

The importance of passing beyond description and advancing a reason that accounts for the existence of an alleged state or condition is illustrated by the law's insistence that a charge of murder may not be proved until a motive has been shown. Mere symptoms or signs of the deed are not in themselves sufficient. If proof is to proceed beyond reasonable doubt a cause for the act must be established.

For a like reason, the debater who makes a blanket condemnation of an existing institution or policy must do more than show that evils are present within it. The drastic charge which he brings cannot be justified unless he proves that these evils are embedded in the very plan and structure of the institution or policy—that this plan or structure causes them. On the other hand, the debater who argues for the adoption of a new policy must, by the logic of the situation, prove his proposed system will act as a cause which mitigates or removes existing evils.

ARGUMENT FROM CAUSAL RELATION DEFINED

Whereas an argument from sign is a *ratio cognoscendi* (a way of knowing), an argument from causal relation is a *ratio essendi*, a reason that accounts for a thing's existing or being so. Instead of answering the question "What?" it answers the question "Why?"

Argument from causal relation assumes that phenomena occur in an invariable sequence. When one phenomenon is present, another will necessarily appear; when one is absent, the other cannot appear. That is, item B does not just happen to follow item A. Rather, A is the generator or producer of B, and B is the inevitable result of A.

Because phenomena are assumed to be invariably connected, argument from causal relation may start at either terminal of the thought process. We may begin by noting the generator, and from its existence infer the existence of that which it is certain to generate; or we may begin by noting the result generated and work backward to the factor that was essential to its production. In the first instance we are reasoning from *cause to effect*; in the second, from *effect to cause*.

As an example of this two-way process, let us suppose that during the spring and early summer the region in which we live has a considerable amount of rainfall. Because of this precipitation we expect crops throughout the area to be lush and plentiful. Here our reasoning proceeds from a known cause to an assumed effect.

Later in the season, however, we drive through a distant state, and observe that the farmers are bringing in an abundant harvest. Consequently, without any direct information concerning the weather conditions that prevailed the preceding spring, we infer that this region also enjoyed frequent rains. In this instance our reasoning follows the opposite direction, and moves from a known effect to an assumed cause. The type of thought relationship involved in both inferences is, however, the same, since both assume an inevitable connection between two phenomena, the first of which produces the second.

USE OF CAUSAL RELATION IN PROOF

To have value as proof, an argument from causal relation must meet three conditions.

1. *That which is assumed to be a cause (or effect) must be a true cause (or effect) of the phenomenon in question.* One phenomenon may follow another sequentially, but have no necessary connection with it. Such a relationship is coincidental or casual rather than causal. For example, if in 1960 a city adopted the commission form of government, and if in 1961 a tornado damaged much property in that city, we could hardly maintain that the two events were causally connected. The second merely happened to follow the first and was in no sense produced by it.

2. *The alleged cause must be adequate to produce the alleged effect.* The mustering-out pay given discharged service men at the close of World War II, while it had an inflationary effect, cannot be regarded as the sole cause, or even as one of the more important causes, of the serious postwar inflation and of the rising price level of subsequent years. These allotments in and of themselves were insufficient to produce such a result.

3. *No intervening cause may operate to prevent the alleged effect.* Advances in medical science have greatly increased life expectancy. At the same time, the competitive pressure and stepped-up tempo of our culture are causing an increase in the incidence of the so-called "stress diseases." Hence, an intervening cause operates to prevent our receiving the full benefit of recent medical advances.

DISCOVERING CAUSAL RELATIONS

In the complex social, economic, political, and moral problems with which the debater deals, the tracing of valid causal relations is, at best, a difficult task. Not only do such problems usually arise out of a number of co-acting causes, but they nearly always produce multiple, and often seemingly unrelated, effects. Moreover, competing and intervening causes are everywhere present.

As an aid to discovering causal relations the debater may, therefore, find it useful to apply five principles developed by the English philosopher John Stuart Mill and sometimes called Mill's Experimental Methods. Limitations of space prevent our doing more than stating these principles here. In considerable measure, however, the Methods may be understood without supplementary explanation, and the student who is interested in exploring them more fully may refer directly to Mill's *A System of Logic* (vol. 1, pp. 451–460).

The Method of Agreement

If two or more instances of the phenomenon under investigation have only one circumstance in common, the circumstance in which alone all the instances agree, is the cause (or effect) of the given phenomenon.

The Method of Difference

If an instance in which the phenomenon under investigation occurs and an instance in which it does not occur have every circumstance in common save one, that one occurring in the former; the circumstance in which, alone, the two instances differ is the effect, or the cause, or an indispensable part of the cause, of the phenomenon.

The Joint Method of Agreement and Difference

If two or more instances in which the phenomenon occurs have only one circumstance in common, while two or more instances in which it does not occur have nothing in common save the absence of that circumstance; the circumstance in which alone the two sets of instances differ is the effect, or the cause, or an indispensable part of the cause, of the phenomenon.

The Method of Concomitant Variation

Whatever phenomenon varies in any manner whenever another phenomenon varies in some particular manner, is either a cause or an effect of that phenomenon, or is connected with it through some fact of causation.

The Method of Residues

> Subtract from any phenomenon such part as is known by previous inductions to be the effect of certain antecedents, and the residue of the phenomenon is the effect of the remaining antecedents.

ARGUMENT FROM RHETORICAL SYLLOGISM

Probabilities or signs expressed in propositional form furnish premises for the type of argument we here call *rhetorical syllogism*.

THE NATURE OF SYLLOGISTIC INFERENCE

As defined by Aristotle, a syllogism is "discourse in which, certain things being stated, something other than what is stated follows of necessity from their being so." [3]

To understand what Aristotle meant by this statement consider these two propositions:

> Every American is patriotic
> Jones is an American

When these propositions are combined, what necessarily follows from them? Obviously, a third proposition which asserts that *Jones is patriotic*.

But, admitting this fact, it still remains to ask why the third proposition follows from the first two. Let us study the matter more closely. Almost immediately we note that while each of the first two propositions, considered by itself, contains two terms, between them these propositions contain a total of only three terms—*American, patriotic,* and *Jones*. Moreover, one of these terms—*American*—appears twice.

Having made this observation, let us next examine how the term *American* is related to the other two terms—that is, to *patriotic* and *Jones*. First, we see that the attribute of patriotism is something every American is asserted to possess. Second, we see that Jones is to be numbered among those persons who are Americans. In other words, he is included in a group or class of individuals, all of whom are asserted to be patriotic. This relationship may be illustrated diagrammatically.

But, as this diagram stands, what is the use of the middle circle which represents the group of persons called Americans? Clearly it has no function and does not, in fact, even need to be present. Since the small-

---

[3] *Prior Analytics,* 24ᵇ.20.

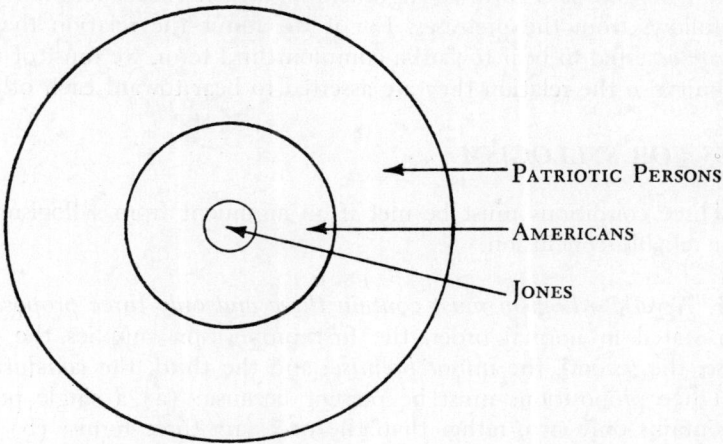

est circle representing Jones lies within the largest circle representing patriotic persons, we could erase the middle circle and still confidently assert that Jones falls into the class of men and women who are patriotic.

But would such an assertion have been possible if at some stage in our reasoning we had not also asserted that Jones is an American? Remember that to begin with all we knew was that every American is patriotic. Suppose, for example, Jones were a Frenchman or a Russian. Could we then have declared that Jones is patriotic? Obviously, we could not, for without the specific information that Jones is an American we should not know whether to place him inside or outside the circle of patriotic persons. Therefore, upon the basis of the given data, we could have inferred nothing concerning his patriotism. Instead, our conclusion grew directly out of our knowledge that Jones was an American.

Yet, interestingly enough, this crucial term *American*, although it appeared twice in the two original propositions, is not present in the conclusion. It has dropped entirely out of the argument.

Before it disappeared, however, the term *American* performed a vital function. It established a relationship between two previously unrelated terms—*patriotic* and *Jones*. It was only by first equating *American* with *Jones* that we were able to make an assertion concerning Jones' patriotism. Stated more formally, the term *American* served as mediator, or common middle ground, through which the terms *Jones* and *patriotic* were compared and their connection established.

A syllogism, then, may conveniently be thought of as a means for establishing the relation that two terms bear to each other by determining the relation that each bears to a common or so-called *middle term*.

Moreover, we are now in a position to understand why Aristotle defined syllogism as a form of argument in which the conclusion necessarily follows from the premises. For if we admit the relation that two terms are asserted to bear toward a common third term, we must of necessity admit also the relation they are asserted to bear toward each other.

RULES FOR SYLLOGISM

Three conditions must be met if an argument from syllogism is to yield a reliable conclusion.

1. *A valid syllogism must contain three and only three propositions.* When stated in normal order, the first proposition supplies the *major premise;* the second, the *minor premise;* and the third, the *conclusion.*

Three propositions must be present because: (a) a single proposition contains only two, rather than the necessary three terms; (b) when more than two propositions stand as premises, they will either contain among themselves more than three terms or at least one of the propositions will be redundant. In neither of the foregoing instances may a syllogistic conclusion be derived.

2. *A valid syllogism must contain three and only three terms.* From only two terms no conclusion may be derived syllogistically because a common basis for comparison is lacking. The presence of four or more terms likewise makes mediation through a common middle term impossible.

The impossibility of drawing a valid conclusion when four or more terms are present may readily be seen in this example:

> All *dogs* chase *cats*
> *Dobbin* is a *pony*

Sometimes, however, it is difficult to determine exactly how many terms are stated in the premises, since the same word may carry a double or unspecified meaning. Here, for instance, is a syllogism which might on the surface appear to have only three terms but which in reality has four because the term *animal* is used in two different senses:

> No animal has the power of rational speech
> Man is an animal
> Therefore, man does not have the power of rational speech

3. *The term which appears twice in the premises (that is, the middle term) must be fully distributed in at least one of the premises.* A term is distributed when it refers to *all* of the individual items which are de-

noted by it. Hence, a distributed term is actually preceded by the word *all, every, no,* or some similar word, or the idea expressed by one of these words is implied. Unless such a word is stated or implied, the syllogism will have an undistributed middle term, and a necessary conclusion may not be inferred, although a probable conclusion is sometimes warranted.

From these two premises, for example, it would be impossible to know for certain whether Smith owned a car, although the probability of such ownership may be strong:

> Most students at X University own cars
> Smith is a student at X University

On the other hand, the following syllogism clearly yields an invalid conclusion because as stated, the middle term *vertebrates* is not distributed so as to refer to all vertebrates:

> All fish are vertebrates
> All birds are vertebrates
> Therefore, all birds are fish

COROLLARIES

From these basic rules of syllogism may be derived five corollaries which further describe the conditions of valid syllogistic inference.

1. *No conclusion may be derived from two particular premises.* Unless one of the two premises of a syllogism exhibits a distributed term, it is grammatically impossible to assert that a given individual or class falls within another class. Under such conditions the principle of *inclusion* cannot be honored, and, as a result, no relationship is established between the major and minor premises.

2. *If one premise is particular, the conclusion must be particular.* Because the middle term, which must always be distributed, does not appear in the conclusion, the total number of distributed terms in the conclusion will be one less than the total number of distributed terms in the premises. But if one of the two premises is particular, the premises between them contain only one distributed term (the middle term). Hence, the conclusion must be particular.

3. *No conclusion may be derived from two negative premises.* Two negative premises state a relationship, not of inclusion, but of mutual exclusion. (No Floridian shovels snow. No Texan is a Floridian.) Obviously, therefore, no syllogistic conclusion is possible.

4. *If one premise is negative, the conclusion must be negative.* A

negative major premise will result in a negative conclusion, since its predicate (*the so-called major term*) automatically becomes the predicate of the conclusion.

> Americans *do not believe in mob rule.*
> John is an American.
> Therefore, John *does not believe in mob rule.*

A negative minor premise results in a negative conclusion because its subject (*the so-called minor term*), which automatically becomes the subject of the conclusion, is, by statement, excluded from the class of phenomena concerning which the major premise makes an assertion.

> All men are (all) rational creatures
> A *cat* is not a man
> Therefore, *a cat* is not a rational creature

5. *No term may be distributed in the conclusion that is not distributed in one of the premises.* Since the conclusion grows directly out of the premises, no more may legitimately be asserted about a term in the conclusion than has already been asserted about it in the premises.

FORMAL VERSUS MATERIAL VALIDITY

As we have already suggested, a syllogism may be regarded as a formula by means of which two independent terms are compared through the office of a common middle term. As is true of most formulas, the syllogism is indifferent toward the subject matter with which it deals. Consequently, it does not guarantee the material validity either of the premise from which it starts or of the conclusion which it produces.

According to the terms of our formula, we have a valid syllogism when we say:

> All automobiles are driven by steam
> The Ford is an automobile
> The Ford is driven by steam

Yet we do not, of course, have a true or materially valid conclusion.

The problems of formal and material validity must be divorced when evaluating the probative force of syllogistic inference. Formal validity may be tested by the rules and corollaries described in the preceding paragraphs; material validity must be subjected to those far different tests by which one determines whether what he says accords with reality.

SPECIAL FORMS OF SYLLOGISM

Thus far our discussion of syllogism has been concerned only with propositions which take the form of categorical assertions: Every American is patriotic. All fish are vertebrates, and so on. We must now recognize that upon occasion the debater also employs hypothetical and disjunctive propositions as the premises for syllogisms. Such propositions standing as premises require special consideration and an understanding of additional rules and principles.

1. THE HYPOTHETICAL SYLLOGISM. The major premise of a hypothetical syllogism is a hypothetical proposition. "If John passes the examination he will celebrate." As such, the premise states not what is known or what has happened, but what will happen provided prescribed conditions are fulfilled. Hence, the relationship between the terms, instead of being set and certain, is tentative and conditional. This tentativeness introduces two important limitations that must be observed in drawing conclusions:

a. *A minor premise that denies the antecedent of the major premise does not yield a certain conclusion.* Examine this pair of propositions:

If John *passes the examination* he will celebrate
John *will not pass* the examination

From these premises alone it is impossible to know for certain that John will not celebrate, for all we are given as data is the assurance that he will do so provided he passes. To be able to determine what he will do if he does not pass would require additional information.

b. *A minor premise that affirms the consequent of the major premise does not yield a certain conclusion.* Consider these propositions as premises:

If John passes the examination *he will celebrate*
John *will celebrate*

Here our conclusion is not certain because, as reflection will make evident, the consequent named may well result from antecedents other than the one stated. For instance, the very fact that he fails may motivate John "to drown his sorrows."

2. THE DISJUNCTIVE SYLLOGISM. The major premise of a disjunctive syllogism states alternative possibilities. If the minor premise denies

one of these alternatives, the conclusion affirms the other. If, on the contrary, the minor premise affirms one of the alternatives, the conclusion denies the other.

> Either John will pass or he will fail
> John *will not pass*
> Therefore, he *will* fail

> Either John will pass or he will fail
> John *will pass*
> Therefore, he *will not* fail

For a disjunctive syllogism to produce a valid conclusion, the major premise must meet two requirements:

a. *The alternatives stated in the major premise must be all inclusive.* The proposition "Michigan will either win or lose next week's football game against Northwestern" would not provide a suitable premise, since a third possibility—that of a tie score—is overlooked.

b. *The alternatives stated in the major premise must be mutually exclusive.* From this disjunction "Either John is a student or he is a Republican" no valid syllogistic conclusion is possible, since John may, of course, be both a student and a Republican at the same time.

ARGUMENT FROM GENERALIZATION

Standing both as independent modes of proof and as means for further supporting the conclusions derived from rhetorical syllogisms are two forms of argument which employ as premises "one or more, known, individual objects or instances, of a certain class as a fair *sample* . . . and consequently draw an inference from them respecting either the whole class, or other, less known individuals of it."[4] When a number of such items are used as a sample for inferring a conclusion concerning the class as a whole or a majority of the members of the class—that is, when reasoning proceeds from some to more—we have *argument from generalization*. When, on the other hand, the sample taken as a premise consists of a single instance and the conclusion also concerns a single instance—that is, when reasoning moves from particular to particular—we have *argument from parallel case*. Although these two types of argument are essentially similar in that each uses "a fair sample as a premise," in the interest of clarity we shall discuss them separately.

[4] Whately, *op. cit.*, 1.2.7.

NATURE OF ARGUMENT FROM GENERALIZATION

The process of inferring a more general conclusion from the examination of a number of specific instances or cases involves three separate steps. First, certain items, assumed to be representative members of a given class, are selected at random. Second, these items are examined critically, and if they are found to exhibit a common character a necessary connection is assumed to exist among them. Third, upon the basis of this assumed connection, a more inclusive judgment concerning all or a majority of the members of the class is made.

For example, in investigating student attitude toward essay-type examinations, a debater selects at random 500 names from among the 10,000 listed in his college directory. Assuming that these individuals constitute a fair cross-section of the student body, he questions each person on the matter and summarizes the results. His figures show that, with thirty-six exceptions, the students interviewed disliked essay-type examinations. Then, making the further assumption that these data are not the result of chance but are connected in the sense that they are specific manifestations of a generally prevailing attitude, the debater concludes that the great majority, if not all of the students on campus, are of a like opinion.

The point frequently overlooked is that an essential step in deriving this conclusion was the postulating of a necessary connection among the 500 judgments recorded. Yet, had these judgments not fitted together into a general system or framework of relationship, they would have remained a collection of isolated facts, from which it would be impossible to draw a conclusion concerning additional members of the student body. Inference did not proceed *immediately* from the given individual facts to a general conclusion, but was *mediate*, since between data and conclusion there intervened an essential third step in which the separate pieces of information were organized according to a general principle.

USE OF ARGUMENT FROM GENERALIZATION

The probative value of an argument from generalization is determined by the degree to which it meets each of the following conditions:

1. *The instances used as premises must be selected entirely at random.* If one wished to prove that the individual states are not able to support sound systems of public education without federal aid, he could easily make out a case by citing as evidence only the so-called "poorer" states of the South. An opponent, however, could just as easily prove that federal aid is not needed by citing instances from a selected group of the rela-

tively "richer" states of the North. In neither case would the resulting argument from generalization be acceptable to a discerning listener; for he would immediately realize that, instead of selecting their data at random from the country as a whole, the contending parties had deliberately chosen figures calculated to support the claims they wished to advance.

2. *The instances used as premises must be sufficient in number to warrant the conclusion.* Perhaps the major danger in argument from generalization is drawing a conclusion from an insufficient number of instances —that is, generalizing hastily. Just because three or four of the top-flight debaters in a particular state also happen to be skilled actors, one is not justified in concluding that all or most good debaters are also good actors. Nor because a few labor unions appear to be dominated by Communists may it be asserted that all unions are so dominated. In neither instance are the cases offered as evidence sufficient in number to support so sweeping a generalization.

It is impossible to lay down a specific rule concerning the number of instances that are required before a general conclusion will be valid. That number will not only vary considerably for different types of subject matter, but will also, in large measure, be determined by whether the audience to which the argument is addressed is friendly, neutral, or hostile toward the debater's central contentions. The only safe procedure is always to present instances in abundance, and then stand ready to offer still more if the resulting claim is questioned.

3. *The instances used as premises must be germane to the claim.* This is another way of saying that the data used as premises must provide valid signs or causes of the claim that is inferred from them. Thus, the fact that a large number of students get good grades without studying long hours does not prove that avoiding study *causes* good grades. Similarly, although thousands of healthy persons are heavy smokers, chain smoking may not be taken as a reliable *sign* of health. In neither instance do the data establish the claim they are alleged to establish. While they may prove a different claim, they are not germane to the conclusion drawn.

4. *Negative instances must be accounted for.* In developing an argument from generalization the debater will frequently encounter one or more cases which run counter to the general rule. Such exceptions are called *negative instances.*

Isolated negative instances may not invalidate a general claim. Such instances must, however, be explained before the claim will be accepted. For example, if it can be shown that the carburetor in Harry's car is improperly adjusted, a generalization may still safely be made concerning the small amount of gasoline normally consumed in cars of this make and model.

ARGUMENT FROM PARALLEL CASE

On the desk before Mary are two unopened packages of Xerxes cigarettes. They are identical in size, shape, weight, and outward appearance.

Mary opens one of the packages and carefully examines its contents. She notes the texture of the paper in which the cigarettes are wrapped and the cut, color, and odor of the tobacco. She determines how firmly the cigarettes are packed.

Then, upon the basis of her exhaustive examination of the contents of the opened package, Mary confidently infers that the contents of the unopened package are in all respects similar.

Here, as in argument from generalization, reasoning is based upon a representative sample. But the sample, instead of consisting of a number of members of a class selected at random, consists of a single member. Moreover, in place of a conclusion concerning most or all of the members of a class, the conclusion is limited to another single class member. In argument from parallel case, therefore, reasoning moves not from particular to general, not from some to more, but from particular to particular. It both begins and terminates with a single representative instance.

ARGUMENT FROM PARALLEL CASE DEFINED

Formally defined, parallel case is that kind of argument in which we attempt to prove that because two phenomena are alike in all relevant observable respects, they will also be alike in one or more additional respects known to belong to the first, but not yet belonging, or known to belong, to the second. Because a plan of delayed rushing has worked at College, A, and because in all relevant respects College B is similar to College A, such a plan would also work well at College B. Because the system of publicly supported medical care used in Sweden appears to have damaged the morale of many Swedish doctors, such a system would have a like effect were it adopted in the United States. These examples are typical arguments from parallel cases.

In order to have probative value, an argument from parallel case must meet two requirements. First, the instance used as a premise must be exhaustively examined. Because this instance alone furnishes the data upon which the conclusion is based, anything less than an exhaustive examination—an examination which reveals all of the instance's facets and explores all of its potentialities and limitations—cannot be trusted as a foundation for inference. Second, the argument must focus comparison on those particular points of similarity which are crucial to the conclusion sought. For example, the fact that Jane and Mary are strikingly similar in appearance does not warrant the claim that they are of equal intelligence, since appearance is not a relevant consideration so far as mental ability is concerned. Nor, because residents of the United States and Great Britain have a similar culture and speak the same language, may we infer that they are alike in their attitudes toward a monarchic form of government.

In argument from parallel case, then, we are concerned not with similarity or difference in gross, but with those specific points of likeness which bear directly upon the claim advanced. Two phenomena may differ in many ways and yet possess one crucial point of resemblance which itself is sufficient to support a valid inference.

PARALLEL CASE AS PROOF

Inferable from the preceding discussion is the basic rule the debater must observe when employing parallel case as proof.

In order to derive a valid conclusion by argument from parallel case, the relevant points of similarity between the cases in question must outweigh the relevant points of difference.

In the realm of human affairs one rarely finds events or situations that are parallel in all details. It is, however, imperative that the phenomena brought into comparison be identical or closely similar in those aspects that bear most directly upon the claim advanced. In proportion as such point-to-point similarity exists, argument from parallel case will have value as proof; in proportion as this similarity is lacking, its proof value will be correspondingly reduced.

ARGUMENT FROM ANALOGY

Like argument from parallel case, argument from analogy involves the recognition of a similarity between two phenomena. Here, however, the relationship, instead of being direct and explicit, is indirect or implied.

Recall the example of analogy presented on page 171: "Just as an overly protective parent who coddles his child undermines the child's initiative and sense of responsibility, so a nation which through welfare legislation coddles its citizens undermines their initiative and sense of responsibility." No attempt is made to establish a direct comparison between the parent and the nation, or between the child and the citizen. Rather, what the argument says is, "As the overly protective parent is to the child, so is the welfare state to its citizens." Or more explicitly, "As the attitude of the overly protective parent affects the child, so does the attitude of the welfare state affect the citizen." What is expressed is merely a ratio or resemblance of relationships; as B is to A, so D is to C.

Because argument from analogy employs a resemblance of relationships rather than a direct literal resemblance, unlike argument from parallel case, it may cross the species line indiscriminately, bringing into comparison phenomena which are themselves quite different. To take Whately's famous example, an egg and a seed are analogous; for although they are not in themselves at all alike, they bear a common relation, the one "to the parent bird . . . and her future nestling," the other "to the young and old plant." [5]

When we compare the head of a government with a captain of a ship or say that changing leaders during a crisis is like swapping horses in the middle of a stream, we are reasoning analogically. Although the items compared are essentially different, each stands in such relationship to its respective referent that it may be regarded as figuratively similar to its counterpart.

USE OF ARGUMENT FOR ANALOGY

Because it establishes only an indirect or figurative relationship, argument from analogy standing alone seldom supplies strong proof for a claim. It may, however, provide a valuable supplement to other types of proof, and often is useful as a means of illustration or of expressing contentions in a striking and memorable fashion.

The test of analogy, unlike the test of parallel case, is not how heavily the essential points of similarity outweigh the essential points of difference, but whether the relationships asserted to exist between the two pairs of items involved in the analogy (B and A, and C and D) are, indeed, alike.

SUMMARY

The forms of inference which the debater most commonly employs in deriving conclusions mediately from data are sign, cause, rhetorical syllogism, generalization, parallel case, and analogy.

A sign is a symptom by which one infers the existence of a state or condition that cannot be directly observed. Valid inference from sign requires a necessary, rather than accidental, connection between condition and symptom, a specific time or place reference, and, usually, the corroboration of other signs.

[5] *Ibid.*

A cause is a reason that accounts for a phenomenon's existence. In a valid causal relationship the assumed cause (or effect) is the true cause (or effect), is adequate to produce the alleged result, and is not vitiated by the intervention of a countercause.

A rhetorical syllogism is a formula for establishing the relationship two terms bear to each other by determining the relationship each bears to a common third, or middle, term. A valid syllogism consists of three and only three propositions which contain among themselves three and only three terms. Moreover, the common middle term must be fully distributed. Special forms of the syllogism have additional rules peculiar to themselves. In a hypothetical syllogism a minor premise that denies the antecedent or affirms the consequent does not yield a certain conclusion; in a disjunctive syllogism the stated alternatives must be both all-inclusive and mutually exclusive.

In argument from generalization, a number of items from a given class are taken as a representative sample and used as a basis for inferring a conclusion concerning additional members of the same class. Special dangers in this form of inference are the use of nontypical instances as premises, hasty generalization, the employment of instances not germane to the conclusion, and failure to account for negative instances.

Parallel case is that form of inference in which we assume that if two phenomena are alike in all observable respects, they also will be alike in certain additional respects already known to belong to the first, but not yet belonging, or known to belong to the second. The crucial test of reasoning from parallel case is to ask whether the essential points of similarity between the phenomena concerned outweigh the essential points of difference.

Analogy is similar to parallel case, except that here the relationship between phenomena, instead of being direct and explicit, is indirect or implied. Analogy expresses not a literal and immediate relationship, but a ratio or resemblance of relationships (as B is to A, so D is to C). The test applicable to this form of inference is to inquire whether the relationships asserted to exist between the two pairs of items involved in the analogy (B–A, C–D) are, indeed, alike.

EXERCISES

Identify and evaluate each of the following arguments:

1. John must be a straight-A student. Every time I see him he has an armful of books.

2. Candidate Smith will make the best mayor because he is the most honest politician in town.
3. The Giants' showing in their first five training games indicates that they are a cinch to win the pennant this year.
4. Not only is war a great evil in itself, but it always has serious consequences in the form of economic depression and social degeneration.
5. Unusually heavy registration figures reported from throughout the nation show that voters desire a change in administrations.
6. Whatever has no parts is simple. The soul has no parts. The soul, therefore, is simple.
7. I am sure that Henry is interested in public affairs. After all, he is a college graduate.
8. The failure of prohibition, which was an attempt to legislate habits and attitudes, shows that compulsory F.E.P.C. legislation would be unsuccesful.
9. Since life is a game, he who would play it well must learn the rules.
10. Tyrants always come to an evil end, as the careers of Caesar, Napoleon, and Hitler clearly demonstrate.
11. Cremo hair dressing must be a fine product. Just see how its sales have increased during the last two years.
12. Just as a fertile soil produces an abundant harvest, so does a fertile, active mind produce a crop of worthwhile ideas.
13. Since Mary is a registered Democrat and most Democrats voted for Kennedy in 1960, we may assume that Mary did so.
14. Blessed are the merciful, for they shall obtain mercy.
15. An expanded program of boys' clubs and supervised recreational activities for young people would reduce juvenile delinquency in Cleveland because it did so in Detroit.

SUGGESTED READINGS

BAIRD, A. CRAIG. *Argumentation, Discussion, and Debate.* New York: McGraw-Hill Book Company, Inc., 1950. Chaps. 10, 13.

BLACK, MAX. *Critical Thinking.* Englewood Cliffs, N.J.: Prentice-Hall, Inc., 1946. Part I, and Part III, Chaps. 15, 16.

CHASE, STUART. *Guides to Straight Thinking.* New York: Harper & Row, Publishers, 1956.

EHNINGER, DOUGLAS, and WAYNE BROCKRIEDE. *Decision by Debate.* New York: Dodd, Mead & Co., 1963. Chaps. 8, 10, 11.

EWBANK, HENRY L., and J. JEFFERY AUER. *Discussion and Debate.* New York: Appleton-Century-Crofts, Inc., 1951. Chap. 8.

McBURNEY, JAMES H., JAMES M. O'NEILL, and GLEN E. MILLS. *Argumentation and Debate.* New York: The Macmillan Company, 1951. Chaps. 8, 9.

chapteR 11

~~~~~~~~~~~~~~~~~~~~~~~~~~~~~~~~~~~~~~

REFUTATION
AND REBUTTAL

by Ralph Y. McGinnis

Whenever two opposing cases on a given issue fail to meet, the listeners or readers tend to discredit both cases. The argumentative processes of attack and defense (with evidence, assumptions, and logical reasoning) determine whether any argument presented is finally either accepted or rejected.

The words *refutation* and *rebuttal* are often confused. Even experienced debaters occasionally use one for the other. If the words were synonymous, then such interchangeability would be justified. However, a debater or anyone engaged in an argument often wants his listeners to understand explicitly whether he is tearing down an argument or rebuilding one. Thus, it is important that the two words, which represent these processes, be used in their proper meanings so that the listener or reader will know beyond any doubt whether an argument is being attacked or defended from attack. Therefore, the following definitions should be kept clearly in mind.

Refutation is the process of attacking, weakening, tearing down, or destroying the argument of an opponent.

Rebuttal is the process of defending, strengthening, and rebuilding arguments, previously expounded, after they have been attacked by an opponent.

J—Methods of Refutation

At a public hearing on the patriotism and loyalty of some public official, a speaker might assert:

We know that all members of the American Legion are patriotic. But this man, who is a veteran, is not even a member of the American Legion. Therefore we must doubt his patriotism.

The crowd might be impressed. But the critical thinker would detect a flaw in the speaker's argument. The process of detecting, exposing, and explaining the weaknesses and fallacies in an opponent's argument is the process of refutation.

APPROACHES TO REFUTATION

There are five general types of attack in approaching the problem of refuting the arguments of an opponent. They are:

Attacks on the interpretation of the proposition
Attacks on material fallacies
Attacks on formal fallacies
Attacks on special fallacies (stratagems)
Special methods of refutation

There is no special order in which these attacks must be used in making refutations. However, identification of the types of attack that you are making when the refutation is begun aids in clarifying the whole refutation process.

ATTACKS ON THE INTERPRETATION OF THE PROPOSITION

Very often two or more persons argue a proposition on entirely different grounds. The arguments of each may be valid, but if they do not clash there is no real argument.

ATTACKING THE ANALYSIS OF THE PROPOSITION

The main issues for most formal debates have been identified as the issues of *need, plan, practicability,* and *desirability* (or *beneficiality*). It is the responsibility of the advocate of any given proposal to analyze the proposition in terms of the major issues and the arguments subordinate to each issue. If the proponent of a proposition (the *affirmative*) does not present an adequate analysis, then the opponent (or *negative*) has the right to challenge the affirmative's analysis. For example, if the affirmative should choose to argue only the *need* for changing the status quo (or even a *need* for the proposal) and ignore the issues of *plan* and *practicability*, then the negative would have good grounds for challenging the affirmative's limited analysis. Sound negative strategy might be to admit the *need* and argue the impracticability of the *plan*. In such a situation there would appear little or no clash between the two cases.

Occasionally an affirmative speaker will attempt to argue a case only on the "philosophy" of the proposal. Depending upon the proposition being argued, the affirmative may successfully maintain the debate at that level. However, the negative usually can make a strong indictment of their opponents for keeping the debate on a theoretical plane. Often the negative can force the affirmative to bring the debate "down to earth" for application to present-day situations.

Disagreement often arises over the extent to which the affirmative should present a detailed *plan*. An affirmative, for example, may attempt to defend a *plan* only in broad terms, whereas the negative may clamor for details regarding the structure, function, and operation of the *plan*. A good example is the proposition regarding the adoption of a welfare state in the United States. For the affirmative to define its *plan* of welfare state as "the assumption by the Federal Government of the general welfare of the people" is definitely an evasion of its responsibility. Certainly the affirmative should specify whether its *plan* includes such factors as increased unemployment insurance, public medicine, more liberal old-age pensions, and federal aid to education. On the other hand, the negative should not try to reduce the debate to useless quibbling over minor details of operation.

ATTACKING THE DEFINITIONS OF TERMS

The method of defining terms has been considered previously. However, debaters often disagree at different stages in the debate about the meaning of terms which they use. It is the affirmative's responsibility to define all terms of the proposition during the first few minutes of the debate. And it is the responsibility of the negative during his introductory statements to accept or challenge the affirmative's definitions. One term that is a stumbling block in many debates is *should*. In debating the proposition, "Resolved: That a federal world government should be established," some affirmative speakers interpret *should* as *will* and carefully pointed out that world trends indicated that world federation was coming whether we wanted it or not. In view of the inevitability of world federation, therefore, they argued that it should be adopted.

Often such debates degenerated into ramblings on whether or not world federation is coming or will come in spite of us. In such cases the original meaning of the term *should* was forgotten. Such exhibitions of poor debating only confuse an audience and injure public appreciation of the art of argumentation and debate.

ATTACKS ON MATERIAL FALLACIES

A material fallacy is an example of argument wherein the basic assumptions and the factual materials used are open to question. In such an argument the reasoning might be sound in form, and the argument itself might be treated directly instead of indirectly through begging or ignoring the question. But if either the basic assumptions or the factual materials used are false or misleading, then the entire argument loses validity. Seven types of material fallacies will be considered.

THE FALLACY OF INACCURACY OF THE FACTS

A fact has been observed to be some concrete or abstract material from which inferences are drawn and relationships are established. Facts deal with the existence of things and their classification and the occurrence of events. For example, there are 50 states in the United States of America (as of March 3, 1963). Not 49. Not 51. Just 50. That is a fact. Also, the Ohio River flows into the Mississippi River. The Mississippi River flows into the Gulf of Mexico. Utah is north of Arizona. Thirty-six inches equal one yard. Japan attacked Pearl Harbor on December 7, 1941. The above statements are facts that have been checked and verified by observation.

In argumentation, assumptions plus evidence plus logical reasoning equal a valid conclusion. But if any one of the three elements (assumptions, evidence, logic) is faulty, then the conclusion is faulty.

THE FALLACY OF FAULTY STATISTICS

"Figures don't lie, but liars do figure" is a familiar comment on arguments which are based on inferences drawn from statistics. The fallacy of faulty statistics does not deal with inaccurate facts or erroneous mathematics. Rather, it deals with the bases upon which the figures are compared. Usually one set of figures or statistics that has one basis (of time, space, place, duration or the like) will be compared with another set of statistics that has a different basis. The following example illustrates the fallacy of faulty statistics:

> There were 7,000 workers killed in industrial accidents in the United States in 1935, but 9,000 workers were killed in the same manner in 1945. Therefore, the percent of workers killed in industrial accidents in the United States increased from 1935 to 1945.

On the surface, the conclusion in the above example appears sound. However, the implication is contained in the assumption that the same number of people was employed by industry in 1935 as in 1945. Such was not the case. More than twice as many workers were employed in industry in 1945 as in 1935. Therefore, 9,000 workers actually constitute a lower percentage of all the workers employed in industry in 1945 than do the 7,000 workers in 1935. Accordingly, the percent of workers killed did not increase, but decreased.

Argument on financial practicability of such proposals as nationalized medicine, government ownership of basic industries, and federal aid to education often confuses the average audience with a maze of statistics. In such cases, the comparisons of all statistics must be examined carefully to determine whether the bases for comparisons are equal.

THE FALLACY OF INVALID TESTIMONY

The rules for argument from authority and for the use of testimonial evidence have already been treated. Generally, the fallacy of invalid testimony can occur in any one of the three following forms:

INTERNALLY INCONSISTENT TESTIMONY. Great similarity exists between the simple fallacy of contradiction and the fallacy of invalid testimony in which the testimony is internally inconsistent. In the former case—fallacy of contradiction—the direct words of an opponent are attacked as being contradictory. In the latter case the inconsistency or contradiction is contained in testimony which is used as evidence. For example, if the speeches of Hitler were quoted as evidence to prove the unjustifiability of the Allies' entry into war against Germany in 1939, it would be an easy matter to point out the internal inconsistency of Hitler's statements.

INCOMPETENT TESTIMONY. Testimony should be considered incompetent if it is made by a person who is not a recognized authority on the subject for discussion, if it is indefinite instead of specific, if it violates the normal laws of logical argument, and if it comes from an unreliable secondary source rather than from a primary source. Congressmen, senators, and even presidents have expressed opinions regarding all of the controversial social and economic problems of the day. But unless even their respected opinions can be treated satisfactorily by the normal tests of evidence, their testimony must be considered incompetent.

PREJUDICED TESTIMONY.   Often an authority may be acceptable from every point of view except that of his own bias. The authority may have spent a lifetime dealing with the problem under consideration. For example, a labor leader in the steel industry may know vastly more about the problems of the steelworkers than any federal mediator in a steel strike. Similarly, the president of a steel company may have much more extensive knowledge about steel factory production and management than the mediator. But the testimony of both the labor leader and the steel company executive could be so biased in a steel strike that the testimony of the government mediator would be more acceptable for the purposes of argument in a debate on a proposal for settling steel strikes.

THE FALLACY OF CONTRADICTION (OR INCONSISTENCY)

As was explained above, if an inconsistency is observed in testimony that a debater is using to support his case, then the fallacy is applied to the testimony, with the result that not only is the debater discredited, but the testimony that he used as evidence is disqualified. However, whenever the debater himself makes claims and assertions that are contradictory, he is charged directly with the fallacy of contradiction. In his enthusiasm for proving the practicability of his proposal, a debater sometimes makes sweeping claims. To illustrate: in developing the practicability of government ownership of the steel industry, the debater may claim that the price of steel would be reduced under the affirmative proposal. Minutes later, he may also claim that under government ownership the wages of the steelworkers would be increased. Unless the debater himself recognized and explained the apparent inconsistency, he could readily be charged by an opponent with being guilty of contradiction.

THE FALLACY OF EQUIVOCATION

A word or group of words in an argument being used more than once with different meanings each time is said to be an equivocation. To illustrate:

> The trend to the political right is increasing and this is what we desire because most people believe in right over wrong.

In this example the word *right* is used in two different meanings.

First, it is used to distinguish conservatism from liberalism in politics. Second, it is used in a moral sense.

> The United World Federalists have many prominent members. Why, even history shows that Washington, Adams, and Hamilton were Federalists. Therefore, in the names of these illustrious fathers of our great country, I appeal to you to support the United World Federalist organization.

Notice the ambiguity in use of the word *Federalist*. The word is used first to refer to those persons who, as organized, advocate a federal union of the various countries of the world with specific sovereign powers of government denied the member states and reserved to the world union. Second, the word is used to describe the adherence of Washington, Adams, and Hamilton to the principles of federalism for American states in the latter part of the eighteenth century. Federalism on a world basis today is entirely different from Federalism for the American States during the early years of the United States.

THE FALLACY OF AMBIGUOUS CONSTRUCTION

An ungrammatical statement that permits two or more meanings to be drawn from it because of the confusion of reference of certain words (usually pronouns) to their antecedents is known as *ambiguous construction*. In argumentation the use of any ambiguous grammatical construction invites immediate challenge by an opponent regarding which of the meanings the advocate intends. To illustrate:

> You had no grounds for false warranty, even though the engine block was cracked, when you signed an agreement "to buy my 1960 automobile, from the original owner in perfect condition."

To what does *in perfect condition* refer? The original owner? My 1960 automobile?

> Whenever we consider adopting additional federal aid to education, we must consider the factor of political control of education. As federal aid to education has increased during the past forty years, political control by the federal government has also increased. It is undesirable, because the local citizen becomes less responsible for supporting education, and it also undesirable because decisions on policy matters are taken out of the hands of the local citizens. National political control can kill the spirit of democracy in local affairs. It should not be encouraged. Therefore, it must not be adopted.

To what does *it* refer? *Federal aid to education? Political control by the federal government?*

THE FALLACY OF FALSE ASSUMPTION

One reason why opposing debaters sometimes do not clash is that they are arguing from different basic assumptions. In a debate on nationalized medicine, for example, the affirmative speaker may present a wealth of evidence to prove that a majority of the people is not receiving adequate medical care. But the negative speaker, ignoring the affirmative arguments, may introduce material to indicate that the adoption of the affirmative plan would handicap the efficiency of the medical profession. The affirmative might be assuming, without saying so, that adequate medical care for the majority is more important than the efficiency of the medical profession. And the negative might be assuming that the efficiency of the medical profession is more important than adequate medical care for the majority of people. Each might be making assumptions that the other is not willing to accept.

In arguing propositions dealing with government ownership of basic industries or even government ownership of all the forces of production and distribution, an affirmative debater will often proceed on the assumption that economic security is preferable to political liberty, whereas the negative speaker will be assuming that political liberties are preferable to economic security. The arguments of each may be presented effectively, each speaker denying entirely or in part the arguments of the other or admitting the arguments of the other. And at the end of the debate the arguments of each speaker may also stand fairly intact. But either speaker would have been vastly more effective if he had pointed out the different assumptions upon which the debate rested.

ATTACKS ON FORMAL FALLACIES

Included in attacks on formal fallacies are the fallacies of faulty generalization, of faulty causal relation, of faulty analogical reasoning, and of faulty deduction.

THE FALLACIES OF FAULTY GENERALIZATION

The rules for argument from specific instances have been discussed previously. Violations of those rules result in the following fallacies.

THE FALLACY OF INSUFFICIENT INSTANCES. When generalizing on a total, how many instances need to be examined in order to form a valid generalization? The number varies. Usually, the smaller the total being generalized upon, the larger the percentage of the total that must be examined. And, conversely, the larger the total that is generalized upon, the smaller may be the percentage examined. Accordingly, 2 out of 3, 5 out of 10, 15 out of 45, 30 out of 80, 50 out of 300, 75 out of 1,000, 150 out of 3,000 and 60,000 out of 150 million have been accepted often as adequate instances for generalizing on the totals indicated. For example, in Montana State University's Registrar's office quick surveys are conducted by examining every twentieth card in the files. That amounts to about 5 percent, or 200 out of 4,000 students.

THE FALLACY OF INSTANCES NOT TYPICAL. One of the most frequently found fallacies in reasoning is the fallacy of handpicking certain instances and claiming that such carefully selected instances represent the general characteristic of all of the instances involved. The illustration given below clearly is not only an example of the fallacy of insufficient instances but also an example of the fallacy of instances not typical. Observe the erroneous conclusion:

> Each of the states of Montana, Idaho, Rhode Island, Utah, Alaska, Hawaii, Wyoming, Nevada, New Mexico, Vermont, Arizona, New Hampshire, Maine, North Dakota, South Dakota, and Delaware has less than one million population. Since 16 out of 50 instances are sufficient for examination, then it can be concluded safely that each state in the United States must average less than one million population.

Under proper sampling conditions, 16 out of 50 instances are enough upon which to base the generalization. However, it is almost a mathematical impossibility that in choosing 16 states at random the first 16 chosen would be the only 16 which have less than one million population each. Obviously, then the 16 states listed were chosen deliberately in order to prove the conclusion.

THE FALLACY OF NEGATIVE INSTANCES. Whether the presence of negative instances destroys a generalization depends upon whether the conclusion claims "therefore most cases of this sort . . ." or whether the presence of a few negative instances will not injure an imperfect generalization ("most cases . . ."). But the presence of a single negative instance will always destroy a perfect generalization ("all cases . . ."), as the following example illustrates:

> All chosen at random, the following states were observed each to have the bicameral type of state legislature: Iowa, Maine, Nevada, Alaska, Florida, Delaware, Arizona, Wisconsin, Arkansas, Kentucky, Colorado,

Ohio, Montana, New Jersey, Oregon, Georgia, Texas, Tennessee, Vermont, Idaho, Virginia, Kansas, Indiana, Alabama, Utah, and Maryland. Since more than half of all of the states were examined, strictly at random, therefore it should be safe to conclude that all states have a bicameral state legislature.

The concluding statement said "all states . . ." But if it had said, "Therefore, most of the states . . . ," the conclusion would have been valid. But since one negative instance, namely, Nebraska, can be pointed to as possessing a unicameral legislature, the conclusion as stated is fallacious.

FALLACIES OF FAULTY CAUSAL RELATION

In Aristotle's sixth category of fallacies in his *De sophisticis elenchis*, he deals with "Fallacies that treat as cause that which is not a cause." Modern writers on argumentation refer to fallacies of faulty causal relation under the headings of Assumed Connection, Post Hoc, Inadequate Cause, and Counteracting Cause.

THE FALLACY OF ASSUMED CONNECTION (*Non Sequitur*). In this type of fallacy a certain cause is observed, and from it a certain result is predicted, even though there is no cause-to-effect relation between the two. Most of our popular superstitions are examples of this form of faulty reasoning.

If you are the third person to light a cigarette on one match, you will certainly have bad luck. Therefore, avoid lighting three on a match.

Don't complete a business deal on Friday the thirteenth, because Friday the thirteenth is an unlucky day and business deals completed on that day spell failure.

If a black cat crosses your path, you will have bad luck. Therefore, stay out of the way of all black cats.

THE FALLACY OF POST HOC (*Assumed Connection between Phenomenon and Antecedent*). "After a fact, therefore because of it" is the meaning of the Latin phrase *post hoc, ergo propter hoc*. It is a common form of fallacy used when a frustrated person observes unpleasant conditions and then looks for a scapegoat cause on which to blame the results. Here are some examples:

It could have been predicted. The *Serpentine* ran aground off the point and broke up and then sank. Why? Because the captain's wife was aboard and every sailor knows that it is bad luck to have a woman aboard ship.

What caused the Great Depression? The Hoover administration, of course, because we did not have the depression until after the Hoover administration took office.

THE FALLACY OF INADEQUATE CAUSE. One of the most frequently committed fallacies is that of inadequate cause. In such a fallacy there actually does exist a connection between the cause and the effect observed, but in reality the cause given is not sufficient to produce the result that is observed or predicted. This fallacy is committed just as easily when going from cause to effect as in reasoning from effect to cause.

Every year spent in college pays a student $40,000. Here is the proof. College graduates now earn on the average of $8,000 per year for forty years, a total of $320,000. People without college educations average $4,000 per years for forty years or a total of $160,000 to the life income, then each year in college pays a student $40,000.

The above example has been quoted many times by education magazines and by college publicity directors who are recruiting students for college. The argument is usually presented as though the only cause for the increased earning power of college graduates is attending college for four years. Other contributing causes are completely overlooked, such as adequate intelligence to start with, initiative, ambition, and physical ability to attend college.

THE FALLACY OF COUNTERACTING CAUSE. Very often the alleged cause is great enough to produce the predicted result, yet the result does not take place because another or a counteracting cause intervenes to prohibit the result from taking place. An example is the following:

The tariff on wool has been lowered by 25 cents per pound. Therefore, a man's suit of clothes, which takes eight pounds of wool in its manufacture, can be expected to come down $2 in its retail sale price.

In this example there is a definite cause-and-effect relationship, and the given cause is large enough to produce the result predicted. But the result might not be able to take place because of an increase in wages of workers in the textile mills or because of an increase in transportation freight rates. Accordingly, when the final product reaches the consumer, it (the suit of clothes) might be $5 more instead of $2 cheaper as forecasted. The two factors of increased wages and increased freight rates are called *counteracting causes;* they prevent the given cause from producing the normal effect. Another example of counteracting cause:

> The stockyards strike in Kansas City was settled on July 5, 1951. Accordingly, the Meat Packing Industry in Kansas City can expect prosperity for the rest of the summer.

Eight days later the flood of Friday, July 13, 1951, intervened as a definite counteracting cause to prevent the cause (the settling of the strike) from producing the result (prosperity).

FALLACIES OF FAULTY ANALOGICAL REASONING

Analogical reasoning never proves an argument conclusively, but it can help to make an argument understandable. There are two general kinds of analogies: literal and figurative. When two similar phenomena are compared, the analogy is termed *literal*. But when two unalike or completely different classes of phenomena are compared, the analogy is termed *figurative*. This latter type of analogy is more often attacked as being fallacious.

THE FALLACY OF ANALOGICAL POINTS OF DIFFERENCE. If the merits and demerits of nationalized medicine are being argued, the affirmative team might draw an analogy between nationalized medicine and the federal post office system. Both are functions of government. Both serve all of the people on a basis of equality. And the speaker might continue to enumerate points in which the two governmental functions are alike or similar. Then after establishing, say, seven respects in which they are similar, he might come to an eighth known quality of the Post Office but unknown in connection with nationalized medicine. He proceeds to argue that because the two systems are alike in seven respects, therefore it is logical to assume that they would be alike in the eighth respect. To a degree the argument should possess credence. But if his opponent could point out that there are nine or ten respects in which the federal post office and a plan of nationalized medicine are different, then he could conclude that the affirmative speaker's argument was fallacious on the basis of the analogical points of difference outweighing or outnumbering the points of likeness.

Analyze the following:

> There will be no war between America and Russia. Why? Because the foreign policies of both the United States and Russia are like two large bullies. Each is a champion in his own neighborhood. Each has made boastful threats, and both are now forced to stand face to face to prove their might. Both are fearful of the other's powers, yet pride and fear of

disgrace drive these two contenders only to mock battle. They resort to the old style of bluffing by flexing their muscles and forceful name-calling. However, such bullies never come to actual blows. Hence Russia and America will never go to war against each other.

Obviously this example of analogy is figurative. The phenomena compared are in totally different categories.

THE FALLACY OF ANALOGICAL NEGATIVE INSTANCES. Often in analogical reasoning one phenomenon will be compared to several phenomena instead of one to another phenomenon. If a speaker is attempting to indicate that since Z is similar in each of five respects to A, B, C, D, E, and F, therefore Z must be also similar to A, B, C, D, E, and F in a sixth respect, then he must be careful that there are not other examples R and S in which the sixth respect did not apply.

For example, a speaker might argue analogically that a system of nationalized medicine for the United States would be similar in each of 10 known respects to systems of medicine in England, Norway, Sweden, New Zealand, Australia, Russia, and Denmark. From this comparison he might conclude that since nationalized medicine in each of the foreign countries possessed an eleventh quality, that of being successful, therefore the eleventh quality would also apply to nationalized medicine in the United States. However, if his opponent were to point out that there existed a system in an additional foreign country, namely, Germany, which had the first ten known points of likeness but which lacked the eleventh quality of successfulness, then the original analogy would be destroyed on the basis of analogical negative instance.

FALLACIES OF BEGGING THE QUESTION

To beg the question, one need merely state the argument in such a manner as to assume the truth of the argument without proving it.

THE FALLACY OF UNSUPPORTED ASSERTION. Merely asserting an argument to be true does not make it valid unless the argument itself represents a widely accepted fundamental philosophy of life. If a basic philosophy is involved, any disagreement between two disputants would evolve around the fallacy of false assumption. However, if both disputants accept the same philosophical approach to a problem and then disagree on a given viewpoint relative to that problem, each will need to prove his contention beyond merely asserting it. Without specific examples, testimony, analogical reasoning, or other forms of support for his respective argument, each debater, by merely asserting as true an argument which needs to be proven true, has become guilty of the fallacy of unsupported assertion.

THE FALLACY OF ARGUING IN A CIRCLE.   Aristotle referred to those arguments which were given to "repetition in relation to the same thing" as "babbling." Whether the ancient Greeks babbled more than modern Americans is not known. At any rate it is very easy to collect many everyday examples of babbling or arguing in a circle.

> Government ownership of industry should not be adopted because it is socialistic; we know that it is socialistic because it is a system which should not be adopted.

> The New York Yankees are a great ball team because they have won many victories, and they have won many victories because they are a great ball team.

THE FALLACY OF FALLACIOUS QUESTIONING.   This fallacy grows out of asking two or more questions as though they were one question that demands a single answer. During the past several years the following example of fallacious questioning has caused considerable furor in the American public affairs.

> Are you now or have you ever been a member of the Communist party?

Actually two questions were asked: "Are you now a Communist?" and, "Have you ever been a Communist?" If a person can answer "no" to each question then he can offer "no" as an answer to the two questions which are asked as one. But it is very possible that a man might have been a Communist at one time previously but no longer be a Communist. In that case, he cannot answer "no" or "yes" to the two questions asked as one without committing perjury.

THE FALLACY OF ASSUMING A MORE GENERAL TRUTH.   In this type of thinking, the point which is being argued is shown to be inclusive within a larger contention that is merely assumed to be true. Actually it is a process of assuming the very argument which needs to be proved.

> Federation of the NATO should be accomplished because it is part of a federation of all the countries of the entire world, and we must admit that world federation is desirable and is even inevitable.

FALLACIES OF IGNORING THE QUESTION

Fallacies of ignoring the question merely shift the attention from the argument under consideration to some factor or condition remotely connected with the argument.

THE FALLACY OF APPEAL TO AUTHORITY. To reason to a conclusion by using logical reasoning and then to substantiate such reasoning by quoting from an authority who makes similar conclusions based on similar reasoning is considered sound technique in public discussion and debate. But to try to establish the truth or falsity of a contention by quoting only from an authority or authorities becomes in reality a fallacious form of reasoning. By operating upon different assumptions with reference to the same contention, two authorities can arrive at opposite points of view and yet both be logically sound in their reasoning processes.

It is possible to find a thousand reputable authorities upholding one point of view, and it is also possible to find another thousand equally reputable authorities upholding the opposite point of view on the same argument. Thus, if one man merely quotes a dozen authorities to prove his point, he really proves nothing. For every authority an affirmative debater quotes, a negative debater can quote a different authority to contradict the previous one. Such a practice can continue indefinitely with neither debater proving anything.

THE FALLACY OF DISCUSSION OF PERSONALITIES. Very often the fallacy of discussion of personalities is confused with the fallacy of appeal to authority. The difference is that in appealing to an authority the authority is recognized as such, while in the fallacy of discussion of personalities the person associated with the argument is represented by description as being a person of good or bad qualities. The conclusion which follows is that the same quality of goodness or badness of the person is associated with the argument with which the person is connected. However, a person's qualities of goodness or badness do not prove or disprove the truth or falsity of an argument with which he is associated.

THE FALLACY OF APPEAL TO PASSION, PREJUDICE, AND HUMOR. (*Argumentum ad hominem,* or *argumentum ad populum—appeal to the people*) is a traditional category found in the older works on logic. Whether such a category should be retained, in its original sense, is questionable. If the speaker exploits his audience by playing upon obvious prejudices, stereotypes, or feelings, he is obviously indulging in reprehensible behavior. However, it is also true that all arguments about human affairs must be built, if they are traced back to their ultimate premises, upon human aspirations, human motives, human feelings. It is the exploitative use of appeals to audience predispositions which is here condemned. Whether such use should properly be classified as a *logical* fallacy, or as an *ethical* matter, may be decided by the reader. The debater, as a speaker, is compelled to consider his audience; and considering his audience, he must inevitably relate his arguments to audience premises (see Chapter 8, Audience Analysis and

Motivation). But relating arguments to basic audience premises need never require the responsible speaker to introduce references to prejudices and passions that are both ethically deplorable and logically unnecessary.

> Members of the jury, I ask you to look closely at the poor, sweet, innocent young girl who stands accused of crime. Look at those tearful eyes. Could a girl so sweet and tender have committed this crime?

THE FALLACY OF APPEAL TO TRADITION. Traditions are broken every day. Some traditions last only a short period of time. Others last for hundreds of years. As long as traditions remain firmly established and unbroken, they constitute an important guide to human conduct and belief. But when a tradition is broken often enough by enough people, then it no longer remains a guide or a validation for human belief and conduct. Accordingly, since tradition can be broken, the mere appeal to the tradition in no way affirms or denies a human belief or conduct which is based solely upon the tradition. The examples follow:

> My father and my father's father always went out into the forest and chopped down a fir tree for Christmas. Therefore, my son, I see no reason for you to buy one this year.

> It has always been the custom in America, the most democratic land in the world, that no man shall be entrusted with the reins of government for more than two terms. If Washington, the father of our country, refused to accept a third term because he believed it would have harmful effects, how can we even consider such a thing as a third term for Franklin D. Roosevelt?

THE FALLACY OF APPEAL TO IGNORANCE OF THE OPPOSITE.

> Socialism will work in America because nobody can prove that it will not work in America.

In the above example the advocate did not prove his point. He merely assumed his point and claimed that his contention was correct because the opposite position had not been, or could not be, established. It is a common fallacy and is easily exposed.

THE FALLACY OF SHIFTING GROUND. If, in discussion or debate, a participant who sets forth an argument is answered by a second participant who ignores the first contention and sets forth an opposing contention, the second participant is said to be guilty of *shifting ground*. The strategy of adopting opposing arguments is one of the effective special methods of refutation. But when it is used properly, the technique of adopting opposing arguments should make some disposition of the opponents' arguments either by admitting them or minimizing them. Ignoring them and shifting directly to opposing arguments burden the contender with the fallacy of shifting ground. Some examples are:

> Q. Mr. Ambassador, if the Chinese Nationalists cannot protect themselves on the island of Formosa without the help of the Seventh Fleet, how can they successfully attack the mainland?
> A. Mr. Senator, if the Chinese Nationalists had more American equipment, they could attack the mainland.

If the second speaker had first admitted his opponent's contention, then the answer would have been one of adopting opposing arguments rather than one of shifting ground.

> Mr. A. If the policy of American high tariffs is continued against Argentine beef, we shall help to protect the American beef industry and keep American dollars at home.
> Mr. B. Well, anyway, the present policy is incurring the ill will of Argentina, and Argentina could easily stir up strong anti-American feelings throughout South America.

In effect Mr. B is admitting the argument of Mr. A, even though Mr. B does not specifically say so. Without admitting, denying, or minimizing it, Mr. B ignores it and shifts over to other ground.

THE FALLACY OF REFUTING AN ARGUMENT NOT ADVANCED. Occasionally during formal debate an advocate, in his zeal to appear effective, introduces refutation on which he is well prepared, of an argument which was not advanced by his opponent. It is a process of setting up a straw man and knocking him down with great showmanship. Of course, the contender who did not introduce the argument in the first place can claim a foul. But unless he speaks up, an audience may not realize that a fallacy has been committed.

THE FALLACY OF FAULTY SYNTHESIS.

> The editors of the *Daily Worker*, the *Wall Street Journal*, and the *New York Daily News* all run successful publications. Just think of what a first-class topnotch paper could be published if those editors would collaborate in the editing of only one paper.

In this type of fallacy, the total is not the sum of its parts. The total might have a greater or a smaller value than the sum of the value of the parts. In the field of sports we often hear people committing this fallacy.

The team cannot be expected to be any good because there is not a single star on the team.

The team should be unbeatable because every man on the team is a star.

As we can guess immediately, the quality of teamwork is a factor that can make a team of no stars into a winning team. Also, the lack of teamwork in a team of individual stars can deny the predictability of the quality of "unbeatable" for the team.

THE FALLACY OF FAULTY DIVISION. In a sense, the fallacy of faulty division is a form of equivocation. A word that is used during a chain of comparisons is used both in an absolute sense and in a restricted (usually average) sense. To illustrate:

The United States has the tallest men, on the average, in the world. Colorado has the tallest men, on the average, in the United States. Denver has the tallest men of all the cities in Colorado. And John Doe is the tallest man in Denver. That makes John Doe the tallest man in the world.

In the above case, each statement can be true except the last one.

SPECIAL METHODS OF REFUTATION

Each of the fallacies treated thus far has been one of the general methods of refuting the arguments of an opponent. These shall be referred to as the special methods (as contrasted to the general or logical methods) or refutation.

REDUCTION TO AN ABSURDITY (*REDUCTIO AD ABSURDUM*)

By accepting the argument of an opponent and applying it in humorous or ludicrous situations, one may destroy the value of an argument without ever having attacked its validity on logical grounds. For example:

The contention is advanced that Mr. X should not be elected President because he has never held a public office. Presumably if he has ever held a public office he would be more qualified for holding the higher public office. But suppose Mr. X was running for the lowest public office. Since he had never held a lower public office (because there could be no lower office than the office he was running for), therefore he could not qualify for even the lowest public office. Only present office-holders could qualify for the various public offices. And years hence, when all present public officials had died of old age and overwork as public officeholders, then our government would be left without a single public official. And yet only the dead officeholders would be qualified to hold office because having held a public office was an essential qualification for holding a public office.

TURNING THE TABLES

Occasionally a debater can accept the arguments and evidence of his opponent and then interpret those materials in such a manner as to help to prove his own case. It is not an easy technique to employ, but when it is used successfully it is highly effective.

An advocate of nationalized medicine usually states as the first issue in the debate the *"need* for changing the present system of medical care in America." In supporting the need issue, he presents evidence to prove such arguments as: many people do not receive adequate medical care; complete medical care is too expensive for the average citizen; and not enough money is spent at present on medical research.

Usually the affirmative arguments will appear impressive in the light of the evidence. A speaker on the negative side, however, instead of trying to present conflicting evidence that disputes the affirmative evidence, can readily accept every chart, graph, fact and statistical table of the affirmative and point out that those same materials also indicate that America has the highest standards of medical care in the world, that medical care is more plentiful to the people in America than elsewhere, that medical care is cheaper in America, and that accomplishments in medical research have already placed America in a position of world leadership. The negative, by using the affirmative's own evidence to support the negative counter arguments, can then conclude that "there is *no great need* for changing the present system of medical care in America." Thus, the negative would have turned the tables.

A negative speaker on the subject of fair employment practices could deny the affirmative's contention that all states should be required by Federal constitutional amendment to adopt fair employment practices by pointing out that all states, except a few, already maintain such practices. Furthermore, he could argue that a natural trend toward such a goal, which the negative also endorses, is more rapid and more certain of development. In other words, he can take the position that what is evolving naturally and inevitably should be allowed to continue normally without delaying its arrival by artificial compulsions. Thus, by using the affirmative's own materials, the negative can turn the table to his own point of view that compulsory fair employment practices should not be required of all states through a constitutional amendment.

POSING DILEMMAS

One of the most effective of the special methods of refutation is the method of exposing dilemmas into which an opponent may be placed. A *dilemma* consists of two courses of action, both of which are untenable. The two possible positions or solutions are called the "horns" of the dilemma. Whichever one the opponent tries to defend can be defeated. If three possibilities are presented to the opposite side, a *trilemma* results; if four, a *tetralemma*; if more than four, a *polylemma*.

A recent example of the skillful use of the dilemma occurred in the intercollegiate debating of the topic of federal aid to education. A question that the negative frequently asked of the affirmative was: "Under the affirmative plan of federal aid to public education, would the present system of segregation of Negro and white children into separate schools in some of the southern states be continued or discontinued?" If the affirmative answered that segregation of Negro and white school children in the South would be continued under federal aid, the negative could respond by showing that (1) the tax money for federal aid to education would involve the flowing of dollars from the northern states (which would receive back less than they were taxed) to the southern states (which would receive more than they were taxed); that (2) the northern states do not believe in and do not practice segregation of white and Negro students; that (3) segregation is more expensive than consolidation of Negro and white students; and that (4) forcing the northern states to help support financially a costly system of segregation in which they do not believe is morally wrong.

On the other hand, if the affirmative answered that under its plan of federal aid the practice of segregation would be prohibited (in order to avoid being caught on the first part of the dilemma), then the negative could point out that elimination of segregation in the South would be less certain of accomplishment than forcing the North to pay taxes to support a system of segregation in which it does not believe. The negative could introduce much evidence to indicate that any attempt to end segregation abruptly in the South would lead to rebellion and violence. Any compromise answer, such as a gradual elimination of segregation over a period of twenty years after the plan of federal aid goes into effect, is not only an evasion of the question but is also an answer which catches the affirmative on both parts of the dilemma instead of on one.

THE METHOD OF RESIDUES

The method of residues in refutation involves reducing the case of a specific number of possibilities and showing that all but one are not practicable. The method of residues is often used as frequently and as effectively by an affirmative debater as by a negative speaker. Sometimes an affirmative speaker will list all the possible solutions to a problem and negate all but one (the one he supports) before his opponent has a chance to list the possible solutions. Occasionally a negative speaker (in his strategy of admitting the affirmative need, denying the affirmative plan, and adopting an opposing plan or counterplan) will list all the possible solutions before the affirmative does and then proceed to rule out all solutions—including the affirmative's—except his own. Thus, the strategy of debate is closely connected to the use of the method of residues in refutation.

EXPOSING IRRELEVANT ARGUMENTS

Setting up straw men and then knocking them down is a favorite sport of people who substitute fluff for real argument in a debate. Frequently a speaker draws the attention of his opponent and of the audience from the real issue of a debate to some irrelevant side point. Such technique only delays and confuses the treatment of the basic arguments upon which attention should be focused.

Demosthenes in his famous oration "On the Crown" skillfully exposed the irrelevant materials which his opponent had introduced into the deliberations. In the United States Congress, much of our modern filibustering involves the consideration of matters that are wholly extraneous or at the best only slightly relevant to the great issues of the moment. The astute debater will develop the ability to see arguments in the light of their relative weight and to classify them according to their relationships, their relevancy, and their importance.

ADOPTING OPPOSING ARGUMENTS

Often an opponent's argument cannot be refuted either by attacking the material validity of its premises or the formal validity of its conclusion. Accordingly, the argument has to be admitted. But it can still be refuted by pointing out that opposing arguments, which also must be admitted, far outweigh the argument under consideration.

In arguing the proposition that all American citizens should be subject to conscription for essential service in time of war, the affirmative established the argument that Russian communism threatened to conquer the world by quoting the Communist Manifesto and the speeches of Lenin, Stalin, and Khrushchev and by pointing to Communist successes in eastern Europe and in Asia. The negative could not deny the affirmative evidence or the inference drawn from the evidence. The negative admitted that argument but still refuted it by adopting the opposing argument that Russian communism "cannot" conquer the world, drawing such an inference from Russian failures in the Greek Civil War, Yugoslavia Titoism, and the Berlin Airlift and from the growing strength of the United Nations and of NATO. Similarly, the negative, in admitting the affirmative argument that present Communist military strength surpassed non-Communist military strength, also refuted the same argument by presenting evidence to prove the opposing argument that American technological and scientific developments in warfare more than compensate for Communist numerical superiority.

Adopting opposing arguments is the most effective method in refutation a debater can use except the method of exposing fallacies in the material and formal validity of premises and conclusions. The danger in using this method, however, is that the user often fails to identify what he is doing. He must make clear that he is admitting the original argument, and adopting an opposing argument or arguments that far outweigh and overshadow the original argument.

ASKING QUESTIONS

The most commonly used special method of refutation in everyday discussion and debate involves the asking of questions. Questions may be asked simply for points of information. Such questions have little refutative value. But in at least four respects the asking of questions can contribute materially to the weakening of an opponent's argument. The questions may take any of the following forms:

QUESTIONS THAT THE OPPONENT CANNOT ANSWER.   If a disputant in an argument is certain that his opponent cannot answer pertinent questions relative to an argument, then the asking of the questions will weaken the argument. In such cases the questions asked must be vital to the argument. Of course, if the defender of the argument can answer the questions, then the argument actually becomes stronger and more important in the debate.

NUMEROUS QUESTIONS TO SIDETRACK THE OPPONENT.   A tactic of some debaters is to ask so many questions of an opponent that whether he attempts to answer all of them or whether he attempts to answer only a few, he can be attacked later by the interrogator for answering ineffectively. If the defender attempts to answer a barrage of questions, he risks spending much valuable time on relatively unimportant points. In this event he might be chided later for having poor perspective and for overlooking the larger, more important aspects of the entire case. But if the defender of an argument refuses to be caught in such a trap and purposely evades the numerous and unimportant questions thrown at him, then he runs the risk of appearing to be unable to answer them.

QUESTIONS THAT EXPOSE WEAKNESSES IN THE PRACTICABILITY OF THE PROPOSAL. The method of posing dilemmas (considered above) involves the asking of questions. It is a very effective technique, especially when the interrogator is ready with strong refutations for all possible answers. Also, the asking of decisive questions can lead to the exposure of inconsistencies as well as to the reduction of the argument, in practical application, to an absurdity.

QUESTIONS THAT EXPOSE OTHER FUNDAMENTAL ISSUES. The best purpose for asking questions is to expose other fundamental issues. A notable example of this technique is seen in the Lincoln-Douglas debates. Lincoln asked Douglas how a free territory applying for statehood under the Popular Sovereignty doctrine could actually prohibit slavery when the Dred Scott decision by the United States Supreme Court had ruled that slavery in free territory was legal. Douglas supported both the Popular Sovereignty doctrine and the Dred Scott decision. Lincoln opposed both. Douglas answered that since property needed state laws for its protection, therefore, if there were no state laws pertaining to certain property (such as slaves), the ownership of such property could not be protected. Douglas straddled the fence. Lincoln remained uncompromising. Although Douglas won the election to the Senate in 1858, he had alienated himself from the southern Democrats. Thus, by asking questions, Lincoln had exposed the most fundamental issue on the problem of slavery.

CUMULATIVE REFUTATION

In the great historical debates, as well as in modern debating in Congress or in intercollegiate speech tournaments, refutation occurs throughout the presentation of contentious materials on a given subject. There is no specific position in debating where refutation should or should not occur. It may occur at any position in any speech after the opening affirmative analysis.

Somewhere during a debate or during argumentative discourse of any other sort, a debater will want to concentrate his refutation in order to make it appear most damaging to the case of his opponent. In collecting and concentrating his refutation he will need to be certain to attack large points rather than small points, and to attack first those arguments that he can weaken or destroy most thoroughly.

GENERAL RULES FOR REFUTATION

In addition to a knowledge of how to refute an argument of an opponent, the effective debater needs a knowledge of when and where to use his skill in refutation. The following suggestions will assist the beginning debater:

EXTENSIVE KNOWLEDGE

Refutation should be built upon extensive knowledge. The more extensive a man's knowledge of his subject, the better he can defend it, or the better he can refute it. Following his astounding reply to Senator Hayne (on the rights of states to nullify federal laws), Senator Daniel Webster was asked how he was able to answer his opponent without first making extensive preparation. Webster replied that he had been preparing the speech for twenty years, and that when the proper time arrived, all that he needed to do was to dip into his vast knowledge of history, law, religion, literature, and philosophy and to grab a "thunderbolt as it went smoking by." The modern debater might not need to prepare his arguments or his refutations for twenty years. But his success or failure in refutation usually will be proportional to the extent of his knowledge on the argument in question.

STRATEGIC ARGUMENTS

Select arguments for refutation on the basis of their strategic importance. Frequently a debater is confronted with a number of arguments to refute and time enough to refute only some of them. Should he refute first the one that he can answer most easily? Or should he answer first the first argument that his opponent introduced? Or the last argument?

Generally speaking, arguments should be selected for refutation on the basis of their strategic importance. If the opposition is basing much of its case upon a certain argument, then that argument should be attacked, whether it was introduced first or last or in the middle of the opponent's speech. If the opposition has posed a dilemma, the dilemma must be answered and, if possible, exposed. Otherwise, the defendant will be accused of not being able to answer questions that are fundamental to the entire proposition. As a debater acquires experience he learns quickly which arguments in the case of his opponents are secondary and which arguments demand first attention because of their strategic importance.

REFUTATION IN CONSTRUCTIVE SPEECHES

Refutation should be distributed throughout the constructive speeches. In formal debating, refutation may occur at any point following the first constructive speech. Usually a debater focuses his refutations at the beginning or end of his speech. Such a practice might add clarity to the presentation of refutation on a given point, but it does not always allow the most integrated presentation of arguments and refutation.

An awkward practice of beginning debaters is that of presenting a prepared case whether or not it follows sensibly the preceding comments. In such cases the speaker sometimes presents refutation of an argument that was not advanced or spends time building up an argument that was admitted by his opponents. Such instances emphasize the need for attempting to attain direct clash between the two cases. Whenever direct clash and intergration of cases are attempted, the refutations will be distributed throughout the constructive speeches as well as in the rebuttal speeches.

FORCING THE DEFENSE

Keep your opponents on the defensive. In argumentation you have a definite psychological advantage in forcing an opponent to meet you on your grounds. If your arguments are well founded upon valid assumptions, true evidence, and logical reasoning, you will welcome the futile attempts at attack by the opponents. Moreover, if you can use superior evidence and reasoning to attack the arguments of your opponents, then your opponents have a psychological disadvantage in trying to defend arguments that cannot be defended. All the methods of refutation discussed previously may be used in keeping an opponent on the defensive. Among the special methods of refutation, the dilemma is particularly effective.

PLANNED REFUTATION

Word the refutation clearly, employing a five-step method. The experienced debater selects carefully the arguments he intends to refute and then proceeds to refute them fully and effectively. The "shotgun" or "buckshot" refutation speech loses strength as it is presented. The "solid shot" refutation speech gathers strength as each argument is developed thoroughly. The five-step method of refutation is as follows:

1. STATE THE ARGUMENT TO BE REFUTED. In all fairness to your opponent and to the audience, the argument should be stated essentially as the opponent presented it. No changing or coloring of the argument should be attempted for convenient interpretation or for any other purpose.

2. POINT OUT THE STRATEGIC IMPORTANCE OF THE ARGUMENT. Why is a given argument chosen for refutation? Is the argument under attack important? If these questions are left unanswered in the minds of the listeners or readers, then the refutation loses some of its effectiveness. An experienced debater will point out how the argument that he undertakes to refute fits into the entire structure of the case. He will recall the extent to which the entire case of his opponent depends upon the argument that he intends to refute. In such a manner he infers or even asserts that if the given argument falls, then the larger issue that depends upon the argument or perhaps even the entire case also falls.

3. STATE YOUR STAND ON THE ARGUMENT. Frequently a debater completes his refutation of an argument (including the presentation of evidence and sound reasoning) without ever stating his position on the argument. Is your opponent guilty of false assumptions? Erroneous evidence? Or faulty reasoning? Do you deny his conclusions? Do you admit but minimize his argument? Do you admit his argument but claim that it is offset by opposing arguments? Whatever stand you take toward the argument, state that stand clearly. Do not proceed automatically with the refutation on the assumption that the audience knows what your stand is. In making a point clear, whether in building up or tearing down an argument, a good rule to be guided by is: Tell them what you are going to tell them; tell them; and tell them what you have told them.

4. PRESENT THE PROOF TO SUPPORT YOUR STAND. After your stand on the argument has been clarified, then present your proof. The proof might consist of new assumptions, new evidence, valid reasoning in contrast to fallacious reasoning that is exposed, or the presentation of opposing arguments. Here again it is good technique to identify clearly the proof process being employed.

5. RESTATE THE ORIGINAL ARGUMENT AS MODIFIED BY YOUR REFUTATION. Too often a refutation is left half-completed. Frequently, a debater will present his proof to dispute an argument and then drop the argument without summarizing it from his own standpoint. In order to clinch the refutation in your favor and to leave no doubts in the minds of readers or listeners regarding your position on the argument, the original argument should be restated as modified by your refutation.

PREPARATION FOR REFUTATION

Prepare refutation cards for anticipated arguments of the opposition because during the heat of debate participants sometimes forget temporarily the most effective form of refuting an argument. Accordingly, a refutation card (or rebuttal card) can recall quickly the previously prepared refutation of an opponent's argument. The opposing arguments and other refutative statements on a refutation card are usually cross-indexed with evidence cards in debater's evidence file. Note examples below and opposite.

NEGATIVE REFUTATION CARD

```
Aff. Argument:  Severe discrimination against
    employment of minority peoples prevails
    in American business industry.

Strategic Importance:  If true, then some NEED
    might exist for changing present methods
    of employment in American business.

Neg. Stand
    1.  Admitted: Some discrimination pre-
        vails, but it is not so severe or
        prevalent as Aff. claims.  (Evidence
        cards 701, 702, 703, 704.)
    2.  Opposing Argument: Discrimination
        practices are diminishing.  (Evidence
        cards 711, 712, 713.)
```

FAIRNESS

Be fair to your opponent. Sometimes a debater in his enthusiasm to refute his opponent will overstate himself to the point of being rude and unfair. An attempt to twist an argument or to read into it an inference that your opponent did not intend should be avoided. Especially in debate, the use of foul play will tend to defeat the person who uses it.

JJ—Methods of Rebuttal

The primary purpose of rebuttal is to rebuild an argument after it has been subject to attack. However, to a great extent, refutation and rebuttal

AFFIRMATIVE REFUTATION CARD (OR REBUTTAL CARD)

<u>Neg. Argument</u>: Federal World Government would
injure American economic security by
usurping sovereignty over tariff laws.

<u>Strategic Importance</u>: If true, then the Aff.
plan would be DETRIMENTAL to the American
people.

<u>Aff. Stand</u>:

    1. Neg. argument is false. The very op-
        posite is true. American economic
        security would be strengthened by
        surrendering sovereignty over tariff
        laws, for:

        A. American markets for foreign in-
           dustries would stimulate foreign
           purchases of other American prod-
           ucts. (Evidence cards 431, 432,
           433, 434, 435.)

        B. Trend toward world free trade
           would stimulate industries
           throughout the world. (Evidence
           cards numbers 441, 442, 443,
           444.)

    2. By obviating the risk of World War
        III, the Aff. Plan by establishing
        peace would more than compensate for
        any possible economic loss to Amer-
        ica. (Evidence cards numbers 471,
        472, 473.)

---

are different parts of the same process. Whereas refutation attempts primarily to tear down the case of an opponent, the very act of tearing down
an opponent's case automatically puts one's own case in better light. Conversely, the process of rebuttal, in rebuilding one's own case, automatically
weakens by comparison with the case of the opponent. Thus rebuttal and
refutation not only function together but are merely parts of the single
process of establishing one case over another.

The methods of refutation, already discussed, may be used generally
in identical fashion for rebuttal. If an opponent attempts to use any of the
general or special methods of refutation to discredit an argument but is

himself guilty of fallacious reasoning in the process, then the mere exposition of the fallacy will help to rebuild the original argument. In other words, the use of good refutation techniques to expose fallacious refutation will actually help to re-establish the original validity of the argument. Thus, valid refutation of invalid refutation constitutes sound rebuttal technique.

ADOPTING OPPOSING ARGUMENTS

The adoption of opposing arguments is used extensively as a technique of defense and rebuttal for arguments under attack. Adopting an opposing argument in effect admits the truth of a charge against one's case. In admitting the charge, however, the defendant maintains that the charge is ineffective when compared to certain virtues of the same case. For example, in debating an intercollegiate proposition relative to compulsory fair employment practices, affirmative debaters would often indict the status quo of employment practices as tolerating discrimination against race, color, and national origin. In defending the status quo and as counter-refutation or rebuttal, the negative speakers often would admit the charge of discrimination against minority groups but at the same time would demonstrate that discrimination practices were diminishing each year. This latter argument, coupled with other negative case arguments would then be held up as having more weight or more importance than the opponents' argument which was admitted. The more special forms of defense, which follow, use this technique extensively for rebuttal purposes.

DEFENSE AGAINST ATTACKS ON INTERPRETATION OF THE PROPOSITION

To a great extent the techniques of defense against attacks on the interpretation of the proposition fall under the general heading of Debate Strategy. However, a few suggestions on this point will aid in developing a general defense for an entire case.

The advocate of a change from the status quo normally will identify early in the contest the issues around which the controversy will center. Usually the issues pertain to the *need* for changing from status quo; a proposed *plan* for a change; and the *practicability* of the proposed plan. If the proponent for a proposition does not present an adequate analysis of the issues, then the opponent has a perfect right to challenge the affirmative analysis. Occasionally, the affirmative will attempt to rest its entire case upon the need issue. In such a case the negative has good grounds for challenging the affirmative's limited analysis, and affirmative rebuttal will appear weak. The same disadvantage would occur to the affirmative if it attempted to ignore the need (possibly assuming the need) and based its case mainly upon plan and practicability.

If the affirmative presents no plan beyond a general definition of what the proposal involves, the negative will be correct in asking for a more comprehensive explanation of what specifications the plan will encompass. For example, in debating the Federal World Government proposition, if the affirmative presents as a plan the rather hazy idea of "all the people of the world working together under a form of government for the peaceful progress of all mankind," the negative would be entitled to ask questions about the sovereign powers to be retained or surrendered by member states, and about matters of fiscal, military, and political organization.

But if the affirmative had presented a fairly comprehensive plan with specific provisions for the legislative, executive, and judicial powers of their world government, then the negative would place itself at a strategic disadvantage by asking questions on minute details.

Whenever controversy develops over definition of terms in relation to over-all interpretation of the proposition, the dispute is resolved usually by appealing to the most acceptable authorities on the subject. In such cases, if either the proponent or the opponent of a proposition attempt to deviate too far from accepted definitions, he will be unsuccessful in defending such a position. As illustrated earlier in this chapter, "should" cannot be interpreted as "will" with any degree of success.

DEFENSE AGAINST ATTACKS ON MATERIAL VALIDITY

In modern deliberative assemblies, as well as in everyday business and professional situations which employ argument, the most difficult part of discourse on which to establish agreement is the validity of facts and basic assumptions. Accordingly, the various types of material fallacies need to be reviewed with emphasis placed upon defense against unwarranted attack.

DEFENSE AGAINST ATTACKS ON THE ACCURACY OF FACTS

It is fairly easy to establish the truth or falsity of such statements as "The Ohio River flows into the Mississippi River"; "Utah is north of

Arizona"; "In 1932 the total national income in the United States was $39,200,000,000." Such statements can be checked for authenticity in authoritative sources and be accepted or rejected.

It is more difficult, however, to establish the truth or falsity of such statements as: "Germany was so discriminated against in the League of Nations that she was forced to withdraw"; and "The United States committed an aggression upon the Japanese people by dropping the atom bomb on Hiroshima." These two last statements are judgments or inferences based upon the observation of events that involved people, places, and time. But very frequently such statements are used as facts in the premises of an argument. In such cases, the so-called fact needs to be defined with time-date-place relationships. Otherwise the same term will be used with two or more persons attributing different meanings to the fact.

DEFENSE AGAINST ATTACKS ON ALLEGED FAULTY STATISTICS

To a great extent the particular date-time-place conditions surrounding the use of statistics also determine whether or not the statistics as used in an argument are faulty. As was pointed out previously, the fallacy of faulty statistics does not deal with inaccurate facts or with erroneous mathematics. Rather, it deals with the basis upon which figures are compared. Frequently, there is genuine misunderstanding regarding the reference in which statistics are used. Often a comparison of statistics is presented that involves two different bases.

In exposing the different bases of comparative statistics, a refutation might easily overlook the fact (intentionally or not) that in reality the two different bases were actually the same basis. Rebuttal—or defense—on the original argument would then need to clarify the basis of the comparative statistics in order to maintain that in truth no fallacy existed.

For example, a debater might argue that the United States national debt of 1963 had increased dangerously over the 1946 figure of $240 billion. In refutation, another debater might claim that because of the increased population and the monetary inflation that took place during the period 1946 to 1963, the national debt actually decreased—comparatively—in proportion to the population and the dollar value. In rebuttal, the first debater could defend his original claim by maintaining that, although both the population and inflation had increased, the prospects for paying off or reducing the debt had decreased, since large savings and the prospect of considerable inflation characterized the nation in 1946, whereas small savings and the prospect of minimal inflation characterized the nation in 1963.

DEFENSE AGAINST ATTACKS ON ALLEGED INVALID TESTIMONY

Whenever the validity of testimony used in an argument is challenged in any of the three respects discussed in the section on refutation (internally inconsistent testimony, incompetent testimony, prejudiced testimony), defense can best be made by explaining how and why the testimony does not have the specific weakness that was charged against it. Primarily, the validity or falsity of the testimony will rest upon the accuracy of the facts relative to the testimony.

DEFENSE AGAINST ATTACKS ON ALLEGED CONTRADICTION

Contradiction is a frequent charge against the proponent of an argument. But here again, the particular date-time-place references will need to be explained to keep the argument in its proper focus. For example, a proponent of federally owned hydroelectric power dams might claim that government ownership of electric power dams would lower the cost of electric power and also raise the wages of the workers. He might readily be charged with inconsistency or contradiction on the ground that if wages are increased, the income must be increased instead of decreased. In rebuttal, the defendant might answer that no contradiction occurs when it is observed that the stock dividends under private ownership are eliminated under government ownership of power dams.

DEFENSE AGAINST ATTACKS ON ALLEGED EQUIVOCATION

If a word or or group of words in an argument is used more than once with more than one meaning, there is no valid defense for the equivocation involved. If the word or words are used with the same meanings each time, then no equivocation can be claimed. The only defense against alleged equivocation is to point out that the same meanings are attributed to the terms each time they are used in an argument.

DEFENSE AGAINST ATTACKS ON ALLEGED AMBIGUOUS CONSTRUCTION

Whenever an ambiguous construction is pointed out in an argument, the best defense of the argument is to reword the argument for the sake of clarity. In refutation, the pointing out of apparent ambiguous constructions often is an attempt to ridicule or make fun of an argument when no vital weakness can be found in it. For example, the following statement could be perfectly clear to an audience of 1,000 or more people: "A better system of old-age pensions is needed for the aged without any time to lose." The general understanding by the audience could be that it is urgent that old-age pensions be improved now. However, an opponent, who had little else to argue about on the point, might claim that the words "without any time to lose" could have reference either to "a better system of old-age pensions" or to "the aged." Actually, the original construction of the sentence could be taken to mean that the aged had no time to lose.

Reference to such an interpretation by the opponent might bring laughs from the audience. But certainly the proponent, while admitting a slight ambiguity in the construction of his argument, could easily claim that the original meaning was clear, that his opponent was engaging in an appeal to humor because he had no substantive answer.

DEFENSE AGAINST ATTACKS ON ALLEGED FALSE ASSUMPTION

Previously it was demonstrated how debates on government ownership propositions often conclude with each side holding divergent basic assumptions. In most cases the assumptions or, more accurately, the major premises in the various units of formal reasoning in the debates are never identified as basic assumptions.

The earnest advocate of any debatable proposal will give careful attention to the basic assumptions which underlie his reasoning. If he is challenged on the validity of his assumptions, he will have a ready defense. Very often in a debate, the person who challenges his opponent on the validity of his assumptions is the person who establishes the acceptability of his premises with the audience. However, whenever a debater is so challenged, he can defend himself by clearly identifying what the basic assumption really is and by explaining carefully the reasons why his particular assumption should be accepted in preference to all other possible assumptions.

In debating a nationalized medicine question, for example, an affirmative speaker might present much evidence to prove that a majority of the people does not receive adequate medical care. The negative speaker might ignore the affirmative argument and proceed to point out how the affirmative proposal would encourage malingering, and hence, inefficiency in the medical profession. The affirmative might be assuming that adequate medical care for the majority of the people is more important than the efficiency of the medical profession, and the negative might be assuming that the efficiency of the medical profession is more important than the amount of medical care which the majority of the people receive.

Generally, the best defense against attacks on alleged false assumption is constant identification and explanations of the assumption (or major premises) upon which the case arguments are based.

DEFENSE AGAINST ATTACKS ON FORMAL VALIDITY

No attempt will be made at this point to present a special defense against attacks on each of the many possible fallacies in the fields of generalization, causation, analogical reasoning, and deduction. The nature of each of these fallacies has been considered previously. The best defense against attacks on the formal validity of one's arguments is to avoid committing these fallacies.

If the debater is guilty of any of the many fallacies possible in the realm of formal validity, two courses of action are open. As explained previously, the fallacy should be admitted readily and openly. Pruning the indefensible part of either side's case will actually strengthen and purify the rest of the case; whereas any attempt to defend and protect an indefensible part of the case will jeopardize the validity of the entire case. Moreover, once the debater has admitted his weakness, he should transfer attention to those arguments of his which are most valid and most easily defended.

There are occasions when an opponent of an argument will himself use one or another of the special fallacies in his effort to expose a fallacy of the same nature. This applies especially to fallacies of ignoring the question. For example, a debater sometimes will decry his opponent's appeal to authority in building a case; then the accuser will himself appeal to authority to establish his own case. In like manner, debaters who charge their opponents with appealing to passion, prejudice, and humor very often commit the same fallacy themselves within their own refutations. Such inconsistencies should be exposed.

DEFENSE AGAINST THE SPECIAL METHODS OF REFUTATION

Each of the seven special methods of refutation is an especially effective method of destroying an argument of an opponent. But when the argument being destroyed is one's own, a defense against these seven special methods of refutation becomes desirable. Of course, if a fallacy has been committed and has been sincerely exposed, the best defense is to admit the fallacy and shift to another argument that is more defensible. But if the refutation itself has been insincere or poorly founded, then the

proponent of the original argument may defend himself in a manner specified as follows for each of the seven special methods of refutation:

DEFENSE AGAINST REDUCTIONS TO ABSURDITY

Often an opponent who tries to destroy an argument by reducing it
to an absurdity does so because he is unable to attack it by using any of
the general methods (exposing fallacies) of refutation. The best defense
against such tactics consists, first, in pointing out that the opponent's
method of reducing to an absurdity is a last resort, since he did not use the
regular methods of refutation, and, second, of asking questions that make
specific reference to the validity of the argument. By pointing out to the
audience that the opponent did not use the available methods of attacking
proof and by asking the opponent directly why he did not find fault with
the argument through the customary channels, the opponent is forced on
the defensive and usually is placed in a position of ridicule himself.

DEFENSE AGAINST TURNING THE TABLES

Whenever the opponent to an argument tentatively accepts the evidence presented and then draws an opposite inference from it, he is using
the special refutation method of turning the tables. The same method is
used when both the proponent and the opponent apply the materials of
the argument first to their own advantage and then to the disadvantage of
the order. In each case the attention will be focused not upon the materials
but upon the inferences and applications made with the materials. Accordingly, any defense against the turning-the-tables technique must be
focused upon applications of the materials and the inferences drawn from
them.

An affirmative speaker on nationalized medicine interpreted factual
data to mean that many American people do not receive enough medical
care. A negative speaker used the same evidence to conclude that the American people have the highest standard of medical care in the world. Whereas
the affirmative inferred *need* from the evidence, the negative used the
same evidence to prove *no need* for change.

The best defense against a turning-the-tables refutation is to question
the frame of reference of the opponent's conclusion and to point out that
the opponent is in effect not only admitting the proponent's argument but
also shifting around. In the example considered here, the proponent can
claim that the turning-the-tables technique of refutation used by his ad-
versary actually exposes three weaknesses in the negative.

First, by making no direct attack against the affirmative's inference drawn from the evidence, the negative in effect is admitting the argument. Second, by drawing a different inference (that the American people possess the highest standard of medical care in the world), the negative is shifting ground. Third, by admitting the affirmative argument and adopting a new argument the negative is actually introducing a new basic assumption in the debate—a premise not acceptable to the affirmative—that whenever an injustice against a part of humanity is smaller than a like injustice against the rest of humanity, the smaller injustice becomes justified. Such a frame of reference for argument can be repudiated by the affirmative, and the negative can be placed in the position of defending the general philosophical stand that an evil is defensible as long as it is smaller than a similar large evil. The affirmative, in defending its original argument, can claim that any evil, whether small or large, should be recognized as an evil and as such should be eliminated.

DEFENSE AGAINST DILEMMAS

A dilemma has been defined as a position in which one is challenged to choose one of two possible courses of action, both of which are untenable. Pure dilemmas (as well as true trilemmas, tetralemmas, and polylemmas) are extremely difficult to find. The simple defense against a dilemma is the position that, instead of only two choices of action being available, there is actually a third choice which is overlooked by the opponent. In the case of a trilemma, a fourth choice would be claimed; in the case of a tetralemma, a fifth choice; and in a polylemma, a sixth or additional choices. Thus, in defending himself against the dilemma the debater exposes the opponent who posed the original dilemma as having ignored other and more likely alternatives.

DEFENSE AGAINST THE METHOD OF RESIDUES

Inasmuch as the special refutation method of exposing dilemmas and the method of residues are similar in construction, the defenses against each are likewise similar. In defense against the method of residues, the debater may do one of several things: (1) he may deny the residue and affirm one of the alternatives which the opponent denied; (2) he may admit the residue and also affirm one or more of the alternatives that his opponent denied; (3) he may either admit or deny the residue and any or all of the alternatives and also introduce one or more new alternatives. If the defense introduces a new alternative, his defense becomes identical with that used in the defense against dilemmas.

DEFENSE AGAINST ALLEGED IRRELEVANT ARGUMENTS

Both attack and defense of so-called "irrelevant arguments" center around a distinction between what is relevant and irrelevant. An affirmative might present possibly as many as eleven arguments under his development of the *need* issue. The negative might answer by claiming that six (let us say) of the arguments are irrelevant and have no important bearing on the case. The original proponent of the six arguments charged with irrelevancy will then need to concentrate his defense on pointing out the connection, the importance, the relationship, and the relevancy of the disputed arguments to the case as a whole.

DEFENSE AGAINST OPPOSING ARGUMENTS

It has been pointed out previously how the development of opposing arguments can be construed either as recommended negative strategy (for the opponent of an argument) or as a fallacy of shifting ground (as seen from the affirmative or proponent point of view). Whenever an opponent claims that he is introducing opposing arguments which supplant or overshadow the constructive arguments of the original proponent, the best defense for the originator of the first arguments introduced is to claim that the opposing arguments are in reality cases of shifting ground.

DEFENSE AGAINST QUESTIONS

The most common method of defense against questions is to ask other questions in return. However, such a defense is weak, and the debater who uses such a defense may be charged with shifting ground. Other defenses against questions are much more effective. The various defenses depend upon the purpose and nature of the questions asked. Accordingly, types of defense are suggested for each of the following types of question:

1. If questions are asked as important points of information, the defender should have a ready answer. If the defender cannot answer, he has materially weakened his case.

2. If questions are asked which the questioner knows the defendant cannot answer, and which are unimportant or irrelevant, the defendant should admit that he cannot answer the questions. Then he should proceed to explain the weakness of the foundation and purpose for which the questions were asked.

3. If more questions are asked than can be answered in the time allotted, the defendant (whether he can answer the questions or not) will

find it to his advantage to point out to his audience that the questions are too numerous to answer in the time remaining, and that they were apparently for the purpose of trying to add confusion to arguments that are basically clear and sound, or to evade vital issues.

4. If questions are asked for the purpose of clarifying practicability (or application) of the affirmative plan, the best response is to acknowledge that major matters of application do need to be considered. The defender then needs to be ready with explanations of how the plan is applied in practice. Further, the defender might need to point out that minor matters of application, although interesting, are relatively less vital than the matters considered.

5. If questions are asked for the purpose of exposing inconsistencies, the defendant will need to measure his answers carefully. In such situations the defendant, sensing a trap, might do well to ask that the questions be defined in their fullest frame of reference.

6. If questions are asked for the purpose of exposing fundamental issues (such as those Lincoln asked of Douglas), then the defendant obviously needs consistent answers. Furthermore, the defendant needs to have all aspects of his case in harmony with his general philosophy and in justifiable relationship to any basic assumptions and premises that the questioner has succeeded in establishing with the audience.

GENERAL RULES FOR REBUTTAL

The general rules that were suggested for refutation apply almost universally to rebuttal. In only a few respects do the recommendations on rebuttal strategy differ from good form in developing refutation. The main point to remember is that most of the refutation techniques used to tear down an argument can be used also as rebuttal techniques to destroy refutation and rebuild an original constructive argument.

EXTENSIVE KNOWLEDGE

Build rebuttal on extensive knowledge. It is just as important to have extensive knowledge for defending an argument as it is for tearing down argument. In fact, in defending an argument a debater may expect attacks from many different approaches.

In defending the argument, the original proponent needs to be prepared to defend it not only from the one angle from which it was attacked, but from all possible angles. In this respect, then, the proponent of an argument needs to have even more extensive knowledge of the argument than is needed by his opponent.

NO NEW ARGUMENTS

Do not introduce new issues in the rebuttal speeches. However, new support for issues already introduced is permissible. In formal debates, as in intercollegiate forensic activities, all constructive arguments should be presented during the main or constructive speeches. Rebuttal speeches should be devoted mainly to three purposes: refuting arguments presented by the opponents in the constructive speeches; rebuilding your own arguments that were attacked by the opposition; and summarizing the two cases from your own point of view.

If new issues were permitted in the rebuttal speeches, insufficient opportunity would be afforded for refutation and rebuttal. And if the last speaker in the debate were to introduce a new issue, there would be no opportunity whatsoever for an answer by the opposition.

FORCING THE DEFENSE

Keep your opponents on the defensive. The foregoing suggestions for the distribution of time on refutation and rebuttal indicate that the effective debater attempts to keep his opponent on the defensive. If the defense of your own case can be made easily and positively, and if your attacks on and refutations of your opponent's arguments can be started in the constructive speeches and repeated and magnified in the rebuttal speeches, your opponent can be kept in a defensive frame of mind. The old maxim that "the best defense is a good offense" seems to have application to debate technique.

PLANNED REBUTTAL

Word the rebuttal clearly employing the five-step method. The five-step method of developing a refutation has a very direct application to the defense of an argument in rebuttal. Slightly reworded for use in rebuttal, the five-step method may be stated as follows:

1. State your original argument, and state briefly your opponent's refutation on the argument.
2. Restate the strategic importance of the argument, and state the extent to which your opponent's attempted refutation constitutes a part of his case.
3. Restate, modify, or otherwise specify your stand on your original argument.
4. Offer the additional evidence and reasoning necessary to rebuild your

argument, or offer your counterrefutation that will expose the fallacy of your opponent's attempted refutation.

5. Restate the argument from your own point of view.

FAIRNESS

Be fair to your opponent. What was recommended to a speaker during his refutation applies with equal vigor to a speaker during his rebuttal. A debater who reveals an unworthy character by overstepping the bounds of fair play undermines the impact that sound reasoning and debate strategy may have produced. As Aristotle maintained so strongly, the *ethos* or inherent character of a speaker will sustain or deny his acquired skill in speaking. Emerson stated this idea in another way: "What you are speaks so loud that I cannot hear what you say."

SUMMARY

Repeatedly, the alert debater will examine the arguments of his opponent by asking himself the following questions:

1. Are material statements made that are based upon inaccurate facts, faulty statistics, invalid testimony, contradiction, equivocation, ambiguous construction, or false assumption?

2. Are hasty generalizations present that are based upon insufficient instances, nontypical instances, negative instances, or misinterpreted coincidence?

3. Are all cause-and-effect relationships real and adequate?

4. Do any false analogies exist?

5. Do the deductions used violate any of the rules of formal validity in critical thinking?

6. Does the opponent beg the question by making unsupported assertions, by arguing in a circle, by asking fallacious questions, or by assuming a more general truth?

7. Does the opponent ignore the question by appealing to authority, by discussing personalities, by appealing to the emotions, by appealing to tradition, by appealing to ignorance of the opposite, by shifting ground, by refuting an argument not advanced, by faulty synthesis, or by faulty division?

8. Can the argument of the opponent be reduced to an absurd position?

9. Can the argument of the opponent be reduced to a dilemma?

10. Can the entire proposition be viewed from a number of standpoints, only one of which is defensible?

11. Can the materials presented by the opponent be turned against him to prove the very opposite of his own argument?

12. Do any irrelevant materials or arguments occur in the case of the opponent?

13. Can the arguments of the opponent be admitted and yet refuted by adopting opposing arguments that are more important than those of the opponent?

An affirmative answer to any one of these questions opens the doors to effective refutation.

In rebuilding an argument that has been attacked, a rebuttal speaker should not attempt to defend an argument in which a weakness of logical construction has been exposed. In rebuttal, an original argument can be defended by offering additional evidence in support of the argument, by adopting opposing arguments to the stand of the opponent, and by going on the offensive to attack the opponent's refutation.

In both refutation and rebuttal, fairness toward an opponent must be observed. Failure on this basis often will defeat normally defensible arguments.

EXERCISES

1. In each of the following examples of fallacious argument, identify the fallacy by name, and explain why the argument is fallacious:

    a. Since it is agreed that whatever interferes with good scholarship in college should be abolished, and since fraternities at Provincial University interfere with good scholarship, therefore all fraternities should be abolished.

    b. If I do not finish by theme tonight, I will get an *F* tomorrow. But since I will finish my theme tonight, I can expect to receive a passing grade tomorrow.

    c. Since all Communists believe in state-supported medicine and since my opponents believe in state-supported medicine, therefore it is apparent that my opponents must be Communists.

    d. Because chain stores can buy goods cheaper, they will, therefore, sell them cheaper.

    e. Liberace practices his music for three hours each day. Therefore, if you practice your music for three hours each day, you too can become a great musician.

    f. Out of the 5,000 automobile accidents which occur on Saturday nights every week in the United States, 4,000 of the accidents occur when the driver has been drinking. Therefore, 80 percent of all automobile accidents are cause by drunken driving.

g. In the attainment of any objective it must be assumed that the end justifies the means. Accordingly, if collaboration with and appeasement of the Russian Communists will bring about world peace, then the United States should follow a policy of collaboration and appeasement toward Russia.

h. If America joins the Common Market, the Western world will attain its maximum economic development. But since America will not join the Common Market, the Western world will not attain its maximum economic development.

i. Candidate Bonsorg must be an honest man for his opponents have never been able to prove otherwise.

j. There are no college fraternities in Communist countries. This confirms that one of our best bulwarks against communism is the fraternity system.

2. From your readings of daily newspapers, from current magazines, and from what you hear in daily conversations, compose a list of examples of fallacies in modern thought and speech. Find at least one example for each type of fallacy discussed in this chapter.

3. Read the Lincoln-Douglas debates carefully and record, for presentation to the class, at least three examples of refutation and three examples of rebuttal used by each speaker.

4. List five beliefs or convictions which you hold concerning present economic, political, or social problems. Prepare a 4-minute speech, using all of the elements of proof you can find, defending one of these convictions. Give the speech to the class. Then prepare a refutation against a speech presented by one of your classmates.

   (Note: Good practice would have each student's speech refuted by another member of the class.)

5. Prepare and deliver a rebuttal speech defending the speech which you delivered for Exercise 4 above.

SUGGESTED READINGS

BEARDSLEY, MONROE C. *Thinking Straight,* 2nd ed. Englewood Cliffs, New Jersey: Prentice-Hall, Inc., 1956.

BLACK, MAX. *Critical Thinking,* 2nd ed. Englewood Cliffs, New Jersey: Prentice-Hall, Inc., 1952.

BOGOSLAVSKI, BORIS. *The Technique of Controversy,* New York: Harcourt, Brace & World, Inc., 1928. Chaps. 1–3.

CHASE, STUART. *Guides to Straight Thinking,* New York: Harper & Row, Publishers, 1956, Chaps. 4–17.

FEARNSIDE, W. WARD, and WILLIAM B. HOLTHER. *Fallacy, the Counterfeit of Argument.* Englewood Cliffs, New Jersey: Prentice-Hall, Inc., 1959.

JAMES, HERBERT L. "Standards for Judging Refutation," *The AFA Register,* 9 (Spring 1961), 21–25.

LARRABEE, HAROLD A. *Reliable Knowledge*. Boston: Houghton Mifflin Company, 1945. Chaps. 9–12.

NICHOLS, ALAN. *Discussion and Debate*. New York: Harcourt, Brace & World, Inc., 1941. Chap. 6.

SMITH, WILLIAM S. "Formal Logic in Debate," *Southern Speech Journal*, 27 (Summer 1962), 330–338.

THOULESS, ROBERT. *How to Think Straight*. New York: Simon and Schuster, Inc., 1947.

TOULMIN, STEPHEN E. *The Uses of Argument*. New York: Cambridge University Press, 1958. Pp. 94–145.

they frequently make mistakes. O
Preparing for Debate, the reader
there anything in debating per se
ing?

School debates in this cour
phasize facts, authoritative testim
vast majority of debate speeches a
sometimes almost nonexistent—au
probably think of the word *tourna*
have seen or been in. Like other
to establish a situation in which
habits may be arbitrarily isolated an
then, can be regarded as a simplifi
concentrate on certain skills before
and complex real-life audience situ

It is clear, therefore, that eve
debate work in tournaments must l
he makes—as a speaker—upon hi:
his concern is the well-known fact
perior delivery help to win decisio
that audiences in later life are goin
in terms of the *total* impression h
gard him not as a debater but as a

Good debating, then, is alwa
more than just effective speaking. I
ing an appropriate audience respons
enough. Good speaking—ideally, a
it should be responsible. That is, it
sane manner, and it reflects the sj
words upon the welfare of society.

Good speaking, therefore, is m
speaking is good communication. A
a message to one or more persons
meanings that are reasonably simil
mind. If debate fails to communic
off the launching pad. No commu
bater finds himself saying, "That
getting at," he should search his so

[1] *A Program of Speech Education* (
of the North Central Association. Present
March 29, 1951). Reprinted in pamphlet
37 (October 1951), 11.

course, after studying the chapters on
ill quickly discern the critical issue: Is
which tends to cause ineffective speak-

try, as is well known, commonly em-
ny, and the processes of "logic." The
re delivered in small rooms to small—
liences. Most readers of this book will
lent when they recall debates that they
earning experiences, debating attempts
ertain attitudes, skills, techniques, and
d hence learned. Tournament debating,
d laboratory in which the speaker can
e is compelled to deal with more subtle
tions.[1]

the student who is doing most of his
e vitally concerned with the impression
listeners. The most trivial reason for
that good speech composition and su-
as. But the most compelling reason is
; to hear him, see him, and judge him
makes—in other words, they will re-
speaker.

s good speaking. And good speaking is
ffective speaking is successful in secur-
e (or judge's decision). But that is not
least—should also be intelligent, and
deals with ideas and facts in a logical,
eaker's concern for the impact of his

uch more than a "bag of tricks." Good
person communicates when he sends
ho then "translate" this message into
r to what the message-sender had in
te, it is like a rocket that fails to get
ication—no debate. Whenever a de-
judge didn't understand what I was
l to determine whether it would not

Recommendations of the Contest Committee
d to the Commission on Secondary Schools,
form from the *Quarterly Journal of Speech*,

be more proper to say, "I failed to communicate my message accurately to that judge."

When we say, therefore, that a good debater is a good speaker, and the good speaker is a good communicator, we mean that the most painstaking preparation, the most acute analysis, the most massive documentation, and the most cogent logic all combined will come to nothing unless the debater successfully communicates to his audience.

In short, no debater is worth his salt who regards himself simply as a thinking engine, as a logic machine, or as a word conjurer. As a good speaker and communicator he is a good thinker, a good researcher and organizer of ideas, and he is an acute logician, but more than that, he adapts his style, materials, and delivery so that his listeners can understand him. He handles his materials responsibly. A debater is under no compulsion in every instance to persuade his audience, but he most certainly is obligated to communicate to that audience.

BASIC PRINCIPLES OF SPEECH COMPOSITION

The word *composition* may call up in some minds the image of a written essay, or even of the sort of thing associated with courses in freshman composition. It should be emphasized at once, therefore, that composing a speech, while obviously having much in common with written composition, is quite a different thing from writing an essay. The reader can study, and re-study if he wishes, what is presented to him in written form; the listener cannot (under normal circumstances) do this with what is presented to him orally. From this basic fact flow many important implications for the manner in which a speaker selects, assembles, and phrases his material. Speech composition, then, refers to the processes involved when a speaker decides how much selected material should be included, how it is to be put together, and how it is to be worded.

For present purposes, these processes can be comprehended under four main headings:

Main ideas (including lines of argument) and subordinate ideas
Supporting materials
Organization
Language or style

Hence, when the debater addresses himself to the task of speech composition, these are the things that will concern him. These four topics, there-

238 [IV] THE DEBATER AS SPEAKER

fore, will constitute the main divisions of the present chapter, except the first which is dealt with in previous chapters.

Before considering these topics, it is important to place the entire subject of speech composition in a proper frame of reference. In other words, the debater must keep before him a clear picture of his *goals*. When the debater works to improve his speech composition, what is he striving for? Is he merely composing the speech for the sake of composing it? Or for the sake of exhibiting his erudition? Or for the sake of producing a "work of art"? It is to be hoped that no reader of this book will be motivated to do any of these. Is it not reasonable to insist that the fundamental goal of speech composition is the two-fold one of combining good logic with good communication? In other words, the suggestion here is that there are two basic criteria to be applied to any debate speech:

1. Does the speech meet *argumentative requirements?* (This means that the speech should represent cogent analysis, thorough research, and sound logic.)

2. Does the speech meet *communicative requirements?* (This means that the speech should be clear, interesting, and adapted to the audience —or judge—and to the occasion.)

The question may be asked, "Can the tournament debater adapt, in any serious degree, to the debate judge?" The answer is that although the debater will seldom possess detailed knowledge of the judge's personality or background he almost always will know enough about debate judges in general to plan his vocabulary and choice of materials appropriately. Regardless of how little or how much advance information a speaker ever has concerning a prospective audience, the essential fact remains that if he is to communicate, he must make whatever adaptations he can, in order to meet the audience on terms it understands. Sometimes these adaptations can be planned far in advance; sometimes they must be made on the spur of the moment. Naturally, the wise speaker—or debater—makes as many of them in advance as possible. It may be said that the good debater is largely a product of the quality of his forethoughts. Even impromptu adaptations to audience and to opponents will be more effective if they arise from a reservoir of reflection, writing, and practice before the debater gets to the platform.

A good debate speech, then, is not necessarily one which convinces or pleases only the debater himself; it must be judged in terms of its communicative impact upon the audience (whether the audience be a large crowd or a single critic-judge).

Since most of the preceding chapters have dealt with the argumentative requirements of a debate speech, and since Chapter 8 has dealt, in addition, with audience analysis and motivation, the rest of this chapter will be devoted to the three remaining topics: supporting materials, organization, and language.

SUPPORTING MATERIALS

In order to do a good job of public speaking (communication), the debater is compelled to do much more than present a mere outline or brief of his case to the listeners. It is essential to recognize the different functions of a brief, with its supporting evidence, and a fully composed speech. The reader is referred to Chapter 6, Outlining the Argument, for a discussion of the manner in which he should marshal his supporting arguments and evidence around the main contentions of his case. This process is one which should take place long before the debater faces his audience. The way in which arguments are arranged, and the way in which supporting evidence is ordered, in a preparatory outline or brief are likely to differ radically from the way in which these materials are actually presented to an audience. (If such were not the case, the debate could be carried on in writing.)

Even with a single critic-judge who may have heard many previous debates on the same topic, the debater should not proceed as if he were addressing an electronic computer. The judge, sophisticated (and weary) as he may be, is still a human being, who can comprehend language and ideas at a certain rate of presentation, at a certain intellectual level, and at a certain experiential level. Hence, the debater who plunges immediately into his speech without even brief preparatory material or without clarifying his frame of reference is risking disaster. Likewise, there is never justification for presenting a debate speech that is a great jumble of arguments and facts, that lacks all vestiges of restatement, illustration, or anecdote.

Too many debaters fill their speeches with as much abstract argument, exposition, and statistical data as the time will permit. They fail to appreciate both the logical and the psychological values of anecdotes, vivid analogies, striking contrasts, and specific instances. In recent years much has been written about possible applications of information theory (the scientific theory of message-transmission in electrical systems) to human communication. One important concept from information theory that appears to be eminently applicable to the human listener is the principle of "channel capacity," and the closely related idea of "redundancy." That is, the receiver of a message can be expected to absorb only a given number of message-units per unit of time. In order to prevent overloading the receiver, it is necessary that the rate of information-flow be slow enough that he can comprehend and assimilate the message. This can be accomplished not only by actually reducing the number of words per minute, but especially by reducing the number of new ideas per minute. In other words, redundancy (in the form of repetition and restatement of various kinds) and the insertion of "filler" (or supporting) material are two important ways of insuring that the debater will not exceed the capacity of the judge to understand and assimilate what he says.

A good rule-of-thumb for the debater to adopt is: always include at least some form of supporting material under every argument and subargument in a speech. Another good rule-of-thumb is: always include a reasonable amount of repetition and restatement of the main arguments. What is "reasonable" will have to be decided by the debater on the basis of his analysis of the audience.

The question next arises: "How should the supporting material be integrated into the argumentative material of the speech?" As an answer to this question, a very rough and informal five-part device is described below.

DEVELOPING A DEBATE CONTENTION: THE S-R-S-R-T PRINCIPLE. This should not be regarded as an inflexible formula but only as a general principle to be adapted to each individual speaking situation.

"S"—*State the contention in its exact terminology.* This should be in the same words used when the contention was introduced, and the same words which will be employed to summarize at the end of the speech or at the conclusion of the debate.

"R"—*Restate (or explain) the contention in different words.* Although not always necessary, at least a sentence or two of restatement will assist the judge or listeners in understanding and remembering the salient arguments. Sometimes a hypothetical example is useful here; the debater says something like this: "Now suppose that all of you in this room were members of the United Nations Security Council . . ."

"S"—*Support the contention, usually proceeding from the specific case to the general situation.* An effective psychological (as well as logical) procedure is to relate a concrete narrative or anecdote if such material is available, to rapidly mention several specific examples without narrative details, to follow up with appropriate statistics summarizing the over-all picture and possibly to conclude with a clinching testimonial opinion from a competent authority. The above can be restated in abbreviated "formula" terms: story, examples, figures, quotes. Naturally, the speaker must make intelligent adaptations to the logical requirements of his case, the available evidence, the time limits, and the audience.

"R"—*Restate the contention (briefly).* This may be done in a single sentence, preferably using words somewhat different from the original statement of the contention, since the original wording will be repeated at the end of the speech, when all the contentions are summarized.

"T"—Transition: supply a linking word, phrase, sentence, or paragraph as a transition to the next contention (or final summary of the speech). Frequently, it is well to make reference here to the over-all structure of the case, showing the relation of the next contention to the debate proposition itself. For example: "I suggested at the first of my speech that we of the affirmative would urge three main reasons for adopting the resolution. I have been discussing the first of these reasons. Let me now take up the second; namely . . ."

The following tabular scheme is offered merely as a convenient memory device:

Developing a Contention:
S—for state
R—for restate
S—for support (story-examples-figures-quote)
R—for restate
T—for transition

Any standard text in public speaking will supply the student with an exposition of psychological principles (such as motivation, reference to the familiar, the use of novelty, suspense, conflict, and similar devices). However, a single example may be provocative. In a debate situation, testifying before the Senate Banking and Currency Committee on July 26, 1950, Bernard Baruch was urging the imposition of drastic economic controls in order to achieve full mobilization. He concluded his argument in the following words:

> Nearly three years ago I clipped an item from a newspaper which seems ominously prophetic today. It told of a boast made by a Soviet general. This general boasted that the Western democracies were bound to be defeated by the Soviet Union because they would not make the sacrifices necessary to arm themselves. They prized their standards of living too highly. They would not be willing to accept the discipline to put "guns" over "butter." In Russia, though, this general boasted, the people were inured to hardship. The Soviet government would force the sacrifices to mobilize. A lean and hungry, but mobilized Russia would overrun a Western world which couldn't bring itself to mobilize—in time.
>
> That is the test which confronts us—not only this country but all of the free peoples of the world. It is the choice of "peace" or "butter," of mobilizing our strength now, while peace can still be saved, or of clinging to petty wants and petty profits, imperilling our freedom and our civilization.

No outside enemy can defeat us. We *can* defeat ourselves. Gentlemen, yours is the decision. Which shall it be—discomfort or defeat? [2]

We may or may not agree with Mr. Baruch's logical analysis, especially his sharp dichotomy between "discomfort" and "defeat." But we will probably admit that his is a well thought-out, logically defensible position, thus meeting the criterion of *argumentative adequacy*. We will probably also admit that he couches the argument in terms which are closely related to basic motives and interests, thus meeting the criterion of *communicative adequacy*.

ORGANIZATION

We are concerned here, of course, with those principles of organization (arrangement, structure, sequence) which the debater must observe if he is to make a proper adjustment to the communicative requirements of the audience situation. It is obvious that the suggestions incorporated in this section complement the principles of case construction and of rebuttal discussed in previous chapters. Therefore, these suggestions should be read in conjunction with the appropriate chapters of this text which take up all those matters having to do with the building of a debate case and of a rebuttal speech.

Perhaps the most helpful and concise way of approaching the problem of organization is to reduce our discussion to a generalized outline for any formal debate speech. A "formal" debate speech could occur in such situations as a radio or television symposium, a contest debate, the constructive portions of a cross-examination debate, or a parliamentary debate. This outline represents only a general structure that can (and must) be modified to suit specific occasions, and this outline is obviously designed for the constructive speeches rather than the rebuttals. However, the basic plan will also be found useful in organizing the rebuttals.

GENERALIZED OUTLINE FOR A FORMAL DEBATE SPEECH. Intended primarily for the constructive argument:

I. *Introduction*
   A. Opening sentences
   B. Exposition
      1. Explanatory remarks intended to conciliate audience hostility (when this is necessary)

---

[2] Bernard Baruch, "Full Economic Mobilization," in A. Craig Baird, ed. *Representative American Speeches: 1950–1951*, The Reference Shelf, Vol. 23, No. 2 (New York: H. W. Wilson Company, 1951), p. 93.

2. References to the significance or importance of the question for debate (when this is necessary); allusion to other contemporary events
3. Historical or other informational background necessary for audience understanding of the case
4. Definition of terms not already self-explanatory

C. Review and preview
1. Very brief and concise summary of the main contentions presented in the debate up to this point (for the first affirmative speaker, obviously, no such summary will be possible), making sure that the listeners are in no doubt about the main currents of the argument
2. A statement of the purpose to be served by the present speech; in most cases, achieved by simply announcing in exact words the chief contentions to be developed in the speech

D. Refutation
Removal of road blocks erected by the opposition, with refutation material mainly a resubstantiation of one's own case.

Remarks on the Introduction

It is clear that all these steps cannot be included in all formal debate speeches. By *opening sentences* is meant any material whose chief purpose is to make a favorable initial impression; for example, greeting to the chairman, to the audience, or to the opposition; pleasantries; humorous remarks or repartee appropriate to the occasion; and allusions to the immediate surroundings or to recent news events.

For a bored or hostile audience, the opening sentences and exposition may have to be quite lengthy, especially in the case of the speaker who opens the debate. Definition of terms can frequently be accomplished most efficiently and most interestingly in the context of the argument itself rather than in a stilted, artificial paragraph set off from the rest of the speech.

The order of presentation of the various parts here indicated may sometimes be interchanged. For example, a devastating attack by the preceding speaker of the opposition may have left such an impression on the audience that the succeeding speaker should refute it as soon as he gets to his feet. Furthermore, refutation may easily precede the preview or the review.

A good technique to follow in the review and preview step is to orient the summarizing around the affirmative burden of proof. A sound general principle of debating, as implied elsewhere in this text, is to keep the whole debate keyed to the requirements of maintaining the affirmative case.

In short, the speaker will probably be guided by these two basic purposes of all introductions: to get from the listeners a fair hearing and to get an intelligent hearing. These purposes imply that the speaker, in his introduction, should concern himself with such matters as obtaining good will, attention, and understanding.

II. *Proof*
    A. Statement of first main contention, followed by development of evidence and argument supporting it.
    B. Similar statement and development of other main contentions (if any).

Remarks on the Proof

    The good debater, of course, is one who is able to make constant reference, during the development of a contention, to the assertions and attacks of the opposition. Therefore, refutation is frequently interwoven with the material supporting the constructive argument. The speaker should be cautioned, moreover, against the inclusion of more than one or two main contentions in a single speech, although occasionally three may be required. But a judge or an audience cannot be expected to remember a whole string of main contentions, nor can the speaker really substantiate a large number of them within the confines of reasonable time limits.

    The speaker should remember that the listener is taxed if he has to keep in mind a large number of subsidiary arguments. However, it is obvious that most main contentions can be partitioned into two or more arguments, each of which can in turn be developed by the S-R-S-R-T method. The debater should not hesitate to introduce subcontentions where the nature of the material requires it, but at the same time, he will be advised to avoid excessive enumeration of points. Would anyone contest the ineffectiveness of the following: "And now, my friends, allow me to take up my next point: the fifth reason supporting my third subcontention under our second main argument?"

III. *Summary*
    A. Precise and accurate restatement of the main contentions developed in the speech, with outstanding subcontentions, if possible.
    B. Concluding reference to the state of the entire case, especially to the burden-of-proof requirements.

    Skeleton plans are suggested below for the four constructive speeches in a conventional contest-type debate. (It is assumed that all speeches are 10 minutes in length.) These plans are for the purpose of demonstrating the manner in which the generalized outline may be adapted to specific cases. They are not intended as models for exact imitation.

First affirmative constructive speech

Introduction (3 minutes)
    Opening
    Exposition
        Significance of question
        Background material
        Definitions of crucial terms
    Preview
        State main contentions of affirmative case; relate to burden of proof
Proof (6 minutes)
    Statement of first main contention
        Subcontention A
            Development (S-R-S-R-T formula)
        Subcontention B
            Development (S-R-S-R-T formula)
Summary (1 minute)
    Restate subcontentions; restate main contentions of entire case with reference to affirmative burden-of-proof requirements; close with with possible reference to significance of question and appeal for support of the proposition

First negative constructive speech

Introduction (2–4 minutes)
    Opening
        Respond to affirmative greetings, sometimes brief rebuttal of salient point
    Exposition (frequently omitted)
        Take issue, when necessary, with affirmative definitions
    Review and preview
        Briefly restate affirmative position, with reference to requirements for maintaining burden of proof (taking issue here with first affirmative speaker, if appropriate)
        Indicate general point of view or philosophy underlying negative case; state the main negative *constructive* contentions
    Refutation
        Attack any crucial affirmative argument—unless: (1) you wish to concede first affirmative speech, or (2) you wish to point out that your constructive argument will simultaneously refute the affirmative

Proof (5–7 minutes)
    (Same as first affirmative outline)
Summary (1 minute)
    (Same as first affirmative, except final appeal, which should be for
    the rejection instead of adoption of the proposition)

SECOND AFFIRMATIVE CONSTRUCTIVE SPEECH

Introduction (2–5 minutes)
    Opening
        Respond to negative greetings; sometimes brief rebuttal
    Exposition
        When necessary, discuss definitions of terms, resubstantiating
        affirmative interpretation or explaining any possible obscurities
    Review and preview *plus* refutation
        Remind audience of basic affirmative position; restate main con-
        tentions of the entire case; *refute* crucial negative arguments
        which may have seriously weakened first speaker's arguments; show
        comparative positions of two cases, with reference to burden of
        proof
Proof (4–6 minutes)
    (Same basic outline as first negative and first affirmative speeches)
Summary (1–2 minutes)
    Remind what the task of affirmative speech is; restate main conten-
    tions of entire case; briefly allude to the negative objections refuted;
    show that burden of proof has been essentially maintained

SECOND NEGATIVE CONSTRUCTIVE SPEECH

Introduction (3–5 minutes)
    Opening
        Respond to some convenient remark of affirmative; sometimes
        brief rebuttal-rejoinder to prominent point in preceding speech
    Exposition (usually omitted)
        If any further discussion of definitions is required, dispose of issue
    Review and preview (sometimes combined with refutation)
        Start by stating negative interpretation of burden-of-proof re-
        quirements; briefly restate affirmative case (usually only the
        main contentions here); restate essence of first negative, show-
        ing in what respects first affirmative was weakened; *resubstanti-
        ate* most crucial refutation arguments of first negative
        State task of second negative; preview remainder of negative case
    Refutation (may be incorporated above)

Handle any further constructive arguments of affirmative that obstruct continuation of negative case

Resubstantiate any remaining constructive arguments of first negative that may have been seriously damaged by affirmative attacks

Proof (4–6 minutes)

(Same basic outline as preceding speeches)

Summary (1–2 minutes)

Restate affirmative burden of proof and chief contentions in affirmative case; point out how negative has vitiated these contentions; conclude by a rapid restatement of negative constructive contentions, showing how much must be done by opposition to resubstantiate affirmative; appeal for rejection of the resolution

With the repeated caution that everything in the preceding discussion of organization must be adapted to meet the demands of particular situations, we pass now to the fourth and last component of speech composition, namely, the use of language.

LANGUAGE

Of all the aspects of speech composition, language is the most elusive to treat within the confines of a brief chapter. Like delivery, language responds more readily to flesh-and-blood practice than to textbook theory.

QUALITIES OF STYLE IMPORTANT IN DEBATE. A complete survey of style, the manner in which a person expresses himself, would be inappropriate here, as well as impossible. We are here concerned with special considerations pertaining to the specific use of language by the debater.

There appear to be five desirable qualities of style for which every debater should strive. The following discussion of these qualities is posited, however, upon certain assumptions.

First, it is assumed that the student does not look upon language as something entirely divorced from either the speaker's personality or his subject matter. A sincere, lively, intelligent person is not likely to use affected, dull, or confused language. The speaker, before attempting any specific corrective measures on his use of language, should first look to himself and to his materials. Does he have an adequate speaking personality? Does he respect his audience? Does he have human-interest examples to relate? Is his thinking based upon sound evidence, clear understanding of relationships, and logical analysis of issues?

Second, it is assumed that any student using this book has achieved a minimal level of language usage in such matters as grammar, common vocabulary, and sentence structure. This means that at least the student does not call unfavorable attention to himself by obvious errors in his use of language.

The five desirable qualities of style which are particularly important for the debater to master may be summarized as follows: (1) clarity, (2) accuracy, (3) conversational quality, (4) vividness, and (5) tact. There are, of course, other qualities of good style, but these appear to be the most important for the debate situation.

1. *Clarity.* Mere textbook admonitions to "be clear" will be of little use to the debater whose language has been called murky, confused, or obscure. The debater should understand the basis of clarity. What is the most fundamental difference between words which are described by a given listener as "clear" and those which are described as "unclear"? A word is perceived as clear by a listener if that word falls within his existing language code or frame of reference. A word is neither clear nor unclear in a vacuum; meaning resides not in words but in people. If the debater uses such a term as "counterplan," and a listener has never used that word before, then it will be unclear to that listener. To another listener, such as a veteran debate judge, it will of course be quite clear. Not only are debaters prone to fill their speeches with the technical jargon of debate, they frequently assimilate the special vocabulary of whatever subject matter they are debating. Even in the later stages of a forensic season, when most debaters and judges have been through a national question dozens of times and when the jargon of that question has become well established, the debater would be well advised to be sparing in his use of such jargon. The debater should study his audiences carefully and examine his language as he prepares his arguments, to determine which phraseology is likely to be within the frame of reference of his listeners. In case his audience consists of no more than a single, experienced critic-judge, he no doubt will use more specialized vocabulary and economy of language than with a general audience; however, even in this instance, he should strive to avoid that form of mental laziness which results in "gobbledygook."

Some of the specific ways in which the debater can usually assure clarity of language may be summarized briefly:

    a. A liberal use of short, simple sentences, avoiding especially the frequent occurence of involved, complex, parenthetical constructions.

    b. The use of colloquial, idiomatic expressions (see "conversational quality," discussed below).

    c. The use of labels, numbering, transitional phrases, and so on, for the purpose of making the structure of the speech explicit to the audience (for example, "my second main contention is . . .").

d. The careful arrangement of crucial sentences so that the most important words or phrases in those sentences are placed first or last (the positions of greatest attention-getting value).

e. The explicit identification of all factual or opinion evidence included in constructive and rebuttal speeches, carefully specifying when the material is quoted verbatim, and when it is merely cited, or paraphrased in the words of the debater; stating the exact source (except perhaps page numbers) of both quoted and cited matter; and identifying the qualifications of all authorities from which evidence is derived.

f. The liberal use of comparisons, literal and figurative analogies, metaphors, similes which achieve clarity by applying the fundamental principle of showing how a term or concept is similar to something the audience already knows.

2. *Accuracy.* Although it should be obvious that argumentative discourse requires extraordinary precision of vocabulary, many debaters casually toss about such vague or ambiguous terms as the following: *our plan, burden of proof, status quo, world federation, anti-trust, the government, labor, subsidies, the American people,* and *better red than dead.* It is not suggested that all such words are forbidden in debate, but only that their referents should be clearly established.

Accuracy is obviously closely related to clarity. However, the difference between the concepts is this: accuracy refers to the precision with which language is related to appropriate referents; clarity refers to the degree with which a listener is familiar with the words received. An accurate term may or may not be clear to a specified listener.

Dictionary definitions, sometimes relied upon by debaters to explain special or technical terms, are frequently unsatisfactory devices for clarifying the referents of such terms. The debater will commonly find that, first, he should choose his crucial words with great care to be certain that they are the exact terms to represent what he is talking about; second, he should define these terms, when necessary, by the use of comparisons and examples (as well as by synonyms).

What some semanticists have called "high-order abstractions" are among the most common hazards in the language of argumentation. What is really meant when a speaker says that "the South" will "reject" a federal F.E.P.C., or that "labor" is guilty of "monopolistic practices," or that government-financed "medical insurance" will constitute a "step" in the direction of "socialism"? Any debater should be unusually alert to this pitfall of sprinkling his speeches with almost meaningless "blah" words. He should constantly examine his vocabulary and ask himself, even about the supposedly "obvious words," "What facts or percentages of facts are referred to when I use such-and-such a word?" "What do I mean (in a given context) by *Russia, labor unions, free enterprise, Congress, the administration, the government, justice, peace with freedom?*"

The concern for accuracy is not limited to high-order abstractions such as these. Concern for accuracy applies to the pedestrian, everyday, utility words that are the bricks and mortar of all speech. The debater, like any public speaker, should command a precision of word choice that will reflect subtle shadings of meaning. He might, for example, study such words as the following, asking himself whether he uses them with precision or merely as crutch words: *cite, quote, prove, say, point out, claim, maintain, small, large, important, explain, evil, good.*

3. *Conversational Quality.* The adjective *conversational* unquestionably covers a wide territory. In the present context, it is intended to describe those attributes of language commonly associated with such terms as *direct, spontaneous, unaffected, unpretentious, colloquial, idiomatic, simple, uncomplicated,* and *informal.* In negative terms, conversational speech is the opposite of such traits as are suggested by the following: *stilted, bookish, ponderous, complex, pedantic, obscure, affected, studied,* and *oratorical.* An example of nonconversational style is given below:

> The philosophy of the affirmative having been adumbrated, as the opening speaker in support of the resolution, I now propose to set forth the basic contentions upon which we shall build our case. Envisaging the Hegelian dialectic which appears to explain the contemporary ideological struggle, we of the affirmative wish to argue, first, that the United Nations, as now constituted, will founder upon the rock of communist intransigence.

Even assuming that the thinking is clear in this horrendous example, can we suggest a more conversational wording of essentially the same ideas? For example:

> I have explained the basic philosophy of the affirmative case. Let me now state, in advance, the main contentions upon which that case will be built. You will observe that both these contentions are logical corollaries of our basic philosophy. Number one: the United Nations, as now constituted, will be frustrated by world communism.

It should be noted that *conversational* refers to *good* conversation, not to casual, off-the-cuff talk. It refers to the spirit of good conversation, not to the literal product as we hear it in everyday life. Its very essence, obviously, is communicativeness. The listener feels no barrier between the speaker and himself. Various writers have attempted to analyze the specific elements or devices that create a conversational style. The following elements are extremely important:

a. The use of repetition and restatement—much more than in written composition.
b. The choice of common, nonacademic words, without sacrificing accuracy.
c. Looser sentence structure, with fewer dependent clauses and qualifying phrases, than in most writing.
d. A large number of short, simple sentences.
e. A freer use of personal pronouns, contractions, colloquial or idiomatic terms, and exclamations than in writing.
f. A relaxation of strict grammatical principles to obtain a more informal sentence pattern, especially the judicious use of parenthetical remarks (or asides), the shifting of syntax in the middle of a sentence, and flexibility in word order.
g. The tendency to use more direct discourse or dialogue than in most writing.

4. *Vividness.* The concept of vividness undoubtedly overlaps many other characteristics. Yet it is easy to imagine a speaker using language that is clear, accurate, and conversational without being at all vivid. By *vividness* we mean that which attracts and holds the attention of the audience for longer than just the fleeting moment of utterance. It is close to what some writers call "force." Vivid language makes it possible for the listener to follow the speaker's line of thought easily.

It is impossible to list all the devices that contribute to vividness, but a few of the most important are:

a. *The specific.* "Prime Minister Winston Churchill, in his speech at Fulton, Missouri" is specific; "an eminent statesman has declared" is not.
b. *The concrete.* "A cold, dingy schoolroom with a splintering wooden floor and tall, narrow windows" is more concrete than "an unattractive classroom."
c. *Variety in vocabulary and in sentence structure.* Debaters need especially to avoid the constant reiteration of hackneyed or stereotyped phrases such as the following: "the gentlemen of the opposition," "point out," "we have conclusively demonstrated," "and so we urge you to support the resolution." Debaters can also be imaginative in varying sentence structure without violating the canon of conversational spirit; for example: "Apparently forgotten by our friends of the opposition is the testimony of Senator Blank . . ." instead of "Our opponents have ignored the testimony of Senator Blank . . ."
d. *Repetition in various forms.* Judiciously used, repetition can be very effective. Especially valuable is the practice of restating main conten-

tions in identical terminology when delivering a final summary. Likewise helpful, when not pushed to the point of tedium, are parallel sentence structure and a refrain of key phrases repeated at intervals.

e. *Association with familiar experiences, emotions, or traditions.* Allusions to the Bible, to Abraham Lincoln, to football, to the cold war, and to equally well-known persons, places, and events make a strong impression on audiences.

f. *Sharp contrasts.* Note this sentence from a speech by Eric A. Johnston: "My point is that I don't like bores, barflies, moochers, the bad-mannered or the foul-tongued, whether they are white or black; whether they belong to the church of Rome or the Sons and Daughters of I will Arise." And another, from the same speech: "The Ku Klux Klanners would never take me in, of course, because I have the old-fashioned idea that bed sheets belong on the bedstead instead of over my head on horseback." [3]

g. *Figurative language—especially metaphor and simile.* Debaters should be cautious in their use of these devices. It is actually quite easy to produce "purple patches," "flowery oratory," and bombast. However, no one can doubt the effectiveness of such a powerful metaphor—now almost a part of the language—as "Iron Curtain."

h. *Questions.* Many writers have stressed the attention-getting values of questions, especially in the form of direct interrogation immediately answered by the speaker himself; for example: "Why do we of the negative take this stand? Because we believe that what the affirmative proposes would result in nothing less than the prohibition of labor's right to strike."

5. *Tact.* Unfortunately, some people confuse tact with obsequiousness; others believe that tact implies deceit, unctuousness, or suavity. To state such misconceptions is to refute them. The student may ask: "Is not tact an aspect of personality rather than a quality of language?" The answer is: "Primarily, yes, but it is a trait that can easily be reflected in a speaker's vocabulary." Perhaps the most specific way of achieving tactfulness in language is to aim at moderation.

The debater, probably more than any other type of public speaker, has a special obligation to avoid overstatement of his cases and to avoid couching his argument in terms that are insulting to the opposition. This implies that no speaker is justified in using intemperate language or in casting sly aspersions upon the character or the intelligence of his opponents or his audience.

Both accuracy and urbanity will be served by such terminology as the examples in the left-hand column below suggest.

[3] Eric A. Johnston, "High Cost of Bigotry," in *Representative American Speeches: 1950–1951,* p. 113.

Prefer:	To:
We do not claim a panacea; we do contend, however, that our plan will bring about a significant improvement.	The plan we offer you today is absolutely essential; it is the only solution to the problem of world peace.
We have shown you where the affirmative speakers have failed to produce substantiating evidence.	We have completely demolished every shred of argument advanced by our opponents.
We recognize that intelligent students of the subject have argued otherwise.	No thinking person could possibly argue in such fashion.

A PROGRAM FOR IMPROVING THE USE OF LANGUAGE. We have noted five attributes of style that are especially important in debating. With these in mind as goals, the student can undertake a systematic program designed to produce tangible results. He should not, however, expect miracles. Language is closely associated with personality and deeply embedded in habit patterns and cannot be quickly or radically changed. The procedures listed below suggest practical ways and means to obtain reasonable improvement in the use of language.

1. *Become sensitized to vocabulary and to different ways of using words.* This involves not only wide reading, but reading with the definite purpose of keeping on the alert for the way in which language is handled. The student should note especially the way in which *speakers* express themselves; he can make a conscious effort to list in a notebook those words or phrases which seem to represent especially apt ways of using language. For example (from Winston Churchill, 1945): "It is no easy cheapjack utopia of airy phrases that lies before us."

2. *Under an instructor's supervision, perform a close sentence-by-sentence stylistic analysis of speech models.* Attempt to identify the specific qualities and devices utilized in a well-chosen speech manuscript. See, for example, how Eric Johnston, in the speech cited at the end of this chapter, meets the special criteria proposed in the preceding discussion.

3. *Set up modest but definite goals in vocabulary and stylistic qualities.* In a notebook, list certain words, phrases, or devices that you intend to use—in everyday conversation—during the forthcoming week. At the end of the week, check off those which, in your sincere judgment, you have really mastered. (Be careful not to attempt flowery, bookish, affected, or artificial locutions.)

4. *Include much writing as a part of preparation for platform debating.* The purpose here is not to suggest that the debater should deliver his

speeches from manuscript or from memory; however, a ready vocabulary and a facile response to opponents' remarks are not usually the result of spur-of-the-moment inspiration. A polished extemporaneous style is largely the product of much writing, rewriting, and more rewriting. The debater can even practice the wording of sample rebuttal-rejoinders in advance, while avoiding the use of "canned" material.

5. *Practice speaking extemporaneously, both from brief notes and from manuscript, introducing variations in the wording as much as possible.* Write out exact phraseology—usually in several experimental versions —of the most important contentions, transitions, introductions, and summaries. Read these aloud to yourself and to others. Solicit criticism, invent new and better ways of expressing these ideas. After you have come up with what appears to be the most felicitous and precise phraseology for main and subcontentions, it may be wise to memorize these few vital passages (but no more).

6. *For developing general language facility, practice paraphrasing selected passages from books, articles, and speeches.* There is value in this exercise, whether you choose awkward, pedestrian passages and try to make them sparkle, or whether you choose models of good writing and try to make them even better.

AN ILLUSTRATION OF THE EFFECTIVE USE OF LANGUAGE.   The following excerpts were taken from a radio–television address made in connection with Brotherhood Week, February 18, 1951. The speaker was Eric A. Johnston, at that time Administrator of the Economic Stabilization Agency. The style is obviously well suited to audience debating. Its essential features, however, are appropriate to the tournament or to any other platform situation.

> I'd like to tell you now what I mean by brotherhood—and the best way to say it is to tell you what I don't mean by brotherhood.
> My belief in brotherhood doesn't compel me to hold open house in my home around the clock, or go to lunch with somebody I don't like. Or go out of my way to be chummy with someone from a different church or with a different kind of ancestry.
> My right to privacy and my right to select my friends are not amended one bit by feeling strongly on the subject of the brotherhood of man. I don't even have to say I'm tolerant to believe in brotherhood. And I don't have to be tolerant. In fact, I don't want to have to tolerate anybody. It's awfully uncomfortable to be in the society of somebody that you think you have to tolerate.
> Maybe I could put it this way: I don't want to be at the same table in a public place or anywhere else with a fellow who makes a heel out of himself.

But I don't like the idea of kicking a man out of any door because he doesn't fit the Ku Klux Klan conception of a hundred percent American. . . .

Brotherhood, to me, doesn't mean showing off your tolerance. I think that's sappy, and it's insincere. Nobody is fooled very long. . . .

Brotherhood means appraising the other fellow for what he's worth inside—as an associate in business—or as a social friend. Maybe the Elsie Dinsmores and the Little Lord Fauntleroys of this world can honestly say they love people in the mass. I can't. I've got to love them as people—as individuals.

And when you boil that down, what does it mean—except living by the American code that says the individual counts ahead of everything else? Let's explore that a little farther.

Now it seems to me that the blame for bigotry in this country is very largely heaped on the head of the native-born, white Protestant. If he'd only be nice and tolerant, why, we'd all get along as cozily as so many sleepy kittens in a basket. The way we get the story, that's the way it seems to go.

It just happened that I am native born, white and Protestant. My ancestors were the life of the party on some of the first ships to drop anchor off America; and if you take me somewhat farther back, the Johnstons of Scotland knew a little bit more about clans than those who spell the word with "K" in this country.

One of the grandest things about America is its human panorama—resulting from the intermingling of so many different peoples from so many different cultures. I hope the day will never come when Holland, Michigan, discards its tulip festival and throws away its title to a little piece of Holland in the heartland of America. I hope the day will never come when we cease to celebrate St. Patrick's day and jig to Irish tunes on the 17th of March. I want to see the rich folklore of other lands live on in America—but only esthetically—not politically. . . .

The armor of courtesy is almost impossible to dent. But bigotry never built a bank balance, bought a bond, or gave a boost to the national income. Withholding jobs and business opportunities from one group doesn't make more jobs and more business opportunities for others. It simply serves as a drag on the whole economic engine. In ordinary times, you can't sell radios and refrigerators and automobiles to people who are denied decent jobs through bigotry.[4]

SUMMARY

The good debate speech is a good public speech; it is not only good argumentation, it is good communication. This means that, besides being

[4] *Ibid.*, pp. 112–116. Reprinted by permission.

logically sound, the good debate speech is clear, interesting, and adapted to the audience and occasion. The student, in order to produce this kind of speech, is concerned with certain basic components of the process called *speech composition:* main ideas, supporting materials, organization, and language.

The lines of argument will be determined by the case plan. Appropriate supporting materials (especially stories, examples, statistics, and quotations) should be selected for effective development of major contentions. This development, it has been suggested, may well be based with necessary adaptations, upon the S-R-S-R-T pattern.

A generalized outline for organizing debate speeches has been proposed, consisting of (I) Introduction (opening, exposition, review and preview, refutation); (II) Proof (development of main contentions); and (III) Summary. This outline was illustrated in the form of possible organization plans for the four constructive speeches in a conventional debate.

Five attributes of language usage are especially relevant for the debater: clarity, accuracy, conversational quality, vividness, and tact. To assist the student in perfecting his use of language, a seven-point improvement program has been suggested. By giving careful study to these principles and techniques of speech composition, the debater will enhance his effectiveness before an audience. He will, in other words, be a competent communicator as well as a good debater.

EXERCISES

Exercises for this chapter have been combined with those from Chapter 13 and placed at the end of that chapter.

SUGGESTED READINGS

Suggested readings for this chapter have been combined with those for Chapter 13 and placed at the end of that chapter.

chapter 13

PRESENTING
THE DEBATE SPEECH

by W. Charles Redding

The preceding chapter has dealt with one aspect of the debater's communicative task: composing the speech. The present chapter will deal with the remaining aspect of communication: actually presenting or delivering the speech to an audience of one or more listeners. The able debater is an effective communicator, concerned not only with sound content but also with its transmission.

Delivery is frequently treated as a distinctly separate problem to be concerned about once a speaker has prepared what he wishes to say. Hence, inexperienced speakers frequently work prematurely on aspects of their delivery—concerning themselves with attempts to correct posture, improve vocal variety, or develop expressive gestures before they have considered certain basic factors from which all delivery must evolve.

All speech behavior reflects the personality of the person speaking. Sometimes this is immediately obvious, sometimes not. Cicero wrote that "all expression is perfect." By this seemingly absurd statement he meant approximately what modern psychologists mean when they say that, whatever a person does or says, he is expressing his personality in some way.[1] Therefore, this chapter will approach the problem of delivery by first considering the total personality of the speaker.

---

[1] See Elwood Murray, *The Speech Personality*, rev. ed. (Philadelphia: J. B. Lippincott Company, 1944); Calvin S. Hall and Gardner Lindzey, *Theories of Personality* (New York: John Wiley & Sons, Inc., 1957).

THE DEBATER AS A PERSON

The debater's effectiveness as a speaker is a function of the way in which his audience perceives him as a whole person.[2] And the way in which the audience perceives him is closely linked to the kinds of attitudes he expresses (or seems to express—which is all the same thing to the audience). For example, if he regards the debate platform as a parade ground where he may exhibit a melodious voice, an impressive vocabulary, a talent for biting sarcasm, or a flashy wardrobe, he will make something less than a favorable impression upon the audience.

Similarly, if the debater has come to look upon the winning of a decision as the paramount goal, overriding all other considerations, it is probable that—as a result of this attitude—his delivery may be characterized by a harsh voice, or a machine-gun tempo, or an aggressive manner. Again, a debater may harbor the illusion that he is obligated to convince the judge of the indisputable 100 percent rightness of his own case, as opposed to the incontrovertible 100 percent wrongness of the opposing case. Is it any wonder, then, that such a debater is accused of bellowing, or table-pounding, or pacing like a caged beast, or insulting his opponents?

There is no intent here to argue that all speech problems can be attributed so obviously to specific attitudes. All of us have met persons who may be charming, fluent conversationalists but awkward, halting public speakers; or we may be acquainted with someone who is rather quiet and reserved when off the platform, yet dynamic and vivid before an audience. Nor is it the purpose of this discussion to suggest that the student can perfect his speaking ability solely by revising his attitudes or tinkering with his personality. The former will frequently be insufficient, and the latter is, of course, foolhardy. But there may be some merit in reminding oneself that many speech problems are best approached as attitude problems.[3] Frequently, an inappropriate attitude, once recognized for what it really is, can be changed with relative ease. Once changed, the consequent improvements in speech preparation or delivery, as actually observed in some instances, may be effortless and almost automatic.

Probably the most important thing to be said here is this: The im-

---

[2] *A Program of Speech Education* (Recommendations of the Contest Committee of the North Central Association, presented to the Commission on Secondary Schools, March 29, 1951), p. 11. Reprinted in a separate pamphlet form from the *Quarterly Journal of Speech* 37 (October 1951), 347–358.

[3] "Successful communication depends upon the understanding, respect, tolerance, and sympathy which speaker and hearer have for each other. Accordingly, certain attitudes should become intimately associated with speech and speaking situations. They are the attitudes of helpfulness, cooperation, tolerance, inquiry, concession, admission, self-reliance, honesty, and conviction." *A Program of Speech Education*, p. 11.

pact of the debater's total personality is likely to be more significant than his mastery of any specific speaking techniques. Authoritative opinion (dating back to ancient Greece), substantiated by everyday observation and recent experimental research, supports the conclusion that a speaker who is well liked or highly respected by his audience will be more effective than one who is the epitome of rulebook perfection but whose personality rubs everyone the wrong way.[4] Of course, it is true that the speaker's personality, as it impresses itself upon the audience, can only be perceived in terms of his actual behavior: the way he walks, his vocal inflections, his choice of words, his grammar, his clothing, and a host of other details.

Hence, it seems likely that the speaker who has mastered the techniques of speech composition and delivery is more likely to make a better impression as a personality than the speaker who has not. The total personality, however, is such a complex, subtle, delicate, and intangible thing that mere techniques or skills, by themselves, will always be insufficient to account for it. It is for this reason that we all have observed effective and pleasing speakers who violated many principles of speech theory; and it is for the same reason that we have observed perhaps just as many speakers who were master technicians but nevertheless ineffective or unpleasant speakers.

The ideal toward which the student should aspire, naturally, is a combination of good techniques and good personality. Fortunately, all the evidence indicates that mastering sound principles of speech helps to build a more effective total personality. Probably most speech teachers, debate coaches, and psychologists would agree with the following statement, taken from the recent report of a Special Contest Committee of the Speech Association of America:

> Personality traits and attitudes seem to be most often revealed in speech, and significant development in speech is usually accompanied by significant gains in personality.[5]

But let it be repeated emphatically: A speaker's total personality (as it is perceived by the audience) is the most important factor in his speaking effectiveness. As Aristotle wrote in the fourth century B.C., the speaker's character is probably "the most potent of all the means to persuasion." [6]

---

[4] See, for example, the researches on "credibility of the communicator" discussed by C. I. Hovland, I. L. Janis, and H. H. Kelley in their *Communication and Persuasion* (New Haven, Conn.: Yale University Press, 1953). Note also Franklyn S. Haiman, "An Experimental Study of the Effects of *Ethos* in Public Speaking," *Speech Monographs*, 16 (September 1949), 190–202.

[5] *A Program of Speech Education*, p. 4.

[6] Lane Cooper, trans., *The Rhetoric of Aristotle* (New York: Appleton-Century-Crofts, 1932), p. 9 (Book I, 1356a).

WHAT IS A GOOD SPEAKING PERSONALITY?

The logical question arises: What kind of personality is usually most effective with the average audience—at least in the United States? Many are the modern prophets who come forward with facile answers—"ten easy steps to personal magnetism, fame, and fortune." But both scientific evidence and everyday observation convince us that nothing so complex as the human personality can be boiled down to a few catchwords. All that seems possible at the present moment is to suggest a few general attributes which apparently, most of the time, characterize good speakers.

So easy is it to slip into hazardous generalizations about psychology that certain cautions will be sounded before we list the attributes of a good speaking personality.

1. So-called .traits of personality may frequently be rooted in the most remote recesses of a person's life. They may be the result of many different forces—wishes, experiences, biological factors. Hence, they may be difficult to modify.

2. Whether deep-rooted or relatively superficial, traits are not simple, unitary segments of a personality; they are the result of the interplay between the person and the situation in which that person is operating at a given moment. Hence, as an example, a speaker may be shy in one given situation, bombastic in another, or quietly confident in a third.

3. Although it is usually difficult to produce significant personality changes after the childhood years, it is also true that some important changes do commonly take place in late adolescence or early adulthood—the high school and college years.

4. Modification of traits or attitudes may take place as a result of the rewards and penalties provided in a given environment. For example, many debaters may rid themselves of excessive sarcasm if they find that coaches, judges, fellow debaters, and audiences obviously disapprove of such behavior.

The suggestions outlined below, therefore, are offered merely as guides. Results will depend upon the kind of practice, the kind of preparation, and the kind of debating encouraged by the student's instructor, both in class and out of class. But it is hoped that these suggestions may provoke fruitful self-analysis and may indicate programs for improvement.[7]

Current textbooks, rating charts, experimental studies, and tourna-

[7] See Gardner Murphy, *Personality: A Biosocial Approach to Origins and Structure* (New York: Harper & Row, Publishers, 1947), especially Chapters 26 and 30.

ment ballots suggest a number of identifiable traits which might go to make up the "ideal" speech personality. It is interesting to note how closely the modern authorities parallel the three requirements of a persuasive personality proposed by Aristotle: intelligence, character (integrity), and good will.[8] Although not a precise scientific instrument, the following description is probably a safe guide for the student who asks, "What is the ideal speech personality?"

The speaker will enhance his chances for effectiveness as he causes the audience to feel that he is:

1. *Honest,* including sincere, ethical;
2. *Communicative,* that is, eager to speak; alert, animated; lively; interested in the audience;
3. *Likable,* that is, genial, modest (without being self-effacing), friendly, tactful, courteous, endowed with a sense of humor, free from artificiality or affectation;
4. *Tolerant,* that is, open-minded, able to see and respect other points of view (without compromising deep convictions), willing to make concessions and to admit errors;
5. *Competent,* that is, well informed, well prepared, thoughtful, logical, poised, confident (without being cocky).

Admittedly other attributes might be added. However, there is some advantage in reducing the basic list to five—a number small enough to be easily remembered. If the student can obtain accurate and honest evaluations from his instructor or from his listeners on these five traits, he may find it possible to locate subtle sources of ineffectiveness. Once these are located, it should be easier to set about their elimination.

HOW DOES THE DEBATER'S PERSONALITY REFLECT HIS ATTITUDES?

An important way of describing what kind of person an individual is consists of making a catalog of all his discoverable attitudes. For present purposes, the word *attitude* will be taken to mean "a predisposition to respond, favorably or unfavorably, toward a specified stimulus." The stimulus may be a person, a place, an object, an idea, a word, or any other object of attention. We have attitudes toward President Kennedy, toward our home town, toward cats, toward Christianity, toward the word *scab*, and so on.

Our concern here, however, is with the debater's attitudes toward three special stimuli of crucial importance to him as a debater: attitudes

[8] See *The Rhetoric of Aristotle,* p. 92 (Book II, 1378a).

toward the speaking situation (including its components—audience, judges, colleagues, opponents), attitudes toward himself, and attitudes toward debate as an educational activity.

THE DEBATER'S ATTITUDE TOWARD THE SPEAKING SITUATION. It has become a truism to say that no speaking situation is complete unless it includes elements such as the audience, the speaker, the subject-matter of the speech itself, and the occasion (time, place, and so on). Occasionally speakers seem to forget this simple truth. They seem to believe that nothing is important but themselves—their voices, their pronunciation, their grammar, perhaps—or that only the facts are important, with the result that the audience is bewildered by an avalanche of quotations, statistics, and closely reasoned arguments; or, at times, that only the audience matters, with the result that jokes and sensational assertions are substituted for a cogent debate case.

The debater can help himself arrive at appropriate attitudes by pondering the following premise: The listener is the final judge of the speaker's effectiveness. No matter how much the debater may protest, "But I made that argument crystal clear!" if the judge or the other listeners failed to get the point, then the debater, as a speaker, was not effective—on at least that one argument. The speaker, of course, is under no obligation to surrender his beliefs or his personality for the sake of placating any audience. He is, however, forced to communicate in the only terms by means of which communication ever takes place: those terms that are adapted to the understanding, the background, and the feelings of the audience. The speaker who ignores this basic truth ends up by talking to himself. The debater who never forgets it may still fail, but he will fail for other reasons.

THE DEBATER'S ATTITUDE TOWARD HIMSELF. In a strictly logical sense, the speaker is of course a component of the total speech situation. However, it is convenient to separate the debater's attitudes toward all those elements of the situation which lie outside his person, from his attitudes toward himself.

How should the debater regard his own role in the speech situation? Should he think of himself as an instructor of the audience (or of the judge, or worse yet, of his opponents)? Should he think of himself as an expert lecturer? Should he think of himself as a clever performer, as a showman, or—in other words—an exhibitionist?

The most reasonable point of view is that the debater should regard himself as an instrument of communication. He is not the prime factor in the total situation; the prime factor should always be the message, not the person. The debater should remember, therefore, that he appears before the audience (and this audience includes critic judges and opponents as well as "lay" listeners) for the purpose, not of exhibiting himself, but of communicating a body of ideas. He is a kind of mediator between subject matter and audience. If the audience were already in possession of the thoughts and the feelings that make up the content of the speech, there would be no need for the speaker. The debater who fully appreciates this fact will be less likely to call attention to himself by such devices as studied gestures, artfully contrived vocal inflections, theatrical pronunciation, or ponderous sentences.

It is also true that a complete grasp of this principle should be of some assistance in relieving excessive stage fright. It seems evident that many speakers lack confidence because they unwittingly assume that the audience exists for the purpose of examining every minutest detail in their platform behavior. Such speakers might deny that they are egocentric. And yet they really are egocentric, for they are assuming (or behaving as if they assumed) that the audience has assembled just to watch their gestures, just to criticize their grammar, just to ridicule their voices, and so on.

Severe stage fright tends to wither as the speaker realizes that he is not the most important item in the total speech situation, that he is there to communicate a subject, and that it is possible to be an effective communicator in spite of technical faults in language, delivery, or speech composition. As he plunges into his speech and as his mind is occupied with trying to convey his ideas to the listeners, he discovers that he does not have time to be worried about himself; hence, he has no time to be frightened.[9]

One way of summarizing this second attitude is to say that the speaker should neither overestimate nor underestimate his true function (a communicative function) in the total speech situation. The student debater might use a check list of such questions as the following: "Was I too casual or flippant in that debate? Or was I a stuffed shirt? Was I apologetic? Or was I dogmatic? Was I thinking, while on the platform: How am I doing? Was I concentrating on my words, my gestures, and my voice instead of on my ideas and my listeners?"

THE DEBATER'S ATTITUDES TOWARD DEBATE. The debater will be a better speaker if he knows in his own mind what debate is all about. He should realize that debate is an educational device, that it is much more than a game or than a speaking contest, that it exists as an instrument of social significance. The debater may well consider the place of debate in modern society; even the most trivial class exercise or practice debate is

[9] The definitive modern statement of the concept of "conversational quality" in speaking comes from James A. Winans and was first published in 1915. For his most recent version, see his *Speech-Making* (New York: Appleton-Century-Crofts, 1938), pp. 23–30.

meaningful only as a device for developing in a student a skill that is supposed to have some sort of social usefulness. The debater can carry forward this line of thinking by recognizing that debate exists not in a vacuum but in a specific social setting.

As a part of a specific social structure, debate should contribute to the understanding of important public questions. There is nothing wrong with mock debates or humorous disputations on such questions as: "Resolved: That this house believes in Leprechauns" or "Resolved: That the Rock should have landed on the Pilgrims." But we are not here concerned with this sort of thing. The debater who has a full awareness of his duty to promote the understanding of public questions is less likely to be the sort of speaker who indulges in pedantic language, frivolous quibbling over technical definitions, distortion of evidence, or a condescending manner of addressing his audience.

A good question for the student to ask himself at the end of any debate (whether it be a private practice engagement in an empty room or a formal forensic meeting before a large audience) could be: "What have I done in this debate to achieve a better understanding of an important problem on the part of myself, of my opponents, or of my audience?"

The debater must never get so wrapped up in a contest that he loses sight of the fact that he is supposed to be learning something in that contest—something more than the way to meet a negative counterplan or what to do about the judge's idiosyncrasies. Educational benefits should accrue both to the speakers and to the audience. Both should learn something about the techniques for analyzing issues, the methods for evaluating evidence, the criteria for drawing logical inferences.

A SPECIAL PROBLEM IN COMMUNICATION: SPEAKING ON BOTH SIDES OF A QUESTION. Before proceeding, it is essential to expose a common source of difficulty. Communication implies purpose. A speaker or writer does not ordinarily string together words taken at random from the dictionary or the telephone book. He is normally concerned with trying to get a definite response from his audience.

Textbooks in public speaking traditionally identify at least three general kinds of audience response, sometimes called the speaker's general purposes. One simplified way of listing them is (1) to entertain the audience, that is, to get the listeners just to enjoy themselves; (2) to instruct the audience—to get the audience to understand ideas, facts, processes, and the like; and (3) to persuade the audience—to modify the beliefs or feelings of the audience, sometimes to obtain specific actions from the audience. Debate, as a technical form with set rules of procedure, may of course be used to accomplish any of these three purposes. It is of crucial importance, however, that the speaker be clear in his own mind about exactly which purpose his is serving in a given debate.

If the debater knows—and if the audience knows—that it is a mock debate, then no damage is done by exaggeration, by playful burlesquing of serious argument, or even by manufacturing supposed evidence for the sake of humorous effect. But in a serious debate, even though humor may be used as a communicative device, most of the techniques are entirely different. Great changes take place in the choice of basic issues, in the authorities, in the statistics, in the organization, in the wording, in the use of vocal inflections, and even in posture and gestures.

In a classroom, in a research seminar, or in a debate tournament, speakers are very frequently heard presenting arguments to support a proposition that has been assigned them and not necessarily one in which they believe or which they desire the audience to accept. In these latter cases, the purpose of the debating would probably be classified as educational rather than persuasive. That is, the speakers are expected to present as good a case as the evidence warrants in order that the participants and the listeners may better understand—or analyze—the problem. This educational type of debate, therefore, can be considered a special case of analysis or exposition. As such, it may legitimately take its place as one of the problem-solving techniques.[10]

It is possible to designate two types of debate, according to the speaker's purpose. For convenience, these will be called the *analytical* and the *persuasive*. The former is concerned with exposing all the relevant facts, opinions, and inferences on one side or the other of a given proposition. The latter is concerned with the attempt, by all legitimate means at the

[10] Cf. Wayne N. Thompson, "Discussion and Debate: A Re-examination," *Quarterly Journal of Speech*, 30 (October 1944), 293–299. Writes Thompson (p. 298): "Discussion and debate, of course, are not identical, but the points of likeness are more significant than the points of difference. Both are concerned with the solving of problems and the finding of truth. . . ." Thompson insists that "Debating is not properly a form of persuasion" (p. 294), arguing that debate is really a division of investigation: "Whereas the purpose of persuasion is to move opinion in a predetermined direction, the form of debate is designed to permit both sides to be heard. Thus, every persuasive plea can be immediately countered, and the effectiveness of the advocate reduced. The debate situation, on the other hand, is well adapted to the careful testing of a proposition and to the suspension of judgment until both sides have been heard. Debate, therefore, is useful in a democratic society because it is *not* a form of persuasion and because it makes difficult the practice of demaguery and authoritarianism." Somewhat similar views are expressed by Clevenger, Ehninger, and Windes.

The present writer suggests that the *form* of debate may be used in many kinds of situations—including the most flagrant types of audience-oriented persuasion. The basic point of view advanced in this chapter is simply that as a *form*, debate may be used to serve any of the purposes to which oral communication can be put.

speaker's command, to gain audience assent. The mental attitude and speaking style will differ in accordance with the type of debate that is being practiced.

The speaker should be able to avoid moral and psychological problems by a clear recognition of which of these types of debate he is using in a given situation. It follows, of course, that the audience (if any) should also understand what type of debate they are listening to. Just as there are conventions in the theatre and the courtroom which make it clear to the audience that the actors or the lawyers are not necessarily arguing their own personal convictions; so those who listen to a debate can easily distinguish whether or not the speakers are attempting to instruct by means of argumentative analysis or to persuade by all the logical and psychological means that are appropriate. If this differentiation is clear to the speaker and clear to all who hear him, there can hardly be anything "immoral" about arguing two sides of the same question. No deception is involved.[11]

It may be suggested that debating both sides is a special instance of *role-playing*. In recent years, training courses designed to improve the "human relations" skills of managers and executives have been conducted— in adult extension classes, in industrial plants, and in a great variety of voluntary organizations. A common feature of such courses has been practice in role-playing; that is, practice in "acting out" the words and attitudes of other people. For example, the supervisor may play the role of a complaining worker; the executive may play the role of a dissatisfied middle-manager; or the bank employee may play the role of a confused customer. A recent issue of *Communication in Action* described how the industrial relations vice-president of a large manufacturing company, "upset over this firm's consistently poor showing in labor arbitration, used role-playing to reverse the trend of unfavorable decisions." What this vice-president did was to put a team of company men, several weeks before a forthcoming arbitration hearing, "through a session of 'pre-trial' role-plays," in an effort

[11] The student will find a thorough airing of arguments for and against the practice of debating both sides (in tournaments) in a series of recent articles: Richard Murphy, "The Ethics of Debating Both Sides," *The Speech Teacher*, 6 (January 1957), 1–9; Nicholas Cripe, "Debating Both Sides in Tournaments Is Ethical," *The Speech Teacher*, 6 (September 1957), 209–212; Richard Murphy, rejoinder, "Debating Both Sides," 6 (September 1957), 255–256; Donald K. Smith, letter to the Editor, "Debating Both Sides," *The Speech Teacher*, 6 (November 1957), 336; George W. Dell, "In Defense of Debating Both Sides," *The Speech Teacher*, 7 (January 1958), 31–34; Douglas Ehninger, "The Debate About Debating," *Quarterly Journal of Speech*, 44 (April 1958), 127–136; Russel Windes, Jr., "Competitive Debating: The Speech Program, The Individual, and Society," *The Speech Teacher*, 9 (March 1960), 99–108; Donald Sikkink, "Evidence on the Both Sides Controversy," *The Speech Teacher*, 11 (January 1962), 51–54.

to "ensure that all arguments of company and union, plus the arbitrator's viewpoint, would be brought out into the open." Furthermore:

> Roles were rotated several times during the series to develop each point of view (arbitrator, union, and company) more fully. This rotation plan never failed to produce additional facts or ideas for strengthening the company's argument. . . . weaknesses showed up when several important points in the company argument didn't stand up under rebuttal.[12]

Recent experimental studies, two of them dealing specifically with college debaters in situations requiring them to argue on two sides of a proposition, support the general conclusion that mere study of the other side is not enough to induce true appreciation of it—that, in Sikkink's words, "one has to take the other side verbally in order to appreciate its actual strength." [13]

Why discuss this matter at such length? Simply because confusion on the part of the debater concerning his real communicative purpose has frequently been responsible for poor speaking on the platform. Such confusion may in some cases encourage a flippant "who cares?" attitude— with obvious and obnoxious results in platform behavior. In other cases, the debater may become so disconcerted by "arguing against his true convictions" that his speaking becomes listless, halting, and monotonous. It is argued here that the debater who knows what he is doing, who perceives the implications of what is meant by "analytical" debating (who perhaps regards it as a form of role-playing), and who realizes what is meant by "persuasive" debating (*never* properly a form of role-playing), should find it that much easier to achieve his maximum effectiveness as a speaker before an audience.

[12] *Communication in Action* (a monthly newsletter published and privately circulated by the American Management Association, New York), 3 (nos. 11 and 12, November–December 1958), p. 1.

[13] Sikkink, p. 54. See also Hovland, Janis, and Kelley, summarizing the research of I. L. Janis and Bert T. King, "The Influence of Role-Playing on Opinion Change," *Journal of Abnormal and Social Psychology*, 49 (April 1954), 211–218; King and Janis, "Comparison of the Effectiveness of Improvised versus Non-Improvised Role-Playing in Producing Opinion Changes," *Human Relations*, 9 (1956), 177–186: ". . . it is possible that even when exposed to the same persuasive communications, people who are required to verbalize the communications to others will tend to be more influenced than those who are only passively exposed" (p. 218). See also Leon Festinger and James M. Carlsmith, "Cognitive Consequences of Forced Compliance," *Journal of Abnormal and Social Psychology*, 58 (March 1959), 203–210; these authors produce research evidence to indicate that if a person is induced to verbalize something contrary to his original convictions, there is a tendency for him to shift those convictions in the direction of the material he verbalizes, especially when minimal pressure is used to elicit the verbal behavior.

DELIVERY

The student should first be clear in his own mind on what a thing is before he attempts to deal with it. When he tries to improve delivery, just what is it that the debater is trying to improve?

For present purposes delivery may be defined as *all those forms of nonlinguistic and nonideational behavior* which a speaker uses in an oral-communication situation. More specifically, delivery consists of all the multitudinous ways in which a speaker can modify his vocal and bodily behavior. In a purely physical sense, all stimuli ordinarily directed by a speaker to his audience consist of visible movements and audible sounds (although other senses may occasionally be involved as well). For convenience, we can arbitrarily abstract from these stimuli the ideational and linguistic content of the message and classify all that remains as delivery. Thus, none of the following should be regarded as forms of delivery: language, lines of argument, main heads and subheads, organization, logic, or supporting material. This is not to imply that delivery and content are unrelated. It is obvious that the two are inextricably woven together into a single, complex message perceived as a Gestalt by the listener. However, it has been found quite possible, for pedagogical purposes, to treat delivery apart from content as such and to practice elements of delivery without paying primary attention to thought or language.

After subdividing vocal behavior into three rather obvious types, we can list four basic *components of delivery*—as follows:

1. *Voice*, that is, phonation.
2. *Articulation*, that is, the production of speech sounds or phonemes: vowels and consonants.
3. *Pronunciation*, that is, the selection of speech sounds along with the stressing of certain syllables to produce recognizable words.
4. *Bodily behavior*, that is, posture, gesture, facial expression, and movement.

(Each of these four components could be further subdivided. For example, voice can be broken down into such entities as pitch level, pitch changes—inflections and steps, volume, quality or timbre, rate, pausing and phrasing, and so on.)

THE FOUR SO-CALLED STYLES OF DELIVERY

It is common knowledge that a speaker may talk "on the spur of the moment," that is, without any specific preparation for a specific speech. This is what is meant by impromptu speaking. Another word, frequently used in everyday discourse as synonymous with impromptu, is extemporaneous. Modern speech teachers, however, generally restrict the use of this word to that kind of speaking characterized by careful advance preparation of ideas and supporting materials, but expressed in language whose precise wording is composed, for the most part, at the moment of speaking. Even if phrases, sentences, or brief passages are given from memory, the speech as a whole would still be classified as extemporaneous. A third approach, very familiar to all of us although falling more into disuse, is verbatim-memory. Finally, there is the method so frequently encountered today—the use of a manuscript which is read word for word to the visible (or invisible) audience.

Obviously, different speakers, subjects, audiences, and occasions will determine which of these four styles will be appropriate in a given situation. However, two observations are in order. First, the debater, whether he be engaging in formal or informal argument, will most frequently use the extemporaneous style. That is, he will prepare his speech, even to minute details, with great care. He may even crystallize the exact wording of crucial contentions and transitions. But the phraseology, with only minor exceptions, will remain the product of the moment. The debater will usually engage in all four styles in a single debate. He must rely upon impromptu speaking for on-the-spot adjustments to the audience and to remarks of the opposition. He uses extemporaneous speaking to present the bulk of his arguments. He uses memory for precise wording of main contentions. And he reads certain quotations from his evidence cards.

In the second place, it should be noted that the terms *impromptu, extemporaneous, memorized,* and *read* really are more accurately used to describe methods of preparation than of delivery. However, it is clear that the way in which a speaker has prepared will exercise a dominant influence upon the way in which he delivers the speech.

THE BASIC CRITERIA OF GOOD DELIVERY

Many students make the mistake of trying to work on vocal inflections or gestures without really understanding what their goals are. A sound philosophy of delivery—an understanding of what function delivery plays in the total communicative situation—is in some instances almost all that a speaker needs in order to correct serious faults. Earlier portions of this chapter have developed the general point of view that communication is the normal purpose of all public speaking. If this is accepted, certain corollaries follow:

1. Content justifies delivery—not vice versa.
2. Delivery is important only as it facilitates the accurate and effective communication of a speaker's ideas to an audience.

3. Although good delivery is an absolute prerequisite of good speaking, it is secondary to good content.

If we continue this line of reasoning, we are forced to conclude that good delivery is that which meets two fundamental requirements. These may be stated as follows:

1. *Good delivery is unobtrusive.* This means that a speaker's voice, posture, or gestures do not call attention to themselves. Voice, articulation, pronunciation, and bodily behavior should all function so smoothly in helping to convey the speaker's meanings that the members of the audience are not even aware of the techniques the speaker is using. If a listener comments, "What graceful gestures, what a beautiful voice," the chances are that the delivery was not appropriate, that is, it was *not* what we are here calling good delivery. If a listener says, "I can't remember anything especially about his delivery," the chances are that the delivery was excellent.

The implications of this requirement are that the delivery must be free from affectation, artificiality, or obviously studied effect. It must be consistent with the personality of the speaker. Vigorous gestures may be quite appropriate for Speaker A but absurd for Speaker B. Furthermore, the delivery must fit the occasion. Larger audiences, for instances, usually require more sweeping gestures and a slower rate of utterance than do small, intimate groups.

2. *Good delivery reinforces the speaker's meanings.* Superior speakers, by subtle shadings in vocal quality and by a wide repertory of changes in pitch, time, and volume, are able to make an audience comprehend infinitely more than the mere words themselves in cold print could ever do. A strategic pause just before a crucial word, a shrugging of the shoulders, a slight movement of the hand, a raising of the eyebrows, a guttural rasp, a rising inflection, all these and many more constitute the complex vocabulary of vocal and bodily delivery. Such techniques as these, regardless of how they are learned in the beginning, are effective only when they are executed so spontaneously that neither speaker nor audience is made aware of them as such.

Ideally, the speaker perfects his command of vocal and bodily expression in the seclusion of private practice. He masters techniques of delivery to the point where they have become established habit patterns. In the public-speaking situation he is then free to concentrate upon his ideas, his words, and his audience. With very little conscious effort, his delivery will be automatically responsive to his ideas.

SPECIFIC GOALS TO WORK FOR IN DELIVERY

These two basic criteria—unobtrusiveness and reinforcement of meaning—may be expanded into a workable list of specific qualities. The speaker may find some profit in using the list suggested below as an aid in self-diagnosis.

VOICE. *Intelligibility through adequate volume and rate.* With the aid of his instructor and other critical listeners, the student can determine whether he is speaking too loudly, not loudly enough, too fast, or too slow.

Appropriate variety to emphasize meanings. Unless persistent mannerisms are discovered, the speaker will do well to analyze the precise shadings of meaning that he may be failing to convey, rather than to plunge into a sterile, mechanical examination of such technical details as pausing and phrasing, syllabic duration, and rising and falling inflections. In other words, he should start with a careful study of meanings before working on techniques.

Pleasing use of voice to help focus audience attention on the speaker's ideas. What makes a voice pleasant to listen to? We think, of course, of quality (timbre). The speaker should be free of such quality defects as nasality, huskiness, and breathiness. But that is not the whole story. Pitch level, over-all rate, and volume level also contribute to pleasing voice. Rhythm, fluency, and syllabic duration are likewise involved. Although these may be considered fine technical details, they are matters with which some speakers must deal directly.

ARTICULATION. The speaker's goal here is to produce accurate, intelligible speech sounds that are easily understood by his audience. It is needless to argue the necessity of eliminating such faults as lisps, muffled vowels, slurred consonants, and aberrant formation of individual speech sounds.

PRONUNCIATION. *Acceptability or Correctness.* The speaker's goal here is to pronounce his words in such a way that he arouses a minimum of discomfort or hostility in his audience. He must study not only the standard dictionaries, but also and particularly those specialized sources which offer a scientific attempt to describe the way in which educated persons actually pronounce words today: for example, the *Pronouncing Dictionary of American English,* edited by Kenyon and Knott (G. & C. Merriam Co., 1953).

Appropriate dialect. We refer here to what C. K. Thomas calls "regional types" or "speech areas." [14] By common observation, even though he may be untrained in phonetics, any student is familiar with certain characteristics which set apart the speech of New Englanders and of Southerners from the rest of the country. It should be emphasized here that there is no implication that any of the large, recognized dialect areas is superior in its speech to any other. The speaker's goal should be to approximate the

[14] Charles K. Thomas, *An Introduction to the Phonetics of American English* (New York: The Ronald Press, 1947), p. 142 ff.

best pronunciation current in his own native region—provided only that his native region is not a narrow, provincial area whose speech patterns are regarded as substandard by everyone living outside it.

BODILY BEHAVIOR. *Consistency with the speaker's personality.* This criterion is no license to do whatever one pleases on the platform. It is merely a caution to the speaker not to attempt postures, gestures, movements, styles of apparel, or facial expressions that are a radical departure from his or her over-all pattern of living.

Appropriateness for the occasion. For example, a formal occasion will usually call for more restrained action than would a gay, chatty meeting made up of close friends. As already mentioned, a large audience generally requires gestures fewer in number but wider in scope than does a small gathering.

Integration. This means that the speaker should be acting as a unit; that his entire body should be coordinated; that fingers, hands, arms, and feet should work together, rather than in such a way as to suggest a marionette.

Animation. This does not mean violence; nor does it imply that the speaker is to huff and puff and charge about the stage. It means merely that, even when the speaker is using very little action, his facial expression, posture, and general bodily tonus indicate that he is alive, awake, alert.

Spontaneity. The term *spontaneity* seems preferable to the ambiguous and hackneyed *naturalness.* It means that all action, whether large or small, should spring on the spur of the moment—without studied, conscious effort—from the ideas and feelings being expressed. It means, therefore, that gestures do not have to be timed—they will automatically time themselves if the speaker will concentrate upon his words and his desire to communicate.

Purposiveness. All bodily behavior should reflect the speaker's purpose to communicate and should reinforce his ideas and feelings. In other words, it should not be aimless, as for example, rocking to and fro, diddling with a pencil, teetering up and down, or buttoning and unbuttoning a jacket.

A PROGRAM FOR IMPROVEMENT IN DELIVERY

In a textbook, only the bare outlines of a program for improvement may be offered. Once more the student must be referred to his instructor and to specialized texts for detailed suggestions, procedures, and drills.

DIAGNOSIS. Keeping in mind both the general and specific goals outlined above as criteria by which to evaluate his performance, the speaker should solicit criticisms from the instructor and from as many listeners as possible. He should supplement these with his own careful self-appraisal.

It is important that this diagnosis be first in terms of the basic issue, namely: How well is the delivery contributing to the communication of ideas? The total impression should be examined before the technical fragments. It is usually more valuable to offer such a criticism as, "All ideas are being equally emphasized," rather than "Your pitch is monotonous." However, there are many cases where the technical details should be singled out. This is especially true when the speaker seems to have a lively awareness of his meanings, but is handicapped by habitual mannerisms of which he is virtually oblivious. Examples of such mannerisms are a persistently rising pitch inflection, a persistently falling pitch inflection, a stereotyped gesture constantly repeated, shifting the weight from one foot to the other.

SEARCH FOR CAUSES. The most common causes of faults in delivery are probably the following: physical or organic deficiencies (disease, malformation, temporary illness, fatigue, and the like), basic attitudes or personality traits, faulty habit formation, misunderstanding of the nature and criteria of good speech, unsatisfactory attitudes toward the subject or toward the speaking, situation, and poor preparation.

DEVELOPMENT OF THE COMMUNICATIVE ATTITUDE. The speaker may be said to have a communicative attitude (1) when he sincerely wants to speak; (2) when he knows exactly what he wants to say; (3) when he is attempting to speak directly to each member of his audience; and (4) when he is aware of the meaning of each idea at the very instant he utters it. He absorbs himself in these awarenesses and hence (ideally) loses all self-consciousness; almost literally, he loses himself in his message and in the communicative situation. The classic statement of this general point of view has been made by James A. Winans, to whose writings the student is referred.[15]

EFFICIENT PREPARATION. Precise methods of preparation will, of course, differ according to the type of speech involved. For example, somewhat different approaches would be required for a persuasive argument to an audience, a constructive speech in a tournament debate, and a rebuttal speech in a tournament debate.

In general, however, some such system as that sketched below will be found practical—with appropriate modifications:

1. Start collecting ideas and evidence far in advance. Avoid the last-minute scramble.

2. Engage a large number of people in casual conversation on as

[15] Winans, pp. 23–30.

many of the crucial ideas and arguments as possible. Note the varying reactions, and follow up suggested leads for further study.

3. Outline tentatively, then read and study the evidence as it seems to fit into this outline. Then revise the outline as further study dictates. In formal debate, develop—in cooperation with other squad members—a brief on both sides of the question, showing sources of important evidence. Do not attempt to use the brief, however, as a speaking outline.

4. Reduce the outline to very concise reminder notes; practice the speech a few times from these notes—either alone or with a sympathetic listener. Rebuttal can be practiced by stating hypothetical (but realistic) opposing arguments, then refuting them in about one or two minutes. For more formal speeches it is frequently well to write out a full manuscript. After writing and revising the manuscript, decide which occasional sentences or phrases are worth memorizing; then destroy the manuscript and practice extemporizing from the outline or speaking notes. Do not hesitate, from rehearsal to rehearsal, to try out variant wordings. Avoid trying to repeat the speech in identical wording from one rehearsal to another.

Do not, however, rehearse a speech so many times that it loses spontaneity. Space the rehearsals over as long a period of time as feasible. Between rehearsals, mull over the detailed outline from time to time, and alternate silent and oral reading of the outline to encourage thorough mastery of subject matter.

DRILL. The student can profit by spending a few minutes every day in activity best described as drill. There are two kinds of drill: meaningful and nonsense. In the former, the student concentrates upon expressing the full meaning of the material that he is reading or speaking. In the latter, he is working solely upon the mechanics of delivery.

First, there is value in the meaningful drill. A simple way of conducting this type of drill is to choose several different kinds of reading matter, ranging from the simplest expositional prose (as in a textbook or newspaper) to dramatic or emotional passages from literature. Set aside about ten minutes each day. Read the material aloud several times, trying each time to express the meaning more thoroughly. Concentrate entirely upon the meaning—not upon the voice or bodily behavior.

Second, it is advisable to mix reading and speaking. A device that has proved effective is to read a short passage aloud several times, then put it aside and attempt to restate it in your own words, using all the vocal and bodily resources you can to communicate the ideas as effectively as when you were reading. This technique helps to bridge the gap between oral reading and extemporaneous speaking.

Third, resort to "nonsense" (or mechanical) drills as a last-ditch expedient if delivery problems remain after other procedures, such as those described above, have failed. These drills are especially appropriate when dealing with unconscious mannerisms, such as voice patterns, fidgety hands, or awkward posture.

Sometimes the method that psychologists call "negative practice" is very effective in extirpating annoying habits. For example, one way of dealing with "and-uh" is to bring it forcefully into the forefront of consciousness by repeating it numerous times on purpose. Read aloud a simple prose paragraph; after every word or two insert a long, loud "uh." Do this for a few minutes every single day. Similar techniques can easily be devised for analogous faults.

Impromptu speaking of a semi-nonsense nature can also be used to supplement reading and mechanical exercises. Another example: It is possible to work on a persistent problem of faulty phrasing by speaking impromptu on such a simple topic as describing the room in which you happen to be standing. With need for very little thought, you can thus practice various ways of grouping words—pausing and phrasing—by concentrating on just this single technique.

It is most important, however, that the student separate in his own mind those activities which are purely mechanical drill and those which represent a real effort to communicate ideas. By no means should the speaker attempt to practice techniques of delivery when he is sincerely trying to communicate meanings to a listener. The only justification for drill work is the hope that certain habits will be formed which will eventually carry over into platform speaking.

We have discussed now the speaker's basic personality, his attitudes, and his delivery. The perceptive reader may ask whether the most important attribute of a person has not been omitted—the speaker's *character*. This topic has been left for the last because it is so important, and because it transcends all that has been discussed to this point.

THE DEBATER'S CHARACTER

This topic will be dealt with under two divisions: ethics and etiquette.

THE ETHICS OF DEBATE

It is almost impossible to write upon the subject of ethics without sounding "preachy." Furthermore, the matter is discussed in other chapters. Therefore, no more will be said here than this: (1) It should be incontestably obvious that the debater who is—or is thought to be—unethical is beyond this book; he really is no debater at all. Once an audience suspects a debater of malpractice, in handling his arguments or in dealing with his opponents, the debate is over. (2) The real nub of the matter, of course, is not whether to be ethical, but how to determine what is ethical. This is not the place to insert a condensation of a course in ethics. But the practicing debater may be helped if he will ask himself, "Am I more concerned with gaining strategic advantage, or with communicating an honest argument? Am I more concerned with making a good personal impression, or with seeing that the crucial issues are considered? Am I more concerned with winning at any cost, or with giving the opposition a fair break? Am I more concerned with hoodwinking a gullible audience, or with encouraging that audience to reach an independent, critical judgment on the issues?" The debater who can honestly give the right answers to such questions as these—whether or not he has taken the trouble to articulate a coherent ethical philosophy—surely cannot go far astray.

THE ETIQUETTE OF DEBATE

Etiquette is more than good manners. It is more than decorum or politeness. It is a reflection of character. In this section the word is taken to mean the outward observable signs of mental attitudes of tact, fairness, and consideration for others. The debater who calls his opponent a "stupid prevaricator" is obviously guilty of a breach of etiquette. Such a person will probably exhibit very little improvement after being reprimanded or told how to conduct himself. But if he can re-examine his basic attitudes— toward himself and toward others on the platform—he is likely to require very little specific instruction in etiquette.

ETIQUETTE BEFORE THE DEBATE. It devolves upon the debaters of a host school, of course, to show every courtesy to representatives of visiting schools. Whenever feasible, guests should be met immediately upon their arrival in town—or at least upon their arrival on campus. All arrangements and rules governing the debate or tournament should be made clear in advance correspondence or notices.

It is pertinent here to describe some violations of etiquette that have come to the writer's attention. In one instance, visiting debaters, with difficulty, located the place of debate and were treated to an empty room. The opposing team went through a perfunctory debate with no judge, no audience. Even the faculty director at the host school was not present, although he did make a brief appearance and then retired without explanation.

Visiting debaters at various times and in numerous places have commented upon the "jerk-water" character of the host campus. Visiting debaters have also frequently flouted—sometimes with considerable flourish

—local rules and traditions of the host school, such as smoking regulations and dormitory hours.

ETIQUETTE DURING THE DEBATE. The subject of etiquette during debate should be considered from two points of view: that of the speaker and that of the listening debater.

ETIQUETTE WHILE SPEAKING. Here belong such matters as the following violations suggest:

Sarcasm, as evinced in tone of voice, choice of words, and facial expression.

Belligerence, reflected in tone of voice, dogmatic vocabulary, hurling of challenges, piling up of questions "which the opposition must answer," and so on.

Discourtesy, as in the words, "The opposition completely misinterpreted what I said!" (Is there any reason for not saying, instead, "We apparently did not make ourselves clear?")

Insincerity, as shown in general manner of speaking and by unctuousness, exaggeration, or affectation.

Unfairness, as in crowding a number of questions or crucial arguments into the last moments of a speech, or failing to make a visual aid available to the opposition, or surreptitiously sneaking constructive arguments into final rebuttals.

Personal rancor, as reflected in such an assertion as: "This is the sort of logic—or so-called logic—I would expect from Mr. (or Miss) _____."

One other violation of good manners cannot be classified among those listed above. That is the practice of addressing remarks personally to the opposition rather than to the audience and judge. With only rare exceptions—and, of course, omitting the necessities of cross-examination—debaters should talk to the listeners, not to the opposing team; and therefore they should almost always refer to the opposition in the third person rather than in the second person.

Several reasons support this advice. The purpose of the debate is normally to expose the arguments on both sides of a proposition for the edification or persuasion of the audience, not the other team. Furthermore, addressing the audience directly and referring to the opposition in the third person lends dignity to the debate; it makes it more difficult to indulge in personalities or sarcasm; and it is simply more effective public speaking. The debater will do well to include in his ready-at-hand vocabulary such phrases as these: "Our friends of the opposition," "Mr. Smith, the first negative speaker has told you . . . ," "We have heard our opponents argue that . . ."

ETIQUETTE WHILE NOT SPEAKING. Such attitudes—and it is to be noted that they are attitudes—as those represented by the list above can be transmitted to the audience even when the debater is silent. Some annoy-ing habits of debaters that are frequently observed are listed below:

Walking up to the platform in a slouchy, devil-may-care manner.

Engaging in constant whispering consultation with one's colleague.

Effecting great surprise, disgust, dismay, or supposed injury by means of obvious facial expressions while listening to an opposing speaker.

Displaying a general attitude of smugness as shown in facial expres-sion and posture while sitting at the table, as if to create the impression that nothing the opposition says could possibly be important or worthy of serious answer.

Many similar examples can undoubtedly be supplied, but those pre-sented here should give debaters a good idea of some practices to be avoided at all costs.

ETIQUETTE AFTER THE DEBATE. No one familiar with contest debate will deny that for some students the debate is never over. Only too common is the ill-tempered and interminable post-mortem in which a debater re-opens the argument with opposition, judge, or any captive listener. Concise, courteous questions to obtain constructive suggestions from the judge are one thing; to badger him about the decision is quite different. In fact, many schools are known to observe an inflexible rule of never objecting to a judge, regardless of the provocation. Such a policy may be too extreme; but at least it reflects a philosophy of debate which recognizes that a decision is, in the long run, the least important of all the educational outcomes of organized debating. It can even be argued that one of the values of debate training is the opportunity it affords the student to take the hard knocks— including the unfair decisions—in stride.

In short, graceful winning and graceful losing are important in debate as they are in other areas of life. Attitudes of smug superiority, condescen-sion, boastfulness, or grudging resentment are really indices of immaturity as well as breaches of etiquette. Let it be repeated: etiquette in debate will be but a small problem if the debater's basic attitudes are satisfactory.

SUMMARY

The debater has not fulfilled his true function until he communi-cates to an audience—whether that audience consists of a single critic-judge, a small group, or a nationwide television audience. His job does not end with analysis, research, case construction, or logical argument. He must view the demanding tasks of speech composition and delivery as the cul-mination of all his efforts.

But communication is not merely a collection of skills and tech-niques. Communication is accomplished by one human being speaking to other human beings. The most crucial factor determining the acceptance of a message is the total personality of the message-sender, as perceived by the message-receiver. Hence, the present chapter has proceeded upon the premise that he who wishes to improve his speaking must look first to the kind of personal impact he makes upon an audience. This means, in turn, that he should be concerned with his basic attitudes, for attitudes largely determine the way in which a person is perceived by others.

It has been suggested that the "good speaking personality" is one that could be characterized, in the opinions of the audience, as: honest, communicative, likable, tolerant, and competent. The debater, in striving to achieve this kind of personality, should examine his attitudes toward the total speaking situation, toward himself, and toward debate. He should constantly remember that his message is the most important element in the situation, and that he is a communication medium—not a star performer. He is there to communicate ideas, not to exhibit himself.

Two types of debate have been proposed: analytical and persuasive. In the first, the debater is functioning primarily as an expositor-analyst-role-player who may be called upon to present the best case possible for a position in which he does not personally believe; in the latter, the debater is not a role-player, he is a sincere advocate appealing for the acceptance of views to which he is personally committed. If the debater is to function at his most effective speaking level, it is essential that he understand the implications of this distinction.

The second main division of the chapter dealt with delivery, which was defined as including four main components: voice, articulation, pronunciation, and bodily behavior. Good delivery satisfies two fundamental criteria: (1) it must be unobtrusive, and (2) it must reinforce the speaker's meanings. A number of specific goals appropriate to the four components of delivery were proposed, concluding with a five-part program for self-improvement: diagnosis, analysis of causes of delivery problems, development of the communicative attitude, efficient methods of preparation, and drill practice.

Finally, the chapter discussed the debater's character. Ethical criteria and accepted standards of debate etiquette were proposed, in a frame of reference which again stressed the pivotal importance of attitudes and total personal impression as determinants of speaking effectiveness.

EXERCISES

(For Chapters 12 and 13 Combined)

1. Using techniques of library research explained earlier in this book, explore books and periodicals in the fields of debate, general speech, and education

for the purpose of compiling a representative list of common attacks upon high school or college debaters as public speakers or as personalities. Extract typical quotations from ten different sources, include precise and complete bibliographical data, and comment briefly upon the cogency of these attacks.

2. Write or deliver orally a report in which you discuss some specific aspect of the general topic: "The Relationships between Speaking and Personality." It is suggested that you consider such matters as motivation, audience perception, the influence of attitudes upon personality, and the problem of attempting to produce significant changes in personality after early childhood. It might be profitable, as one option, to analyze the personality of a well-known public speaker or advocate. (You may wish to start by examining appropriate titles listed in Suggested Readings.)

3. Examine the specimen debate in the Appendix. Be prepared to analyze and evaluate, in class, the following aspects of this debate:

a. The argumentative adequacy and the communicative adequacy of the main contentions, subcontentions, and speech organization.

b. Instances of what you regard as good and poor use of language (style).

c. Instances or passages in which you believe the argumentative adequacy and the communicative adequacy are probably far apart.

4. Ask a colleague to list the words you repeat most often in your debates or in practice. Write down several synonyms, if possible, for each. Attempt to use these synonyms in your next practice.

5. Compose several different ways of expressing each of the following:

a. Explain that what you, or your colleague, said in a previous speech has apparently been misunderstood.

b. Attempt to extricate yourself from an apparent inconsistency which has been pointed out by the opposition.

c. Challenge the competence of an authority cited by the opposition.

d. Admit that you have been caught in an inadvertent misstatement of fact.

e. Point out what appears to be a serious error in the wording of a quotation used by the opposition.

f. Quote an authority of your own: include transition into the quotation, establishment of the authority's competence, reading of the quotation itself, relating of it to your case, and transition into the next passage of the speech.

6. Choose a passage of around 500 words from a speech made by a well-known figure in American history such as Daniel Webster, Henry Clay, William Jennings Bryan, Abraham Lincoln, Charles Sumner. Explain orally the features of the style that you believe make it different from today's style; write out and read aloud your re-wording of the passage as it might be adapted for a modern audience.

7. Compose a brief reply to each of the following: aim for both cogency and power in your speech composition. Consider the applicability of the S-R-S-R-T pattern.

a. "Controversy equalizes fools and wise men. . . ." Disputes in which this "equalization" is likely to occur are, of course, a waste of time. The *reductio ad absurdum* of this kind of discussion is often to be found in the high school and college "debate," as still practiced in many localities. Since both the "affirmative" and "negative" can do little other than exaggerate their own claims and belittle the claims of the opposition, the net intellectual result of such encounters is usually almost negligible, and decisions as to who "won" the debate must be made on such irrelevant points as skill of presentation and the pleasing personalities of the contestants.—S. I. Hayakawa, *Language in Action*, 1941, pp. 136–137.

b. It is recognized that the solution of common problems in the democracy is not best arrived at through dramatic, eloquent, emotional speeches. On the contrary, deliberations on a highly intellectual plane should be more prevalent than they are in the solution of community, national, and international problems. . . . Very little space in our democratic life is left for the long over-used dramatics and emotions in speech making. Nor is there much purpose in a democracy for formalized debates wherein parties resolve to win through eloquent presentations of a side with little if any regard to examination of the facts in the problem. The purpose of debate is to win a point, not necessarily to arrive at a solution to a problem.—Recommendations of a Committee of the North Central Association (later revised), March 1950, in *Speech Activities*, 6 (Winter 1950), 145.

c. The position of the orator is frequently in an intermediary zone between that of criminals and honest men. . . . Orators who rave should probably be classed with the criminally insane. In cultivated society to be accused of oratory should be equivalent to a charge of moral turpitude. —H. R. Huse, *The Illiteracy of the Literate*, 1933, p. 170.

8. One veteran debate director has explained his objections to the practice of debating both sides of a question in a tournament:

Is this abrupt change of sides a situation one is likely to face in real life? Does the salesman have to urge people to buy his product in the forenoon and warn them against it in the afternoon? Does the preacher have to defend the Church on Sunday and the Devil on weekdays? . . . It may be granted that it is highly desirable for a citizen to see both sides of a question, but does he have to become an advocate to do so? . . . It seems to me that this searching for the truth, this investigation of all the facts and argument on both sides should come *before* a person becomes an advocate; it should be a part of the process of discussion or inquiry. I would not consider a debater fit to represent the college until he had weighed carefully all possible opposing arguments and looked for all possible damaging evidence. But I have never found it necessary for him to attempt to persuade *others* that this proposition is justified in order to see both sides.—Brooks Quimby, *Speech Activities,* 9 (Summer 1953), 30.

> In a paper or oral report, respond to this view—agreeing or disagreeing, in whole or in part. However, *before* doing so, compare them with divergent points of view (and evidence) presented by other authors mentioned in Suggested Readings.

9. Respond to the following assertions:

> a. When measured against the full body of rhetorical principles, the debate speech is truncated; the emphasis is on development of the body with little consideration for introductions and conclusions. . . . Little thought need be given to selecting and arranging materials to gain the interest and attention of the listener. Organization of the debate speech is based on logical rather than rhetorical necessities.
>
> b. The debater's central aim is to be judged the better debater, the criterion for judgment being how well he handles the logical elements of discourse. Delivery has little opportunity to fulfill its function in a contest where the emphasis is on the science of argumentation. It is bound inextricably with commitment and purpose, neither of which the debater has. . . . In view of the central purpose of tournament debate and the resulting depersonalization of tournament rhetoric, one might question if delivery should be evaluated. . . . Take this category off the ballot altogether . . .

These passages are from: Hermann G. Stelzner, "Tournament Debate: Emasculated Rhetoric," *Southern Speech Journal,* 27 (Fall 1961), 34–42.

> c. Since debate is a human institution and the debate judge is likewise human, there admittedly may be some persuasion involved. But it is more of a by-product than the end-product, which in debate is conviction. . . . The whole world is one big salesroom in which everyone is a salesman of something—an idea, a product, or himself. If considered in such a broad sense, it could be reasoned that the debater is a persuader, even of the expert judge. . . . While there may be a thousand factors which will influence a judge favorably or unfavorably, the core of the debate process is conviction more than persuasion. . . . The judge, the one important listener, is almost out of reach as far as persuasive communication goes. . . . The great bulk of the weapons of persuasion are denied the contest debater.—E. C. Buehler, "The Role of Opinion as Related to Persuasion and Contest Debate," *Southern Speech Journal,* 25 (Fall 1959), 21–26.

10. From one of your current debate speeches, select a major contention that can be developed orally in about three or four mintes (the S-R-S-R-T pattern is suggested). Write and deliver this developed contention in four

ways, adapting elements of content, language, and oral presentation to these hypothetical audience situations:

a. A junior-high school assembly.
b. A televised debate, carried over a nationwide network.
c. A small, select audience of experts on the debate proposition.
d. A large, tumultuous mass meeting of emotionally aroused partisans.

SUGGESTED READINGS

(For Chapters 12 and 13 Combined)

ALLPORT, GORDON W. *Pattern and Growth in Personality*. New York: Holt, Rinehart & Winston, Inc., 1961. See discussion of "traits."

BRIGANCE, W. NORWOOD. *Speech: Its Techniques and Disciplines in a Free Society*. 2nd ed. New York: Appleton-Century-Crofts, Inc., 1961. See discussions of ethics, persuasion, and delivery.

CHRISTOPHERSON, MERRILL G. "The Necessity for Style in Argument," *The Speech Teacher*, 9 (March 1960), 116–120.

CLEVENGER, JR., THEODORE. "Toward a Point of View for Contest Debate," *Central States Speech Journal*, 12 (Autumn 1960), 21–26.

DAVIDSON, DONALD. *American Composition and Rhetoric*. New York: Charles Scribner's Sons, 1959. Pp. 504–524.

DICKENS, MILTON. *Speech: Dynamic Communication*. 2nd ed. New York: Harcourt, Brace & World, Inc., 1963. Chap. 20.

EHNINGER, DOUGLAS. "Decision by Debate: A Re-examination," *Quarterly Journal of Speech*, 45 (October 1959), 282–287.

FAIRBANKS, GRANT. *Voice and Articulation Drillbook*. 2nd ed. New York: Harper & Row, Publishers, 1960.

FLESCH, RUDOLF F. *How to Write, Speak, and Think More Effectively*. New York: Harper & Row, Publishers, 1960.

GRAY, GILES W., and WALDO W. BRADEN. *Public Speaking: Principles and Practice*. New York: Harper & Row, Publishers, 1951. See discussion of ethics.

HANLEY, T. D., and WAYNE THURMAN. *Developing Vocal Skills*. New York: Holt, Rinehart & Winston, Inc., 1962.

HAYAKAWA, S. I. *Language in Thought and Action*. New York: Harcourt, Brace & World, Inc., 1949.

LUCAS, F. L. *Style*. London: Cassell & Co., Ltd., 1955.

McBATH, JAMES H. "Speech and the Legal Profession," *The Speech Teacher*, 10 (January 1961), 44–47.

McBURNEY, JAMES H., and ERNEST J. WRAGE. *The Art of Good Speech*. Englewood Cliffs, N.J.: Prentice-Hall, Inc., 1953. See discussions of speech purposes, ethics, delivery.

MILLER, GEORGE A. *Language and Communication*. New York: McGraw-Hill Book Company, Inc., 1951. Pp. 1–9; 41–45; 47–52; 76–79; 100–117.

MILLS, GLEN E. *Composing the Speech.* Englewood Cliffs, N.J.: Prentice-Hall, Inc., 1952.

MINNICK, WAYNE C. *The Art of Persuasion.* Boston: Houghton Mifflin Company, 1957. Chaps. 1, 2.

PERRIN, PORTER G. *Writer's Guide and Index to English.* Rev. ed. Chicago: Scott, Foresman & Company, 1950.

RUESCH, JURGEN, and WELDON KEYES. *Nonverbal Communication.* Berkeley: University of California Press, 1956.

SHERIF, MUZAFER, and CAROLYN W. SHERIF. *An Outline of Social Psychology.* Rev. ed. New York: Harper & Row, Publishers, 1956. Chaps. 15, 16, 17.

STRUNK, WILLIAM. *The Elements of Style* (with introduction, revisions, and a new chapter by E. B. White). New York: The Macmillan Company, 1959.

VAN RIPER, CHARLES, and J. V. IRWIN. *Voice and Articulation.* Englewood Cliffs, N.J.: Prentice Hall, Inc., 1958.

WEST, ROBERT. "The Prospect for Speech Education," *Quarterly Journal of Speech,* 30 (April 1944), 143–146.

WINDES, JR., RUSSEL. "Competitive Debating: The Speech Program, The Individual, and Society," *The Speech Teacher,* 9 (March 1960), 99–108.

V.

chapteR 14

~~~~~~

FORMS
OF DEBATE

by Gifford Blyton and
Bert E. Bradley, Jr.

TRADITIONAL DEBATE

Little needs to be said at this point concerning the traditional form of debate. Earlier chapters have made clear the rules and techniques governing this form of debate in collegiate tournaments. In traditional debating there are four constructive speeches and generally four rebuttal speeches. Occasionally because of time limitations or unusual circumstances the number of rebuttal speeches may be reduced to two. The time limits for these constructive and rebuttal speeches may be varied in other situations, but in intercollegiate debating the time limits are customarily ten minutes for constructive speeches and five minutes for the rebuttal speeches.

CROSS-EXAMINATION DEBATE

Since J. Stanley Gray first set forth in 1926 a description of what he called the Oregon Plan of debating,[1] cross-examination debate has undergone several changes and claimed many new adherents. Probably the largest number of supporters came in 1952 with its adoption by the National

[1] J. Stanley Gray, "The Oregon Plan of Debating," *Quarterly Journal of Speech Education*, 12 (April 1926), 175–180.

Forensic League. Cross-examination debate appears to be the most frequently used type on the high school level. In many states it is used exclusively. Although the traditional format remains the most commonly used in intercollegiate tournaments, there are a growing number of popular annual cross-examination tournaments. Other tournaments have used one or two rounds of cross-examination debating as a variation from rounds of traditional debate.

The significant distinction between cross-examination debate and traditional debate is a period following each constructive speech during which a member of the opposing side has an opportunity to question the constructive speaker. This chance for a direct clash of issues and personalities attracts many followers to this form of debate; for this reason cross-examination debate is generally most popular with audiences.

A typical arrangement of speeches is as follows:

First affirmative constructive speech
Cross-examination of first affirmative by second negative
  (First negative may handle this cross-examination, but it makes an
    awkward arrangement)
First negative constructive speech
Cross-examination of first negative by first affirmative
Second affirmative constructive speech
Cross-examination of second affirmative by first negative
Second negative constructive speech
Cross-examination of second negative by second affirmative
Negative rebuttal
Affirmative rebuttal

The time limits on these speeches may be varied. Following is a shortened format for presentation before audiences:

Affirmative constructive	8 minutes
Negative cross-examination	4 minutes
Negative constructive	8 minutes
Affirmative cross-examination	4 minutes
Negative rebuttal	4 minutes
Affirmative rebuttal	4 minutes

The constructive speeches in a cross-examination debate are developed and presented in the same manner as in a traditional debate with the exception that after the first affirmative constructive the results of the cross-examination should be incorporated in the next constructive speech. One of the most common errors in cross-examination debating is the failure of debaters to utilize in the constructive and rebuttal periods material elicited in the cross-examination.

The key to effective questioning of the opposition is thorough preparation. Many debaters seem to feel that the cross-examination period is a time for impromptu speaking, and their questions readily reveal this fact. But if the questions are to probe the issues intelligently and usefully, most of them must be carefully prepared in advance. Of course, as in any kind of debate, some lines of argument will be raised that have not been anticipated. Under such circumstances, the questioner obviously must adapt to the specific lines of argument as much as possible. In most instances this does not mean that he will have to abandon all his previously prepared questions. It means simply that he will have to coordinate them with the new questions appropriate to the case being met. Moreover, unexpected replies of the opponent will suggest previously unthought of questions to the examiner if he has sufficient knowledge to place the answers in perspective.

"The purpose of cross-examination," says one expert, "should be to catch truth, ever an elusive fugitive." [2] More specifically, questions used in cross-examination debate are generally designed to accomplish one or more of three purposes: (1) To elicit information for clarification; (2) To aid in the development of a constructive case; or (3) To assist in the tearing down of the opponent's case.

SUGGESTIONS FOR THE QUESTIONER

1. The time allotted for questioning is a brief and valuable period in which significant information may be obtained from the opponent. The questioner should confine his speaking to questioning the opponent; this is not the place for interpretative or evaluative comments upon replies of the witness. Follow-up questions may be used to make the listeners immediately aware of the significance of a particular reply by the witness.

2. The questioner should not approach cross-examination with the aim of forcing the opponent to concede that his case is a hopeless one built on specious arguments and invalid evidence. No opponent in his right mind is going to do this. A significant objective will be attained if the questioner is able to discredit some of the evidence on which one or more of the key points is based, if some of the reasoning is shown to be shallow

[2] Francis Wellman, *The Art of Cross-Examination* (Garden City, N.Y.: Doubleday & Company, Inc., 1948), p. 204.

288   [V] *EDUCATIONAL DEBATE ACTIVITY*

or improbable, or if the opponent is forced to admit the existence of alternative proposals.

3. Cross-examination should be organized. The questioner who jumps from point to point will not only confuse the opponent and listener, he will be unable to pursue a thought long enough to force the opponent to unwilling conclusions.

4. A line of questioning should be pursued to its logical conclusion. As a general rule, the examiner should not stop the questioning before the conclusion has been made clear. A conclusion that is obscure to the opponent will most likely be even more obscure to the listener.

5. Cross-examination should be conducted in a friendly, albeit trenchant, spirit. One writer has observed:

> During the examination, the cross-examiner is in charge. His task is a test of tact and good judgment. He must avoid offending his opponent or the audience, and yet he must not be timid in his questioning. So long as he retains his good nature, self-control and a sense of fairness, he may conduct a vigorous and aggressive examination without fear of giving offense.[3]

Though the questioner may be aggressive in his probing of the opponent's case, there is no place in intercollegiate debate for the bullying, domineering approach too frequently seen in cross-examination. Moreover, there is much doubt that bullying tactics are effective: "More cases have been won by putting leading questions casually than by employing vigorous and belligerent methods of cross-examination."[4]

6. The questioner should always be in control of the cross-examination period. A talkative opponent should not be allowed to monopolize the time. The examiner may interrupt to inform him that his answer is sufficient. This does not mean that the examiner has a license to restrict the witness to monosyllabic replies; it does mean that he has the right to prevent filibustering on the part of the opponent. An evasive witness should not be permitted to avoid answering the questions.

7. The questioning period would not be used simply to reiterate in question form the material the opponent has presented in his constructive speech. Examine the assumptions underlying his approach, and attack the authorities, facts, reasoning, and arguments in such a way that he is forced to reveal information that he normally would not have disclosed.

[3] Darrell Parker, "The Use of Cross-Examination in Debate," *Quarterly Journal of Speech*, 18 (February 1932), 100.
[4] William Gallagher, *Technique of Cross-Examination* (New York: Practising Law Institute, 1955), p. 28.

8. The questioner should avoid the "Isn't it a fact" form of cross-examination unless it is used to acquaint the audience with that information or to get the opponent's position on record. As one lawyer has pointed out:

> An examination which consists of such questions merely gives the witness an opportunity to flatly contradict the testimony of one's own witness and is . . . a poor substitute for no cross-examination at all. Such questions may find a place now and then in an extended cross-examination, but a cross-examination should never consist of a series of such questions and nothing more.[5]

9. Cross-examination should be concentrated on the weak portions of the opponent's case. The examiner should not allow the opponent to render the strong parts of his case even more invulnerable by asking questions about those parts.

10. Though the purpose of questioning is to establish the validity or nonvalidity of an argument, keep in mind that the cross-examination is being conducted for the benefit of the listeners. The questioner, therefore, should speak distinctly and loud enough for the listeners to hear. He should not turn his back to the listeners while questioning. Not only is the direct address more effective, but it also permits the questioner to observe listeners' responses and capitalize on those reactions.

11. The questioner should make no personal attack on his opponent. Unlike the lawyer who is interested in discrediting either the testimony or the witness, the debater is interested in discrediting only the opposition's evidence and arguments.

12. Answers of the opponent should not be repeated unless they are being repeated for emphasis. The questioner wastes valuable time repeating the answers as many beginning cross-examiners do.

13. The examiner should be cautious of asking questions to which the answers are unknown. Wellman indicates that the examiner does not have to know the answer to every question he asks, but he warns that no examiner "should ask a critical question unless he is reasonably sure of the answer." [6]

14. Only questions that are fair and relevant should be asked. Question-begging terms should not be included in the questions.

15. Questions should be brief, simply stated, and phrased positively. Long, involved, complex questions only create confusion for everyone concerned.

[5] *Ibid.*, p. 70.
[6] Wellman, *op. cit.*, p. 23.

16. Once the cross-examination has begun, the questioner may not confer with his colleague until it is concluded.

SUGGESTIONS FOR THE WITNESS

1. The witness should realize that the responsibility for courtesy and fairness rests just as much with him as with the examiner. The respondent should maintain control of his emotions despite pugnacity, sarcasm, and discourtesy on the part of the examiner.

2. The witness should not be afraid to say "I don't know." It is better to admit early that one does not know than to have the examiner demonstrate it after the witness has tried previously to conceal it.

3. The witness should not talk solely to the questioner. He must keep in mind that it is the listeners' evaluations that are most important.

4. All fair questions should be answered in a straightforward manner. The witness should not try to use the opponent's time by giving long-winded answers. Debate loses its value and function if the participants engage in evasive tactics. It has been pointed out, however, that the witness

> may exercise some control over the question period by controlling the timing of his answers. If he feels that the questioner is rushing him, he can slow down his answers. If he feels that the questioner is dragging out the question period, he can answer rapidly, exposing the questioner's ineptitude.[7]

5. The witness may legitimately refuse to answer some questions. If a question-begging term is included in the question, the witness should point this out and refuse to answer the question until it has been worded properly. If a question seems obscure, the respondent may request a clarification before answering.

6. The witness should not try to cross-examine the examiner during his question period. Remember that the time belongs to the examiner for questioning; the witness will have a chance to cross-examine later.

7. The witness must be on guard continually for the traps the examiner is constantly setting for him. However, this must not prevent the witness from giving definite answers where they are appropriate. A witness who gives only equivocal replies destroys the listeners' confidence in his ability to give any valid answers.

8. Once the cross-examination has begun, the witness may not confer with his colleague until it is concluded.

[7] Lloyd Fuge and Robert Newman, "Cross-Examination in Academic Debating," *The Speech Teacher*, 5 (January 1956), 69.

DIRECT-CLASH DEBATE

Direct-clash debating is an excellent device for teaching concentration on a specific issue inasmuch as all attention is focused upon one argument in each of a series of clashes. Credit for this form is given to Edwin Paget who in 1931 sought a more effective means for eliminating discussion of insignificant points, irrelevancies, and weaknesses in reasoning. Although this style has not been widely used in American intercollegiate circles, some tournaments are devoted exclusively to direct-clash debating.

Many coaches find that direct-clash debating offers valuable training because of the emphasis placed upon sound preparation, quick thinking, and effective use of language. Debaters are often stimulated by the direct clash technique because it has all the excitement of an intellectual fencing contest.

As with other debate formats, the direct-clash permits variations as to topics used and time limits. In general, however, the national intercollegiate resolution is used. The rules are flexible, but a commonly used pattern is as follows:

1. A team consists of from two to five members. The speaking order may be varied, but no one speaker may speak twice in succession, nor may he initiate successive clashes.
2. The debate begins with the affirmative taking up to five minutes to define terms, outline basic arguments, and present a plan.
3. The negative is allowed equal time to accept or reject the affirmative analysis, state those affirmative issues on which the negative agrees to clash, and present additional issues as desired. The negative may also outline a counterplan, and exclude from the argument points on which the two teams agree. The debate is then confined to the issues on which the two teams differ.
4. Following the two opening speeches, each side is allowed a short period (usually three minutes) to clarify the issues on which clash is to occur, and, if desired, to strengthen definitions.
5. Before the debate proceeds the judge should rule on areas of basic difference. If, for example, there is a fundamental difference on meaning of terms, he may ask that the first clash be confined to this area. The judge may also, if he chooses, state the order in which the issues are to be considered. He may likewise vote against a concession if he feels it concedes the debate. Furthermore, he may award the decision at this point should he think one side clearly the winner.
6. If the decision has not been awarded by this time, the affirmative is given four minutes to argue in favor of one of its issues as described

in its initial analysis. The argument should be stated clearly, should be well documented, and should exclude all petty points. An alert judge will penalize a debater who resorts to trivia in an effort to prove the validity of an issue.

7. Upon the conclusion of the affirmative's four-minute speech, the negative is permitted two minutes to answer the argument proposed by the affirmative. The affirmative and negative teams then speak alternately for two minutes until each side has spoken three times. Unless the judge stops the debate, the clash ends with a two-minute summation by the affirmative. As soon as the clash is ended, the judge awards the clash to the more effective team. The judge may award the clash sooner, but he must show just cause for such action. In general, most clashes run the full seven speeches (some tournaments limit the number of speeches to five as a time-saving device).

8. Subsequent clashes use the same procedure, with the two sides alternating in originating the clashes. When one team has won three clashes, it is proclaimed winner of the debate.

9. No issue may be used twice in one debate unless the losing side wants to pursue the same issue, or unless the judge demands further clash on the issue in question.

PROBLEM-SOLVING DEBATE

The problem-solving debate is a combination of discussion and traditional debate. "It aims at placing debating and public discussion on a basis that is scientific in its approach, logical in its procedure, educationally sound in its objectives, and wholly constructive in its results." [8] Thus, emphasis is placed upon an intellectual cooperative effort to solve a problem as opposed to the "win at all costs" attitude often characteristic of traditional debate. Problem solving concentrates on an honest effort to seek the truth as it applies to the solution of a problem. The productiveness of this form depends on the cooperative mood brought to it by participants. Not as popular as traditional, cross-examination, or direct-clash debating, it does provide training in realistic multilateral analysis.

The rules and procedures of a problem-solving debate as first stated by Professor Orr still remain as the guiding principles for this exercise:

1. The question for discussion is stated in the form of a problem, as "How can we best maintain a high standard of living for all citizens of the United States?"

[8] Frederick Orr and Albert Franzke, *The University of Washington Plan of Problem Solving Debate*, Bulletin Number 8, Seattle, 1938.

2. Teams shall be composed of either two or three speakers.
3. Teams shall be designated as "A" and "B," rather than "Affirmative" and "Negative." Such designation shall be determined by drawing just before the debate begins.
4. The order for the speakers on team "A" shall be first, third, and sixth. The order for team "B" shall be second, fourth, and fifth.
5. Analysis speakers shall be allowed ten minutes, solution speakers twelve minutes, and evaluation speakers eight minutes (times may be modified by mutual consent).
6. It is the duty of the first speaker on each team to present an unbiased analysis of the problem. He should give all the facts necessary to an understanding of the situation which has produced the problem, and he should discover the fundamental factors involved in the solution of the problem, and when possible set up certain criteria by which advocated solutions may be judged. He should not, however, attempt to present a solution. His sole problem is that of analysis.
7. The second speaker on each team shall present the solution that his teammate's analysis and his own research, reasoning, and convictions tell him is the best solution. He shall show clearly why his solution is the best and just how it would solve the problem.
8. The third speaker on each team shall examine the solutions presented by both sides, agreeing or disagreeing as the case may be. He must be judicial and unbiased in his attitude, fair and logical in his conclusions. He may question any of the previous speakers on any point presented by them, and they must give a direct, brief answer. His purpose in questioning must be to clarify the issue, not to trick the speaker into an admission. His conclusion may either agree or disagree with that of his colleague. His chief aim is to discover the best solution regardless of his past beliefs. He may even offer a new solution if the situation seems to warrant it. His main purpose, however, is the unbiased evaluation of the solutions presented.
9. When a team is composed of only two speakers, the first speaker on each team shall also present the third or evaluating speech.
10. If a decision is desired, the following ballot should be used. No percentages should be given. Speakers are ranked in pairs, and the team receiving the lower total rank wins.

Notice how the ballot reproduced on page 294 facilitates evaluation of participation characteristics in a problem-solving debate, yet de-emphasizes the element of team decision. Speakers are judged in pairs: first there is the analysis, then the solution, and finally the evaluating speakers are heard.

PROBLEM-SOLVING DEBATE BALLOT

Specific bases for judgment	Team A	Team B
	Rank 1 or 2	*Rank 1 or 2*

1. *Analysis speeches*
   a. Unbiased approach
   b. Adequate presentation of facts
   c. Successful discovery of difficulties
   d. Adequate criteria for judgment
   e. Effective presentation

2. *Solution speeches*
   a. Freedom from prejudice
   b. Cooperative effort
   c. Logical argument
   d. Adequacy of solution to meet analyzed difficulties
   e. Effective presentation

3. *Evaluating speeches*
   a. Fair, judicial attitude
   b. Analysis and comparison of solutions presented
   c. Soundness of conclusions
   d. Cooperative effort
   e. Effective presentation

COMMENTS:

TOTAL

JUDGE _____

The rules and procedures and the evaluation blank are reproduced by permission of the University of Washington.

MOCK-TRIAL DEBATE

In an attempt to find a debate format that would retain audience interest, Warren A. Guthrie developed mock-trial debate at Western Reserve University.[9] Mock-trial debate follows rules that are slightly modified from the legal procedure used in a law court. The national debate proposition may be utilized, but must be modified to call for a decree of specific performance or a writ of mandamus by the court.

Twenty-two participants are needed to conduct the mock-trial debate. One serves as judge to preside over the debate. A second debater performs as the bailiff to open court, swear in witnesses, and keep time. A third impersonates the Attorney General of the United States in the capacity of defense. A fourth debater executes the duties of the attorney seeking the writ or injunction. Six participants—three for each side—take the role of witnesses. Each witness assumes the identity of some outstanding authority. Unlike the practice in a law court, expressions of opinion are not ruled out of order, but the witness must restrict his testimony to historical fact or published statements of the person represented. Twelve members of the audience sit as the jury.

The procedure for the mock-trial debate is as follows:

1. The bailiff calls the court to order.
2. The judge has three minutes in which to present necessary, pertinent background material and to define the proposition's terms.
3. Three minutes are allotted to the attorney for the plaintiff to outline objectives he expects to achieve in examination of witnesses.
4. The Attorney General is given three minutes for the same purpose.
5. Each of the three witnesses for the plaintiff is called, sworn in, and subjected to four minutes of direct examination, after which the Attorney General may ask three questions in cross-examination.
6. Each of three witnesses for the defense is called, sworn in, and subjected to four minutes of direct examination, after which the plaintiff's attorney may ask three questions in cross-examination.
7. A three-minute final summary speech is delivered by the Attorney General.
8. A three-minute final summary speech is given by the attorney for the plaintiff.
9. The judge presents his charge to the jury.
10. The jury renders its decision.
11. Following the jury's decision, the meeting may be opened to general discussion from the floor.

[9] Warren Guthrie, "The Reserve Plan for Intercollegiate Discussion," *Quarterly Journal of Speech*, 25 (February 1939), 392–396.

Use of the mock-trial format offers several advantages for a debate squad interested in more than tournament activity. The dramatic impact of the simulated courtroom scene is especially appealing to an audience, and the large number of participants permits greater utilization of the team. The minor roles involved allow the use of less-experienced debaters whose participation in tournament debating would be severely limited.

LEGISLATIVE-PARLIAMENTARY DEBATE

There are many variations of legislative debate, or parliamentary debate, as it is often called. While many may argue that these are distinct forms, the differences are apt to be academic. Parliamentary debate is used in legislative bodies, and legislative debate utilizes parliamentary principles. Without trying to describe all aspects of all the forms of legislative-parliamentary debate, this section will outline general rules with the recognition that each group may make its own special adaptations.

The essential characteristics of legislative-parliamentary debate are: (1) It aims to solve problems through oral discourse; (2) its participants constitute a relatively large group with representatives from several institutions who meet to solve problems with the aid of recognized rules (such as *Robert's Rules of Order*); (3) officers are selected to direct the activities according to the agreed-upon rules; (4) issues are decided by majority rule, while minority rights are protected; (5) problems are usually announced weeks in advance to allow participants to prepare bills which will form the bases for debate; (6) the actual debating centers on investigations of the problems covered by the bills; (7) effort is made to emerge with workable solutions to these problems.

The group convenes as an assembly, with seating according to personal convictions on a resolution, or according to some other division, such as geographical. Each assembly determines its own procedure, so the following is intended only as a guide:

1. A resolution is read (usually by the first speaker who moves its adoption), then two persons are allowed to speak for, and two against it for from five to eight minutes each.
2. The floor is then opened for general discussion, with all speakers given equal time (such as three minutes). Each side is permitted the same number of speakers.
3. The speaker may be interrupted by permission from the chair. The speaker may or may not yield.

4. Debate is generally ended by a motion to close debate, or by general consent. All bills and amendments are acted upon by majority vote.

Much of the success of legislative-parliamentary debate rests with the chairman, who directs the action, maintains decorum, and equalizes participation.

Legislative-parliamentary debate is a valuable teaching device as it offers many opportunities to practice public speaking, parliamentary usage, and problem solving. It places a premium upon quick thinking while dealing with significant issues of the day.

THE HECKLING DEBATE

The heckling debate combines certain features of cross-examination and the legislative form. It seeks to focus attention on an issue by direct questioning, and it permits interruptions by the opposing team. These interruptions may come at any time except during the first three minutes and final two minutes of the constructive speech. Because this debate form often disorganizes the speaker, he must be thoroughly conversant with the proposition, and in complete control of his faculties. A person who is easily disturbed by an attack upon what he is saying would not do well in a heckling debate.

Many rules have been adopted by different groups using the heckling debate, but in general contestants are guided by such matters as:

1. Each of the four speakers is allowed fifteen to eighteen minutes to present his speech and to answer the heckler.
2. There are no rebuttal speeches (this rule is sometimes altered by mutual agreement).
3. The heckler may address the chairman with, "Mr. Chairman, may I ask the speaker a question?" Once given permission, the heckler addresses the speaker. If he does not get a satisfactory answer, he may pursue his cause until he is satisfied.
4. The floor belongs to the speaker, so his opponents are not allowed undue heckling, nor may they interject long, complicated statements. All questions and comments must be brief and to the point.
5. A speaker should not be heckled on every point; rather the heckler should wait until an issue has been presented, then attempt to undetermine the whole argument.
6. When a speaker is interrupted, he must answer for himself and not allow his colleague to speak for him.
7. The purpose of the heckling should be clear. The intent is to clarify, not confuse issues.

8. Heckling by the audience is not permitted.
9. The chairman is responsible for proper decorum. He rules on all appeals, and he enforces procedure.

TELEVISION DEBATE

The 1960 Nixon-Kennedy presidential debates gave striking evidence of the enormous potential of television debate. They demonstrated that large numbers of the American public can be brought into contact with divergent viewpoints on important issues of public affairs in an interesting and dramatic way. Early in 1962 the NBC Television Network presented a series of televised intercollegiate debates. The weekly program, *Championship Debate*, moderated by James H. McBath, was broadcast live from New York City. It was carried on 160 stations across the country. Other significant television debates such as those on *Face the Nation* and *The Nation's Future* have confirmed the value of television debating. The television industry is beginning to recognize that in a debate they have a program that inherently possesses conflict, suspense, and many other factors that attract the attention of the viewing public.

Several factors must be considered when a television debate is being prepared. The debate must be adapted to television. Since this is a relatively new medium of communication, a single format for a televised debate has not as yet been evolved.[10] Experimentation may prove there is no one best format. At the moment, however, it seems safe to conclude that the traditional, hour-long format of intercollegiate debate would be deadly dull to the viewers. On the other hand, showmanship is no substitute for sound analysis and clear thought. Debate formats must permit a sound analysis of the issues and at the same time maintain a brisk pace that will retain the viewers' attention. It appears that a format which employs cross-examination, preferably by the debaters themselves, evokes the personal clash so intriguing to the general public and yet encourages a probing analysis of the issues. It would also seem that no debater should be allowed more than five minutes for an uninterrupted statement.

Placement of the debaters is also important in producing a successful television debate. The use of a central speaker's stand to which each debater must walk is impracticable. Too much time is lost in exchanging places, and the resulting break in speaking causes a much slower-paced program. A separate podium should be provided for the chairman and each

---

[10] For a detailed account of the use of one format for a television debate, see: Edward Stasheff and Edd Miller, "Televising a Debate in a Courtroom Setting," *The Speech Teacher*, 3 (September 1954), 215–219.

debater unless they are seated informally in chairs. The participants may stand or sit behind their rostrums. The Nixon-Kennedy debates had the debaters standing, with the chairman and examiners sitting. In the *Championship Debate* program the moderator is seated, while the speakers stand both during the speeches and during the cross-examination period. *Face the Nation* debates generally have the chairman and debaters standing, while *The Nation's Future* has all three participants sitting. The most effective arrangement seems to be for the three to form a triangle with the chairman at the apex of the triangle. *Championship Debate* uses this order with the debaters facing each other and the audience seated behind each team, and the moderator to the rear. *Face the Nation* places debaters face-to-face about twelve to fifteen feet apart, and the chairman behind them. *The Nation's Future* also uses the triangular plan with the participants closer together and the debaters facing the chairman who is directly in front of them. If more than two debaters are used, the triangular arrangement may be less satisfactory.

Physical and vocal delivery must be adapted to the television medium. All bodily movement must be confined to the prescribed area that will keep the debater "on camera." If the speaking is done from a studio, the relationship of the television speaker to his viewing audience is comparable to that in a small, intimate conversational situation. In this case, the debater must restrain his gestures, facial expression, and bodily activity. Courtesy demands that one refrain from shouting and orating to listeners only a few feet away. If there is a large, enthusiastic audience in front of the speaker, however, the home viewer seems to react to the speaker more as a member of the larger audience than as a home viewer. The debater who speaks from the studio has a unique opportunity to maintain eye contact with every listener. For by looking directly into the correct lens of the television camera, the speaker is looking straight at each home viewer.

Debaters accustomed to the extemporaneous method of debating should experience little difficulty in adjusting to the strict time limits of television programs. If visual aids are to be used, they should be prepared by a professional. The high standards established for television props have made viewers highly critical of anything amateurish. In addition, the director of the program should be consulted for technical advice on how to design the visual aid for the best effect and how to work it into the program at the most appropriate time.

INTERNATIONAL DEBATE

The International Debate program is a joint project of the Committee on International Discussion and Debate of the Speech Association of America and the Institute of International Education. Begun in the 1920's, the program halted during World War II, and resumed in 1947. Under present arrangements two foreign teams usually visit the United States each year. One team tours east of the Mississippi during one school semester, while the other team tours west of the Mississippi during the other school semester. Customarily, the teams are from "Oxford and Cambridge alternately every fall since this is the only time of the year students from these universities are willing to come." [11] In the past ten years teams have come in the spring from such countries as India, Wales, Scotland, and New Zealand as well as England. Every other year a team is chosen from the United States to visit Britain or some other country.

An honorarium is charged each host school in this country to cover the cost of the program. For this initial fee only one debate may be held; an additional charge is made for each extra debate. Regardless of the number of times the foreign team debates, only one debate may be scheduled per day. In addition, the host school must provide housing and meals while the foreign team is on its campus.

The topics for debate are suggested by the visiting team. A ballot containing the propositions is sent to the host school from the Institute of International Education several weeks in advance of the foreign team's visit. Since most foreign debaters will debate only from conviction, the ballot indicates their preference for each proposition. Thus, if the host school desires to have a split team debate, it must select one of the propositions on which the foreign team members are split.

Most schools participating in the International Debate program have found it to be a provocative, invigorating showcase for the campus debate program. Opportunity is provided to display outstanding varsity debaters to campus audiences, while less experienced debaters can be identified more definitely with the debate activities by using them for such duties as ushering and timekeeping. Prominent members of the school's faculty and administration may be brought into direct contact with the debate program by asking a different one to serve as chairman of the debate each year. The audience can be given a sense of involvement in the debate by placing at the bottom of the printed or mimeographed program a ballot by which they can vote at the end. These can be collected quickly by the ushers at the conclusion of the debate, tabulated during a brief open forum, and the results announced by the chairman before the audience departs. A small social gathering following the debate including only the debate team members and the visitors offers a cultural occasion of immeasurable value.

[11] Judith Sayers, "The International Debating Exchange," *The AFA Register*, 9 (Spring 1961), 2.

SPLIT-TEAM DEBATING

Split-team debating places a debater from one school with a colleague from another school. Although not a frequently used variation from the traditional format, a few popular, well-attended split-team tournaments are held annually. There are, however, several disadvantages to this form of debate when used in a tournament. More time is required for each round of debate. Since the debaters on each team, affirmative and negative, are meeting for the first time, they must have an opportunity to discuss the approach to be used and the means of developing and defending it. With only a limited time available for each round of debate in a tournament, the brief consultation too frequently permits only a superficial analysis of the divergent approaches, with the result that poorly thought-out compromise cases may replace well-conceived cases developed from long reflection and sound research. It is also difficult to achieve effective teamwork in a split-team debate. Working together initially, the debaters have not had a chance to coordinate their attack and defense. Nor have they discovered through the trial and error of previous debates or through judges' critiques how best to distribute responsibilities.

Despite the disadvantages of split-team debating, many adherents think that advantages outweigh weaknesses. They believe that split-team debating may stimulate the debaters to do new thinking on the proposition. Confronted with the necessity of devising a different case in cooperation with another debater each round, the debater will be forced to probe in fresh directions in evaluating ideas suggested by his new, temporary colleague, and thus derive new insights into his own case and the debate proposition. In addition, split-team debating generally results in the minimizing of rivalry between institutions. This is especially true if a team is composed of debaters from schools which are arch rivals. They will be forced to forget their own differences in order to work together to defeat a common opponent. Split-team debating thus provides a greater opportunity to create new friendships.

SUMMARY

This chapter has dealt with the more common forms of debate, other than the traditional type. While each has distinctive features, all emphasize the need for sound research as a basis for effective problem solving. Cross-examination stresses a legal question-answer technique which enables the participants to test the validity of hypotheses during actual debate progress. When it comes time to teach concentration upon a single issue, no other debate style excels the direct clash. The debaters focus attention on one argument, with the result that insignificant points tend to be eliminated. Problem-solving debate aims to combine discussion and argumentation. Because an honest effort is made to find the best solution to a problem, skillful debating per se is secondary to an unbiased, cooperative approach.

The mock trial is akin to a courtroom in that parts are played by a judge, bailiff, attorneys, and witnesses. A large number of students participate and audience appeal becomes an important by-product. Legislative-parliamentary debate takes place in an assembly comparable to senate groups. Resolutions and bills are presented with the participants guided by traditional parliamentary rules. The heckling debate utilizes certain features of cross-examination and legislative forms. Speakers may be interrupted and subjected to direct questioning.

The popularity of public debating has increased with the advent of television. Many variations are used and considerable interest is shown, particularly when national figures or outstanding collegians oppose each other. International debating maintains a colorful character as teams from England, India, Wales, Scotland, and other countries tour the United States. These teams generally engage American debaters on a variety of subjects while using the traditional format. An interesting variation is the use of split teams, a procedure which has found support in many sections of the United States. In this case the respective teams are composed of debaters from different schools. Thus team "A" may have one member from Oxford joining an American student to oppose his traveling companion who forms team "B" with another American student.

EXERCISES

1. Prepare a series of questions designed to lead an opponent to a conclusion that establishes an affirmative argument supporting this year's intercollegiate debate proposition.
2. Attend a practice debate involving intercollegiate debaters on your campus. Write a critical evaluation of the debaters.
3. Conduct a direct-clash debate on the current intercollegiate debate proposition.
4. Arrange to hold a problem-solving debate before a campus audience on some significant local issue.
5. Assume you are the judge in a mock-trial debate. Prepare a three-minute statement covering definition of terms and background materials.
6. Prepare in writing a detailed format for a television debate.
7. Watch *Meet The Press* on television. Write a critical analysis of the questions and answers.

8. Attend the International Debate on your campus. Write a 500-word essay on the differences between the English and American debaters.
9. Watch *Championship Debate* on television. Write a critical analysis of the debate. Evaluate the influence of the audience on the debaters.
10. Make a list of ten questions suitable for use in a heckling debate on the current intercollegiate debate proposition.
11. Write an evaluation of legislative-parliamentary debate.

SUGGESTED READINGS

FUGE, LLOYD and ROBERT NEWMAN. "Cross-Examination in Academic Debating," *The Speech Teacher*, 5 (January 1956), 66–70.

GALLAGHER, WILLIAM. *Technique of Cross-Examination*, New York: Practising Law Institute, 1955.

GRAY, STANLEY. "The Oregon Plan of Debating," *Quarterly Journal of Speech Education*, 12 (April 1926), 175–180.

GUTHRIE, WARREN. "The Reserve Plan for Intercollegiate Discussion," *Quarterly Journal of Speech*, 25 (February 1939), 392–396.

HAAKENSON, ROBERT. "Adapting Debate to Television," *Western Speech*, 17 (May 1953), 165–173.

KRUGER, ARTHUR. *Modern Debate: Its Logic and Strategy*, New York: McGraw-Hill Book Company, 1960. Chaps. 24, 25.

ORR, FREDERICK and ALBERT FRANZKE. *The University of Washington Plan of Problem Solving Debate*, Bulletin Number 8, Seattle, 1938.

PARKER, DARRELL. "The Use of Cross-Examination in Debate," *Quarterly Journal of Speech*, 18 (February 1932), 97–102.

REYNOLDS, C. H. "A New System of Debate," *Quarterly Journal of Speech*, 26 (February 1940), 6–11.

SAYERS, JUDITH. "The International Debating Exchange," *The AFA Register*, 9 (Spring 1961), 1–4.

WELLMAN, FRANCIS. *The Art of Cross-Examination*, Garden City N.Y.: Doubleday & Company, Inc., 1948.

chapteR 15

ORGANIZING FORENSIC PROGRAMS

by Gregg Phifer

Superior forensic programs are the result of careful planning and hard work. They do not just happen; they are the end product of a co-operative effort by the faculty director of forensics, his assistants (if any), debate captains or managers, student speakers and debaters, and the school administration. The program can be no stronger than its weakest link.

This chapter is written especially to help those directing or preparing to direct forensic programs. Student debaters will also profit from understanding some of the problems of administering a forensic program. Although the orientation of this chapter is to forensic activities in college, many of the same principles and practices are also applicable to high school forensics.

BASIC PRINCIPLES

There is no such thing as a model forensic program. The size and location of the institution, to say nothing of the nature of the school and its students, do much to condition the type of forensic program that would be possible and desirable. Not every institution should aim for national competition or try to sponsor a major tournament.

If this is true, then the best guide to forensic excellence is a study of basic principles rather than a description of one or more ideal programs. Seven principles are considered here.

1. *The forensic program is an integral part of the total educational program of the institution.* Forensic activities provide valuable laboratory, co-curricular, or extracurricular experiences in all forms of original speaking. If student participants gain increased ability in reflective thinking and advocacy, if they acquire complex skills of speech composition and delivery, if they learn to organize and analyze and outline a case, frame and define propositions, do research in the library and elsewhere, then the forensic program serves defensible educational aims and deserves a place in an educational institution.

The ultimate test of education through forensics is the same as that of all education: Are students, because of their work in forensics, better able to take their places in society? Do they learn valuable vocational skills? Are they better citizens of a democracy? Are their lives richer and fuller? Unless the answers are affirmative, the administration has no business supporting the forensic program.

2. *The forensic program should be integrated as closely as possible with curricular offerings.* Courses in public speaking, discussion, debate, argumentation, and parliamentary law are usually offered by the Department of Speech; in a few institutions written and spoken communication are administered by a Department of English or in a School of Communications.

Forensic experiences provide invaluable training in oral communication, as well as a liberal education in practical problems of government, economics, sociology, and international relations. Students who begin by participating only in extracurricular activity should be encouraged to enroll for classroom study; those in academic courses should be urged, sometimes required, to take advantage of out-of-class experiences.

Many institutions give academic credit for approved participation in forensics. If restricted to those whose achievements reach a high level, this credit arrangement may help both students and director by combining the advantages of the extracurricular activity with those of the academic course.

3. *The forensic program should provide opportunities for any student who wishes to participate and is willing to work.* This does not mean that all students are capable of representing the institution in intercollegiate competition or that any student must be permitted to join the varsity debate squad. It does mean that there should be room somewhere in the forensic program for any serious student seeking to profit from such experiences. The inexperienced and unskilled may find room in the intramurals, from which the best and most faithful graduate to intercollegiate competition.

Novices should not be foisted upon the public nor involved in competition beyond their capabilities. The balanced program provides a range of opportunities for the least skilled to the most accomplished.

Some insist that forensics belong to the superior student.[1] In a sense that is true. He will be most attracted by forensics and will go farthest in tough competition. American education spends much money and provides special help for students handicapped physically or in speech, reading, writing. Forensics offer a challenge to the abilities of the sometimes neglected superior student. Where possible, however, the door to forensics should stand open to anyone with the will to participate.

4. *The forensic program must fit the time and energy of those in charge.* In many liberal arts colleges the director of forensics does the whole job. As his program grows in variety and number of participants, he is sorely tempted to try to meet all needs. But the forensics person must not spread himself too thin. Life is too short, and regular classes are too important. It is better to do a good job with a limited program and to expand that program as the administration recognizes its value and underwrites its expansion with more money and faculty or graduate assistant time.

5. *Victory in intercollegiate contests is a by-product of a successful forensic program, not the central objective of forensic activity.* The trophy case must never be made the measure of success. No school can win all the time. If the forensic director does a good job of teaching and preparing his students for competition, a proportionate share of honors will come his way. This is all any department head or dean should ask. The director whose trophy case bulges may actually be doing a poor educational job. He may be concentrating on a few hand-picked stars, neglecting many others who deserve and would profit from intercollegiate competition. He may be overcoaching his students, doing research or preparing speeches— work they should do for themselves.

6. *The forensic program should include many different original speech activities.* Tournaments alone do not make a forensic program. Good programs are diversified to include intramural, international, home-and-home, and radio-TV debates. Forensics also include cooperative group discussions, student congresses, orations, and extemporaneous and after-dinner speeches.

7. *Finally, successful forensic programs frequently put student speakers before live audiences: campus clubs, church groups, civic organizations, and high school assemblies.* Broadcast or televised discussions and debates provide invaluable experience for capable students. Debate must leave the classroom, with its tournament audience of sleepy timekeeper and bored judge, and earn a place with men and women outside the ivy-covered walls.

[1] Bert E. Bradley, Jr., "Debate—A Practical Training for Gifted Students," *The Speech Teacher*, 8 (March 1959), 134–138.

ATTRACTING QUALIFIED STUDENTS

Some fortunate campuses with a long and well-established forensic tradition present the director with the problem not of attracting qualified students into forensics, but of selecting teams from the many experienced speakers available. In such institutions many well-worn channels bring superior high school speakers to the campus and the freshman class. At many institutions, however, there is stiff competition for the superior student. The director must work hard to present the challenge of forensics to those students who have most to gain from our activity.

1. Experienced high school speakers and debaters may be drawn to the campus by direct contact, through the recommendation of alumni, and from teachers in neighboring high schools. Many institutions recognize that superior speakers and debaters are usually superior students and offer partial or full scholarships.

2. Among the best sources of forensic material are classes in fundamentals of speech, usually the largest speech classes on campus. Instructors may be asked to recommend forensics to superior speakers.

3. Help can be solicited from other departments: philosophy or religion, where pretheologues congregate; government or business or sociology, which attract prelaw students.

4. Members of the squad often recommend forensics to their friends and the institution to graduates of their high schools.

5. Students active in campus politics—class officers and members of student government—offer a challenging field for forensic recruiting. Student congresses may prove especially attractive to them.

6. A mimeographed or printed bulletin on the program in public speaking, discussion, and debate may be prepared and distributed to nearby high schools and to college students expressing interest.

7. If kept informed of all forensic activity, the college public relations office can do much to inform the general public about forensics. Timely stories in the campus newspaper help.

8. Programs can be taken to high school assemblies and civic organizations. These show students, parents, and teachers what you are doing.

9. In many institutions the forensic program opens with a "mixer" at the regular time and place of squad meetings. Personal invitations should be mailed to all who have participated in previous years or have expressed an interest during orientation or elsewhere. Announcements may be made through fundamentals-of-speech classes, in the student newspaper, and on posters around campus.

Successful mixers attract favorable attention and present effectively the challenge of the year's forensic program. A central part of the mixer should be a talk on the value of forensic participation and a description of the proposed forensic program for the year. Those present should fill out an information sheet or card including some or all of the following items:

Name	High school
Date	High school forensic experience
Campus address	Other college
Campus phone	College speech courses
Home address	College speech experiences
Year in college	Membership in campus organizations
Academic major	Participation in campus activities
Vocational ambition	Class schedule

A humorous debate may add entertainment to the mixer. Veteran debaters enjoy burlesquing traditional procedure and poking more or less gentle fun at each other and at those in charge of forensics. Simple and inexpensive refreshments give the mixer some of the informality and friendliness of a party. The fall mixer succeeds to the extent that prospects are inspired with the value of forensics, impressed with the size and quality of the year's program, informed concerning the time, place, and program of regular forensic sessions.

PLANNING A DIVERSIFIED FORENSIC PROGRAM

Sometimes even those who should know better think of forensics only in terms of a varsity squad attending a series of debate tournaments. Debate is an important and well-established intercollegiate contest activity, but a forensic program so limited lacks the many values found in other original speech activities. A well-rounded forensic program includes a variety of speech experiences.

DISCUSSION

Democratic self-government functions through both problem-solving discussion and decision-making debate. Out of prolonged public discussion of a problem situation comes a specific resolution for debate, representing only one of many possible solutions to the problem. Our society needs both the advocate, deeply devoted to his cause and seeking by all legitimate means to win others to his views, and the group discusser, skilled in cooperative problem solving.

Some debate enthusiasts insist that discussion has failed as an intercollegiate activity.[2] Numerous established collegiate discussion conferences show that competition in intercollegiate discussion is possible. Discussion cannot and should not put the same emphasis on competition as debate. Nevertheless, judges can evaluate the ability of students to cooperate in group reflective thinking. Both in intercollegiate conferences and intramural forums, discussion has proved its right to a place in a well-rounded forensic program.

STUDENT CONGRESS

Debate appears in various patterns, many of them described in Chapter 14. One event is the student congress. Intercollegiate congresses bring together representatives of several colleges and universities for a series of caucuses, committee meetings, and legislative sessions. Debate on various controversial "bills" is governed by rules of parliamentary law. Discussion in the committee sessions, persuasion in the hallways and party caucuses, and debate on the floor provide varied experiences. Even log rolling and delaying tactics teach the student through personal experience to appreciate the difficulties of the legislative process and the values of compromise.

The National Forensic League encourages area and district congresses for high school students and brings together the best senators and representatives from all districts in a national congress. Probably the best example of a national student congress on the college level is the annual spring congress sponsored by Delta Sigma Rho. Both Tau Kappa Alpha and Pi Kappa Delta have sponsored student congresses as part of their national conventions in past years.

Regional congresses are more frequent, sponsored by such groups as the Northeast Ohio Debate League and the Northern California Forensic Association. Mississippi has its own Youth Congress. In the South, the Southern Speech Association sponsors the Congress of Human Relations at its annual convention, with high school students making up the House, college students the Senate. Some institutions have sponsored a model

[2] Grace Walsh, "A Report on Student Reaction to Intercollegiate Discussion," *The Speech Teacher*, 7 (November 1958), 336–339. Martha Salsbury, "Can We Compete to Cooperate?" and Cunera Van Emmerik, "Discussion on Trial for Its Life," *The Forensic*, Series 47 (October 1961), 3–5. Wayne Brockreide and Kim Giffin, "Discussion Contests Versus Group Action Tournaments," *Quarterly Journal of Speech*, 45 (February 1959), 59–64. Kenneth E. Anderson and Jerome B. Polisky, "The Application of the Symposium-Forum to Contest Discussion," *The Speech Teacher*, 9 (March 1960), 131–134. David W. Shepard and Forrest L. Seal, "The Discussion Contest: Requiescat in Pace," *The Speech Teacher*, 6 (September 1957), 221–223. Robert S. Cathcart, "The Case for Group Discussion Contests," *The Speech Teacher*, 6 (November 1957), 315–318.

United Nations assembly or (in election years) a mock political convention. Certificates may be awarded for excellence in parliamentary speaking.

INDIVIDUAL EVENTS

Any well-rounded forensic program includes many forms of public speaking with different patterns of preparation from impromptu speaking to carefully prepared and often memorized manuscripts. Speech purposes likewise run the gamut from entertainment through information to persuasion.

Some tournaments in all areas of the country include varied individual events. Tournament directors occasionally encourage participation in these events by a sweepstakes trophy in all events. Schools in the Northern Oratorical League have a unique opportunity for this traditional speaking experience. Among the forensic honoraries, both Tau Kappa Alpha and Pi Kappa Delta have sponsored various individual speaking events as part of their national conferences. Many campuses feature intramural oratory and often other individual speech contests. Sometimes there is an endowed cash prize or a revolving trophy or plaque for the victor.

VARIETY IN DEBATE

No one would argue that "real life" debating is all of one pattern. Cross-examination, congressional, parliamentary, conference style, and courtroom style debates provide a variety of learning experiences often more valuable than the traditional tournament pattern. Tournaments and dual debates may be organized in varied patterns. Cross-examination and heckling debates are especially attractive to audiences.

In addition, an alert forensics director will provide for his debaters experiences in various kinds of competition. A series of tournaments does not make a well-rounded forensic season. To these should be added dual or home-and-home debates, perhaps with a traditional rival. Intercollegiate or intramural debates may be scheduled before civic clubs. Almost every year a foreign debating team tours the eastern or western United States. To be advised of such a tour one should be on the mailing list of the Institute of International Education, 800 Second Avenue, New York 17, New York.

INTERPRETATION

Other occasional forensic contests include oral reading, Bible reading, dramatic interpretation, address reading, poetry reading, declamation, and radio news reporting. These are not original speech activities, since the student makes use of material prepared by someone else. Such events as these diversify still further the speech experiences of students in forensics.

PREPARING STUDENTS FOR INTERCOLLEGIATE COMPETITION

Superior performance in forensic competition requires long, hard work. Some of this can and should, wherever possible, be done in the classroom in courses in argumentation and debate, in public speaking and persuasion. Students attracted to debate as an extracurricular activity may be persuaded, perhaps required, to register for such courses. Students registering for these courses may be encouraged, perhaps required, to meet with the debate squad.

On a few campuses the class in debate and the varsity debate squad may be one and the same. In most situations, however, the director of forensics finds it necessary to schedule regular meetings for his squad. Depending on the campus and the individual situation, these may come once, twice, or even three times a week. Only a college holiday or real emergency should be permitted to break this regular routine.

WORKING WITH THE VARSITY DEBATE SQUAD

The cornerstone of most forensic programs is the varsity debate squad expending much of its effort in preparation for tournament debating on the national debate resolution. These same debaters should, of course, appear before service clubs or campus audiences in dual debates. They should debate topics other than the national resolution; frequently, for instance, they have opportunities for demonstration debates on the national high school subject. These paragraphs, however, emphasize the primary responsibility of most debate squads.

As early as possible in the school year, experienced debaters and new prospects should start work on the national resolution. Some veterans may even begin reading during late August or early September, if notified by the director as soon as the national topic is announced. Perhaps a sheet or two of preliminary bibliographical items can be ready for students as they return to the campus in September. The only safe assumption is that debaters know little or nothing about the chosen resolution; even if in high school they debated a similar topic, their information is likely to be half-remembered and out of date.

A target date for early-season intrasquad debates should be set early. This and an early season tournament or two serve as motivation for early preparation, before midterm and other examinations interfere. Some forensics directors put their debaters on their feet debating early in the year;

others insist that they keep an open mind on the subject as long as possible. Perhaps the best solution is a compromise: give the debaters an early target date for intrasquad debates and in the interim fill them as full of up-to-date information and analysis as possible.[3]

A good beginning is to start the squad discussing. In successive meetings they can begin to provide answers for such questions as these:

1. What did the framers of the proposition intend by the resolution? What do the terms mean, singly and as a whole?

2. What problem situation is brought to a focus in the proposal for action embodied in the year's debate resolution?

3. What symptoms illustrate the existence of a problem? What are the causes? What trends may be noted in the present situation?

4. What alternative courses of action may be proposed for solution of the problem(s)? What is the relationship of these alternatives to the proposition by which the affirmative is bound? Are they mutually exclusive? supplementary? complementary?

5. What plans may be offered by those (a) supporting the debate resolution and (b) by those who advocate an alternative, a counterplan?

6. What are the probable consequences of adopting the resolution? What benefits may be claimed by its proponents? What dangers, difficulties, evils, and costs may be urged by its opponents?

Many factors help the director to determine the timetable for his squad's development: the length of each meeting, the frequency of meetings, the previous experience of the squad, the amount of time that must be taken from study of the debate subject for survey of debate technique.

Early squad meetings may involve both new and old members in symposium or panel discussions. Subject matter specialists in the area of the proposition (probably in the social sciences: government, economics, sociology, and history) may be invited to talk to the debate squad. When this is done, it is a good idea to explain to the guest speaker that squad members must debate both sides of the resolution, and that an analysis or general review of the issues would be more valuable than the faculty member's own conclusions on the proposition.

An approach of this kind encourages students to look first at the problem situation, secondly at all possible solutions, and only after this background has been laid, at the specific solution embodied in the debate resolution.

[3] For another discussion on "Training Debaters" see Arthur N. Kruger, *Modern Debate: Its Logic and Strategy* (New York: McGraw-Hill Book Company, 1960), pp. 377–381.

During the course of the season the forensics man inevitably becomes at least a second-hand expert on the debate subject matter. He cannot hold himself above the battle and concern himself with method only; this would be a sterile abdication of his responsibility to analyze arguments as well as criticize their presentation. His approach must remain balanced, even when his colleagues in other disciplines take sides most strongly. If he has strong convictions on the debate subject, it will probably be impossible to hide them from the squad; he must be careful, however, not to force them on his students.

The director of forensics must determine for his particular group of debaters the proper balance between content and technique, between knowledge of the subject and mastery of the skills of argumentation. Neglect of either one will reduce the educational value of his instruction and will usually (barring exceptional high school training) make his debaters look bad in intercollegiate competition. Most forensics men find it necessary to schedule special sessions for beginners on the squad and to break them in gently. Debate as an educational part of the college program must not exist only for the already skilled; it may contribute more educationally to the beginner than to the veteran.

Once the season is under way, sessions of the debate squad may be closely integrated with the intercollegiate debate schedule. Debaters will recognize the need for practice debates to prepare for intercollegiate competition. Afterward they will find value in post-mortem discussion of cases and arguments offered by debaters from other schools. As time goes on, they will enjoy variations of the traditional debate pattern: cross-examination, heckling, or problem-solving debates. They will find valuable training for rebuttal in direct-clash sessions.

A squad that meets once a week during the intercollegiate debate season, skipping holidays, examination weeks, and semester breaks, will have around twenty-five sessions in the academic year. This is not many, though the director may think otherwise as the season begins. Double the number could easily be used. Only by careful planning can student debaters be adequately prepared.

PREPARING STUDENTS FOR OTHER EVENTS

Students assigned to participate in a discussion conference all too often regard this as a snap for which little or no preparation is required. Such an attitude makes a mockery of intercollegiate discussion. If each forensics director would require that his school's representatives in discussion were as well prepared—with information, individual discussion outlines, and practice sessions—as his debaters, discussion events would have a better reputation in intercollegiate forensic circles.

Essentially the same principles hold for the various individual events frequently associated with debate tournaments, occasionally held separately. If the squad learns at the last minute that "somebody has to enter impromptu speaking," "you will get an oration ready," and "somebody must enter after-dinner speaking," they will take these events casually and give them scanty last-minute preparation. But if a speaking event is worth doing at all it is worth doing well; those entered should be encouraged and trained to give nothing but their best. This policy holds both educational and tangible rewards.

Debaters registered for courses in public speaking, persuasion, extempore speaking, or speech composition can often combine class assignments with preparation for a tournament event. Likewise, squad members taking courses in oral interpretation may handle tournament assignments in this area.

Prospective orators or participants in an event frequently called persuasive speaking should be encouraged to consider many different subjects, choose one in conference with the instructor, write and rewrite, subject the manuscript to criticism by the instructor, then rewrite again. If possible, the oration should be delivered repeatedly to class or club audiences before it is used in intercollegiate competition. Possibly the winners in an intramural contest may represent the school in some important contest or contests.

General preparation for extemporaneous or impromptu speaking takes place in original speech classes. Frequently, however, tournament sponsors announce a general area within which specific topics will be chosen. The forensics director may draw up topics of his own within this general field and give speakers practice under contest conditions. Participants must learn to help themselves through reading, note taking, and oral discussion.

After-dinner speakers have a particularly difficult problem. They must study the probable audience and speaking situation and discuss their analysis with squad veterans and faculty members. Choosing a topic for the entertaining speech and selecting suitable developmental material are difficult processes. Each illustration or anecdote must be weighed in terms of the occasion, audience, time limit, and the speaker's individual style of humor. And despite careful preparation, the speech must never become so fixed that it lacks the spark of spontaneous adaptation that characterizes the successful after-dinner speech.

GENERAL SUGGESTIONS FOR THE DIRECTOR

If several faculty or graduate assistants are working with forensics, the debate squad may be divided. Some institutions maintain separate squads for men and women. Others divide the experienced from the inexperienced.

The best plan probably varies with the nature and tradition of the individual institution. All responsible directors, however, regard the group meetings as only part of the job. Individual and team conferences are held on cases, evidence, strategy, and speech composition.

The faculty director of forensics should be a teacher and counselor. He should teach skills of argumentation, not dictate case or speech outline. Students must learn to think for themselves; they are not puppets performing as the coach pulls the strings.

Students work hard only when motivated. Many students on the debate squad will not be enrolled for courses in speech, and the instructor in charge gives neither credit nor grade. Motivation is needed. The director should keep the values of forensic activity before squad members throughout the year. Through constructive criticism he may help each student understand his own achievements, limitations, and needs for self-improvement. The fact that important national issues are being studied also encourages hard work. The strongest motivation in forensics, however, probably comes from intercollegiate competition. Forensic competition is an intellectual intercollegiate sport, a contest of brain against brain. Many excellent students learn to love this clash of ideas as well as the trips, tournaments, and audiences before whom they speak.

Members of the debate squad should learn to cooperate as well as compete. An early group project should be the preparation of a joint annotated bibliography listing and evaluating many sources of information. Some schools maintain a common "brains box" into which all squad members put duplicate copies of valuable evidence; others encourage less formal methods of sharing discoveries. In practice debates veterans are often teamed with novices to their mutual benefit. The novice learns debate strategy and technique; the veteran is reminded that genius and a mastery of debate jargon are not necessarily synonymous.

SCHEDULING THE FORENSIC PROGRAM

Colleges and universities vary in size, location, means of support, academic emphasis, forensic tradition, and many other matters. A successful forensic program in one location would fail in another. Every forensic program must be designed for one particular campus and student body.

Schools in or near metropolitan areas may, if they choose, arrange a heavy schedule of home-and-home and service-club debates. Schools farther off the beaten track must invest heavily in a few highly publicized debates and rely more on trips to debate tournaments. Some institutions emphasize open forums, speakers' bureaus, or radio-TV discussions.

BALANCING THE PROGRAM

Most good programs strike a balance among forensic activities: debate tournaments, a discussion conference, a student congress, oratorical league, or regional speech contest. International debates are scheduled when available, and home-and-home rivalries encouraged with a few select opponents. Intramural debates, forums, and contests round out the program.

Anyone assuming direction of an established forensic program should find out about the previous year's program and study ways in which it could be improved. Among the factors determining the nature of his program are (a) the size and location of the institution, (b) size and responsiveness of the community, (c) amount of the forensic budget, (d) availability of radio and TV stations (commercial or educational), (e) forensic events within a reasonable distance, (f) honor society affiliation of his institution (if any), and (g) number of students reporting for his squad.

PLANNING THE SEASON AS A WHOLE

Before the fall term begins, it is a good idea for the director of forensics to make a tentative plan for the season as a whole. He should strike the best possible balance among various forensic events and patterns of debate, seeking through a varied series of experiences to provide motivation and educational experience for his students.

An excellent guide for this planning is the calendar prepared by the American Forensic Association and printed in its journal. Events all over the country are listed, by date and location, with minimum information about events, eligibility, and the person in charge.

In scheduling events, you are likely to find many or all of the following suggestions applicable in your region:

1. There are likely to be several early-season events from October to December. Some are limited to novices; others are designed to help the varsity "warm up." Many will offer the contributions of subject-matter experts.

2. Many invitational tournaments for varsity debaters are scheduled for January through March. Some include special sections for novices; many include individual speaking events. A few of these feature cross-examination or split-team patterns of debate.

3. National tournaments of the honor societies, as well as West Point regional tryouts and the West Point and other national tournaments, usually come in the two-month period from mid-March through mid-May.

4. If your school is affiliated with one of the forensic honoraries, you will have regional and national conferences or tournaments nearly every

year. Or your school may participate in a state or regional league. Events in this category are usually closed to nonmembers.

5. Many schools have the tradition of a short or long debate tour. Maybe your school has such a heritage. Or you may encourage others to stop at your institution for a debate. Invitations to dinner and a night's lodging are seldom refused.

A full and varied program of intramural and intercollegiate forensics will probably last from the September mixer through the May squad banquet and election of officers for the next school year. Beware of concentrating forensic activity so sharply in two or three months that student debaters miss more classes than they should.

TRAVEL

Many institutions own station wagons or college automobiles obtainable for debate trips if reserved in advance. Frequently the director is expected to use his own automobile and is reimbursed at a mileage rate paid from the forensics budget. Some schools make all trips by public carrier, usually bus or train, sometimes plane. This settles major problems of liability, since this is assumed by the carrier. When using college-owned transportation the director should discuss with the college business manager or his insurance agent the subject of liability. When traveling by private automobile he should be sure that the trip is covered by adequate insurance.

Each director must decide, within the limitations of the budget and with or without the counsel of his debaters, how far to travel. It is true that more students can be sent on short trips, but superior people may have earned and may need the stimulation of a long trip and national competition. A distant location gives tournaments glamor; sometimes the trip may be worth the cost, but a heavy expenditure on a few people should be examined closely.

For each off-campus trip all participants should be informed early of the date and time of departure, date and probable time of return, schedule of events at the destination, and arrangements for travel, quarters at the destination, meals, and method of reimbursement for necessary expenses. Schools with limited budgets sometimes ask each student making a major debate trip to pay part of his own expenses.

AGREEMENT FOR DUAL DEBATES

Nothing that you can foresee should be left to chance when you schedule debates with another school. Whenever possible, exchange written agreements on a form similar to that given on the next page.

INTERCOLLEGIATE FORENSICS AGREEMENT

Between
_____ and State University.
1. Place: The debate or discussion will be held at _____
_____ On arrival, the traveling team should go
to _____ The event will be held before
_____

2. Time: The event will be held at _____ $\frac{A.}{P.}$ M. on _____ 19_____
3. Subject will be: _____
_____

4. In debate, State University will support (strike out two):
   affirmative,   negative,   both sides
5. Program: The event will be conducted as follows: _____
_____
   Number of speakers from each institution: _____
   Length of speeches: _____
6. Is a decision desired? Yes___ No___ Oral critique? Yes___ No___
   Suggestions for judge or critic: _____
7. Entertainment: What entertainment, if any, will the host school
   provide? _____
8. Dress: _____
9. Publicity material concerning the visitors should be sent to:
_____

10. Special notes or comments: _____
_____
_____

_____   _____
Director of Forensics, State U.

                                        _____
                                        Title and Institution

     Schools entertaining British or other foreign teams traveling under the auspices of the Institute of International Education understand clearly their responsibilities. They are to provide housing and meals, as well as the fee (currently $100) to defray traveling expenses. Insofar as possible, the Institute keeps everyone informed of progress enroute and of any changes in the itinerary.

FINANCING FORENSICS

Most of the time the college or university director of forensics has no direct responsibility for raising funds to support the forensic program. He is often responsible, however, for presenting the case for debate as persuasively as possible to department head and dean, or perhaps to a student-government budget committee. If a student manager can "carry the ball," so much the better, but the faculty director must at least counsel and advise, if not more.

SOURCES OF FUNDS

Most forensic funds come either from student activity fees appropriated by student government or by the administration, or from direct college or university appropriation.[4] It is doubtful that a new director of forensics can change the way his funds are allocated, but he should certainly learn how this is done.

Forensic budgets may occasionally be supplemented for special projects: a national convention, a special invitation to West Point for its national tournament, an international debate. Administration or student government sources may look with favor on such projects and be willing to provide financial support. Less frequently the alumni or other friends of the institution may be willing to help. Occasionally (more often in high school than in college) forensics secure added help from tag days, special entertainments, civic organizations, and appeals to toastmasters.

SIZE OF THE BUDGET

Surveys of the status of forensic budgets are made frequently. Anyone who follows *The Speech Teacher* and publications of the American Forensic Association will probably locate more up-to-date statistics than are presented here. In 1961, a survey conducted under the sponsorship of the American Forensic Association revealed:

> Travel budgets reported ranged in size from $50 to $5400. One hundred and forty-three schools, 58 percent of all reporting, had travel budgets of $1000 or more. This group broke down as follows: four had budgets of $5000 or above, three were in the $4000 bracket, nine were

[4] Nicholas M. Cripe, "A Survey of Debate Programs in Two Hundred and Forty-six American Colleges and Universities," *The Speech Teacher*, 8 (March 1959), 157–160.

in the $3000, thirty-six had budgets between $2000 and $2900, thirty-two schools were between $1500 and $1900, fifty-nine schools had travel budgets ranging from $1000 (14 schools) to $1400 (10 schools).

Of the schools with budgets below $1000, seven had a $900 budget, twenty-three were $800 or a bit more, thirteen were in the $700 class, twelve were between $600 and $675, fourteen were between 500 and 550 dollars, nine had budgets of 400 to 450 dollars, ten were $300 or a little above, five were in the $200 range, and seven were $150 or less.[5]

The location of a school has much to do with the amount of money required to support a strong program. Schools in or near a metropolitan area can conduct an extensive program on a $1,000 budget. Schools in Tallahassee, Florida; Albuquerque, New Mexico; or Missoula, Montana must travel long distances for intercollegiate competition. Travel costs money and an equivalent program costs several times as much money.

Most directors naturally consider their appropriation—any appropriation—too small. They ask for more money. Competing activities make similar demands, and administrative officials and student councils quickly develop strong resistance. A strong forensic program, serving many students, and kept in the public eye through good public relations, will in most environments earn adequate support from whatever powers control the purse strings.

MAKING A PRELIMINARY ESTIMATE OF EXPENSES

Before each forensic season (usually in the previous spring), the director of forensics will be asked to prepare a tentative budget. He may consult with or shift part of the task to student managers, but the ultimate responsibility is probably his.

The following items should be considered as the budget is prepared:

1. Costs of each trip planned: transportation, housing, meals, registration fee.
2. Costs of an international debate (if this is part of the program): fee to the Institute of International Education, housing and meals for the visitors while on campus, costs of promotion.
3. Entertainment of visiting schools: housing, meals. Cooperation of dormitory officials or fraternities and sororities may reduce this item.
4. Fees and expenses of critic judges where decisions are desired.
5. Expenses in connection with tournament or contest sponsored by the institution: awards, fees, and expenses for visiting teachers, entertainment.

[5] *Ibid.*, p. 157.

6. Intramural trophies and awards.
7. Postage and duplicating services.
8. Annual forensic awards.
9. Incidentals, such as refreshments purchased for the fall mixer or spring party.
10. Reference materials purchased for use by the squad. (Often materials may be bought through the library budget.)
11. Publicity or promotion of forensic events: posters, cards, or letters for direct mail advertising, photographs of leading members of teams. The college paper or public relations office may share these expenses.
12. Contingencies: a sum set aside for emergencies or unforeseen needs.

RECORDKEEPING

The college or university business manager will describe the records that must be kept of expenditures from the forensics budget. Usually the school will provide the faculty member responsible with a cash advance to cover the costs of a major trip, any balance to be returned with the report of expenditures. Receipts are often required, at least for major disbursements. The director of forensics needs a careful record of expenditures both to know how much money he has left in his budget, and to make next year's planning more accurate.

ENCOURAGING STUDENT RESPONSIBILITY

Modern college debate grew by natural stages out of nineteenth-century student literary societies.[6] Here and there the student-organized debate society, with a faculty adviser who has no real authority, still persists. At the opposite extreme, some faculty directors make all plans and decisions concerning the forensic program. The best course of action probably strikes a middle ground.

A faculty director of forensics gives the program mature judgment and continuity. Student participation in the planning and administration adds youthful vigor and enthusiasm. Theoretically the ultimate responsibility for important decisions usually remains with the faculty director. In practice, a considerable share of this responsibility may be assumed by student veterans in forensics.

[6] David Potter, *Debating in the Colonial Chartered Colleges.* Teachers College, Columbia University, Contributions to Education, No. 899. New York, 1944.

The amount of student participation depends on many factors: the climate of the campus, the age of the forensic program, the number of experienced students. In any case, the director may at the beginning of the year explain to the varsity squad the state of the budget and probable costs of various trips. Students can express preferences concerning the tournaments they would like to attend and the schools they want to meet in dual competition.

STUDENT MANAGERS

Responsible students often are singled out by election or appointment as student managers of debate. Sometimes there is a single manager; frequently there is one for men and another for women. Occasionally the system of student managers is highly developed with a different manager for each class, freshmen through seniors, and for various aspects of the program: radio and television, speakers' bureau, away debates, home debates, tournaments.

Occasionally a small hourly or monthly stipend is provided for the senior manager. More frequently, the post has become one of honor on the campus—with real competition for the position.

RESPONSIBILITIES GIVEN STUDENT MANAGERS

The requirements of each individual situation and the personnel available for each job determine the responsibilities delegated by the director to the student managers. If chosen toward the end of his junior year, a senior manager may, in cooperation with the faculty director and members of the varsity squad, prepare the schedule and tentative budget for the following year. A good manager often handles correspondence with other schools, makes agreements for individual debates, plans and arranges for transportation to off-campus debates or tournaments, sees that entertainment is provided for visiting speakers, and keeps records of all expenditures and a running estimate of the balance in the forensic budget.

RESPONSIBILITIES OF EVERY PARTICIPANT IN FORENSICS

Each student in forensics should be taught to assume his share of the total responsibility. The forensic program does not belong to the director or to the institution in the abstract; it belongs to every member of the squad, to every participant in any event.

On campus, each participant should consider attendance at every squad meeting a minimum essential of good citizenship. Assignments to report or to debate should be carried out as they would be for a favorite class—as, indeed, debate should often be. In case of unexpected emergencies, the director of forensics should be notified at the earliest possible time. Meetings are for business. There is a time for work and a time for play in all activities—including forensics—and woe to the student who insists on playing when there is work to be done.

When the student represents his institution away from his own campus, his conduct comes under special scrutiny. Squad members must act like ladies and gentlemen at all times; this should be enough of a guide if taken seriously. Frequently the director will specify a curfew during a tournament or insist that students stay together in their recreation. And there is no excuse for the student who is still packing when the director drives up ready to go or who rushes up just as the train pulls out or the plane takes off.

WINNING AN AUDIENCE FOR DEBATE

Silver-haired forensic veterans sometimes swap stories of the "golden days . . . when the Old Armory was packed to the rafters with cheering throngs, all in evening clothes; and . . . torchlight processions formed to welcome teams returning from battles on alien fields." [7] But that was before football and basketball mounted their thrones. Modern debate audiences too often consist of the friends and acquaintances of debaters, and only victory in a major tournament rates a headline in the college paper.

PUBLICIZING FORENSICS

Someone must assume responsibility for giving the college and community press, and radio-TV outlets, accurate information about forensic activities while they have maximum news value. But if at all possible the forensics director should not allow himself to be saddled with this additional chore. If given the raw material the college public relations office will often write the stories. Sometimes a member of the varsity squad also writes for the college paper and may ask for the forensics assignment.

One of the most effective methods, where possible, is the appointment of a student publicity director.[8] A conscientious man with some writ-

[7] Raymond F. Howes, "Finding Debate Audiences," *Quarterly Journal of Speech Education,* 11 (November 1925), 364–368. See also James Gordon Emerson, "The Old Debating Society," *Quarterly Journal of Speech,* 17 (June 1931), 362–375.

[8] Wilbur E. Gilman, "Can We Revive Public Interest in Intercollegiate Debates?" *Quarterly Journal of Speech,* 14 (November 1928), 553–563.

ing skill can do much to make the campus conscious of forensics. And this is a first step, at least, in winning an audience for debate.

Pictures and posters are useful ways of advertising special events. Needed skills can often be secured through the cooperation of the college photographer and the Art Department.

TAKING DEBATE TO THE AUDIENCE

Slim audiences for college debates suggest the advisability of taking debates to civic clubs and campus organizations where "the audience . . . is furnished *by* not *for* the occasion . . .' [9] Program chairmen, faced with the need to plan for a seemingly unending series of weekly meetings, usually welcome an offer of student speeches, discussions, and debates. The Chamber of Commerce in a city of any size knows the meeting times and officers of the Lions, Elks, Optimists, Rotary, Kiwanis, and similar organizations.

The same contact may be made with campus clubs and religious organizations. Members of the debate squad frequently belong to these groups and may easily talk to responsible program chairmen. In a large community or on a large campus the problem may be to limit rather than expand the number of invitations for discussions and debates.

Never undertake more of these assignments than can be done well. Quality must be kept high or interest lags and program chairmen start saying "no." Offerings may be presented informally to selected chairmen or announced to all in mimeographed or printed brochures. Colleges are often anxious to establish and support a student speakers' bureau. Alumni offices frequently use student speakers to keep in touch with alumni clubs in neighboring communities.

USING AN ATTRACTIVE PATTERN OF DEBATE

For all debates before audiences—face-to-face or over radio or television—the director of forensics should take special care to use an attractive pattern of debate. Few tournament debates are presented with a general audience in mind; few audiences are sophisticated enough in debate strategy or in the subject matter of a particular debate to appreciate an unrelieved diet of closely reasoned argumentation.[10]

Debaters before service clubs, high school or college assemblies, or over radio and television must frequently conform to a shorter time sched-

[9] E. D. Schonberger, "Debate and the Audience Problem," *Quarterly Journal of Speech*, 16 (June 1930), 291–296.

[10] Lloyd H. Fuge and Robert P. Newman, "Cross-Examination in Academic Debating," *The Speech Teacher*, 5 (January 1956), 66–70.

ule than the hour-plus of the standard pattern of tournament debate, four ten-minute constructives followed by four five-minute rebuttals.

ATTRACTING SPECIAL AUDIENCES

Only special effort for an outstanding attraction has any chance of bringing respectable numbers of faculty or students to forensic events. For an outstanding item, such as an international debate, direct mail advertising to faculty, alumni, and interested townspeople may prove effective. A mailing list may be compiled from neighboring alumni and the college-theatre patron list.

One device frequently used in college is the "draft." Students of debate and discussion, and even classes in fundamentals of speech or communication, may be required to attend some forensic event. As an occasional practice this can probably be defended as a valuable listening experience for students of speech. It may help if the director of forensics suggests possible listening assignments to instructors of fundamentals classes.

USING RADIO AND TELEVISION

These mass media provide another way of taking debate and discussion to wider audiences. If the college has a radio station, forensic activities should be able to secure time without difficulty. It will be harder to sell discussion or debate to the program director of a commercial station. However, each station is required by law to operate in the public interest, and college discussions and debates help the station fill its legal obligations. High-quality programs with a local slant can earn a place in the programming of even a busy commercial station. The original selling job may be easier if the director can offer several tapes or kinescopes of high-caliber debates or discussions.[11]

Television offers special challenges and opportunities. Debate or discussion can provide good televiewing if skill and effort are devoted to the task.[12] In February 1962, the American Forensic Association with the American Student Foundation launched a sixteen-week series, "Championship Debate," over the NBC Television network. The intercollegiate debates of the initial series were viewed by a weekly audience of more than four million.

[11] Milton Dickens, "Adapting Debate to the Air," *Quarterly Journal of Speech*, 27 (April 1941), 255–261.

[12] Edward Stasheff and N. Edd Miller, "Televising a Debate in a Courtroom Setting," *The Speech Teacher*, 3 (September 1954), 215–219. Wayne E. Brockriede and David B. Strother, "Televised Forensics," *The Speech Teacher*, 6 (January 1957), 30–35.

HIGH SCHOOL FORENSICS

Most of the problems of college forensics are true of the high school as well. The forensic program must, moreover, be adapted to the school itself, to a small-town high school with a graduating class of ten or a big city giant with a student body larger than most colleges. No two forensic programs have quite the same setting, tradition, or administrative support. The following section, however, raises three problems especially perplexing to many high school debate coaches.

ADJUSTING TO THE ACADEMIC ENVIRONMENT

In most colleges the director of forensics counts his assignment part of his academic load; that is, if the normal teaching load is fifteen hours, he may be assigned twelve plus debate, or even, less frequently, nine hours. Usually he has a class in debate for which students receive regular academic credit. Frequently his debaters may earn credit (one hour a semester up to a prescribed total) for approved participation in forensics.

Debate in high school often fails to enjoy such status. Work with debaters should be but often is not a part of the teacher's academic responsibilities; too often the principal or superintendent sees debate as "just another outside club" to be assigned to a new or unwary English or social studies teacher, *in addition to* his regular teaching schedule. Too often there is no class in debate for which students receive academic credit.

Any qualified high school debate director will work toward the best academic conditions possible both for his own sake and for his students. He may have to accept unsatisfactory conditions temporarily, but not permanently. A judicious move or two sometimes works wonders.

FINANCING HIGH SCHOOL FORENSICS

A self-respecting college or university sponsoring a forensic program arranges at the same time for its financial support. The budget in a small institution may not be large, but it is a definite sum on which the director can count. An assured budget is a luxury in high school forensics. Frequently, in big schools as well as small, the coach must raise the funds before he can spend them. This places an extra burden on the forensics person, since time and energy that should be devoted to instruction must go instead to fund-raising.

High school forensics typically finds its financial support in varied fund-raising expedients. One school prepares a forensics calendar and sells these throughout the community. Another sponsors a Forensics Follies each fall, a fund-raising entertainment program for school and community. Many resort to bake sales, candy sales, or selling refreshments at football and basketball games. These are not ideal solutions, but they work. Money comes in, often at the beginning of the school year, and the forensic program can rely on its own budget, however restricted.

Two other expedients may be mentioned. In a large city one or more of the civic clubs often provide financial assistance to forensics. This may be especially useful in case of a national conference or unexpected opportunity. The debaters often reciprocate by providing one or more programs for the civic clubs. Another expedient is to require those making debate trips to pay part or all of their own way: meals or housing or transportation or fees, or some combination thereof. This is potentially unfair, since it adds a financial test to those normally required for membership on the traveling squad.

COMPETITION WITH OTHER CLASSES AND ACTIVITIES

Speech classes and activities compete with other classes and student activities, whether in high school or college. Despite its long academic tradition, speech does not belong to the modern sacred trilogy of science, mathematics, and foreign language. A written composition may creep into a charmed circle with the plea, "Johnny can't write," but few people seem worried about whether or not Johnny can speak or debate.

It may be comforting to note that speech instruction is still a marketable commodity, that public speaking and parliamentary law are popular adult education programs. A teacher doing a superior job in speech and debate classes will find students reacting favorably to the challenge. Through them and their enthusiasm effective community and administrative support usually may be obtained.

SUMMARY

This chapter emphasized the basic principles applicable to all forensic programs justifying sponsorship by an educational institution. We considered the practical problems faced by the director of forensics in (1) drawing qualified students into the program, (2) diversifying what sometimes tends to be standard-pattern national-question tournament debating only, and (3) developing an intramural forensic program. The director often fills his teaching function best as he works with the varsity debate squad in preparation for competitive debate. Detailed suggestions for effectiveness with the squad have been made.

Additional administrative problems facing the director of forensics are

(1) scheduling a balanced forensic program and planning for travel to other campuses and entertainment of visiting teams, (2) securing adequate financial support from the college administration or from student activity funds, (3) delegating responsibility to student debaters and managers, and (4) winning an audience for debate. Finally, attention was given to several special problems of high school forensics.

The art of directing forensics cannot be learned from lectures or textbooks alone. To organize and administer a forensic program for maximum impact, to prepare students for excellence in competition are difficult tasks. Most men and women who undertake the direction of forensic activities can look back to their own high school and undergraduate debating days. These are valuable experiences, but now the director must remember that he has a new environment, a new perspective, and new problems. He cannot transfer to his new institution either the program he experienced as an undergraduate or that in which he may have worked as a graduate assistant. But colleges and universities have their likenesses as well as differences. A well-trained director of forensics can, with initiative, time, judgment, and effort, organize a program reflecting credit on himself and his profession.

Experience is the ultimate teacher.

EXERCISES

1. Do you agree with the seven general principles stated in the first section of this chapter? If not, why not? If so, how well does the forensic program at your institution measure up to those standards?
2. Where does the forensic budget at your institution fit into the pattern? Considering the number of students active in forensics, the location of your institution, and similar criteria, how adequate is your present forensic budget?
3. Assume that the head of your department or the dean of your college is carefully examining all budgets. Defend your forensic budget (or a larger one) in terms that a responsible educational administrator can appreciate.
4. Does your institution participate in a competitive discussion conference? If so, where, and how do your representatives like it? If not, why not? Do you agree with those who argue that discussion has failed as a competitive forensic event? (See the references listed in the footnote on page 309 of this chapter.)
5. How many audience debates did your institution sponsor last year? Is this number adequate for the number of students in forensics and appropriate to opportunities available on campus and in the community?
6. How do you try to make debating attractive to audiences? What pattern of debate do you use? What role do you give the audience during or after the debate?
7. List the opportunities for radio or television discussion or debate open

on your campus or in your community. Then hold a brain-storming session on ways and means of attracting and holding a good audience over radio or TV.

8. Assume that your debate squad plans to enter a tournament one month after the fall forensics mixer. Outline a program for weekly (or twice-weekly) group meetings together with essential team conferences and practice debates.
9. What is the relationship in your institution between curricular instruction in public speaking, discussion, and debate, and the co-curricular program in forensics? Is this relationship a happy, complementary one? If not, how can it be improved?
10. Assume that in your institution a faculty committee is considering a proposal to grant college credit for approved participation in forensics. As the new director of forensics, you are called to testify before this committee. What would you say? Remember that unless you favor the proposal it will almost certainly die, and that there may be strong resistance to its approval.

SUGGESTED READINGS

The Bulletin of the National Association of Secondary-School Principals. See "Speech in the Extracurriculum Program," 29 (November 1945), 116–124. Also 38 (January 1954), Chaps. 6, 11, 12.

CHENOWETH, EUGENE C. *Discussion and Debate.* Dubuque, Iowa: Wm. C. Brown, 1951. Part 5.

EHNINGER, DOUGLAS. "Six Earmarks of a Sound Forensic Program," *The Speech Teacher,* 1 (November 1952), 237–241.

FRIEDERICH, WILLARD J., and RUTH A. WILCOX. *Teaching Speech in High Schools.* New York: The Macmillan Company, 1953. Chaps. 6, 7, 8.

HARRIS, KENNETH. *Innocents from Abroad.* Cambridge, Mass.: Houghton Mifflin Company, 1951. The story of an Oxford Union Society debating team touring the United States.

LAHMAN, C. P. *Debate Coaching.* New York: H. W. Wilson Company, 1940.

MELZER, ARNOLD. *High School Forensics.* New York: H. W. Wilson Company, 1940.

NICHOLS, ALAN. *Discussion and Debate.* New York: Harcourt, Brace & World, Inc., 1941. Chap. 7, Appendix 8, 9.

OGILVIE, MARDEL. *Teaching Speech in the High School.* New York: Appleton-Century-Crofts, 1961. Section 3.

PETERSON, OWEN M. "Directing the Extracurricular Forensic Program," Chap. 10, in *Speech Methods and Resources: A Textbook for the Teacher of Speech,* ed. Waldo W. Braden. New York: Harper & Row, Publishers, 1961.

"Program of Speech Education: Recommendations of the Contest Committee of the North Central Association with Respect to Speech as Submitted by the Speech Association of America," *Quarterly Journal of Speech*, 37 (October 1951), 347–358.

REID, LOREN D.　*Teaching Speech in the High School.* Columbia, Mo.: Artcraft Printers, 1952. Chap. 12.

ROBINSON, KARL F.　*Teaching Speech in the Secondary School.* New York: Longmans, Green & Co., 1954. Part 3.

WEAVER, ANDREW THOMAS, GLADYS L. BORCHERS, and DONALD K. SMITH. *The Teaching of Speech.* Englewood Cliffs, N.J.: Prentice-Hall, Inc., 1952. Pp. 310–317, 340–344, 362–374.

chapter 16

DEBATE TOURNAMENTS

by Robert B. Huber

Born in the latter part of the nineteenth century, intercollegiate debating grew steadily during the early part of the twentieth century. Beginning with dual contests between colleges, forensic programs soon expanded into the triangular debates and small leagues. Schools with adequate budgets arranged tours through nearby regions. During the 1920's, this kind of travel was not uncommon. Even so, colleges with limited budgets found it difficult to afford debate training for more than a handful of students.

It is generally believed that the first debate tournament was held at Southwestern College, Winfield, Kansas, March 14–16, 1923. The national forensic fraternity Pi Kappa Delta held a tournament for the first time during its 1926 convention.[1] However, it was the depression of the 1930's that gave impetus to the tournament idea. Small budgets made it necessary to give forensic training to more students at less cost. Squads of ten to fifteen students could engage in several rounds of debating and individual events during a weekend. The large debate tournament, as well as small practice tournaments, developed throughout the Midwest, the South, and Far West during the depression. However, tournament debating did not invade the East until after World War II. Tournaments have become so numerous during the past decade that several are held every weekend from November through April in every section of the country.

Originally, debating was the primary contest at tournaments. Now

---

[1] Egbert Ray Nichols, "A Historical Sketch of Intercollegiate Debating," *Quarterly Journal of Speech* 23 (April 1937), 272.

a wide variety of individual events are held such as extempore speaking, oratory, oral interpretation, discussion, and congressional sessions.

High schools were quick to follow the college trend in adopting the tournament format. State leagues soon employed these tournament procedures. The National Forensic League instituted a system of national high school forensic championships early in the 1930's.

VALUES OF DEBATE TOURNAMENTS

Debate tournaments provide excellent training for the debater. First, a beginning debater can enter a novice tournament and know that he is meeting debaters of his own caliber. Second, tournaments provide all debaters with the drill essential to the development of excellence in argument. Third, they give each debater a chance to have a challenging program throughout the year. Fourth, tournaments provide an opportunity for the debater to match wits with many outstanding students from a variety of schools. The inauguration of national tournaments has given debaters the opportunity of competing with some of the best debaters from all sections of the country.

Many benefits accrue to schools who choose to operate such tournaments. The joint effort of the debaters plus nondebating students lends prestige to debate within the school. In those schools which operate large tournaments many students become acquainted with debating by serving as chairmen-timekeepers or administrators of the tournament. A large tournament often focuses the attention of the entire community upon debate and promotes interest in it. The impact of debate teams from twenty, thirty, or forty colleges and universities upon a community can hardly be ignored.

WHAT TOURNAMENTS WILL NOT DO

Since the audience in tournament debating is frequently limited to merely the judge and a chairman-timekeeper, tournament debating is not a superior method of training students to become audience speakers. The tournament debater does not have to adjust to various types of audiences. Tournament debating, with its emphasis upon the logical mode of persuasion, tends to develop a neglect for the psychological. Sometimes tournament debating encourages bad habits: a too rapid rate of speech, a poor sense of communication, and neglect of stylistic devices by which speeches are made more vivid. Because of these drawbacks, there are those who are highly critical of tournament debating, some even to the point of advocating abolishing it. However, the value of repeated drill, the larger squad, and lower costs tend to outweigh the shortcomings. Directors who recognize the shortcomings of tournaments usually compensate for them by adding to their schedules home-and-home debates and other events such as oratory and extempore speaking or by operating a speakers' bureau.

TYPES OF TOURNAMENTS

Tournaments tend to be classified on the basis of the goal to be achieved. A novice tournament is one that aims to give training to beginning debaters. A varsity tournament is one limited to experienced debaters. However, coaches may use superior novice debaters on their varsity squad. Particularly is this true of tournaments which emphasize the learning experience and de-emphasize the winning aspect.

By far the greatest number of tournaments today are invitational. An open invitational tournament is one that is available to all who wish to come. Anyone wishing to attend merely writes for an invitation. A closed invitational tournament is one in which the director invites only a selected number of colleges. Various regional tournaments, leagues, and national debate fraternities hold closed tournaments. Among these are the Western, Southern, Eastern, and New England. Such tournaments are closed to schools outside the region. The national honorary forensic fraternities have their national conferences which are usually closed events; only those schools which hold charters within the fraternity are eligible to participate.

Anyone who is thinking of operating a tournament should first determine whether there is a need for one. The easiest way to answer this question is to find out whether the various schools in the particular region have students who need increased participation. A survey of the coaches soon provides this information.

MAKING A "BLUEPRINT" OF THE TOURNAMENT

It is extremely important for the tournament manager to picture in detail everything that will be required in the successful operation of the tournament. He must determine the date which should have minimum conflict with other events both on his own campus and with respect to the invited schools. The type of tournament will have to be determined, whether it is to be novice, varsity, practice, decision, open or closed invitational. The events will have to be planned, including the number of rounds of debate and whether other events such as extemporaneous speaking, oratory, or oral reading will be included. In addition, social events such as banquets and dances will have to be planned. The number and type of schools to be invited will depend upon the space available on the particular campus. The schedule should insure sufficient time for everything.

Many tournament managers make the mistake of packing too many events within too short a period of time; they forget the difficulties of getting to and from meals or the time necessary to move from one building to another.

In making the blueprint of the tournament, problems that may need special attention should not be overlooked. Visiting schools will always appreciate help on housing. Attention should be paid to facilities for obtaining food. Particularly is this important if the influx of visiting debaters might overwhelm the usual eating places available.

Problems of transportation need to be anticipated. Schools coming by means other than automobile will need means of getting back and forth from their rooming and eating places. Even those coming by automobile may have difficulty in populous cities. To avoid complications a tournament manager must know his locale and the effect that the convention of debaters and coaches will have on the city.

When conducting decision tournaments plans for proper awards need to be made. Trophies, medals, and certificates take time to prepare. They require either special printing or engraving.

Having determined the tournament schedule from hour to hour, it is essential that the director blueprint all the steps in preparation for the tournament. This is no small task because he will have to anticipate every job that needs to be done, who is going to do it, and exactly what time it needs to be done. For example, he will have to plan when the original invitations are to be sent out, when he wants the early replies back, whether he will want a final entry blank sent out to each school, and if so, exactly when it should be returned. In addition, he will need to think in terms of selecting and training his student administrative staff.

SELECTING AND TRAINING THE STUDENT ADMINISTRATIVE STAFF

This staff should be chosen far in advance of the tournament. If one is operating an annual invitational tournament it is wise to choose important staff members one year in advance; they will have the experience of one tournament before they assume major responsibility.

One of the most important staff members is the student chairman. He takes on the role of tournament manager with the forensic director as the supervisor. Such a person should be intelligent, congenial, and, above all, reliable. This individual then proceeds to choose an assistant chairman and the chairmen of the various committees needed to operate the tournament. The chairmen of the respective committees in turn pick their own personnel. A meeting should be held with the student chairman at least two months in advance of the tournament to ensure the early selection of the assistant chairman and the chairmen of the various committees.

Original invitations to the various schools should be sent out at least two months in advance of the tournament. It is wise to have all chairmen and committee members picked at least three weeks prior to the tournament. At that time the director should have a meeting with each student chairman to go over in detail the jobs that need to be done. The director should make certain that each chairman knows just how many people he needs at any given moment to perform the tasks required of his committee. It is wise to have each chairman report periodically during the days prior to the tournament so that the director can be certain that the jobs are being performed on time.

JOB CHECK LISTS WITH DEADLINES

It is helpful to make a job check list with each chairman and set a deadline for the various tasks to be accomplished. This should be done at your first meeting with each chairman.

Securing chairmen-timekeepers is one of the biggest tasks the administrative staff will have, particularly if the tournament is large. In the large tournament operated annually by the writer, some seventy-five to one hundred chairmen-timekeepers are needed for each round. Recruiting begins three weeks prior to the tournament. The student chairman selects an individual in each living unit to act as his lieutenant to aid in recruiting. These lieutenants report daily to the chairman, who in turn reports progress to the director. Speech classes are canvassed by their professors. All this must be done two or three days prior to the tournament.

In many tournaments there is little chance to give specific training to these chairmen-timekeepers, some of whom have never heard a debate. Instructors in the speech classes often can coach them. On the other hand, it can be done without any training if prepared, detailed instructions are supplied.

INSTRUCTIONS TO CHAIRMEN-TIMEKEEPERS

1. BE PROMPT
2. Be sure to bring a watch which has a second hand.

3. Report to the registration desk on the ___ floor of _____ 15 minutes before the debate is scheduled to begin.
4. At the registration desk pick up:
   a. Instruction Sheet, if you have forgotten yours.
   b. Your room and debate assignment
   c. Judge's ballot
   d. Time cards
5. Proceed to your assigned room.
6. Before the debate begins:
   a. Get the names of schools debating—which is debating affirmative and which negative
   b. When possible, write the names of the debaters on the blackboard, the affirmative debaters' names to the left as you face it, the negative to the right. Have each debater sit on his side of the room.
   c. On the judge's ballot (using ball-point pen or pencil) fill in the blanks with the following: round, affirmative, negative, 1st affirmative, 2nd affirmative, 1st negative, 2nd negative, also the division and room. The judge will fill out the rest after the debate.
   d. Hand the judge his ballot.
   e. Check with the judge to see if he is from the school named on the schedule.
7. Start the debate by:
   a. Welcoming all present to the debate tournament in round 1. For rounds 2, 3, 4, and 5 say "We hope you are enjoying the tournament and visit to _____."
   b. Announcing the topic for debate.
   c. Then announcing: "Each debater will give a 10-minute constructive speech and a 5-minute rebuttal. I have time cards arranged to reveal the number of minutes left to speak. At the end of the time allotted I will stand. There will be a 5-minute intermission between the constructive and the rebuttal speeches."
   d. Introducing debaters individually by name in this order: 1st affirmative, 2nd affirmative, 1st negative, and 2nd negative.
   e. Then saying, "We will proceed immediately to the debate."
8. Take a seat in the audience about the 2nd row from the front. Proceed to time the speeches accurately and be sure to give warnings as directed.
9. Time the intermission and then start rebuttals saying, "Now we shall proceed to the rebuttals with the 1st negative speaking first."
10. Time the rebuttals starting with the time card indicating 5 minutes to go.
11. After the debate is over:
    a. Have the judge fill out the ballot and hand it to you.
    b. Introduce the judge who will then give his critique.

c. Bring the ballot and time cards back to the registration desk. Be sure to get checked in.

The transportation committee becomes an important group in any large tournament. If all the events can be held within one building there will be little need for more than transporting participants to and from their rooming places. Once the tournament becomes large and is held in a variety of buildings the duties of the transportation committee become greater. They not only serve to transport participants but they should be available constantly to help in case of trouble. Thus, in blueprinting the transportation committee's job it is wise the first time you meet with the chairman to go through the tournament hour by hour to determine the number of cars that will be needed at any given time. It will lessen your problems in transportation if the final application blank for tournament admission returned by the schools contains the following information:

We will arrive _____ at _____ by car _____ plane
                  date   time
_____ train _____ bus _____
We will depart _____ at _____
                  date   time

Having this data you will know which schools will need to be transported constantly to and from their debates and you will also know when and where to pick them up should you care to provide such transportation service. With this knowledge you will be able to predict how many cars you will need before and after each event. Even while debates are in progress it is wise to have one or two cars standing by in case the tournament is held in buildings located at great distances from each other.

For each forensic event other than debate there should be a committee. Each committee should have its own job check list—planned with the tournament director. The following are some of the jobs to be done:

1. Preliminary list of participants obtained from entry blanks.
2. Determination of the number of sections of each event (usually not less than six nor more than nine per section).
3. Procurement of rooms.
4. Procurement of chairmen-timekeepers.
5. Allotment of judges. (These will be selected from among the visitors and may have to be augmented from your own campus.)
6. Printing of ballots.
7. Assigning participants to their proper section.
8. Sending the judging and participant assignment to the schools at registration.

9. Running of events as scheduled.
10. Collecting the ballots and determining the winners.
11. Mimeographing or dittoing the results.

The preceding list will cover most of the events with the possible exception of extemporaneous speaking. For this event the following additional steps must be included:

1. A series of thirty to fifty topics upon which the participants will speak will have to be drawn up prior to the tournament.
2. A time and place for drawing topics, half an hour before the contest, will have to be chosen and manned.
3. Each participant must be assigned two different times, first when he draws his topic and second when he speaks.

Convocations, social events, and banquets should be given careful consideration. General convocations take up time and should be avoided unless they promote tournament efficiency. Debaters are peculiar about social events; often they prefer to entertain themselves rather than to be part of a large organized group. Dances and university plays, for example, usually attract only a few. Banquets, on the other hand (with the price included in the registration fee), usually are well attended. The banquet, however, should be thoroughly planned and provide proper variation from the other events in the tournament. Remember—guests hear much speaking in the debates and other contests, so it is wise to avoid the use of speakers unless someone unusual is available. The chairman of the banquet should have a check list for the performance of his tasks.

1. Choose and procure the banquet hall.
2. Plan the menu with the caterer.
3. Determine the seating arrangement.
4. Determine the type of program and procure the entertainers. Warn all entertainers to keep within the time limits.
5. Plan the seating arrangements. Often this will be limited to the seating at the head table.
6. Choose a good master of ceremonies who knows how to keep things moving.
7. Procure a public-address system if needed.
8. Notify those serving to use the informal method so that the food moves in rapidly and the dishes are cleared from the tables quickly.

Ceremonial speeches, such as welcoming or presenting, should be kept to a minimum and as short as possible. Introductions of people and thanks to those who contribute should be done quickly and sincerely. Throughout all keep a strong rein on the proceedings so that everything moves rapidly.

Registration and tournament headquarters chairmen should be instructed in their tasks. Registration procedures can be simplified if a registration envelope is utilized. This envelope should be large enough to contain all the materials needed for each school. On the outside of the envelope be sure to write the name of the school and the amount due in registration fees along with other fees that may have to be charged. Inside the envelope place a schedule of events for each person, the banquet and other tickets, and the sheet of information for guests. This information sheet can often take the place of a convocation. All the information that is needed can be placed on it: composition of the tournament, location of buildings, where to go in case of emergency, how to obtain transportation, where to get meals, how to find rooms, where rest rooms are located, and so on. It is a good idea to include maps of the city, maps of the campus, and judges' instruction sheets as well.

The procedure at the registration desk should go as follows:

1. Check to see if the people in attendance are the same as those names appearing on the entry blanks mailed in prior to the tournament. If such a method was not used have them complete an official entry blank with the names of those in attendance. This information will help in case of emergencies which require quick location of personnel.
2. Record where the groups are staying.
3. Record the means of transportation, discovering whether they have their own car or will need assistance.
4. Have them pay the fees and receipt them.
5. Record their time of departure.

By using such simple procedures as these, registration can move rapidly.

At the tournament headquarters you will need one person sitting at a desk marked "Information." You will need one or two people to check the chairmen-timekeepers out and in. The chairman of the transportation committee should be close at hand ready to designate a car to go to any trouble spot. He and the student chairman should be readily available in case anything goes wrong.

Another group will be needed to tabulate the results. Two or three people will suffice. Their procedure should be as follows:

1. Check each ballot for accuracy to see that the winning team has the highest rating points or the lowest ranking score. This is extremely important because about one out of every twenty to twenty-five bal-

lots will contain errors. At the same time the winning team can be encircled on the schedule for that round.

2. Repeat the process to see that no mistakes have been made.
3. Start printing the results. List schools alphabetically with the affirmative teams first, and record the victory or defeat for each.
4. Prepare ballots for distribution to the various schools. Use a fairly large envelope for each school. The part of the ballot designated as the affirmative's copy will go to the school of the affirmative team. The copy designated for the negative will go to the school of the negative team.

To hasten the tabulation of results, chairmen-timekeepers for the last round should pick up the ballot before the judges give any critiques and return them to headquarters. Rapid tabulation plus keeping the printing of results up to date permits quick publication of results after the tournament is over. Efforts of the tournament administration to have the ballots available for distribution and the results in final printed form leave a pleasing impression upon guests.

THE DEBATE SCHEDULE

There are certain principles that your schedule should embrace:

1. Schools should meet only once during the tournament.
2. Judges should judge a school only once.
3. Since coaches are usually the judges, a judge should not judge a team that his team will meet later.
4. In tournaments where teams come from a wide region, avoid having neighboring schools meet.

The director should make a master schedule. The following is an example of a schedule for nine schools in a four-round tournament. The schedule is virtually a perfect one with every school meeting every other school once and each judge judging every school once, no judge judging a team that his team will meet later.

The principles involved in the chart are:

1. The first column stands for the affirmative teams.
2. The successive columns contain the negative team which debates that affirmative in successive rounds of that tournament. In the chart, affirmative 1 successively debates negative teams, 9, 8, 7, and 6. Such a master schematic form is made by dropping the negative of team 1 down

| | Negative | | | |
Affirmative	Rd. 1	Rd. 2	Rd. 3	Rd. 4
1	5	9	4	8
	9	8	7	6
2	6	1	5	9
	1	9	8	7
3	7	2	6	1
	2	1	9	8
4	8	3	7	2
	3	2	1	9
5	9	4	8	3
	4	3	2	1
6	1	5	9	4
	5	4	3	2
7	2	6	1	5
	6	5	4	3
8	3	7	2	6
	7	6	5	4
9	4	8	3	7
	8	7	6	5

one for each successive round. Thus, negative team 1 debates successively affirmative teams 2, 3, 4, and 5.

3. The schema for the judges also takes a definite pattern. In the first round the judge of school 1 is placed in the column of the affirmative team just below the team which his negative will debate in the last round of the tournament. In the chart, since there are four rounds and negative 1 meets affirmative 5 in the last round of the tournament, judge 1 is placed in the spot of judging affirmative 6 versus negative 5. In round two judge 1 is moved up to judge affirmative 2 and the negative team he has just met. In round three, judge 1 is moved to the horizontal column below his spot on the first round—namely, in the column of affirmative 7. In round four, judge 1 is then moved back up to the column just below where he judged in round two; in this case to judge affirmative 3.

From the foregoing illustration you can see that there is a pattern of judging assignments from round to round as the tournament progresses. If you have as many as eight rounds the pattern will be the same except that judge 1 in the first round in an eight-round tournament would start at affirmative 10 versus negative 9. In round two his place would be the same as for the shorter round; in round three he would judge affirmative 11, in round four affirmative 3; in round five affirmative 12 and in round six affirmative 4, and on through the same procedure for eight rounds.

The value of the foregoing master sheet to the tournament director is that he can see the schedule of the whole tournament on one page. The other great advantage is the fact that he does not have to check every single debate. What happens to school and judge 1 happens in a similar fashion to all others. Upon the arrival of the schools they can draw for positions and the school that draws number one will take those places on the schedule throughout the tournament.

Then to promote clarity the actual schedule of the tournament should be redrawn from the master schedule. The first printed schedule would appear somewhat like this on a mimeographed or dittoed sheet.

	Round 1				Round 2		
A	N	J	Room	A	N	J	Room
1	9	5	Arts 101	1	8	9	Arts 101
2	1	6	Arts 102	2	9	1	Arts 102
3	2	7	Arts 301	3	1	2	Library 302
4	3	8	Science 202	4	2	3	Science 202
5	4	9	Science 208	5	3	4	Library 304
6	5	1	Science 314	6	4	5	Science 314
7	6	2	Thornton 103	7	5	6	Thornton 103
8	7	3	Thornton 105	8	6	7	Gym 201
9	8	4	Thornton 206	9	7	8	Gym 202

This type of schedule is used when the tournament is a simple local one and no additional variables have to be considered. Should you have a large regional tournament in which schools are permitted to enter two or three pairs of teams, and you desire to avoid having neighboring schools meet, creating a schedule is not as easy. Utilizing the master, draw the schedule completely before the tournament begins. Schools that have three multiple units are placed on the master relatively equal distances throughout the schedule. Next, draw those with two units and place them at equal distances. Finally, draw those that have only one unit and place them in the remaining blanks. However, in order to see that the neighboring schools do not meet juggle the positions.

Suppose you have a five-round tournament. The affirmative team 6 will meet in succession the five schools above it, while the negative 6 will meet the five schools in succession below it. Thus, if a neighboring school falls within that range merely move it to another spot in the schedule. The complete schedule with the names of schools instead of numbers is printed prior to the tournament.

In a large regional or national tournament permitting only one unit to enter, it is possible to avoid having schools from the same geographic area meet. If there are eight rounds of debate, for example, the country can be divided into five geographic areas, with each school being scheduled to meet four teams from each of the other areas. (Schools participating are distributed as equally as possible into the five divisions.)

Many tournaments are operated with only a single two-man team alternating sides from round to round. An odd number of schools will necessitate some schools receiving byes.

	R–1–N	R–2–A	R–3–N	R–4–A	R–5–N	R–6–A	R–7–N	R–8–A
	17	4	15	6	13	8	11	10
1	2	28	26	24	22	20	18	16
	19	6	17	8	15	10	13	12
3	4	2	28	26	24	22	20	18
	21	8	19	10	17	12	15	14
5	6	4	2	28	26	24	22	20
	23	10	21	12	19	14	17	16
7	8	6	4	2	28	26	24	22
	25	12	23	14	21	16	19	18
9	10	8	6	4	2	28	26	24
	27	14	25	16	23	18	21	20
11	12	10	8	6	4	2	28	26
	1	16	27	18	25	20	23	22
13	14	12	10	8	6	4	2	28
	3	18	1	20	27	22	25	24
15	16	14	12	10	8	6	4	2
	5	20	3	22	1	24	27	26
17	18	16	14	12	10	8	6	4
	7	22	5	24	3	26	1	28
19	20	18	16	14	12	10	8	6
	9	24	7	26	5	28	3	2
21	22	20	18	16	14	12	10	8
	11	26	9	28	7	2	5	4
23	24	22	20	18	16	14	12	10
	13	28	11	2	9	4	7	6
25	26	24	22	20	18	16	14	12
	15	2	13	4	11	6	9	8
27	28	26	24	22	20	18	16	14

The principles of drawing up this schedule are:

1. Put the odd-numbered teams in the first column to the left.
2. Put the even-numbered teams in successive columns to the right, depending on the number of rounds.
3. At the top of each of the columns, beginning with the second one, put the round number and the side for the even-numbered teams. In other words, the R—1—N means that the even-numbered team takes

the negative in round one against the affirmative team listed in the column to the left. R—8—A means that the even-numbered team takes the affirmative in round eight against the negative listed in the column to the left.

4. The odd-numbered judges will judge the first, third, fifth, and seventh rounds. In a tournament as large as this, each can be placed at the spot indicated. If there are only twelve teams in the tournament you will have to move judge 1 upwards into the column to judge affirmative 3 and negative 4 and then move down in the same schematic form. The even-numbered judges may be placed in the same manner.

Many tournament directors, realizing that certain schools can have a lucky draw or that powerful schools may defeat each other, choose to utilize an elimination series in addition to the four, five, six, or even eight seeding rounds. In this case the top sixteen, eight, or four teams are put into elimination rounds. This has the advantage of making a little more certain, particularly in large tournaments, that the winners are really top-notch teams. On the other hand, it prolongs the tournament.

Power matching has been introduced into some tournaments in the hope of avoiding the pure luck of the draw. After each round winners are matched with winners and losers with losers. Although it may not be perfect, this system insures the emergence of the best debate teams.

The main steps in power matching are:

1. As the ballots come in, check them for accuracy. Make sure that the rating points and ranking correspond with the decision.

2. Record the wins and losses on a win-loss chart.

3. After each round, list the schools by the total number of wins.

4. Match the schools by wins and losses. From round to round avoid either the formation of undue obstacles or the giving of advantage by your method of matching, that is, a team that is paired with a lower-ranking team at one time should be paired with a higher-ranking team the next time. This is made necessary when there is not an even number of teams having identical wins or losses.

5. In two-man debate switching sides, the matching on the second, fourth, sixth, . . . , rounds must be modified by making sure that the teams are debating on the opposite sides from the sides debated in rounds one, three, five, . . .

DETERMINING THE WINNERS

The universal method of determining the winner is by totaling the number of debates won. Should there be ties, there are a variety of ways in which they may be broken. One is by using ranking points. Various ballots have the judge rank the debaters 1, 2, 3, and 4, in their order of excellence in that particular debate. Teams tied in numbers of wins would be ranked on the basis of total ranking scores, the lowest being ranked first, . . . Many people prefer the ranking-point method of breaking ties since there is little leeway for subjective reactions of judges to the debaters. Those favoring this point of view argue that certain judges in a tournament in using rating points are either too generous or too conservative and thus have undue influence on the outcome.

Various ballots utilize rating points and some prefer this method of breaking ties. The American Forensic Association ballots have rating point scales of 25, 15, and even less for each debater. Other ballots have as many as fifty rating points for each speaker. Thus the debaters are rated on this point scale by the judges. When this method is used to break ties the team or school with the highest number of rating points is declared the winner.

Still another way to determine the winner is by the number of wins first; then by making use of medians. For example, if the tournament is five rounds, the combined points for that round which is third from the best is used in breaking ties. Supposing a 25-rating-point ballot were being used in a four-man-debate tournament. For each round add the total number of rating points. Let us presume that in the first round the four debaters get a total of 82 rating points; the second round 79, the third 80, the fourth 76, and the fifth only 62. The median in the five rounds is 79. These points determine where the school ranks in the tournament should it happen to be tied for first or any other place. The median score is supposed to overcome the tendencies of those judges who are unduly generous or conservative with points.

BALLOTS AND INSTRUCTIONS TO JUDGES

Ballots for use by the judges should be procured or printed in sufficient time before the tournament. The American Forensic Association has several types of ballots that may be procured from its Secretary-Treasurer. These ballots have the distinct advantage of providing three copies. One copy can be retained by the tournament manager, the second can be given to the affirmative team, and the third to the negative team. Should one choose to print or mimeograph ballots, there are certain essential features that should be included. At the top of the page the division is needed (whether it is novice or varsity), the round, the room number, the blanks for the names of the four debaters, columns for rating points

NATIONAL CONFERENCE OF TAU KAPPA ALPHA

Judges Ballot for Speaking Events

Contestant	Topic	Rank	Rating

In the first column place the name of the contestant.

In the second column write the topic being discussed. (Omit if ballot is used for discussion.)

In the third column rank the participants in order of excellence: 1, 2, 3, 4, & 5. The four best should receive the first four ranks, while all the rest should receive the rank of "5."

In the fourth column assign rating points to each speaker on the basis of the following scale:

90 and above = Superior
85–89 = Excellent
80–84 = Good
75–79 = Fair

Name of Judge: _____

School of Judge: _____

Reprinted by permission.

or ranking points or both. At the bottom a place should be provided for the name of the school winning the debate, the name of the judge and the school from which he comes. It is wise to have the ballot printed in such a manner that one portion of it can be given to the affirmative team and the other portion to the negative when the tournament is over. Examine the sample debate ballots in Chapter 17.

Ballots for other events will have to be printed by the tournament manager. The simple ballot reproduced here is one utilized in the 1962 Tau Kappa Alpha National Conference. It can be used for oratory, persuasive speaking, after-dinner speaking, extempore speaking, discussion, oral reading, or similar events.

It is wise to have an instruction sheet for judges so that they may know what is expected of them for the tournament. It should indicate whether or not oral critiques are desired for the debates or individual events, and if the decision is to be announced. It should also contain instructions about the ballot and how to fill it out. Some tournament managers give general instructions on how to judge debates if there is a likelihood that the judges need such help.

There will always be the grave problem of getting competent judges at tournaments. There is no way to assure high quality, but there are some things that can be done: try to get members of the speech faculty, present or past directors of debate, or former college debaters. Many tournament directors make the mistake of offering to procure judges. However, by the time the number of judges necessary to cover the tournament director's teams and all those who want to be hired are utilized, the quality becomes rather poor. Insist that the visiting teams be accompanied by their coaches. Many directors of novice tournaments make use of debaters who are in their third or fourth year of college debating.

PREPARING FOR THE WORST TO HAPPEN

Do not be prepared for the best to happen—be prepared for the worst. Participants on their way to tournaments may have accidents; deaths occur in families; debaters quite frequently get sick. In every tournament someone is late in arriving, there are judges that don't show up, there are chairmen-timekeepers who fail to appear. Likewise, somebody is always getting lost; wrong teams get together to debate; because some teams are late a self-appointed assistant director of the tournament will put two teams together that are to meet later on in the tournament. Of primary importance in handling emergencies is a good system of communication. If the tournament is small and all events are held in one building the problems will be greatly decreased. If it is large, the following suggestions will help solve the "worst" when it happens.

First, in the system of communications, be sure a phone is available at tournament headquarters; second, that phones are available in the various buildings throughout the campus where the events are held so that problems can be reported quickly to headquarters. Another aid in communication is to have the transportation system equipped with walkie-talkies.

Be ready to solve quickly the problem of scheduling should you have last-minute drop-outs. Many tournament directors print up as many as three or four first-round schedules for just such an emergency. This can be done easily in those cases where you permit only one unit entries. Once a tournament is under way then the schedules for rounds two, three, four and so on can be printed. Should yours be that type of tournament requiring a printed schedule with the names of the schools present, you should develop a simple plan for quick rescheduling.

Be ready to prevent the long delays caused by latecomers or teams which fail to arrive. Request all schools entering the tournament to call long distance, reversing the charges, in case they are going to have to drop out or be late for the first round. In this way the second round of the tournament can begin on time. Should you delay starting one debate too long in the first round, four debates will be late in the second round.

Another problem is the failure of chairmen-timekeepers to show up. If your tournament is a large one and you are using the general student body, you can expect about 10 percent to fail you. The solution is to get 10 percent more chairmen-timekeepers for each round than you will theoretically need. Often it is wise to have members of your own debate squad serve as these reserve timekeepers. Another solution is to have a source you can tap, such as a fraternity, sorority, or club that will furnish them at a moment's notice.

Another problem is judges failing to show. Depending on the size of the tournament it is wise to have one, two, or three judges who will be available for such an emergency. Rather than to have them come to the tournament headquarters and wait, they can be requested to remain in their offices on campus, should they be college professors, or in their nearby homes. Thus, you can call them and have one of the cars transport them quickly to the debate.

Finally, problems arise when debaters become ill. Since schools pay a lot of money to travel great distances it is unwise to cancel debates. One way to solve this problem is to have a member or members of your own squad take the place of sick debaters. If such a thing is not possible, you have left the alternative of having the remaining member of the team afflicted debate both spots. Ordinarily you would count it a loss against the afflicted team. However, the three debaters would get much needed experience which should be the basic aim of most debate tournaments.

SUMMARY

For a successful tournament: make sure that the tournament is needed; make a detailed blueprint of everything that should occur during the tournament; have a good student administrative staff with the chains of command very clear in the minds of everyone; have a complete check list along with deadlines for the accomplishment of every task for each of your student lieutenants; have a detailed check list for each individual who has a particular task in the tournament; draw up the debate schedule yourself so that you can solve any last-minute problems that may arise; and have special methods by which you can do all tasks more expediently. From year to year as you run a tournament improve on these. Always operate expecting the worst to happen. If you plan for it, you will have a solution readily available.

EXERCISES

1. Explain:
   a. The values of tournament debating for the debater.
   b. What tournament debating will not do for the debater.
   c. The benefits of operating a tournament.
2. Make out the following debate tournament schematics:
   a. Five schools participating in two rounds of four-man debating.
   b. Twelve schools participating in five rounds of four-man debating.
   c. Sixteen schools participating in six rounds of two-man debating, alternating sides debating.
3. Make a practice run-through of a 20-team, power-matched, two-man, alternating sides, two-judge tournament similar to the one in the text.
   a. Draw all needed charts except rating and ranking points.
   b. Schedule the debates by power matching each round for eight rounds.
   c. For each round utilize two judges.
   d. Determine winners of each debate by drawing or flipping a coin.
   e. When finished rank the teams in order of excellence except for ties.
4. What principles should you observe in choosing and directing the administrative staff of a tournament?
5. How can you make registration simple and rapid?
6. Specifically, how would you procure fifty chairmen-timekeepers per round for a five-round tournament at the school where you are now located?
7. Draw up a set of rules for the following forensic events:
   a. Extempore speaking

b. Oratory
c. Discussion (six rounds)
d. A student congress
e. Poetry reading
f. After-dinner speaking
g. Radio announcing

8. List the factors to be observed in order to solve the "worst" which may happen in tournaments.

SUGGESTED READINGS

CONSTANS, H. P. "The Role of Intercollegiate Debate Tournaments in the Post War Period," *Southern Speech Journal,* 15 (September 1949), 38–44.

CROCKER, LIONEL. "The Values of Tournament Debating," *Southern Speech Bulletin,* 3 (March 1938), 5–7.

EUBANK, WAYNE C. "A View of the Forensic Situation," *Southern Speech Journal,* 14 (November 1948), 108–114.

EWBANK, HENRY L. "Speech Contests as Educational Techniques," *Quarterly Journal of Speech,* 22 (April 1936), 187–196.

FREELEY, AUSTIN J. *Argumentation and Debate.* Belmont, Calif.: Wadsworth Publishing Co., Inc., 1961. Chap. 24.

LAHMAN, CARROLL P. *Debate Coaching.* 2nd ed., New York: The H. W. Wilson Company, 1936. Chaps. 7, 9.

MILLS, GLEN E. "Audiences and Tournaments: Two Forms of Over-emphasis," *The Speech Teacher,* 9 (March 1960), 95–98.

ROBINSON, ZON. "What Happens to Speech Values in Tournament Debating," *Southern Speech Bulletin,* 7 (March 1942), 122–125.

WALSH, GRACE. "Tournaments: For Better or Worse?" *The Speech Teacher,* 6 (January 1957), 65–67.

chapter 17

∿∿∿∿∿∿∿∿∿∿∿∿∿∿∿∿∿∿∿∿∿∿∿∿∿∿∿∿∿∿∿∿∿

EVALUATING
THE DEBATE

by Nicholas M. Cripe

SECURING COMPETENT JUDGES

The problem of securing competent judges of debate is not a new situation created by the continued and growing interest in extracurricular debate and the subsequent increase in the number of debates and participants in the activity. Rather, it has been a recurrent problem ever since the inception of intercollegiate debating in the latter part of the nineteenth century. Prior to that time, when a decision was rendered, it usually was by the audience, which voted on the merits of the question rather than on the quality of the debating.

This system obviously did not lend itself to fair verdicts, especially if the debate were before a biased audience. Consequently, in the early contest debates, the decisions were rendered by a board of judges usually composed of three to five distinguished men who were requested to base their judgment solely on the merits of debating. Governors, senators, jurists, clergymen, and college presidents were in great demand as judges for these debates. That these eminent men were not always competent, at least in the minds of the losing school, is only too evident from comments in various college newspapers of this period. And as the popularity of interschool debating spread, it became increasingly difficult to secure a panel of even three eminent, unbiased, and competent judges. (The care given to the selection of the panel of judges by the two competing schools would compare favorably with that given by opposing attorneys in selecting a jury for an important trial.) This process in the opinion of many educators was too expensive (the three or more judges usually were paid a fee plus expenses) and placed entirely too much emphasis on winning.

So, in the early nineteen-hundreds the competing schools began using a single expert or critic judge. This change in selection of judges from a board comprised of eminent citizens to a single professional debate judge was deplored by those who feared it would destroy the "real-life" aspects of contest debating and make it simply an academic exercise. One outspoken critic of the new order argued that the "one feature of debating which is indispensable to its success as a *device for securing training in public speaking* is the retention of able nondebaters as judges. Judged by them, debating will remain where it belongs—very close to actual life." [1]

Today the emphasis is on the single expert judge who may or may not be required to give a critique of the debate and the individual debaters. However, in many major tournaments, while a single judge may still be used in the qualifying rounds, three or more expert judges are frequently used in the final elimination rounds to determine the tournament winner. And while the judges in any of the rounds seldom are required to give an oral critique, they frequently are expected to prepare written comments on the individual speakers and the debate as a whole.

That the present system of judging is not without fault is a fact learned early in the career of every debate director. The causes are many. One is that giving the title of *coach* to an individual does not by necessity mean that he becomes an expert in debate. Still another is the conviction on the part of many judges that contest debates and real-life debates do not differ in the manner in which they are to be evaluated.

Perhaps at this point we should establish the relationship between real-life debating and contest debating. They have much in common. Both types of debate consist of actual discussion of real-life problems. Frequently, at the same time that legislators in their assembly, clergymen in their pulpits, and businessmen over their luncheon tables are debating such problems as extending diplomatic recognition to a foreign power or the merits and demerits of nationalized medicine, interscholastic debaters in contests throughout the United States are debating the same problems. And this is as it should be, for after all, the ultimate purpose of contest debating should be the training of the participants to better take part in

[1] William H. Davis, "Debating as Related to Non-Academic Life," *Quarterly Journal of Public Speaking*, 1 (July 1915), 112. For a more detailed discussion of the arguments of "contest" debates vs. "real-life" debates sees as follows in the *Quarterly Journal of Public Speaking*: Editorial—"A Disconcerted Editor and Others," by James Milton O'Neill, vol. I, p. 79; Editorial by O'Neill, "Able Non-Debaters," vol. I, p. 201; Editorial by O'Neill, "Judges Again," vol. I, p. 305; W. H. Davis, "Is Debating Primarily a Game?" vol. II, p. 171; Editorial by O'Neill, "Game or Counterfeit Presentment," vol. III, p. 135; Hugh Neal Wells, "Judging Debates," vol. III, p. 336.

real-life debates. But because the specific goal of contest debating is to train debaters we find an educational reason for distinguishing between the evaluation of real-life and contest debating.

DIFFERENT FORMS OF JUDGMENT

In the real-life situation a citizen may not only listen to but may also participate in the debate for which he may be called upon to render a decision. First, and probably the most frequent decision he is expected to give is called the "layman's" vote. As a member of his church, he votes whether or not to build a new church building; as a member of a union, he is asked to vote for a strike or agree to a new contract; as a member of the board of directors of a business, he decides whether or not to vote for a stock dividend; as a citizen he is called upon to vote for candidates for public office or for a new bond issue. In all these instances he listens to the arguments, perhaps even offers a few of his own, and then votes his decision on merits of the question. And the odds are fairly high that he decides the merits of the question by simply answering one question— "Which side is the best for my interests?"

The other type of vote he may be asked to cast is the "juryman's" decision. As a member of the jury, he is supposed to exclude from his consideration of the decision all except the evidence admitted in the trial. Genuine feeling as to right or wrong, prejudices, any honest conviction he may have, and knowledge he may possess from another source other than the trial itself are to be suppressed. Thus, to the best of his ability, he attempts to answer the question, "Is this defendant guilty according to the law and the evidence presented here?" and votes accordingly.

This is the decision-making for real-life debates. But are these verdicts desirable for interscholastic contest debates? In other words, should decisions be rendered solely upon the evidence submitted, or to the side with which the judge agrees? To win the decision, should the contest debater have to convince the judge that either the affirmative or the negative is the correct side? Granted, that if the sole aim of school debate is to reproduce as nearly as possible the real-life situation where the speaker presents his arguments in a conference, or to a court, or to the voting public, then the decision should be some form of audience decision. These types of debate decision are used in law schools where moot court trials are held before actual court judges, and in audience situations where a "shift-of-opinion" ballot may be used to measure the debaters' ability to change opinions.[2]

[2] Howard S. Woodward, "Measurement and Analysis of Audience Opinion," *Quarterly Journal of Speech*, 14 (February 1928), 94–111.

If, however, the aim of the debate contest is to effectively train participants in the methods of oral argument, then the judging should be by a critic capable of offering expert opinion on the comparative excellence of the debating. The judge should vote as a critic. It is his job to decide which of the teams in his opinion did the better debating. He does not vote as a layman according to his best interests; he does not vote as a juryman only on the evidence presented; he does not vote on the basis of everything he knows about the question and of his own views as to the correct course of action. Instead, he lays aside his personal views and renders his decision solely on what the teams say and how they say it in a particular debate. Religious creeds, political beliefs, and social philosophies should have nothing to do with the decision if the judge is a true critic. The team doing the better debating, not the team fortunately assigned the side in which the judge believes, earns the decision. Granted, there is always a tendency to overrate the speaking abilities of those with whom we agree and to be more critical of those with whom we disagree, but the good critic-judge recognizes this tendency and guards against his personal beliefs coloring his reactions.

The ideal critic-judge of debate is an impartial individual who has a thorough knowledge of debate theory and debate practice, who possesses analytical ability, has had considerable experience both as debater and debate judge, and is capable and willing to give an effective oral critique of the debate. Finding these attributes in practicing debate judges is not especially difficult. A much greater problem is the lack of a uniform philosophy of judgment among these judges.

FINDING A UNIFORM
PHILOSOPHY OF JUDGMENT

There are numerous schools of thought regarding the grounds for a debate decision. One minority group might be labeled "the correct grammar" school. These judges have one criterion: correct grammar. Split an infinitive, dangle a participle, mispronounce a word, and the team loses the decision. Granting the true value of correctly spoken English and that one of the duties of a critic judge should be the pointing out of any mishandling of the language, most expert judges feel there are more important criteria for judgment.

Another school of thought is that of the proponents of "good delivery." These judges regard debating primarily as an exercise in public speaking. Their chief concern seems not to be with *what* is said, but with *how* it is said. With these judges an Abraham Lincoln would never win a decision from a Patrick Henry.

The third group of judges, and probably a much larger school than either of the first two, is the "real-life" or "convince me" school. These are the judges who seem to forget the hours and even years that they have spent building their own beliefs about a topic, and so they say in effect to the students, "All right, you have thirty minutes. Convince me." These are the judges who forget that they are judging a contest debate; that no matter what they think, there are two sides to the proposition; that they are supposed to be determining which team is doing the better debating; that they are critic-judges and not members of a policy-making group. These judges forget the purpose of their role and the purpose of the debate. The debate is held not to settle a question of policy but simply to reveal which of the two teams has shown the greater skill in debate.

While some debate judges encountered today belong to one of the above three schools, they are not expert critics. Obviously they are not well versed in debate principles and patently lack an understanding of the educational purpose of contest debating. There are, however, two divergent philosophies among acknowledged expert judges that point up the lack of a uniform yardstick for judgment. These can be classified as the "issues" school and the "skills" school.

Both views will admit that in judging a debate, like judging anything else—a beauty contest, a work of art, or the comparative merits of two automobiles—certain criteria must be accepted and applied. Both schools agree that unless definite standards of measurement are used, a meaningful decision is impossible. Most expert judges agree that debate, for all its contest aspects, is more than a mere game and that it is important that sound principles guide the rendering of the decisions. The disagreement arises regarding what these sound principles should be.

Many judges contend that the debate decision should be rendered primarily on the basis of issues. They argue that it is the job of the affirmative team to prove the proposition to be probably true, and that the negative team must either disprove the proposition as being true or establish to the satisfaction of the judge that the affirmative has failed to prove its case. Since issues, they argue, are "those inherently vital points affirmed by the affirmative and denied by the negative, upon the establishment of which depends the establishment of the proposition," issues should be the ultimate criteria used in formulating a debate decision. If the affirmative wins all the issues contended in a particular debate, they win that debate; if the negative wins one of the key issues or creates sufficient doubt that the affirmative has won the issues, then the negative wins the debate. In other words, to prove a proposition probably true the affirmative must win all the key issues; if they fail to do so, they lose the decision. Members of this school are many and strong in the defense of their philosophy.

The members of the *skills* school take a slightly different stand than do their colleagues in the *issues* school when selecting the criteria for rendering a debate decision. These judges contend that the immediate goal of a team is the demonstration of its superior debating ability. According to this philosophy, a team might lose an issue or two but still win the decision because they did the better debating; that is, they showed greater skill in using the techniques of debate. Proponents of this view contend that the purpose of school debate is the training of its participants in the methods of sound debating, that becoming proficient in such aspects of debate as analysis, reasoning, the use of evidence, organization, refutation, and delivery is the ultimate goal of this activity.[3] Therefore, the final decision should not rest upon who won the issues in the debate, but rather on how proficient were the teams in the various techniques demanded from the skillful debater. The members of the skills school freely admit that we do not keep a running score on the minister's Sunday sermon or the politician's speech, awarding him five points for delivery and four points for organization and so on. Rather, they grant whether or not he has successfully established his issues and accept or reject his point of view accordingly. But, they contend, the contest debate is a different situation; the purpose is not convincing a judge, but training debaters in perfecting certain skills so that in real-life situations the blending of these skills may achieve conviction. The ultimate test should not be whether the debaters have changed any minds, but rather the amount of skill shown in the use of the processes by which minds are changed.

Proponents of the skills point of view maintain that in their analytical approach to a debate, the judge is less inclined to let his personal beliefs color his judgment. Also, judging the debate on skills rather than just issues, they contend, is fairer because of time restrictions imposed upon the debaters. Frequently the debate proposition is such that some issues either cannot be developed or destroyed simply because there is not sufficient time to do so. Under these circumstances, to render a decision strictly on who won the issues probably places an unfair burden, either of proof or rebuttal, on one of the teams. For instance, many judges felt the proposition debated in college circles a few years ago, "That Congress should have the power to reverse decisions of the Supreme Court," placed an undue burden on the affirmative to show a pressing need for changing a century and a half of American tradition in ten minutes. There was not sufficient time to discuss adequately the complex legal cases involved. The skills school contends that it is conceivable that a team could thus have lost the need issue and still have done the better debating. Their delivery,

---

[3] Kim Giffin, A Study of the Criteria Employed by Tournament Debate Judges," *Speech Monographs*, 26 (March 1959), 69–71.

their organization of arguments, their use of evidence and reasoning, their defense of their case as a whole might well have been better than that of the negative team. But they lost the need issue. Should they lose the decision? Did the negative team do a better job of debating? A skills school judge would say "no" and vote for the affirmative. An issues judge would say "yes" and vote negative. Conceivably, a team could win two of three main issues overwhelmingly, but lose one issue by a narrow margin, and thus lose the debate. On the other hand, a judge from the skills school would probably give the decision to the team losing the one issue because it demonstrated better use of analysis, delivery, evidence, and the other criteria.

Whatever their disagreement regarding the final criteria to use, both the issues and the skills schools of judging agree that deciding which team did the better debating demands more of a judge than determining the correct use of grammar, good delivery, or the ability to strengthen beliefs already held by a judge.

ATTRIBUTES OF THE EXPERT DEBATE CRITIC

BE A GOOD LISTENER

One of the first requirements of the judge evaluating a debate is that he be a good listener. To be an effective listener demands more of the judge than merely being within earshot of the debaters. Good listening is an active process which requires that the judge must see and understand the various ideas presented in the debate in their proper relationship to each other. Such a listening process demands critical thinking on the part of the judge; it allows no room for daydreaming; it demands of the judge a disciplined control of his own thinking. To put it bluntly, the ability to listen critically, to be a good listener, is one of the first talents a debate judge should acquire if he desires to do an effective job of evaluating the debate.

This being the case, some practical suggestions for being a critical listener should be considered. He should:

1. BE PREPARED TO LISTEN. The judge should select a place to sit where he can see and hear the speakers without conscious effort on his part. He should pick a location as free as possible from distractions—such as people passing an open door or chatting in the hall, the pounding of a radiator, a draft on his back, moving objects outside a nearby window. Probably he will want to take notes, so he should arrange a convenient

place to do his writing. In other words, before the debate starts, he should eliminate as many outside distractions as possible. He should be prepared to listen.

2. PLAN HIS LISTENING. The judge should not just listen; he should listen with a purpose. In a debate he might want to listen for:

a. Each side's interpretation of the proposition. Was it a fair one? How were the terms defined? (A practical suggestion: write them down as a check in case later in the debate either side should attempt to shift position.)

b. The over-all patterns of the cases to be presented. A good debater probably will mention his intentions early in his speech. If he does, this serves as an excellent guide for listening. If he does not, this should alert the judge to listen even more carefully because the lack may be due to poor analysis or hazy thinking on the proposition, or it may be part of the strategy of the team as it attempts to occupy certain positions undetected by the opposition. Whatever the reason, it is a signal to listen carefully to discover the pattern of the case.

c. The main points of the speech. Usually the good debate speech is built around two or three main points. What are they? How are they related?

d. The way each speaker and each team meets the arguments of the opposition. Are the arguments met head-on or are they evaded? Is the speaker meeting the main points or isolated points? Is the refutation of points presented in an easy-to-follow manner? Does the speaker make clear why a point is being refuted?

e. The use of language. Is the vocabulary adequate? Are words being used correctly?

f. The delivery of the speeches. Is the speech easily heard? Is it easily understood? Is the bodily action adapted to the verbal action? Are both adapted to the audience and the room?

3. LISTEN WITH AN OPEN MIND. The critic judge is asked to cast his vote for the team doing the better debating, not for the team endorsing his personal point of view. His responsibility is to give his decision on the basis of what he saw and heard in the debate.

HAVE A SET OF CRITERIA FOR EVALUATING THE DEBATE

The judge not only must be a critical listener, but he must also have a set of criteria to use in measuring the abilities of the two teams. Frequently, the debate ballot provides this standard of measurement for the judge. While the number and terminology of the criteria may vary, the following elements are most frequently included.

1. ANALYSIS OF THE PROPOSITION. This consists of defining terms in a satisfactory manner and selecting and developing the main issues in the debate proposition. The judge should note any attempt at very narrow or tricky definition of terms. He should be aware of any attempt to define a term one way and debate it another. The judge also should remember that school contest debates are necessarily restricted by time limits; therefore, a team must select those lines of argument which their analysis shows to be fundamental. However, in his critique, the judge may suggest an alternative analysis should he deem it necessary.

2. USE OF EVIDENCE. Facts and opinions are used to generate proof. There is no substitute for knowledge of the proposition, and it is through the use of evidence that a team displays this knowledge. The judge must decide to what extent and how well evidence was used by the two teams. Again, in his critique, it is the duty of the judge to point out good and bad use of evidence or, if appropriate, lack of evidence.

3. SOUNDNESS OF ARGUMENT. In this instance the judge is concerned with the reasoning being used. Does it meet the tests of sound logical reasoning? If a debater draws illogical conclusions or in other ways uses faulty reasoning and it is not detected and attacked by the opposition, one side is as guilty as the other of poor argument and both should be penalized. The judge should point out the errors and make corrections in his critique.

4. ORGANIZATION OF MATERIAL. Good organization is simple, clear, and easy to follow. This criterion should apply to rebuttal as well as to constructive speeches and to the negative as well as to the affirmative efforts. While the negative in most cases should not be expected to have the tight organization that can be required of the affirmative, especially in the first affirmative speech; nevertheless, it should show good general organization, and individual points should be clearly organized. There is no excuse for the negative case being a disconnected, haphazard attack on the affirmative.

5. REFUTATION AND REBUTTAL. This particular criterion is concerned with the ability of the debaters to adapt their case to that of their opponents. The judge will want to pay particular attention to the arguments selected to attack or defend. Are they the important points or are they minor points? Are the debaters trying to attack every point made without any attempts at selectivity?

6. EFFECTIVENESS IN DELIVERY. Too frequently in contest debates the speakers, in their effort to get everything said, seemingly forget that they are participating in a public speaking exercise. They forget that bodily action, facial expression, vocal quality, personal appearance, and correct

pronunciation are all items that the critic should consider under the heading of effective delivery. There is need for coherence, emphasis, and variety in the delivery of the debate speech. The critic judge should commend good delivery and deplore its absence.

The extent to which criteria are used largely distinguishes the philosophy of the "skills" school of judging from the "issues" school. To the issues judge the above criteria or similar ones merely serve as a convenient means of measuring how the issues were won. The skills school, on the other hand, considers issues important and integral parts of the analysis criterion, but not all-important. How well the criteria are satisfied is the determining factor in the decision. If the affirmative failed to establish a prima facie case and the negative failed to recognize the fact, to the skills judge both would be guilty of poor debating but the negative would not get an automatic win as they probably would with an issues judge. Actually, however, judges embracing the two philosophies frequently give their decisions to the same team. This happens when the team showing the greater skill has also in the opinion of the issues judge won all the issues.

Having explored the judge's role, the lack of a uniform philosophy of judgment and the demands placed upon the judge from a philosophical point of view, let us examine some practical suggestions for evaluating and criticizing a school debate contest.

PRACTICAL SUGGESTIONS FOR EVALUATING DEBATES

GENERAL SUGGESTIONS

1. A DEBATE SHOULD BE JUDGED AS IT PROGRESSES. At any given time in the debate the judge should be able to give the decision to one team or the other if asked to do so. This is not to suggest that the judge should arrive at certain conclusions early in the debate and then refuse to change or revise them regardless of what transpires later in the event. Rather, it means that the judge constantly should be deciding which team is bettering or harming its position and why, and he should be doing this from the start to the finish of the debate, regardless of how many times it means revising his estimation of the teams.

2. THE JUDGE SHOULD RETAIN HIS OBJECTIVITY. He should not let his preconceived notions as to how a particular issue or point should be developed cause him to penalize a team for not developing it according

to his particular point of view. While the judge must have preconceived notions regarding the use of evidence and reasoning to establish proof, of the obligations of the affirmative and the negative, of the burden of proof and the burden of rebuttal, of the criteria he will use as standard of judgment in evaluating the teams, he should not allow his conception of the issues, the main points, and subpoints to so dominate his judgment as to demand only these issues and points from the teams he judges.

3. THE JUDGE SHOULD BE WILLING TO OFFER AN ORAL CRITIQUE. School debate is primarily a learning activity. The judge should be willing to discuss the comparative merits of the two teams and the individual debaters. He should be willing to explain the reasons for his vote and to offer suggestions for improvement. However, this should not be the time for another debate nor should the judge submit himself to the vituperative comments of an irate loser. In a school debate the critic judge is not a baseball umpire and he is not paid to be one.

4. THE EXPERT JUDGE FREQUENTLY RE-EVALUATES HIS JUDGING. He compares how he arrives at decisions with other judges whom he respects as competent debate critics. He looks for weak spots in his judging where he may be overly critical or perhaps not critical enough. He strives to remain objective and to do the most competent job of judging of which he is capable.

SPECIFIC SUGGESTIONS

Almost a half century ago, Lew Sarett, one of the great teachers in the field of speech, suggested a plan for debate judges to follow in analyzing a debate and arriving at a decision. During the debate, the judge would have before him a set of questions for which he would be seeking answers. This set of questions, or one similar to it, if used by all judges, would aid in promoting uniformity of philosophy among debate judges while assuring both teams in the debate that their efforts would be thoroughly and carefully analyzed. Professor Sarett suggested that the expert judge should seek answers to eleven questions in the debate.[4]

1. Which team was superior in the clear, coherent, and effective organization of its material?
2. Which team better supported its contentions with sound proof?

[4] Lew R. Sarett, "The Expert Judge of Debate," *The Quarterly Journal of Public Speaking*, 3 (April 1917), 137–138.

3. Which team established and maintained the most crucial issues?
4. Which team was superior in destroying its opponent's crucial issues?
5. Which team, through greater freedom in departing from prepared speeches, and through superior extempore speaking and resourcefulness, more readily adapted its arguments to the arguments actually made by its opponents upon the platform?
6. Which team in its constructive argument manifested a superior analysis of the questions?
7. Which team manifested a superior analysis of the debate as it actually progressed on the platform, that is, which team was superior in discovering and following the strategic issues rather than the minor or irrelevant points?
8. Which team was superior in team work?
9. Which team was superior in delivery, aside from the effective delivery presumed in other questions?
10. Which team in general—aside from the rebuttal work presumed in other questions—was superior in rebuttal?
11. Which team was superior in debate strategy?

While it is obvious that these questions are not mutually exclusive, it seems that this or a similar set of questions could bring to the judging of school debating a clarity, a thoroughness of analysis, and a unity of criteria that was lacking when Professor Sarett first offered them and that frequently is lacking today.

SUMMARY

Competent judging of academic debate is neither a simple task nor an easy one. It is a task requiring special abilities. Because of the contest aspect of the debate, there is a tendency to place considerable emphasis on the decision. Actually who won should be of but momentary importance to the teams and of even less importance to the judge. The truly important point is *why* did one side win. The competent judge should clearly understand the reasons for his decision, and should be able to explain them with equal clarity. In other words, he should realize that the role of the judge differs as the type of debate to be evaluated differs—that real-life debates demand different forms of judgment than do contest debates. He should know whether he subscribes to the "skills" school of judging or to the "issues" school, and why he belongs to one or the other. He should be a good listener with consistent criteria for evaluating the debate. He should be constantly striving to make himself a better critic-judge.

American Forensic Association Debate Ballot

FORM C

Division_____ Round_____ Room_____ Date_____ Judge_____

Affirmative_____ Negative_____

Check the column on each item which, according to the following scale, best describes your evaluation of the speaker's effectiveness, and indicate the RANK for each speaker in the space following his name.

1—poor   2—fair   3—adequate   4—good   5—superior

	1st Affirmative					2nd Affirmative					1st Negative					2nd Negative				
	1	2	3	4	5	1	2	3	4	5	1	2	3	4	5	1	2	3	4	5
Analysis																				
Reasoning & Evidence																				
Organization																				
Refutation																				
Delivery																				

Total_____   Total_____   Total_____   Total_____

Team Ratings: AFFIRMATIVE: poor   fair   adequate   good   superior

NEGATIVE: poor   fair   adequate   good   superior

COMMENTS: COMMENTS:
1st Aff. (name)_____RANK ( )   1st Neg. (name)_____RANK ( )

2nd Aff. (name)_____RANK ( )   2nd Neg. (name)_____RANK ( )

In my opinion, the better debating was done by the _____
                                        (AFFIRMATIVE OR NEGATIVE)

_____
(JUDGE'S SIGNATURE AND SCHOOL)

DEBATE BALLOT

(Bear down—you are making three copies)

Division_____Round_____Room_____Date_____Judge_____

Affirmative _____ Negative _____

Rank the debaters in their order of excellence in this debate: 1 for best,
2 for second best, 3 for third best, and 4 for least best.

Rate the effectiveness of each debater in a manner similar to the way you
grade in school, i.e., A,B,C, etc. However, on the ballot use rating points
as indicated by the following table:

A+ — 15	B+ — 12	C+ — 9	D+ — 6	E+ — 3
A — 14	B — 11	C — 8	D — 5	E — 2
A— — 13	B— — 10	C— — 7	D— — 4	E— — 1

	Name	Rank	Rating points
1st Affirmative	_____	_____	_____
2nd Affirmative	_____	_____	_____
1st Negative	_____	_____	_____
2nd Negative	_____	_____	_____

(NOTE: Rank and Rating points should correlate with the decision; i.e.,
the winning team should receive the higher total in rating points and get
the lower total in ranking. In close debates the rank might be tied but
the rating points should favor the winning team.)

COMMENTS: COMMENTS:

1st Aff.   1st Neg.

2nd Aff.   2nd Neg.

In my opinion, the better debating was done by the _____
                                        (Affirmative or Negative)

_____
(Judge's Signature and School)

TO THE AUDIENCE

The debaters will appreciate your interest and help if you will, both before and after the debate, indicate on this sheet your PERSONAL OPINION on the IDEA PROPOSED FOR DEBATE.

As soon as the debate is finished, opportunity will be given you to question the debaters on any matter that pertains to the question.

BEFORE THE DEBATE

☐ I believe in the affirmative of the resolution to be debated.
☐ I am undecided.
☐ I believe in the negative of the resolution to be debated.

THE REASONS FOR MY OPINION ARE:

Date _____
Place _____

This blank is filled by a

☐ man   ☐ woman, whose age is

_____

AFTER THE DEBATE

I have heard the entire discussion, and now

☐ I believe more strongly in the affirmative of the resolution than I did.
☐ I believe in the negative of the the resolution.
☐ I am undecided.
☐ I believe in the affirmative of resolution.
☐ I believe more strongly in the negative of the resolution than I did.

THE REASONS FOR MY OPINION ARE:

Howard S. Woodward, "Measurement and Analysis of Audience Opinion, *Quarterly Journal of Speech*, vol. 14 (February 1928), 109. Reprinted by permission of the Speech Association of America.

EXERCISES

1. Write an essay of 300 words or less as to whether or not, in your opinion, real-life debates demand different forms of judgment than do contest debates.
2. How would you describe the ideal critic-judge of debate?
3. Write an essay in which you develop a philosophy of judgment to guide you in judging contest debates.
4. Prepare a five-minute speech to convince advocating either the "issues" philosophy or the "skills" philosophy of judging debates.

5. Write an essay on critical listening as applied to the judge of debate.
6. What criteria should a judge use in evaluating a contest debate? Write an essay setting forth and defending the criteria you would use to judge a contest debate.
7. Write a critical essay comparing and evaluating this chapter on "Evaluating the Debate" with similar chapters in three other textbooks of your own choosing.
8. Write a critique of the debate contained in the Appendix of this book. To which team would you award the decision? Why?

SUGGESTED READINGS

BROCKRIEDE, WAYNE E. "A Standard for Judging Applied Logic in Debate," *The AFA Register*, 10 (Spring 1962), 10–24.

CLEVENGER, THEODORE. "Toward a Point of View for Contest Debate," *Central States Speech Journal*, 12 (Autumn 1960), 21–26.

DRUM, DALE D. "The Debate Judge as a Machine," *Today's Speech*, 4 April 1956), 28–31.

GIFFIN, KIM. "A Study of the Criteria Employed by Tournament Debate Judges," *Speech Monographs*, 26 (March 1959), 69–71.

GIFFIN, KIM, and PAUL R. MCKEE. "An Analysis of Evidence in Debates," *The AFA Register*, 10 (Winter 1962), 1–5.

HALSTEAD, WILLIAM P. "Who Wins Debates, a Statistical Study of 1320 Debates," *Quarterly Journal of Speech*, 26 (April 1940), 213–220.

ROBINSON, JAMES L. "Are We 'Overlegalizing' School Debate?" *The Speech Teacher*, 9 (March 1960), 109–115.

ROEVER, JAMES, and KIM GIFFIN. "A Study of the Use of Judging Criteria in Tournament Debate," *The AFA Register*, 8 (Winter 1960), 12–14.

SCOTT, ROBERT L. "On the Meaning of the Term *Prima-Facie* in Argumentation," *Central States Speech Journal*, 12 (Autumn 1960), 33–37.

SHEPARD, DAVID W. "Logical Propositions and Debate Resolutions," *Central States Speech Journal*, 11 (Spring 1960), 186–190.

WOOD, KENNETH SCOTT. "Is the Decision Element a Detriment to High School Debating Objectives?" *Quarterly Journal of Speech*, 25 (April 1939), 254–261.

APPENDIX:
SAMPLE DEBATE

John T. Austin, University of Akron
Albert C. Hingston, Pacific University

The unabridged debate offered here as an example for study and class discussion should prove useful in demonstrating the importance of (1) organization of the debate speech, (2) composition of argument, (3) arrangement of evidence and refutation, and (4) team strategy. The debate will be more meaningful if the reader bears in mind that these were the arguments and speeches employed in an actual tournament situation. The editor and contributors to this volume felt that a note on the setting for this debate would prove interesting and enhance appreciation for the performance of these two teams.

Out of the distinguished history of dialectic at the United States Military Academy there evolved at the close of World War II an interest in sponsoring a national debate tournament. As a result of a nationwide poll of 1,000 colleges and universities, the West Point Debating Society, in April 1947, formulated its first National Debate Tournament.

Since that first tournament, the "NDT" structure has been modified to meet requirements brought on by increasing national interest in debate. Today eight self-governing districts representing fifty states are responsible for selecting between 30 and 40 teams who debate eight seeding rounds of "strength versus strength pairings" to determine the sixteen finalists who move through four elimination rounds on the third and final day of the tournament.

The debate reported here, with only minor editing, was the final round of the 1961 National Debate Tournament and was judged by the following panel of experts who voted 4–3 in favor of Harvard University: Glenn Capp, Baylor University; Thomas Dolan, Fordham University; George Henigan, George Washington University; James H. McBath, University of Southern California; Frank Nelson, Northwestern University; Holt Spicer, Southwest Missouri State College; Grace Walsh, Wisconsin State College, Eau Claire.

It was during this tournament that a 30-minute film-TV documentary of "NDT" was prepared.[1] At the sixteenth "NDT" in April, 1962, a Champions Plaque was dedicated as the first step toward establishing a "Hall of Fame for Debaters."

FIFTEENTH ANNUAL NATIONAL DEBATE TOURNAMENT

FINAL ROUND OF DEBATE
West Point, New York, April 29, 1961

Harvard University——Affirmative   Kings College——Negative
PROPOSITION——*Resolved: That the United States Should Adopt a Program of Compulsory Health Insurance for All Citizens*

FIRST AFFIRMATIVE CONSTRUCTIVE SPEECH: GENE CLEMENTS, HARVARD UNIVERSITY

Ladies and gentlemen, because Larry and I feel that the dollar sign has no place in medicine, we resolve: "That the United States Should Adopt a Program of Compulsory Health Insurance for All Citizens": a program of spreading the risk of medical expense throughout society, "compulsory" in the sense that it would be financed through federal taxes. Now in this first speech we would like to show you that there is a compelling need for a change, that a program of compulsory health insurance could meet that need and that such a program would be beneficial to the American people.

Turning first to the need for a change, Larry and I will present three contentions. Number one, the neglect of health today is causing needless death and suffering; number two, the primary reason for this neglect of health is that people are led to make medical decisions on economic grounds; number three, this problem is inherent in the present system.

First then, we contend that the neglect of health is today causing

---

[1] "The National Debate Tournament; West Point," (30-minute television-film program). *For Information write:* Donald Sandberg, National Educational Television and Radio Center, 2320 Washtenaw Avenue, Ann Arbor, Michigan.

needless death and suffering. The Conference on General Welfare reported in 1959, "Due to inadequate medical care, over a third of a million lives are needlessly lost each year." Frankly, Larry and I are appalled by this tragic waste of human life, but, of course, the problem extends far beyond those who die to the many more who suffer without the care they need. The U.S. Public Health Service reported last year that 49.9 percent of all acute disabling medical conditions received no medical attention whatsoever, and that this neglect endangers the health of everyone of us, when they said in *Public Health Reports* last February that 800,000 Americans with serious contagious diseases need medical supervision to protect the health of the general public. But, 400,000 of these—that's one-half—are receiving no medical supervision of any kind. The Conference on the General Welfare pretty well sums up the situation when they say that the health needs of the nation are grossly neglected.

The question, then, is why, and that's our second point. The primary reason for this neglect of health is that people are led to make medical decisions on economic grounds. In other words, in seeking medical care, all of us have to ask ourselves—how will the bill be paid? Our first point here is that many people just can't pay it. Professor A. F. Wessen of Washington University wrote last December, "Families are often forced to decide against seeking care that they desperately need because of the high cost of necessary medical services." Professor B. J. Stern of Columbia was a little bit more explicit when he wrote in *The Sociology of Medicine* in 1960, "For the vast majority of the people adequate medical care has grown increasingly beyond reach because of its cost." And Professor Strauss of Colombia wrote last July, "The result of such high cost is that many health needs are neglected."

Our second point is that for still more people, even if they can pay some medical bills, uncertainty as to what the ultimate cost will be leads them to postpone the care or to forego it entirely. This point is substantiated by Professor of Sociology E. L. Kuhs when he says, "The possible cost of treatment of more serious disease—if later discovered—must remain an unknown factor and this uncertainty often determines whether to seek care in the first place."

Our third point is that for all of us, even if we can pay all of the medical bills, the economic deterrent remains; because although we know that diagnosis and early treatment are necessary, we just may not feel sick; so we decide to economize by avoiding care. As Jerome Rothenberg said in the *American Economic Review*, "Consumers tend to economize by seeking medical attention only when they feel very ill, discouraging early diagnosis and treatment." In other words, because we must all make economic decisions in seeking medical care, we often postpone in the hope that our symptoms will just go away. Sometimes they don't.

We conclude then that the primary reason for the neglect of health is that people are led to make medical decisions on economic grounds. We must always ask—how will the bill be paid? No matter what mechanism of the present system we try to rely on, this question still remains, and that is our third point. This problem is inherent in the present system because, as Professor of Economics B. A. Weisbrod pointed out last June, "No voluntary system can remove the need to make economic decisions in seeking medical care. In self-financing where the cost of care is directly a factor, of course, this defect is obvious. But even voluntary insurance suffers from the same inherent problem."

First, as Professor Haverman wrote last month, "Nobody can afford all the insurance he needs, and in deciding which of life's risks to brave, most individuals decide to take a chance on the family's health." And that's not too difficult to understand when you realize, as did Professor Stern of Columbia, that even the better voluntary prepayment plans offer too little and cost too much to be included in the budgets of the majority of the population. In short, you have still to ask—how will the bill be paid?

Second, as *Public Health Reports* observed in June of 1959, even when people decide to pay the premiums for some kind of insurance policy, the economic factor remains because the amount of coverage they can buy depends, of course, on how much money they have. That's why we say that the problem is inherent in any voluntary system of medical financing. There is thus a compelling need to combat the unnecessary death and suffering in the United States. The program we adopt must be universal since everyone is faced by economic decisions in seeking medical care. And it must be compulsory because no voluntary method of financing removes the need to make those economic decisions.

The plan we advocate is pretty simple. All medical bills would be sent to local boards composed of doctors and representatives of the public. These boards would set the fees, control abuses, and send cumulative bills to the Department of Health, Education, and Welfare which would pay them out of an insurance fund financed through compulsory taxes. It would be run just like any other insurance program except that the premiums would be based on the ability to pay, and the benefits would be comprehensive, covering the diagnosis, cure, medication, treatment, or prevention of diseases. Unlike the present system, the affirmative plan, by making insurance compulsory for all citizens, eliminates the need to make economic decisions in seeking medical care, for a compulsory tax based on financial ability has prepaid it. Our plan thus meets the need by freeing the American people to decide whether to get medical care on the basis of whether or not they need it.

Finally, Larry and I think that our plan could accomplish something really constructive in addition to meeting the need, and we would like to present the major advantages of our plan right now so that the negative team will be able to consider them right from the beginning of the debate. Our first advantage is that compulsory health insurance would prevent medical costs from causing severe economic hardship. Now the logical way to prevent an expense from causing financial hardship is, of course, to distribute that expense on the basis of financial ability, and that is exactly what compulsory health insurance would do through a progressive tax mechanism. Under the present system any one of us might some day be struck by a financially crippling illness. In fact, Professor J. H. Richardson of the University of Leeds wrote last year, "There is conclusive quantitative evidence that a major cause of financial hardship and even poverty in the United States is heavy expenditure for medical care." Compulsory health insurance has a very real advantage here. If we remove the dollar sign from medicine, the cost of illness will no longer be allowed to transform medical tragedy into financial disaster.

Our second advantage is that compulsory health insurance would relieve the financial drain on our hospitals. Edward T. Chase pointed out in last May's *Reporter*, "The indigent often do without the care they need in order to receive medical charity, but when they do receive that charity it often happens that nobody pays the bill, and then the hospitals are in serious trouble." Dr. J. P. Dixon testified in Congress July, 1959, "Unpaid bills have become such a drain on resources that the quality and availability of hospital services are seriously threatened. Many of our hospitals are on the brink of financial disaster." By paying those bills through compulsory health insurance we could eliminate this crisis before it cripples our hospitals.

Our third advantage is that compulsory health insurance would provide adequate medical care to many who must now rely on inadequate welfare services. In fact, our plan would completely eliminate second-class citizenship from medicine by providing care to all on an equal basis as a matter of right. But reviewing the present system, the Advisory Council on Public Assistance disclosed last February that there are glaring defects in the ways the medical needs of the indigent are being met. Less than half the states fully meet welfare needs by even their own minimal standards. For those millions who must now rely on "poor man's medicine," then, compulsory health insurance provides something which the present system has failed to provide—medical equality. The affirmative plan then would relieve economic insecurity it would prevent hospital insolvency; it would remove medical inequality.

In every one of these areas there is a pressing need for action. Some suggestions have been made. Perhaps the negative team may even make some here today. That's why we don't claim that these are needs in the debate sense for the affirmative resolution. But the advantage of that affirmative program is that it strikes at the heart of each one of these problems by removing economic considerations from medicine. And you remember why we must adopt such a program. We must adopt it because a third of a million lives are needlessly lost each year; because half of the disabling acute illnesses remain untreated; because 400,000 contagious disease carriers receive no medical supervision and all of this primarily because people must ask themselves—"How will we pay the bill?" a question that neither they nor the present system can answer. Compulsory health insurance answers that question by removing the dollar sign from medicine.

FIRST NEGATIVE CONSTRUCTIVE SPEECH: FRANK HARRISON, KINGS COLLEGE

Mr. Chairman, distinguished guests, ladies and gentlemen, I might begin by paraphrasing Winston Churchill, "Never have so many things been found so wrong with so little in so short a time." Keeping that in mind, I'd like to analyze the proposition presented to you by the gentlemen of the affirmative in somewhat of a reverse order; that is, I would like to turn first to the question of these additional advantages. Now I think it very interesting that the first affirmative speaker told you these are not needs—they are just additional advantages—sort of "bonus points" that come along with the affirmative resolution. We are going to suggest that each one of them, when looked at in a more realistic light, becomes a distinct disadvantage which the affirmative will have to cope with before it can substantiate the desirability of this plan.

First, you were told it's going to prevent hardship on the part of individuals. Now we are going to ask the gentlemen of the affirmative: since when did it become the duty of the federal government to make sure that no person in the United States undergoes financial hardship? If a person's home burns down, this is a tragedy. If his city is flooded, this is regrettable; but the federal government does not have the obligation to make sure that no one undergoes economic hardship. We suggest then the governmental theory of paternalism—the government is going to take care of everybody for every reason. We suggest a disadvantage; it tends to make people too dependent on the state.

All right, second, we were told that the indigent often go without care rather than seek charity. Well, that was an interesting assertion, ladies and gentlemen. I am going to ask you to search your memories and see if you have ever found any evidence presented on it. And after we have evidence I would like the gentlemen of the affirmative to quantify their problem. How many people actually do not seek what care for what particular reason?

Well, we were told, however, some of them do—you see—and this puts hospitals in trouble because the government doesn't pay sufficiently for the free patients which the hospitals accept. Now we are going to agree that the hospitals are in trouble, and we are going to suggest that the major fault of it belongs to the hospitals because, you see, they are inefficiently administered. James Brindle, the director of the Social Security Department of the United Auto Workers, said in the *Social Welfare Forum* for 1959, "Rapidly rising premiums are caused not only by justifiable improvements in hospital wage levels and working conditions and better technical facilities, but also inadequate concern for the operating efficiency of hospitals, unwillingness to enforce legitimate controls and a reluctance to experiment with new ideas." What is our point here ladies and gentlemen? Simply this: the gentlemen of the affirmative say quite rightly that hospitals are in trouble, and they, instead of proposing to correct the problem, propose to have the federal government step in and subsidize inefficiency and bad administration. We don't think that is an advantage; we think it is a distinct disadvantage. Indeed, Dr. Herman M. Somers, who is chairman of the Department of Political Science at Haverford College, told the National Council of Social Workers in May 1959, that the advocates of the affirmative resolution ". . . assume that if the government moved in they could continue present expensive and wasteful practices with assured payments, whereas now the countervailing pressure of organized consumers calling for more rigorous cost accounting and quality control appears to be growing steadily." Not only are the gentlemen of the affirmative subsidizing inefficiency, they are retarding the trends in the present system which will stop this inefficiency.

All right, advantage number three. We are going to eliminate second-class citizenship. How? Well, we are going to make sure that the states no longer discriminate. It seems that in some states, people get good welfare care; in other states, they get bad welfare care, and this is a distinct problem. All right, gentlemen, we agree with you; it is a problem, and we suggest, as the first affirmative anticipated we would, that there is a far more simple answer to the problem than he has discussed with you. We simply pass a federal law standardizing state requirements for public assistance in medical care. It was done in social security; it was done in unemployment compensation. I see no reason why it couldn't be done under the present system. What's the disadvantage? Well, the gentlemen by saying that the states are doing it today, admit that it is within the potential of the state to take care of the problem. They say, "Yes, the states can take care of the medically indigent; they are doing it today." The gentlemen of the affirmative just don't like the way they are doing it. Well then, what are you doing? You are having the federal government assume a burden that the states can and are handling. We suggest a further centralization of our government, a further breakdown in the responsibilities of the states, a further disadvantage of that resolution.

All right, having viewed the advantages claimed for it, let's turn to the resolution itself. You will recall that, in the first place, neglect of health today is causing death and suffering. I don't think anyone can dispute that the medical care of the American people is not what it should be. Nor do I think that anyone can dispute that there has ever been in the history of the world a nation whose medical standards were as high as they could be. In short, ladies and gentlemen, the medical needs of the people are always met less fully than they could be. What the gentlemen of the affirmative have to do in this debate is show you that the reason that these needs are not being met is economic and that their plan will take care of the need. Let's see whether this is true.

First, we should ask ourselves how many people are there in the country affected by the need of the gentlemen of the affirmative? In other words, gentlemen, and we ask you directly, what percentage of the American people are not getting adequate medical care today because they can't afford to pay for it? Now I think that this is a very fair question. The entire need of the gentlemen is that there are people not getting care for financial reasons. Gentlemen, how many? How great is your need for a universal program? Now let's ask ourselves some additional questions. First of all, if anyone in this country seeks medical care, is he prevented from getting it? Dr. Leonard Larson, then president of the American Medical Association and later chairman of the Medical Care Subcommittee of the White House Conference on the Aging, told the Senate Finance Committee in 1960, "We have proved again and again that no person in the United States need go without medical care because he is unable to pay for it." After an extensive study of the subject, the *Texas State Journal of Medicine* concluded in January, 1959, "Evidence is lacking that any American, aged or otherwise, who has needed and actually sought health care has been denied it."

All right, point one—no one is being denied care for financial reasons, and the negative agrees. Why is this? Well, we suggest the reasons are subjective in nature. They aren't going to be cured by the resolution. For our authority we'll turn to the most recent government statement on the problem, the *Background Paper on Health and Medical Care*, the White House Conference on the Aging, January 1961: "The reasons why people do or do not seek medical care are many. These in turn are often interrelated and complex, but they include such important factors as fear, habit, tradition, mores, religious belief, social dicta, degree of general education, degree of health education, and convenience of the service or facility for medical care." And in that whole long list—the most recent government statement on the problem—ladies and gentlemen, in that whole list I didn't hear cost. Let's ask ourselves more explicitly, is cost a significant factor? George Bugbee, president of the Health Information Foundation, in the *Bulletin*, April 1959: "Economic factors seem to be a relatively minor element in this reluctance to see a physician." *National Survey of Old-Age Survivors Insurance Beneficiaries* conducted again by the Department of Health, Education, and Welfare, 1957: "On the whole there appears but little systematic relationship between the amount of medical cost incurred by an elderly person and the amount of case income, or if he is married, the combined income of the couple."

All right, we suggest then three things: first, no one is denied care because he can't afford it; second, people are undermining their health primarily for subjective reasons that this resolution will not take care of; third, the economic factor is not determining in the question of medical care. Well, the gentlemen say, "Yes, but you see that the problem, the problem which we deny, is inherent." Why? Well, first because no one can afford all the necessary insurance. Again an assertion of the gentlemen introduced without evidence. Let's turn to Michael M. Davis, who was a member of various medical-care commissions set up by the government, who wrote in 1956 in the book, *National Health Insurance,* "Though the population covered by comprehensive plans is as yet only a few million, these plans have demonstrated that comprehensive high quality medical care can be made available through health insurance at an annual cost of $150–$200 for a family." This is between 4 and 5 percent of a family income of $4,000. Perhaps this is the reason that Dr. Jerome B. Cohen of the City College of New York concluded in his 1958 book, *Decade of Decision,* "As comprehensive is now written under group plans it is within the financial reach of even the modest income employee." Well, we were told, yes, you see, we were told even after these people get insurance it simply isn't enough. Why? Well it doesn't cover all of the cost. Now, gentlemen, we are going to accuse you of inadequate analysis here. We suggest that everyone here in this room after debating the topic or listening to it this year knows that there are five ways of paying medical care: you can take the money out of your pocket; you can borrow it from a bank; you can get it from private charity; you can get it from public charity; you can get it from voluntary insurance. Gentlemen, you have to show us that these five means taken *in toto*, taken together, taken as a unit, taken as a whole are insufficient. Not just that one part is insufficient. Maybe that is why Marion Folsom, the former Secretary of Health, Education, and Welfare, wrote in his pamphlet, *Voluntary Health Insurance and Medical Care,* February 1958: "Of course, no one expects voluntary insurance arrangements to meet medical costs completely."

All right, the last question the negative will ask you in this debate: To what extent are these voluntary companies meeting their task? Well, three surveys have been taken; Odin Anderson, 1957; Cornell University, 1956; Columbia University in 1959. They all reached the same conclusions. I would like to quote from Dr. Anderson, "Studies which relate health insurance benefits to the medical expenses of insured persons indicate that some 75–94 percent of hospital expenses and 62–76 percent of all surgical costs are covered."

Our conclusion: those people who have insurance have their hospital bill covered up to 94 percent, have their surgical bill covered up to 76 percent. Insurance isn't supposed to do everything. You have to tell us that all the means taken *in toto* are inadequate, gentlemen, not just a fragmentary analysis presented for affirmative reasoning. We suggest then the rejection of the resolution stated. Thank you.

SECOND AFFIRMATIVE CONSTRUCTIVE SPEECH: LAURENCE TRIBE, HARVARD UNIVERSITY

Ladies and gentlemen, I felt a little strange clapping for what Frank had said as I am afraid I cannot agree with very much of it. I don't think Frank really denied the basic contentions that Gene made in his first speech.

Let's go back to that first speech and see what we tried to establish. We suggested to you that the neglect of health is today causing needless death and suffering in the United States, and it is important to note that the negative team admits that contention. We have a third of a million unnecessary deaths every year; we have 400,000 contagious disease carriers receiving no medical treatment; we have half of all acute disabling medical conditions going untreated. All right, we suggested to you next that the primary reason for this neglect of health is that people are led to make medical decisions on economic grounds. And what did Frank say? Well, he said, number one, no one is denied needed medical care according to a very objective source, Dr. Larson of the American Medical Association. We are going to suggest that that is not responsive to our contentions; that whether or not anyone is denied care has nothing to do with whether people do not seek it for financial reasons, and we are going to suggest that in addition to being irrelevant, Frank's statement is false. *The American Journal of Public Health* in May of 1960 says, "Incredible as it may seem in this enlightened century, we know only too well how tragically true and how increasingly frequent are the cases in which people are denied access to prescribed care because of their inability to pay." So we are going to suggest to you that here is an increased advantage of the affirmative plan. People under the present system are indeed denied care because they can't pay for it; under compulsory health insurance they wouldn't be.

All right, the second point that Frank made was that there are many reasons for the neglect of health. They include fear, education, attitude, etc., and he seemed to make a great deal of the fact that out of the one publication that he very judiciously selected there is no mention of cost. But, unfortunately, we think that the problem cannot be dismissed in terms of lethargy or lack of education or improper health attitudes. The former Assistant Secretary of the Department of Health, Education, and Welfare, E. L. Richardson, wrote in August of 1959, "We now have in America a citizenry that is deeply interested in health and that is generally aware of what is necessary and available in medical care. The problem is not basically one of attitude or education, but one of economics."

If the gentlemen are not going to discuss the authorities that we presented so far, let's look further—let's look to Professor J. Henry Richardson, writing in *Economic and Social Aspects of Social Security*, 1960. He says, "Illnesses are often neglected in their early stages primarily because of the expenses involved in medical care." *The New York Times*, December 7, 1959: "Millions of Americans defer needed medical treatment primarily because of the fear of cost." Professor Hazel Kyrk, *The Family in the American Economy*, 1953: "Field Studies have shown quantitatively that diagnosis and treatment are postponed or even foregone for economic reasons." That's why now we concur with the University of Michigan report to the Senate Finance Committee in June of 1960 when they say that income is the overwhelming determinant of the ability to get needed medical care. That's why we agree with the Conference on the General Welfare, December 1959, when they say that the problem of health neglect in the United States is essentially economic.

We aren't denying the existence of other factors. We should move to solve other problems too, but the primary problem is one of cost and nothing that Frank said denied that.

Third, he turned to George Bugbee, again the president of a voluntary agency, another objective source, telling us that there is no correlation between care and income and therefore that the economic factor is not determining. We are going to challenge Mr. Bugbee's standards here. The *Social Security Bulletin* of February, 1961, says the latest national health survey shows that the amount of medical care received by a family was significantly related to the family's income. We think that Mr. Bugbee is just plain wrong; and, furthermore, we don't think that any of the statements that either Mr. Bugbee or Mr. Harrison made really refute any one of our three points. You will recall, number one: we said many people just can't pay the bills. Frank's response—how many people? Let us look again. Professor B. J. Stern, *The Sociology of Medicine*, 1960, states: "For the vast majority of the people," (and Gene read this in his first speech) "adequate medical care is simply beyond reach." We turn to Professor Stern, who states that this affects the vast majority of the people. We turn to Professor Strauss, who says that the result is a neglect of health. That really wasn't denied by the opposition. All right, then we suggested that even more people fear the ultimate cost though they can pay some of the bills. Frank had nothing to say on that point, and the negative team refused to discuss with you our third point here, and that is that even if we can pay all of the bills, all of us just tend to economize. We tend to economize because we may not feel sick enough to get care, and we think that this constitutes in itself a very important reason for removing the dollar sign in medicine. Because until we do, we've got a very important national problem of health neglect that we'd like to solve and that the negative team will do nothing about.

The question then is: Is this problem of health neglect inherent in the present system? Frank went through a rather rapid enumeration of the mechanisms—there were five of them—through which somehow one could pay for medical care. If you will recall, the reason we suggested to you that the problem is inherent in the present system was as Professor B. A. Weisbrod pointed out: none of these mechanisms in the present system can remove a need to make economic decisions in seeking medical care. Most of these things Frank said can be lumped under self-financing, and here of course cost is directly a factor, and he didn't deny that that proves, of course, the problem isn't solved here. What about voluntary health insurance? We suggested to you that no one can afford all the insurance he needs, and this wasn't just a matter of assertion. We cited Professor Haverman saying that most people decide to curtail their health insurance expenditures. The negative team couldn't deny that. What about the next point, that even if you didn't decide to buy some kind of insurance, the amount you can buy depends upon how much money you have? The negative team distorted that to mean that insurance doesn't cover all the cost. That wasn't what we said at all, but now that the negative team has brought it up, what did Frank actually tell us? He said you could get comprehensive care for two hundred dollars a family. Now a little quick arithmetic shows you that if you multiply that by the number of families in the country, that means that this mythical company's policy would be collecting ten billion dollars for twenty and a half billion dollars worth of medical care. I think it would go out of business pretty fast. I'd like to see that policy. We don't think it is really comprehensive, and Professor Dickerson in his text on health insurance, 1960, corroborates that view. He says, "The Federal Trade Commission objects to the term 'comprehensive' in health insurance advertising. There is simply no comprehensive policy offered." And you know we have shown you that if you don't cover expenses, the economic decision in that area remains. We've got to have coverage. The negative team can't provide us that coverage. They can't even argue about the inherent defects of voluntary insurance. And finally, they suggest that the problem isn't inherent because perhaps some people can get welfare.

We suggest to you, number one, that welfare really isn't universal, and you will remember that Gene said that the need was for a universal program because everyone is faced by economic decisions in seeking medical care, and frankly, we don't know why the gentleman from Kings would restrict compulsory financed medical care only to the indigent. Number two, you will recall that under the second advantage, Gene cited Edward Chase, and again it wasn't an assertion. Edward Chase was cited to the effect that a great many people are deterred from getting welfare by the stigma of the "means test," and here Frank said that there just isn't any evidence available on the subject. Well, the April 1961, *Report of the Iowa Department of Social Welfare* seems to think that there is. They say that there is no questioning the fact that a great many people have gone without needed medical care because they couldn't bring themselves to apply for this type of assistance through a welfare office. The report of the House Commerce Committee on March 10, 1954, concluded, "Economic means tests are in many areas serious barriers to hospital admission, threatening the public health through the perpetuation of serious infectious disease."

So, we think that public welfare just isn't the adequate solution to our problems. We think it isn't universal; we think it is inadequate; we think there is a "means test" which deters people from getting care.

All right, what about the question of inadequate public welfare? This you recall was part of our third advantage, and Frank tried to relate that to the need by saying that perhaps by improving welfare we might be able to meet that need. Well, you will remember that welfare doesn't allow people to decide whether or not to get medical care on the grounds of whether or not they need it. They've got to decide first of all whether or not they want to be degraded. We'd like to suggest to you that Frank hasn't given us a workable counterplan for expanding welfare to the point where we can rely on it. In the Senate Finance Committee on June 29, 1960, Governor Nelson Rockefeller, and I suspect he knows something about financial matters, said that, "The financing of state plans for expanded welfare will present serious financial strains on the states. It is likely that even under federal participation, a number of states couldn't participate at all." So we think that the negative's nebuluous counterplan wouldn't meet the need; we don't think it is even related to the need because welfare doesn't remove the need to make decisions of economic origin in seeking medical care, and we are still left with a problem that the present system cannot meet.

It can be met by removing the question of how will the bill be paid through a program of prepayment. Now what about those three advantages that would result from such a program? Number one, we suggested that we would relieve economic insecurity, and Frank says, "Is this the duty of the federal government?" We aren't suggesting that it is a duty of the federal government; we are simply suggesting that it would be advantageous for the federal government to prevent medical tragedy from leading to financial disaster. And frankly, I think the gentlemen are being a little inconsistent here. They advocate welfare to take care of people when they have already been forced into destitution, but they are not willing to prevent anyone from being forced into the welfare program.

All right, what about the second advantage that would prevent hospital insolvency? I think Frank misinterpreted this point, and said we were talking about higher premiums, and then suggested that we would be subsidizing inefficiency. I think that is a distortion. The fact is that more efficient administration of our hospitals is independent of the affirmative plan. We could accomplish it with or without the affirmative plan. The problem is those unpaid bills that are putting our hospitals out of business and, as a matter of fact, Frank hasn't suggested any other way in which we could solve the very important need for some kind of action.

And the third area—that we would remove medical inequality—that we would provide adequate care to states that have inadequate care for welfare services. Well, Frank says that here is a problem. What he would have us do is standardize welfare levels. Presumably since we showed you that there aren't more funds at the state level, he'd like to standardize them at the low levels that exist at the present time. We don't think that that is a solution. We think that again there is an undenied advantage to the affirmative plan here.

For those reasons, then, we still believe that we should remove the dollar sign from medicine—that we should adopt a program of compulsory health insurance for all citizens.

SECOND NEGATIVE CONSTRUCTIVE SPEECH: PETER SMITH, KINGS COLLEGE.

Ladies and gentlemen, as second speaker for the negative in this debate, I'd like to go over the objections which we might have—which we do have—to the affirmative plan as it was suggested in the first affirmative speech, and then attempt to reanalyze some of the so-called affirmative advantages and attempt to look at them in a light a little bit more realistic than the gentlemen from Harvard have done.

First of all, with regard to the affirmative plan, we would like to point out that although we were given some very, very general details as to the cost and method of financing, we weren't told by the members of the affirmative team anything at all as to the general cost of their proposal. Now this, we think, is most interesting, because the members of the affirmative team are, on the one hand, contending that the American people have a barrier of money between them and medical care which they need, and that the whole philosophic basis of the affirmative case is this very interesting thesis: if we take the dollar sign out of medicine, we can solve this problem.

How are they going to take the dollar sign out of medicine? By that very old utopian method—let the government pay for the program and let the people take advantage of it, based upon their need. This is all very interesting, but I think, as even the gentlemen on my right realize, the government gets the money from somewhere. The government is going to collect this money from the very means which they suggested—some kind of compulsory tax. Now I would like the members of the affirmative team to justify the fact that, on the one hand, the American people don't have enough finances to pay for this system through the present method no matter what it might be; and, on the other hand, somebody somewhere is going to have enough money so the federal government can get it in compulsory taxation and give it back to hospitals and doctors, providing the American people with free medical care. The illusion that one can remove the dollar sign from medicine is just that—an illusion, and the members of the affirmative team realize it. The only way in which that could be done is if hospitals, doctors, and all of our medical facilities were to go completely without pay and give free service. The dollar sign isn't being removed; it is being transferred. We are going to have a middle man, and the members of the affirmative team cannot—at least they haven't so far—and I don't think that they can—say that it is going to be done at any greatly reduced cost. First of all, according to the *Source Book of Health Insurance Data* for 1960, the total cost of medical care for the American people last year was approximately 18 billion dollars. Now, we would like the members of the affirmative team to show us where the affirmative and where the federal government is going to get the funds to finance the program.

Secondly, we would like the members of the affirmative team to justify one very important thing for us. We've been told in very general terms that the federal government is going to take over the entire system of financing medical care. By this we would presume that the federal government is going to pay everybody's medical bill for all of his medical expenses, and yet throughout this debate (though we have been given some general philosophic needs and some general arguments about some people who don't get medical care), there is nothing specific at all in this affirmative proposal. What do I mean by specific? Well, the members of the affirmative team have not once given us any reason why the federal government should pay the total medical bill. They haven't shown us that the American people experience any difficulty paying for nonprescribed drug expenses. They haven't shown us that we experience any difficulty paying for sunglasses that doctors might prescribe. They haven't even shown us any particular reason where the need exists in hospital care, surgical care, or personal-physician care. They have given us some general statements as to people who don't get the care. We would like the members of the affirmative team to justify this particularly, so that they can prove to us that we should allow the federal government to take over the entire system. Granted (and we will grant this for about ten seconds), there may be a need in some specific area, but we would like the members of the affirmative team to show us that it exists in every facet of our medical system today, because this is the only ground upon which they could justify a plan which supposedly pays everyone's medical bills. The plan it seems is about X times larger than the affirmative need. I had to say X because I don't know exactly how big the affirmative need is.

But again, we asked the members of the affirmative team to show us exactly what is the need for the federal government to pay the full amount of everyone's medical bill. Then the members of the affirmative team went a little bit further. They told us they are going to have local boards to regulate any abuses which might creep into the system. This is all well and good. The affirmative team is suspecting that there are going to be some abuses. We contend that local boards aren't a satisfactory means of solving the problem. My colleague pointed out that the hospitals are in a financial mess due to the present system. I can read some quotations here that point out that there are abuses on the local level. Some doctors don't live up to the code they are supposed to live up to. Many patients take advantage of the system. Many hospital administrators and persons in hospitals, either through negligence or through crookedness, will take advantage of such a proposal.

Now the members of the affirmative team have provided some type of regulation, but it is on a local and not on a federal or even on a state level. In other words, the very persons who under the present system (and under their proposal also) may perpetrate violations are going to be judges in their own cases under the affirmative proposal. This too will add to the general cost—the X cost of that affirmative proposal—a significant disadvantage to the affirmative team.

Well, in regard to the so-called over-all points given to us by the affirmative team and their advantages, we were told there are three things wrong with the present system. Now these things aren't needs in the debater's sense—they are needs as far as the United States is concerned. The affirmative proposal it just happens is going to solve these needs. Now it is the contention of the members of the negative team that, first of all, the affirmative proposal won't solve these problems, and, secondly, it is going to make some of them a great deal worse than they are under the present system.

You will recall that one of them is the contention by the members of the affirmative team that we are going to remove the drain of financial burden of free care on the hospitals. Well, my colleague pointed out that they weren't giving you the whole story there. A great part of the reason why hospitals are in financial difficulty is through their own inefficiency—

through practices—bad practices—which occur in the hospitals. What was the answer of the second affirmative speaker to this point? He told you that first of all we are going to get rid of the free care which hospitals have to give, and secondly we didn't propose any alternative. Now we don't think it is the obligation of the members of the negative team to provide a counterplan. We'd only like to point out, first of all, that this affirmative proposal won't specifically be solving the whole problem since a great part of the problem is hospital inefficiency and they are taking no federal or state means to solve the problem of hospital inefficiency. Secondly, the members of the affirmative team have more or less, by asking us to provide a solution, admitted that the problem exists within the present system. But let's carry it one step further. We don't think it is just a problem of hospitals being run wrong or hospitals having to give a lot of free care to people who can't afford to pay their bills. We think it is something which goes much deeper, for there is a general shortage of hospital and general medical facilities throughout the United States, and it is the contention of the members of the negative team that the affirmative proposal won't come anywhere near to solving this problem. Now why is this so? Well, I made a big point out of the lack of substantial and adequate regulations before. Why did I do this? Well, I did this because it's one of the things that comes about when you have a complete—and nothing could be more complete than this affirmative proposal—a complete system of prepayment of medical expenses. F. J. Snyder, a research analyst for the Public Affairs Institute, *Health Insurance for the Aged*, 1960: "An unfortunate by-product for the increased use of hospitilization insurance is the over-utilization of hospital facilities. The abuse of medical insurance results in further packing overloaded hospitals." And Mr. Snyder concludes his statement by saying, "Any successful government-sponsored health insurance will have to meet the problem of unnecessary use of hospitals and unnecessary surgery."

I stress the word *unnecessary* because I realize the affirmative are quite willing to come up here and say that this increased use of hospitals will be for the people who don't get the care now. I say unnecessary because it will be persons who don't need medical care who will flock to these hospitals and to these doctors and overutilize these facilities. And there is very definitely a shortage. I don't think I have to prove it, but I would like to point out exactly how seriously it exists and where it exists. *U.S. News and World Report*, May 9, 1958: "Because of the short supply of doctors, hospitals often cannot obtain the physicians they need even when they seek to hire them." Now the members of the affirmative team may well try to point out that their program—their program of X amount of compulsory health insurance—is going to solve this problem; this problem of hospitals being abused; this problem of an overutilization of facilities or a shortage of doctors, but it just isn't so. Professors Baisden and Hutchinson, University of California, *Health Insurance*, 1958, "The mere act of providing more money for medical care does not necessarily result in an increase in either the quantity or the quality of the services."

Mr. F. J. Follman, Jr., Director of the Research and Information Bureau of the Health Insurance Association of America, *Voluntary Health Insurance and Medical Care*, 1958: "The existence of a broadly established insurance mechanism no matter how effective does not nor can it increase the medical personnel or facilities available." What conclusion can we reach here? One of the advantages that we are supposedly going to have when we adopt this affirmative proposal is the fact that medical care is going to be made more adequate. Everyone is going to have the wonderful advantages of adequate medical care just due to the adoption of this affirmative plan. But we pointed out that we do have a problem of a shortage of facilities and doctors. The affirmative has no adequate measures in its plan for providing against unnecessary overutilization of these facilities and compulsory health insurance per se won't solve this problem, and what's going to be the result? Well, Mr. Selig Greenberg, a medical reporter for the Providence *Journal*, in *Harpers*, 1960: "The frequent instances of careless medical care given by overworked doctors is among the most frequent complaints of patients today." In other words, we can see that overworked doctors, overstrained facilities, give inadequate medical care, and the affirmative proposal is going to worsen this situation leading to a greater amount of inadequacy in medical care given to the American people. They aren't meeting the advantage; they are creating an even greater disadvantage through the adoption of the affirmative proposal.

For these reasons and objections to the need which my colleague brought up before, and which he will continue in the first negative rebuttal, we beg that the affirmative proposal be rejected. Thank you.

FIRST NEGATIVE REBUTTAL SPEECH: FRANK HARRISON, KINGS COLLEGE

Ladies and gentlemen, as first speaker for the negative, returning to this podium, I would like to discuss with you again the question of whether or not there is a need for the affirmative resolution, and I would like to discuss with you some of the refutations of arguments which the second affirmative speaker wishes I had made.

Now the first thing you will recall which I asked the affirmative team was specifically, gentlemen, how many people in the United States are not getting adequate medical care because they can't afford to pay for it? I said, "Gentlemen, give us the statistics." And that was a very clever answer we heard. We were told, according to some authority, the vast majority of the American people can't on their own resources afford to pay for medical care, and that simply doesn't answer the question. The question, gentlemen, to repeat, is: How many people aren't getting care because they can't afford to pay for it? Perhaps the vast majority can't afford on their own resources—you will recall there are five ways in which they can pay for medical care, only one of which is out of their own resources. They can borrow; they can go to charity; they can have insurance; but, simply, the answer given does not reply to the question.

Then we were told, "You will see people making medical decisions on economic grounds." I came to the rostrum and I quoted Dr. Larson (who is not very objective—I'm sorry—he was testifying under oath at the time). However, some authority (and I think that this is cute), some authority knows of circumstances in which people are denied care because they can't afford it. I wish that authority would call the American Hospital Association because their president appeared before the Ways and Means Committee in July, 1959, and he said, "I am not aware of cases where people have been refused hospital and medical services because of their inability to pay for it." And furthermore, the representative of the AFL-CIO, Mr. Cruikshank, was asked the now famous debater's question by Congressman Alger of Texas, "Please give examples of the circumstances—give specific cases in which people have been denied care," and I think the gentlemen can search the record of the House Committee on Ways and Means and will find that Mr. Cruikshank notably did not reply. All right, we went on a little further. You will recall I quoted from the most recent source I could get, the White House Conference in January, 1961. They said there were many reasons why people aren't getting care. The gentlemen said, well, it was nice of the negative team to pick out the one source that would go along with them. It was also nice for the negative team that that source happened to be the most recent and the most authoritative. But, they said, "There are a lot of other problems involved. We admit this. The problem is that economics is the main problem." Now, gentlemen, even if we concede that for a minute, you are missing the point. The point is your need isn't going to meet your plan because you have admitted that there are other barriers beside economic barriers, so even assuming this grand hypothesis, even assuming that we are going to be able to strike down the financial barrier, other barriers remain. Other barriers are still effective. People still aren't going to doctors, and that very lovely need isn't met by that comprehensive plan.

Well, we were told, "Income is the overwhelming determinant." All right, ladies and gentlemen, I'd like to take a look at what happens when that overwhelming determinant is taken away. Drs. Odin Anderson and Paul Shipley, *Comprehensive Medical Insurance*, 1959, began by discussing the fact that there are three plans: the General Health Insurance Plan, the New York Health Insurance Plan, and the Windsor Insurance Plan, which prepay the patient's visit to the doctor's office in the first place. They pay for the patient every time he goes to the doctor's office. Obviously, no cost to him.

Now according to the theory of this affirmative team, wouldn't you think that people would be going to doctors far more frequently than when they don't have such insurance? Let's look at the conclusions of a recent release of the *National Health Survey* which showed that 37 percent of the population had not seen a physician within a year. Under the most favorable financial conditions, the absence of such barriers to physicians' services in G.H.I., H.I.P., and Windsor, we find: 25–32 percent of the enrollees will not seek physicians' services within a year; 37 percent don't go when they don't have insurance; 32 percent don't go when they do have insurance. Gentlemen, we suggest that your economic determinant isn't determining too much. Well, then we were told that all of the negative sources in the debate simply don't stand because Mr. Bugbee is president of an insurance company. Now I am a little tired of hearing Mr. Bugbee assailed for bias in this debate. He happens to be president of the Health Information Foundation, which is not employed by the insurance companies. And even if he is, we suggest that the Department of Health, Education, and Welfare has not yet come under the pay of the insurance companies and I cited them too, and the gentlemen never replied.

You recall, I said there are five ways to pay for medical care. I said the gentlemen had to indict each one of them, and I ask you to search your memories; they haven't indicted the ability to borrow. They said, "No, gentlemen, you don't get the point. This point is that these don't remove the necessity for economic decisions." Gentlemen, you haven't shown us what evils are following from these economic decisions; you haven't shown us that they are leading to concrete harm, but only that there are three advantages to the affirmative resolution. The first one, you see, is it's going to prevent hardship. Now I suggested to the gentlemen that it is not the duty of the government to prevent people from going into debt to any degree. The gentlemen said, "Oh, that isn't the problem; they are going to become destitute under the present system." Gentlemen, would you present some statistics to prove that a significant number of people are becoming destitute? We suggested it is going to create a paternalistic welfare state. No comment from the gentlemen. Then we were told the indigent would go without care. I said, "Very interesting, in fact. Indigent go without care rather than seek it." And according to the second affirmative speaker I said there was no evidence available. No! I said the second affirmative had to tell us how many people in the indigent group don't get care because they can't afford it, and we still haven't heard the answer. But we were told, you see, that a more efficient administration of hospitals would occur independent of the resolution. I read an authority on hospitals in this debate, Dr. Somers, who said it wouldn't. It would occur under the present system and not under the resolution. I think that we can conclude that the resolution still deserves to be rejected. Thank you.

FIRST AFFIRMATIVE REBUTTAL SPEECH: LAURENCE TRIBE, HARVARD UNIVERSITY

After fifteen minutes of optimistic negative discussion about what the gentlemen of the opposition consider a very lovely need, we are led to believe that perhaps there is no problem at all, that perhaps it is just some wild rumor started by 400,000 contagious disease carriers. We are going to resist the temptation to reach that conclusion because there are a couple of objections we have to cover before we can go back and see why that conclusion is fallacious.

The gentlemen asked, "How much will the plan cost?" They were very concerned about the fact. We turn to Dr. Alan Gregg, *Challenges to Contemporary Medicine*, 1957. He says that by spending 6 percent more than we currently spend on medical care, the government, through compulsory health insurance, could provide completely comprehensive medical services for everyone. By using the gentlemen's own figure of 18 billion dollars, that means that we would spend about 1.08 billion dollars more than we currently spend on medical care. Frankly, we think that the needless death and suffering under the present system really is worth about one billion dollars at least.

Now, the gentlemen say that actually there is some big problem here because we couldn't get enough money under the affirmative plan because we haven't got enough money now. Well, number one, we weren't talking only of the inadequacy of funds; we were talking about decisions. Number two, people pay taxes progressively; they don't pay medical bills progressively. Then the gentlemen said, "Where is the money going to come from?" Well, it is going to come from income taxes. In *Public Finance*, 1960, Professor Troy Cauley points out, "Because of the interrelationship between government spending and the economy, far higher tax levels would in no way impair our economic growth." Then the gentleman suggested that there were all kinds of things like dental expenditures, drug expenses, and sunglasses. I suppose that we ought to have discussed these very specifically. Frankly, I thought Gene covered quite a bit in those first ten minutes without time to apply all of his arguments to every one of these areas. We think that the area of dental care is typical. *Public Health Reports*, March 1959, says, "Only 31 percent of the American people who seriously need dental work are getting it at the present time, primarily because of the high cost inolved." So, frankly, we think that our need really does apply to all of these areas. They told us that local boards are unsatisfactory. We've got 430 of them working pretty satisfactorily now. They said over-utilization would result. Well, number one, that contradicts their idea that there is no cost barrier. Number two, it could be effectively controlled. *The Evaluation of Medical Care Programs*, 1961, points out, "It has been shown empirically that unnecessary or wasteful use of medical services can be effectively controlled with no adverse consequences." It is suggested that doctors would be setting their own fees, but the negative forgets that doctors and laymen sit on those boards. They told us there were going to be abuses, and yet James Brindle in the *American Journal of Public Health*, 1957, says, "Services must be completely prepaid if the economic barrier to needed care is to be removed, and if unnecessary surgery and hospitiliza-tion is to be discouraged." That shows the need for comprehensive care, doesn't it? Not the reason for rejecting the affirmative plan.

Finally, they suggested that we've got too few facilities now. Number one, we say that even if we've got fewer facilities than we would like to have, that's no reason to determine who gets to use these facilities on the basis of the highest bidder. Number two, we say that we don't really have a serious facility problem. *The New York State Medical Journal* on May 15, 1959, said, "If the public fully utilized the preventive, diagnostic, and treatment services and facilities already available, a great many of the ill-nesses now fatal could be effectively treated." So let's look back on some of those illnesses—let's see what the primary neglect of health is in the United States today. It was suggested that no one is denied care, and we were told finally that it is true because Dr. Larson was under oath. Well, frankly, we still think that the *American Journal of Public Health* really wasn't speaking purely out of its imagination when it suggested that people are denied care. The issue was peripheral to the direct question but we still think that constitutes an advantage to the affirmative proposal. The question wasn't who is denied; the question is why don't people seek that care? And we presented Professor Richardson, Professor Kyrk, the Univer-sity of Michigan Report, and the Conference on the General Welfare, all saying that the primary reason that they didn't seek that care was economic. The gentlemen come back and tell us that the economic factor isn't de-termining because there is no real correlation between money and medicine in the United States, and they say that the Department of Health, Edu-cation, and Welfare National Survey for last year concluded that utiliza-tion rates go up 23 percent as income goes down 25 percent. So we are going to suggest to you that there really is a very basic problem in all of these areas; that when the negative team asks us what happens when the economic factors are removed, they know what we have already shown you, and that is that when the economic factors are removed—as in the case of Georgia, for instance—(according to the Medical Association in

1954), millions of people got care who hadn't gotten it before. In that particular instance, one million three hundred and eighty thousand people, when screening surveys were offered on an experimental basis, received free medical care that they hadn't gotten before the cost barrier had been removed. That's what happens. Cost is a major factor, not education.

All right, what about the question of the inherency within the present system? The gentlemen first suggested that comprehensive policies could be given to all of us for $200. When they saw the absurdity of that suggestion they dropped it completely in the debate. They no longer contend that they can provide that kind of policy. They have nothing left here really, because they aren't denying, number one, that the economic decision remains when you have to decide whether or not to buy voluntary health insurance. They aren't denying, number two, that the amount you can buy depends on how much money you have. They aren't denying that in welfare or in any free program, people are deterred by the "means test," so it doesn't free people to make medical decisions on medical grounds. Yet they're not denying, finally, if we adopted the affirmative plan we could prevent a great deal of economic hardship, we could improve our welfare program, and we could prevent our hospitals from going broke as a result of unpaid bills. All they say is that there still will be other problems that our program may not solve. We don't think that's a reason to reject our plan. We think we still should remove the dollar sign from medicine.

SECOND NEGATIVE REBUTTAL SPEECH: PETER SMITH, KINGS COLLEGE

Ladies and gentlemen, as last speaker for the negative, I would like to summarize the debate for the final time. First of all, the objections which I raised to the affirmative plan were answered rather hastily by the first affirmative rebuttalist. We were told that some experts say that we can finance the program at a cost only 6 percent greater than the present system, and this is something which our economy can bear; so therefore there is no real problem. Now gentlemen, I think anyone associated with this debate topic knows that I could bring up ten sources saying that your administrative cost would be 6, 8, 12, 15, even 18 percent; just as you brought up one that it was 6 percent. But the essential question that I asked was: Are you supposedly going to remove the dollar sign from the area of financing medical care? At least that was the basic affirmative thesis in this debate. Yet I pointed out in my second negative speech that you aren't really doing this at all. All you are doing is transferring it, so that the federal government takes the money from the citizens of America to provide their medical care, instead of the people paying it directly or indirectly through various facets of the present system. You aren't really removing the dollar sign. It is still going to be of cost to the American people to bear financing of their medical care. Now, according to your statement, the present system is too much for the American people to bear. I asked you to break it down and consider it separately so I wouldn't have to do it. I'm about to do what you wouldn't do.

The only estimate we have so far of just what the affirmative proposal is going to entail is the fact that it is going to pay everyone's expenses for every type of medical care. This is fine. In the present system everything costs 18 billion dollars. Theirs is going to cost 6 percent more, and yet the American people, according to the affirmative stand on this floor, can't afford the present system in its totality. So, therefore, we think the members of the affirmative team have pulled one of the greatest illogical conclusions of all time. They are contending the American people can't afford a system, and in order to help them pay their way out of this problem, we are going to provide them with a system which is going to take more money from them, remove the dollar sign from the area of medical aid and economics, and make everybody happy. Gentlemen, this is Utopia carried to its furthest extreme.

Again, an example of where the affirmative proposal does not show too much correlation to the affirmative needs. We pointed out that regulations by local boards would be deficient. They say doctors and laymen will sit on the board. This doesn't prove again that you are going to stop all the kinds of abuses which exist at various levels. My colleague pointed out that the reason why hospitals are in trouble is because hospitals have inefficient practices. No real answer here given by the members of the affirmative team. The affirmative proposal of compulsory health insurance is going to make this problem worse. As far as overutilization of facilities is concerned, the affirmative team "whitewashed" it. I pointed out that one of the things they are going to do—one of the needs they are supposed to solve—is the adequacy of American medical care. And the result of this overutilization of facilities is going to be a decrease in the adequacy of medical care made available to the American people. The members of the affirmative team had no answer here; an advantage turned into a distinct disadvantage.

Now in regard to the affirmative need, I have no intention of running through every single quote fired at you by the first affirmative speaker and fired right back by my colleague, and then refired by the members of the affirmative team. But I think one thing stands clear. First of all, despite the fact that a great many people die in the United States every year, it hasn't been established by the members of the affirmative team that these people die because they can't afford treatment, and this is the only logical basis on which we should adopt the affirmative proposal. And the reason why is very simple—because my colleague has contended throughout this debate that there are other factors besides purely economic ones which keep people from seeking needed medical care—everything from negligence to pure ignorance. The members of the affirmative team at first flirted with the idea of completely refuting it. When we came to the first affirmative rebuttal, they were accepting it. They were saying, "But the primary reason is economic." Primary or not, my colleague matched the first affirmative speaker's source saying that you won't solve the problem by giving the people the money to go to the doctor, and he gave the specific example of where it has been done and showed how the utilization of services didn't increase one bit. In other words, we can see that the affirmative proposal won't get at the heart of the problem—making the American people get adequate medical care when they have the means available to them.

Well, the members of the affirmative team moved a little bit further. They indicted the so-called "present system" by considering voluntary health insurance, and they told us that because the amount of voluntary health insurance depends on the amount of money you have, there is something wrong with voluntary health insurance. Well, my colleague pointed out that the other facets of the present system were completely ignored by the members of the affirmative team. They go back constantly to their basic thesis, that we've got to take financial problems out of the area of medicine in the United States today. Now this we don't think is the obligation of the federal government. It certainly isn't being very well handled by the members of the affirmative team for this very simple reason: the federal government, or the United States as a political body, has no obligation to make sure that everyone in the United States gets lavish special care or has all his economic problems solved. This would be quite a job for the federal government. But the federal government does have some kind of an obligation to make sure that the American people get medical care when they need it, and this has no bearing upon the affirmative contention that the American people sometimes die when they don't get adequate medical care. The affirmative in this debate haven't established an essential specific reason for adopting this resolution, and the second affirmative speaker in his rebuttal must show you that their specific plan per se will solve the evil that they say exists in its totality, or the affirmative proposal won't meet that evil. The need can be solved by other means, and we need not adopt their resolution. Thank you.

SECOND AFFIRMATIVE REBUTTAL SPEECH: GENE CLEMENTS, HARVARD UNIVERSITY

Before we return to the need, let's look again at the few objections which the negative team managed to sustain after Larry refuted them. They brought back the idea that we were just transferring a dollar sign, but the crucial thing is that we are transferring it from the individual, where it deters care, to the government. When the government pays it from a progressive tax, the individual no longer has to make an individual economic decision every time he wants care. And we've shown you, I believe, that that individual economic decision is the main cause for health neglect. That, we contend, is where we are transferring the dollar sign. And the gentlemen ask us how in the world we can possibly pay for it if we contend we cannot pay for it now. Again they mistake the fact that we are doing it on an individual basis. We say there are many who can't pay for care. All of us are deterred. However, through a progressive tax we can let everyone's care be paid for because, of course, the individual no longer has to meet all of his expenses if he has low income—if indeed, he can't pay for his care. We certainly wouldn't think that the gentlemen of the negative are contending that this nation is too poor, too cheap, to provide adequate care for all its citizens. So we think that these objections to the affirmative proposal certainly don't stand.

Let's go back to the need itself. In the first area, we said that there was a neglect of health which led to needless death and suffering. For a while this was admitted; then the gentlemen wanted to know if these people died because they couldn't afford care. Well, my colleague directly related the one third of a million who die needlessly (that is one of five deaths each year) to essentially economic problems—in this area, for instance, one half of all disabling acute illnesses. We sort of assumed that it was apparent that, if these people are flat on their backs, they know that they need care, and there must be a pretty good reason why they aren't getting that care. We suggested that that factor was the economic factor. And I think we proved it when we gave you Professor Richardson, *The New York Times*, Professor Kyrk, the University of Michigan Survey, who all concluded that income was the overwhelming determinant. But the gentlemen said, "no," that there are other factors. There certainly are other factors, gentlemen. We never contended there weren't. We gave you testimony that these factors were relatively insignificant, which as yet has gone undenied. We showed you surveys in Georgia, for instance, where over a million people came out to get free preventive examinations. Eighty-five percent of those people had not been diagnosed previously.

Let's go a little bit farther, however, let's go to Philadelphia where the A.F. of L. Medical Center in Philadelphia provides preventive examinations for certain union members at no cost. A survey recently conducted revealed that were it not for this free center, 92 percent of the members receiving preventive care never would have sought diagnosis. It suggests to us that indeed there may be a cost barrier to medical care, a cost barrier which in fact transcends all other barriers, and encompasses all of us, and this is the point which the negative has never refuted. The idea that it's not the cost of care alone, but the fact that we must make an economic decision in seeking that care, extends the need to everyone of us in this room. Everyone of us, every time we put off a physical examination because we want to economize (we want to save the ten, fifteen, twenty dollars it costs for a physical examination), has made an economic decision which has harmed our health. We contend that compulsory health insurance can remove the need to make those economic decisions. *Public Medical Care* by Dr. Franz Goldman pointed out that ". . . by providing easy access to early diagnosis and thorough treatment, compulsory health insurance would greatly reduce the frequency of serious stages of illness." Compulsory health insurance can certainly meet the need in this particular area.

The gentlemen introduced the peripheral idea that people aren't denied care. Well, of course, this isn't particularly relevant to our case. We are worried about the people who never seek care in the first place. But, indeed, people are denied care, and the hearings of the House Ways and Means Committee is ample evidence, documented by studies in Michigan, Boston, California, and throughout the nation, that because of inability to pay for it, literally millions of Americans go without needed medical care. So very definitely there is a problem in this area, and certainly we feel that the removal of the need to make those economic decisions can solve the problem. We showed you in that area of inherency that voluntary insurance—basically all these so-called other five factors could be lumped as either voluntary insurance, welfare, or self-financing—voluntary insurance could not remove the need to make economic decisions. In fact, it depended upon the income of the individual purchasing the insurance. The negative never responded to either of these ideas. They presented a comprehensive policy which proposed for ten billion dollars to give 20 billion dollars worth of care. When we pointed out the absurdity of that, they dropped the point. We showed you in welfare that the "means test" deterred care—in fact that welfare was inadequate. In this particular area, again, the negative has dropped its point.

Ladies and gentlemen and members of the opposition, the negative have made cost a primary consideration in this debate. They ask us how we'll pay the bill. We've shown you that we can pay the cost of the affirmative proposal in dollars and cents. The negative proposal is today being paid for through human death and suffering. How, gentlemen, will you pay the bill?

INDEX

Refutation (*continued*)
general rules for, 215–218
methods of, 193–215
planned, 216–217
planning for, 85
preparation for, 218
special methods of, 209–215
defense against, 225–229
Refutation cards, 218, 219
Refutation case, 113–114
Reid, Ronald F., 48–69
Relics, as evidence, 159
Research
analysis and, 66
background for, 71–72
bibliographies and, 74–78
for debate, 70–87
individual, 79–83
material
acquiring, 70–83
filing, 84–85
recording, 83–84
notes and, 83–85
procedure for, 71
sources of information, 74–83
steps in, 70
supplementary materials and, 78–79
Residues
in causal relation, 178
method of
defense against, 227
in refutation, 212
Rhetorical syllogism, argument from, 178–184
Role-playing, 266–267
Rostrum, The, 40

S-R-S-R-T principle, in developing a contention, 240–241
Sample debate, 367–393
Scheduling
forensic program, 315–321
tournaments, 340–344
Second affirmative speaker (*see* Affirmative speakers)
Second negative speaker (*see* Negative speakers)
Sign
argument from, 171–174
distinguished from cause, 172–173
function of, in proof, 172

Signs
reliability of, 173–174
use of, in proof, 174
Sketches, as evidence, 158
Social classes, as groups, 132–133
Social responsibility, of debaters, 10–11
Societies
forensic honor, 33–47
development of, 40–44
future of, 44–47
organization of, 33–40
See also names of societies
literary and debating, 19–22, 23
growth of, 20
importance of, 19–20
typical, 20–22
Speaker, The, 40
Speakers (*see* Affirmative speakers; Negative speakers)
Speaking
extemporaneous, 268–269
impromptu, 268
memorized, 269
Speech, 235–284
composition of, 235–256
basic principles of, 237–255
language and, 247–255
organization, 242–247
outline for, 242–247
supporting materials, 239–242
presentation of, 257–284
Speeches
constructive, refutation in, 216
main
first affirmative speaker, 116–117
first negative speaker, 118–119
second affirmative speaker, 118
second negative speaker, 119–120
Split-team debating, 301
Stage fright, 263
Stand-pat case, 114
Statistical Abstract of the United States, 82
Statistical facts, sources of, 82
Statistics, faulty
alleged, defense against attacks on, 222
fallacy of, 195–196
Status quo case, 114
Strategic arguments, 215–216
Student congress, 309–310
Student managers, 322

INDEX

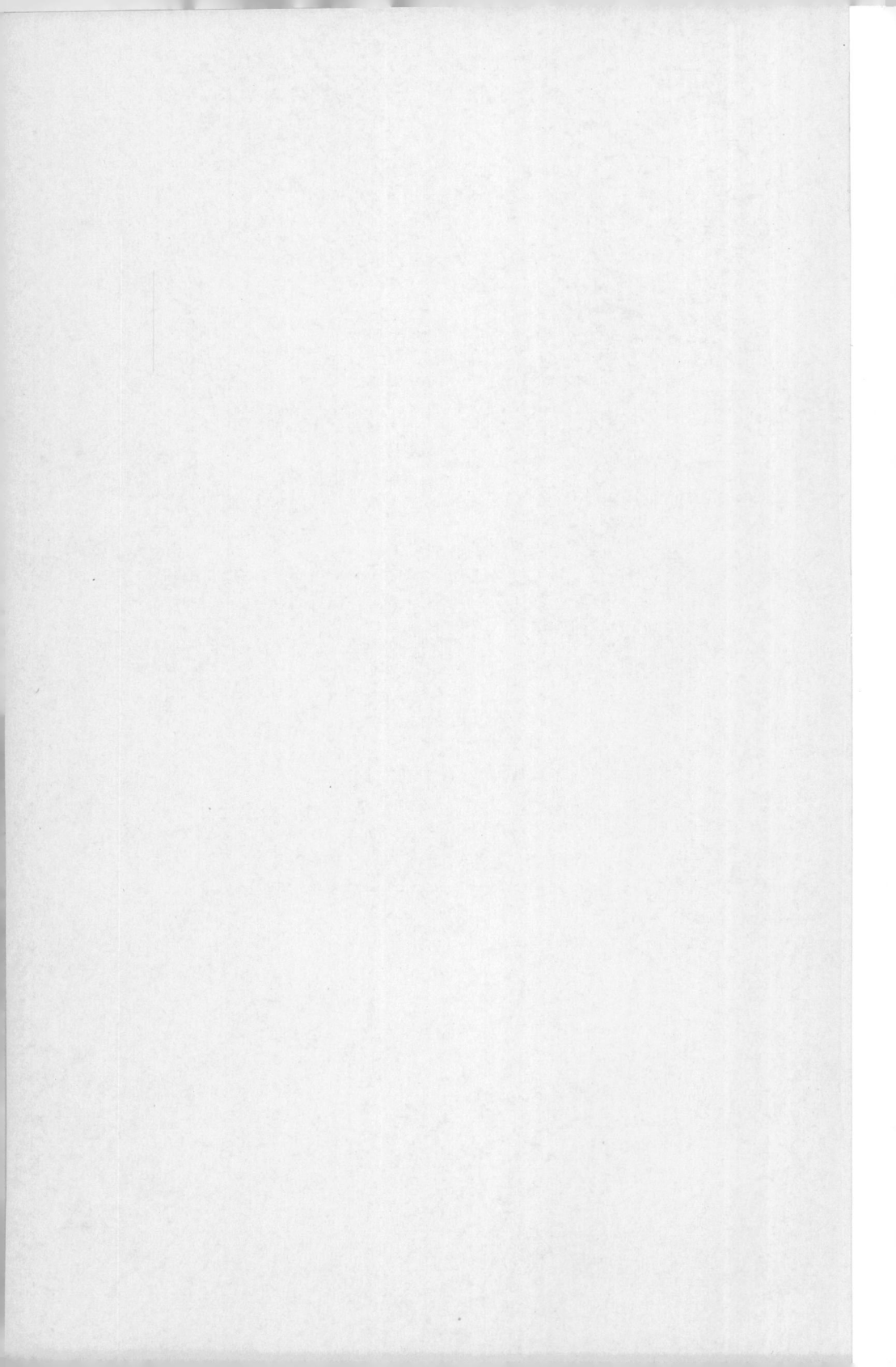